C0 CBU 562

THE FALL OF THE ROMAN HOUSEHOLD

In his *Decline and Fall of the Roman Empire*, Edward Gibbon laid the fall of the Roman Empire at Christianity's door, suggesting that 'pusillanimous youth preferred the penance of the monastic to the dangers of a military life ... whole legions were buried in these religious sanctuaries; and the same cause, which relieved the distress of individuals, impaired the strength and fortitude of the empire.' Gibbon's idea still presents a challenge for historians. Certainly, Christian values and institutions changed the landscape of possibility during this key period of Roman history, but how? This surprising study suggests that, far from seeing Christianity as the cause of the fall of the Roman Empire, we should understand the Christianization of the household as a central Roman survival strategy. By establishing new 'ground rules' for marriage and family life, the Roman Christians of the last century of the Western empire found a way to reinvent the Roman family as a social institution to weather the political, military, and social upheaval of two centuries of invasion and civil war. In doing so, these men and women – both clergy and lay – found themselves changing both what it meant to be Roman, and what it meant to be Christian.

KATE COOPER is Director of the Centre for Late Antiquity and Senior Lecturer in Early Christianity at the University of Manchester. She is the author of *The Virgin and the Bride: Idealized Womanhood in Late Antiquity* (1996) and editor (with Julia Hillner) of *Religion, Dynasty, and Patronage in Early Christian Rome, 300–900* (2007).

THE FALL OF
THE ROMAN HOUSEHOLD

KATE COOPER

University of Manchester

CAMBRIDGE
UNIVERSITY PRESS

BT
707.7
.C66
2007

CAMBRIDGE UNIVERSITY PRESS
Cambridge, New York, Melbourne, Madrid, Cape Town, Singapore, São Paulo

Cambridge University Press
The Edinburgh Building, Cambridge CB2 8RU, UK

Published in the United States of America by Cambridge University Press, New York

www.cambridge.org
Information on this title: www.cambridge.org/9780521884600

© Kate Cooper 2007

This publication is in copyright. Subject to statutory exception
and to the provisions of relevant collective licensing agreements,
no reproduction of any part may take place without
the written permission of Cambridge University Press.

First published 2007

Printed in the United Kingdom at the University Press, Cambridge

A catalogue record for this publication is available from the British Library

ISBN 978-0-521-88460-0 hardback

Cambridge University Press has no responsibility for the persistence or
accuracy of URLs for external or third-party internet websites referred to
in this book, and does not guarantee that any content on such
websites is, or will remain, accurate or appropriate.

173499093

For Hester and Hildelith

Contents

So it has been since the days of Hecuba and of Hector, Tamer of Horses: inside the gates, the women with streaming hair and uplifted hands offering prayers, watching the world combat from afar, filling their long empty days with memories and fears: outside, the men in fierce struggle with things divine and human, quenching memory in the stronger light of purpose, losing the sense of dread and even of wounds in the hurrying ardour of action.

George Eliot, The Mill on the Floss

Preface

This study considers the end of the Roman empire from the point of view of household and family life. This is an aspect which has been comparatively neglected in the otherwise voluminous literature on the empire's decline and fall. At issue here is how late Roman householders drew on an emerging Christian wherewithal of ideas and resources – I do not mean theology but practical ethical ideas and personal relationships with Christian *virtuosi*: nuns and bishops, priests and monks – to help them find a path through an unprecedented period of social change. At the end of antiquity, I will argue, the older vision of Roman family life based on the legal powers of the *paterfamilias* gave way to a new ideal, in which the *paterfamilias* had essentially ceded to the Christian bishop his role of arbiter in matters of piety and justice. But this development did not occur in a vacuum. Rather, it had roots reaching back into the third century, to an erosion of the powers of Roman heads of households that had more to do with tax-collecting than with religious ideas.

Our concern is with the Western, Latin-speaking part of the Empire, which after the death of Theodosius the Great in 395 became first an administrative unit separate from the eastern territories, and then a cluster of independent kingdoms under Gothic, Vandal, and other non-Roman kings. In the West, the 'long fifth century', from the death of Theodosius up to the invasion of Italy in 535 by Roman armies based in Byzantium, saw a revolution in the ground-rules of two related but distinct Roman social institutions, the family and the household. One aspect of this social revolution – relatively well understood by modern historians – involved the choice, by the sons and daughters of Roman families, to avoid marriage, and rather to live as professed ascetics either at home or in dedicated communities. Yet a second aspect of the revolution in family life, the widespread adoption of an evolving ideal of marriage as a commitment for eternity, has received far less attention. It is this revolution in the role of married householders that forms the subject of the present study.

Iustum matrimonium, the traditional form of marriage practised by Roman citizens whether pagan or Christian from the time of Augustus to the end of the empire, was a limited reproductive contract, ideally established between two men. One of the two parties to the contract was a man at the height of his powers, the father of a marriageable daughter. The other, perhaps though not necessarily younger, was the aspiring father of sons. The partners to the marriage were the former man's daughter and the latter man himself. (The rules of *patria potestas* meant that there was variation: in some families the bride was *sui iuris* and able to enter the contract herself, while in others the groom was still *in potestate* and his father acted on his behalf. But since the bride was ideally in her mid-teens, and the husband ideally a decade or so older, he was more likely to be *sui iuris*, whether because of his father's death or through the father's choice.)

Roman marriage was fundamentally sequential. It served a private purpose, of course, that of producing legitimate heirs to continue the father's line. But its public purpose, that of producing a new generation of citizens and thus of securing the population against staggering mortality rates for childbirth, disease, and infection, was if anything even more urgent. All parties agreed that it was desirable for the union to last until the death of one or the other partner, but even so the conditions of ancient medicine and public health meant that this might well happen before the children reached maturity. If one partner died, or the changing circumstances of either family made it advantageous to dissolve the union, the firm expectation was that the surviving partner or partners should remarry as swiftly as possible.

In the last century or so of the Roman empire in the West, marriage was reinvented as a specifically Christian institution. On the one hand, I argue, the civic importance of marriage was heightened by the progressive erosion of Roman political stability and the subsequent attempt by barbarian kings to re-establish the peace on new terms. At the same time, the new attention to the theoretical basis of Christian marriage reflected a self-conscious attempt on the part of bishops and other Christian writers to steer powerful lay patrons toward understanding sexually active marriage as a second-tier form of asceticism. Ironically, we suggest, the new attention to marriage can be understood as a knock-on effect of the success of ascetic Christianity. Across the fifth and sixth centuries, the understanding of *adfinitas*, kinship by marriage, changed. Traditionally, a man could choose his affines in a way he could not choose his consanguine kin, but traditional

Roman marriage, with its pragmatic approach to divorce, offered only a weak, because reversible, form of kinship. The new mode of affinity, by contrast, was meant to be as binding as blood kinship while retaining the advantage of being chosen. The increased hold of the marriage bond, whether or not it involved reproduction, would have far-reaching repercussions for both women and men.

Historians have tended to assume that a far-reaching 'Christianization' of marriage did not really take place until after the first millennium, as a corollary to the celibacy of the priesthood championed by the 'Gregorian Reform' (e.g. Georges Duby, *The Knight, the Lady, and the Priest*). Before 1000, the laity and their marriage bonds are seen to be improvised and inchoate, awaiting the formative intervention of the ecclesiastical hierarchy. This influential hypothesis is at least partly untrue: on the evidence presented here, the Christianization of marriage is a late Roman, not a medieval, problem. Already at the end of antiquity the need to re-theorize marriage had begun to be addressed, and the Christian identity of the married laity was far from inarticulate.

To capture in a single gesture the movement within marriage at the end of antiquity, we may focus our attention on the position of the female partner, the daughter who becomes first bride, then wife and mother. In Roman marriage, the wife was a liminal figure, standing on the threshold between two households. Rather than joining her husband's *familia*, the circle of dependents who by law were under his *potestas*, including both children and slaves, the wife remained part of the *familia* of her father. In the fifth and early sixth centuries, however, Christian writers did their best to bring the wife into the sphere of her husband's authority.

Under the Roman empire, however many successive husbands a woman might acquire following widowhood, divorce, or both, in legal terms she remained first and foremost her father's daughter. Despite the harsh realities of divorce and infant mortality, Roman parents loved their children, and there is copious evidence that Roman marriage was at least in many cases a bond of lasting mutual affection. But the fact remains that Roman marriage was a reproductive contract between *two* families, not the creation of a new, third family around the conjugal bond.

Her position at the intersection of two kin-groups had many advantages for the Roman wife, who was able to draw on the protection of her blood kin, the *familia* to whom she belonged by law, while enjoying many rights as a distinguished guest of the *familia* of her husband. By modern standards, her independence from the husband was surprisingly high. She had her own property and up to the time of Constantine if she wished to divorce, she might depending on her status require the permission of her father, but the consent of the husband was not required. At the same time, she had correspondingly little protection if her husband or his kin wished to be rid of her. Her husband had no claim on the property she had brought into the marriage (while the husband had usufruct of her dowry, it returned to her or her family if the marriage ended), but if she were poorer than he, or had no surviving kin, she might well find herself vulnerable if the marriage ended unexpectedly.

More importantly, the Roman mother had no legal claim on the children of a marriage. If they were born in wedlock and her husband had accepted them as his own, they belonged to his *familia* – not, like herself, to that of her own father. This made things easier for Roman magistrates – there were no grounds for a custody battle between divorcing parents – but it made for a staggering imbalance of power between husband and wife when divorce was on the horizon. Although modern studies often perceive the freedom to divorce as an advantage for Roman women, in the context of Roman family law it is fair to assume that most women with children went to extraordinary lengths to *avoid* divorce, with its resulting limitation of access to beloved children.

The most striking of the changes proposed to Roman marriage by Christian bishops was the prohibition of divorce. Christian literature had always taken a dim view of divorce and remarriage, but there is significant evidence to suggest that, like the scriptural view that Christians would do better not to marry in the first place, the literature against divorce had little measurable effect on Christian practice up to the fourth century. Even after the emperor Constantine and his successors began to limit the conditions under which a man or woman could claim a unilateral divorce (i.e. against the will of his or her partner), there is good evidence that Christians as well as pagans made free use of divorce by mutual agreement. But from the late fourth century there is evidence that this began to change.

Naturally, ecclesiastical writers and lay patrons had different points of view where marriage was concerned, and where the sources allow, we will explore these differences in the study that follows. Our evidence for the laity is restricted for the most part to the senatorial aristocracy, but the story of their struggle with the clergy over the nature of the marriage bond is well worth telling. We will try to capture the distinctive flavour of aristocratic lay Christianity – the Christianity, for example, of the poetess Proba, whose biblical cento, a history of Old and New Testaments composed exclusively from lines of Virgil, seems to have been a staple of the medieval school-room. Steeped in both the memory of Rome's greatness and anxiety for Rome's future, aristocratic lay Christianity reflected vividly both the harsh realities and the cultural aspirations of the age.

Meanwhile, churchmen in the fifth and sixth centuries crafted a spirituality of marriage expressed in the distinctively martial imagery of the period. Thus were married women encouraged to think of themselves as soldiers of Christ, whose persistence in virtue would crush the armies of Satan. It is not difficult to see how this imagery reflects the atmosphere of military alert during the years of the fall of the Theodosian dynasty and the uncertain tenure of the Visigothic, Ostrogothic, and Vandal kingdoms (the first of which would endure for centuries, while the latter two collapsed within decades). At the same time, Christian writers were attempting to reinvent married life as a spiritual path of daily martyrdom. Central here was the need to explain why 'opting out' of conjugal relations, as a number of influential married couples were seen to do from the late fourth to early sixth centuries, did not mean that the marriage bond itself was dissolved.

The chapters that follow consider contrasting aspects of the Roman household as a progressively Christian institution. The structure may be somewhat unexpected, since the outlines of a history of marriage and household are repeatedly interwoven with attention to source material, and scholarly debates from other aspects of social and cultural history, that have seemed to me to be important for understanding the context within which late Roman men and women made decisions about marriage, reproduction, property, and religious identity.

Chapter One, 'The Battle of this Life', offers an introduction to Christianity from the late fourth to the early sixth centuries, with special attention to two little-known Latin conduct manuals addressed to aristocratic laypersons: the anonymous *Ad Gregoriam in palatio* written in the late fifth or early sixth century for an otherwise unknown Gregoria, the wife of a Roman senator, and a second treatise addressed by Ferrandus of Carthage to Reginus, *dux* in North Africa around 535, shortly after the Roman reconquest of the territory. Chapter Two, 'The Obscurity of Eloquence', considers the distinctive sub-culture of senatorial lay Christianity during our period, arguing that the 'patronage class' of aristocratic lay householders played a far more active role in shaping the Christian ethics of the day than has previously been understood. Chapter Three, Household and empire, considers the ethical perspective of the senatorial laity with specific reference to their role as landowners, suggesting that a consideration of the economic position of the late Roman estate makes it possible to understand the moral urgency of fifth-century debates on the duties and obligations of rich Christians.

Chapters Four and Five turn from social context to the efforts of Christian writers to create a compelling and distinctive spiritual world-view for their lay correspondents. In Chapter Four, 'Such Trustful Partnership', letters of advice from bishops to married Christian couples take centre stage, with special attention to the attempt to understand sexually active marriage as a form of *askesis* or spiritual training. Thus the Christian wife is portrayed on the one hand as the mistress of a citadel besieged by the satanic army of the vices, at the same time as her ability to endure the routine indignities of life with a husband is rendered heroic through the lens of Christian martyrdom. Chapter Five, The invisible enemy, develops a discussion of the wider Christian vision of life as a spiritual battle, showing how the reinvention of marriage contributes to a distinctive late Roman and early medieval Christian spirituality. Finally, I have included, as an appendix, a translation of *Ad Gregoriam in palatio*, a text which I believe to be of unparalleled importance for understanding the social and spiritual tensions centred on the Christian household in our period.

* * *

In preparing this study I have acquired many debts, the greatest of which I would like to record here. Many institutions have made time, books, and other resources available during the course of the project, and I would like especially to thank the University of Manchester, the Ludwig Maximilian University of Munich, Georgetown University, Dumbarton Oaks, The British Academy, and the Austrian Academy of Sciences for their assistance. I am especially grateful to the staff and students of the History Department of the University of Padova, who offered a congenial home within which to think out the final shape of the study.

I have benefited from unusual generosity on the part of friends and colleagues who have shared their time, expertise, and inspiration. Gillian Clark and Judith Evans Grubbs each read the whole manuscript, and parts of it more than once, revealing exemplary forbearance, generosity, and expertise. Other friends have kindly read chapters, or shared their considerable wisdom in discussion: Kim Bowes, Averil Cameron, Paul Fouracre, Julia Hillner, Christopher Kelly, Gavin Kelly, Henrietta Leyser, Anneke Mulder-Bakker, Philip Rousseau, Kristina Sessa, Bryan Ward-Perkins, Chris Wickham, and Jocelyn Wogan-Browne. At different stages of its evolution, Janet Martin, Nicholas Horsfall, and Carole Hill read through drafts of the translation of *Ad Gregoriam in palatio* appended to the study. My gratitude for this act of friendship and encouragement is deep, especially since it opened a window on the kind of literary friendship so important to late Roman men and women. None of the above, it goes without saying, bears responsibility for the errors and interpretations to be found in what follows. To Michael Sharp and his team at Cambridge University Press, I am grateful for shepherding the book through production as swiftly and painlessly as possible, and I owe thanks to Sarah Tatum for preparing the index. Translations, where not explicitly acknowledged, are my own.

A last group of friends, Robert and Margaret Markus, Peter and Betsy Brown, and Jim and Mary Douglas, have offered indispensable criticism and encouragement since the project's inception many years ago, always accompanied by memorable hospitality. Among these, I would especially like to remember Mary, who, over the course of a twenty-year friendship, repeatedly brought the conversation around to deceptively straightforward questions about how Romans coped with their in-laws. If a confident line of inquiry about how Roman kinship systems work can be traced in what follows, it is thanks to this intellectual generosity. Her death this past spring, with Jim's in 2005, have left their friends, and the world of letters, immeasurably poorer.

Finally I am grateful to my family. My parents, Robbi and Kent Cooper, did their best to draw me away from a Casaubonesque obsession with detail toward aspects of the project that might be of use or interest to readers whose starting-point differs from my own. Conrad Leyser, my husband, revealed an astonishing ability to remain inspired and inspiring through dozens of drafts and a thousand conversations, though no one who knows him will really be surprised. Our two daughters, both born while this project was already in progress, are now old enough to have shown real generosity of spirit in encouraging their mother to lend her attention to something they could see was important to her, even if far less important than themselves. To Hester and Hildelith, in thanks for countless small kindnesses, I dedicate this book, with my love.

Abbreviations

Periodicals are abbreviated according to the conventions in *L'Année philologique*

AA	*Auctores Antiquissimi*
AASS	*Acta Sanctorum*
ANF	*Ante-Nicene Fathers*
BHL	*Bibliotheca Hagiographica Latina*
BMCR	*Bryn Mawr Classical Review*
CC	*Corpus Christianorum, Series Latina*
CCCM	*Corpus Christianorum Continuatio Medievalis*
CIL	*Corpus Inscriptionum Latinarum*
CSEL	*Corpus Scriptorum Ecclesiasticorum Latinorum*
MGH	*Monumenta Germaniae Historica*
Epp.	*Epistolae*
ILS	*Inscriptiones Latinae Selectae*
NPNF	*Nicene and Post-Nicene Fathers*
PCBE	*Prosopographie chrétienne du Bas-Empire*
PG	*Patrologia Graeca*
PL	*Patrologia Latina*
PLS	*Patrologiae Latinae Supplementum*
PRLE	*Prosopography of the Later Roman Empire*
SC	*Sources chrétiennes*
SRM	*Scriptores rerum Merovingicarum*
TLL	*Thesaurus Linguae Latinae*
TU	*Texte und Untersuchungen*

CHAPTER I

'The battle of this life'

When it was noised abroad that Attila the king of the Huns, overcome with savage rage, was laying waste the province of Gaul, the terror-stricken citizens of Paris sought to save their goods and money from his power by moving them to other, safer cities. But Genovefa summoned the matrons of the city and persuaded them to undertake a series of fasts, prayers, and vigils in order to ward off the threatening disaster, as Esther and Judith had done in the past. Agreeing with Genovefa, the women gave themselves up to God and laboured for days in the baptistery – fasting, praying, and keeping watch as she directed. Meanwhile she persuaded the men that they should not remove their goods from Paris because the cities they deemed safer would be devastated by the raging Huns while Paris, guarded by Christ, would remain untouched by her enemies.[1]

This passage, the most famous episode of the sixth-century *Vita Genovefae* or *Life of Saint Genevieve*, reflects a late Roman certainty that miraculous powers and historical events could not be understood in isolation from one another. By organizing the women of Paris to protect Paris from Attila the Hun through their prayers, Genovefa ran a considerable risk. Having followed her advice, the citizens then lost their nerve and threatened her with stoning or drowning as a false prophetess. Yet the saint's ability to mobilize both the male and female property-holders of Paris toward complementary tasks also demands our attention. In the eyes of her sixth-century biographer, the ability of Genovefa and her matrons to turn away a military invasion through the power of prayer, and the ability of a leading, female member of the *curia* to direct a risky but ultimately successful strategy for safeguarding the moveable goods of the town's principal citizens are, fused

---

[1] *Vita Genovefae* 10 (*MGH SRM* 3, 219), tr. Joanne McNamara and John Halborg, *Sainted Women of the Dark Ages* (Durham and London, 1992), 13. Note that the *MGH* edition gives the 'A' recension, *BHL* 3335, now accepted as the earliest version (see n. 6 below). *AASS Jan.*, 1, 138–43 gives the later 'B' recension, *BHL* 3334; this is the text translated in *Sainted Women of the Dark Ages*.

into a single image of extraordinary *virtus*. As the story is told, the practical decisions of the men of Paris depended directly on their faith in their women-folk, particularly with their ability to call down the powers of heaven to protect the city, and the good judgement of their leader Genovefa.

From the point of view of the Frankish author of the *Vita Genovefae*, the fact that the riches of Paris had not been lost to the Huns, as they would have been had they been moved to the other cities which had indeed been sacked, meant that Paris was a richer and more powerful city when it came into the Frankish kingdom. Even more importantly, it was known that the city had been chosen for protection by divine favour. This was an attribute of great consequence in the early medieval context – that Paris had fallen to the Franks themselves was merely a sign of their own even greater favour – and the importance of this divine sign helps to explain the desire of the Frankish king Clovis (d. 511) to be buried near Genovefa in Paris, in the basilica which he and his queen Clothild built over her tomb.

The story thus illustrates the important interaction between military power and religious ideas at the end of antiquity, a theme to which we will return more than once during the course of the present study. But it has another significance for historians who wish to understand the place of women in this troubled period. Fifth- and sixth-century women could not expect to hold themselves apart from the harsh military realities of their day. The unlucky *domina* could find herself the target of an invader's gratuitous violence – and this even if the army in question was Roman. The *Liber Pontificalis* records the brutality of Belisarius' siege of Naples:

But hearing that the Goths had made themselves a king [Witiges] against Justinian's wish, he came to the district of Campania close to Naples and with his army embarked on a siege of that city, since its citizens refused to open up to him. Then the patrician gained entry to the city by fighting. Driven by fury he killed both the Goths and all the [Roman] Neapolitan citizens, and embarked on a sack from which he did not even spare the churches, such a sack that he killed husbands by the sword in their wives' presence and eliminated the captured sons and wives of nobles. No one was spared, not *sacerdotes*, not God's servants, not virgin nuns.[2]

---

[2] *Liber Pontificalis*, ed. Duchesne, 3, s.v. Silverius, tr. Ray Davis, *The Book of Pontiffs (Liber Pontificalis to AD 715)* (2nd edn, Liverpool, 2000), 54. This passage comes from the first half of the life of Silverius, written c. 538–9 according to Duchesne, rather than from the second, later half, which seems to have been composed in the mid 550s (*Liber Pontificalis*, 1, xxxix–xli, ccxxx–ccxxxii, and 294, n. 15).

It is clear from the above that far from being spared, the 'wives of nobles' were in fact a target category for Belisarius' soldiers. A few lines down, the anonymous compiler recounts the year-long siege of Rome by Witiges; the account makes it clear that the invasion party was only one of the dangers threatening the besieged population:

During those days the city was under such a siege as totally to prevent anyone leaving or entering it. All private, state and church property was destroyed by fire, while men were cut down by the sword. The sword killed those it killed, famine killed those it killed, pestilence killed those it killed.[3]

Under these circumstances, even clerics and women were called upon to cultivate a version of Christian forbearance little different from the warrior stoicism of the menfolk. In certain circumstances, clerics and Christian women could take an active role in shaping the warrior ethos. That military virtues were not in principle reserved for men only can be seen from a letter addressed by Cassiodorus to the Roman senate in 533, justifying the sole rule of the Gothic queen Amalasuintha, daughter of Theoderic the Great. Amalasuintha had served as regent for her son Athalaric; after his death she attempted to bear the Ostrogothic crown in her own right.[4]

If we are to believe the *Vita Genovefae*, the women of the late Roman provincial aristocracy were perceived as a distinct grouping, sometimes cooperating with, and at other times complementing or correcting the efforts of their men-folk. To pursue the theme, let us turn back to Genovefa and her efforts to support and even guide the Roman military effort, and then to manage the turbulent transition from Roman to Frankish rule in the northern province of Belgica Secunda, covering the period from 429 to 502.[5]

The *Vita Genovefae* has been the subject of an interpretative revolution in the past two decades. Long dismissed by many scholars as a Carolingian legend drawing on the myth of an ancient corn goddess who eventually became the city's patron saint, the *Vita* was not believed to bear reliable information about the fifth or even the sixth century. In 1986, however,

[3] *Liber Pontificalis*, s.v. Silverius, tr. Davis, 54.
[4] Cassiodorus, *Variae* 11.1.10, 14, *MGH AA* 12, 329) stresses her warlike character and virtue, '*quod habet eximium uterque sexus*'; see the discussion in Patrick Amory, *People and Identity in Ostrogothic Italy, 489–554* (Cambridge, 1997), 77.
[5] After a victory of Clovis over Syagrius c. 486/7, whose precise significance is disputed, at least part of Belgica Secunda was ruled as an independent kingdom by the Franks. A useful summary of the problems involved in assessing the Frankish takeover can be found in Penny MacGeorge, *Late Roman Warlords* (Oxford, 2002), at 114–36.

Martin Heinzelmann and Joseph-Claude Poulin published a study which changed the terms of reference for all future study of the saint. Poulin's detailed assessment of the early manuscript tradition and Heinzelmann's comparison of the earliest recension with other contemporary material including inscriptions and late Roman legal sources brought forth a Genovefa who was nothing like the peasant girl familiar to historians of an earlier generation.[6]

Heinzelmann was able to show, thanks to the earliest version of the *Vita Genovefae* identified by Poulin, that the woman known to the anonymous hagiographer's informants had in fact held the rank of *clarissima femina* within the Roman system of honours.[7] The first *Vita Genovefae*, almost certainly written c. 520, preserved important details about the saint that were airbrushed out by later editors, perhaps because they did not suit the emerging legend. Daughter of Gerontia and Severus, Genovefa seems to have been born around 420 to a distinguished Frankish military family on one side and a member of the Roman administrative class on the other. In the early fifth century distinguished Franks often acquired Roman honours, gave their children Roman names, and 'assimilated' fully to the existing Roman order, so either of Genovefa's Roman-named parents could in principle have come from a Frankish background; one of them must have, given Genovefa's own Frankish name, since Roman families did not give barbarian names to their children.[8] While the details of her parents' background are a matter of speculation, Genovefa clearly inherited substantial land-holdings, along with the rights and obligations of an influential member of the Roman *curia* first of Nanterre and then of Paris (where she came to live, sponsored by a powerful godmother, after the death of her parents).[9]

Her encounters with 'the people of Paris', as well as her exercise of public functions such as organization of the finance and construction of public buildings and supervision of the *annona*, suggest that well into middle age Genovefa's authority was based on property ownership and exalted social standing as much as on her Christian virtues.[10]

---

[6] Martin Heinzelmann and Joseph-Claude Poulin, *Les Vies anciennes de sainte Geneviève de Paris, études critiques*, Bibliothèque de l'École des Hautes Études, IVᵉ Section, Sciences Historiques et Philologiques 329 (Paris and Geneva, 1986).
[7] Heinzelmann and Poulin, *Vies anciennes*, 92.	[8] Heinzelmann and Poulin, *Vies anciennes*, 83.
[9] Heinzelmann and Poulin, *Vies anciennes*, 92, suggests that Genovefa would have held one of the following titles: *principalis, patrona civitatis, defensor civitatis, mater civitatis, curator civitatis*, any of which would have carried duties and responsibilities to act on behalf of the city council.
[10] Heinzelmann and Poulin, *Vies anciennes*, 93–8.

Once Clovis' father Childeric (d. 481) had established himself in Northern Gaul,[11] Genovefa, now probably in her sixties, is portrayed as a sort of affectionate thorn in the side of the Frankish monarchy. An early episode of her relationship with Childeric plays with irony on the all-important question of gaining entrance into a fortified city.[12]

I cannot express the love and veneration that the illustrious Childeric bore her when he was King of the Franks. On one occasion, he went out of the city and ordered the gates to be closed so that Genovefa could not rescue some captives he meant to execute. But a faithful messenger conveyed news of the king's intentions to Genovefa and without delay she set off to save their lives. The people's amazement was wonderful to see when the city gate opened by itself when she touched it without a key. Then, gaining the king's presence, she persuaded him not to behead his captives.[13]

Naturally the warrior king's attempt to close his city against the woman who had stopped Attila comes to nothing. Just as his city cannot remained closed against her, so his will can not hold fast against her powers of persuasion.

There is reason to suspect that the author of the *Vita Genovefae* had in mind an idea of how Genovefa's ability to rally the women of Paris might have been shaped by her own engagement with Christian devotional literature. Shortly after his description of Genovefa's protection of Paris, the hagiographer catalogues the allegorical figures of virtue of the second-century Christian manual, the *Shepherd of Hermas*, suggesting that 'the twelve spiritual virgins described by Hermas ... kept her company'.[14] In fact, the *Shepherd* was precisely the kind of early Christian devotional text that could well have been available to Genovefa or her biographer. It is a particularly appropriate choice. In Book 3 of the *Vita Geonvefae*, the description of the twelve allegorical virgins cited in *Similitudes* 9.15 of the *Shepherd* occurs in the context of the building of a mystical tower from which the virgins themselves are

---

[11] Heinzelmann and Poulin, *Vies anciennes*, 100, discusses the possibility that Childeric had been appointed as a Roman administrator to Belgica Secunda at the same time as holding royal title among the Franks before taking up arms against the Roman government of Syagrius. The definitive break seems to have taken place with Clovis' victory over Syagrius in 486/7. Although the chronology and topography of the *Vita Genovefae* have yet to be definitively mapped against our fragmentary understanding of the decline of Roman power in the province, the present discussion does not require their resolution.

[12] MacGeorge, *Late Roman Warlords*, 118, identifies the city as 'probably Paris', but admits that the text is ambiguous.

[13] *VGen* 26 (*MGH SRM* 3, 226; tr. McNamara and Halporn, 28).

[14] *VGen* 16 (*MGH SRM* 3, 221; tr. McNamara and Halporn, 24).

visible. While the link between the 'mystical tower' of Hermas and the walled city of Paris is not made clear in the *Vita Genovefae*, the equation between tower and city becomes clearer when we consider the link made between a 'tower of contemplation' and a besieged city in another source from the late fifth or early sixth century, the anonymous *Ad Gregoriam in palatio*. Genovefa's biographer may well have seen the tower of Hermas as an inspiration for, or a key to understanding the significance of, the virgin's prayers from within the walls of her city. To be sure, the ascent to the tower of contemplation should by no means be seen as a retreat from engagement with the Christian's concrete predicament; the spiritual power of the praying women had both a practical and a mystical importance.

One of the more striking elements of the text is its invocation of the message carried to Genovefa by travelling merchants from the great Syrian saint Simeon Stylites (d. 459), asking her to remember him in her prayers as he stood on his pillar outside Antioch. The point here is that the Church was perceived as developing new and alternative modes of relationship; that men and women of Christian virtue could call upon not only the powers of heaven but also on networks of religious solidarity which reached right across the span of the former empire. If Roman military prowess was no longer invincible, the Roman legacy of Christian solidarity became even more important in the ensuing political free-for-all.

We shall have occasion to meet Genovefa again, as she is one of the very few genuinely well-documented women of our period. At the same time, she raises a spectre for the historian, because in the progressive stages of her *Vita* we can trace the distortion in memory of a prosperous lay landowner of senatorial standing into a peasant nun. This transformation served not only the purposes of devotional literature, as the well-connected *materfamilias* is progressively revised into a fuzzy and romantic figure. It also met the needs of a later Church whose institutions of memory – the monastic libraries – had little reason to devote resources to the celebrating of lay householders acting as 'free agents', and every reason to furnish hagiographical literature with details aligning a saint to devotional models in which monastic readers could find edification. The afterlife of Genovefa is a cautionary tale for anyone wishing to understand the social history of the late Roman householder class in general, or its women in particular, because it offers concrete evidence of the filtering process by which monastic librarians – and copyists – successively eroded our base of evidence.

Still, the late fifth and early sixth centuries offer little-explored terrain for trying to trace the history of the aristocratic laity, in part because a number of letter collections have survived from the period. Most are linked to bishops such as Sidonius Apollinaris,[15] Avitus of Vienne,[16] Ennodius of Pavia,[17] or Fulgentius of Ruspe;[18] networking with the powerful laity was clearly a *métier* for many of them.[19] In the later chapters we will discuss the emergence of a conduct literature addressed by bishops and deacons to this class. Something about the context and expectations of these men and women can be gleaned from the language in which advice to them is couched, and from the points of reference which the writers seem to expect the readers to recognize. Perhaps most valuable among these texts for our purposes are the moral writings of Fulgentius of Ruspe, much of whose advice to political men (Theodorus, Felix), aristocratic virgins (Proba), widows (Galla), and married couples (Optatus, Venantia) still survives.[20]

To draw conclusions about lay values from the prescriptive context of moral exhortation is a treacherous task. Occasionally, an opportunity for cross-referencing arises when letters are addressed to a single layperson by more than one writer, and in these instances we can glimpse the distortions which must inevitably govern all our materials. So, for example, the Arcotamia whom we encounter in the letters of Ennodius as a pious and ascetically minded Christian kinswoman[21] appears in the *Variae* of Cassiodorus as a landowner who, having allowed her daughter to divorce and remarry, now pursues the first son-in-law in a lawsuit over a piece of choice real estate.[22] Two lay aristocrats of the early to mid sixth century stand out as candidates for such an approach: first, Senarius the patrician, who appears in the correspondence of Ennodius, as the recipient of a theological treatise by Avitus of Vienne, and a treatise on baptism by John, deacon of Rome (possibly the future Pope John II), and a number

[15] Sidonius, *Epistolae* (*MGH AA* 8), Philip Rousseau, 'In Search of Sidonius the Bishop', *Historia* 25 (1976), 356–77, and Jill Harries, *Sidonius Apollinaris and the Fall of Rome* (Oxford, 1994).
[16] Avitus of Vienne, *Epistulae* (*MGH AA* 6/2). An accessible introduction is offered by D. Shanzer and I. Wood, *Avitus of Vienne: Selected Letters and Prose* (Liverpool, 2002).
[17] Ennodius, *Epistulae*, *MGH AA* 7; See now Stéphane Gioanni, *Ennode de Pavie, Livres 1. et 2. texte établi, traduit et commenté* (Paris, 2006).
[18] Fulgentius, *Opera* (*CC* 91); tr. Robert B. Eno, *Fulgentius: Selected Works* (Washington, D.C., 1997).
[19] On letter collections in this period, see Ian Wood, *The Merovingian Kingdoms: 450–751* (London and New York, 1994), 24–7.
[20] As above, n. 18.
[21] Ennodius, *Epistulae* 6.24 (*MGH AA* 7, 226) and 7.14 (*MGH AA* 7, 237–8). On Arcotamia, S. A. H. Kennell, *Magnus Felix Ennodius: A Gentleman of the Church* (Ann Arbor, 2000), 36 and 137.
[22] Cassiodorus, *Variae* 4.12 (*MGH AA* 12, 120).

of times in the *Variae* of Cassiodorus;[23] and secondly the *dux* Reginus,[24] the recipient of a theological treatise on docetism from Fulgentius, and a moral treatise on the conduct of a military leader from Ferrandus, deacon of Carthage. We will return to the handbook of Ferrandus below, since it stands as a valuable parallel to the conduct literature addressed to women, and reveals something of the peculiar flavour of Christian life during a period characterized both by cultural flowering and by military upheaval.

At the same time, a rich landscape of conduct literature survives, for which neither author nor addressee can be firmly established. These texts, which mostly circulated under spurious attributions to Augustine, Ambrose, Jerome, or John Chrysostom in the surviving copies, are very difficult to make sense of, since the basic parameters of date, authorship, and context often cannot be established with any certainty. Generations of scholars have constructed hypotheses about when and why these texts were produced, but since these attributions are occasionally overturned, every effort has been made in the present study to make it clear where a revision of the received wisdom about dating would alter the validity of any argument made.

The present study has, nonetheless, drawn very heavily on this anonymous literature, on the view that late Roman history really does not need to be divided into two historiographical streams, one oriented to economic, political, and military infrastructures while the other considers religious matters and 'private life', in each case with a minimum of reference to the other end of the spectrum.[25] One of the principles of this study is that this is not how history works.

The Duke of Wellington is believed to have said that the Battle of Waterloo was decided on the playing fields at Eton. He seems to have meant that the profound induction of a generation of Britons into a culture of sportsmanship allowed them, years later, to prevail in a conflict their masters could never have imagined. As children, they had been drilled in cooperation, mutual reliance, intelligent anticipation of an opponent's strategy, and the capacity to endure seemingly pointless suffering – all to the point that these became instinctive. So too, we may imagine that the end of the

---

[23] John the Deacon writes to Senarius about baptismal liturgy responding to his questions: John the Deacon, *Epistula ad Senarium* (*PL* 59, 399); see J. Sundwall, *Abhandlungen zur Geschichte des ausgehenden Römertums* (Helsinki, 1919), 153; also Avitus *Ep.* 39 (36) (MGH AA 6/2, 68) – writing to him about Eastern theological quarrels. On Senarius, see now Andrew Gillett, *Envoys and Political Communication in the Late Antique West, 411–533* (Cambridge, 2003), 191–202.

[24] For Reginus, see *PCBE*, 958; *PLRE* 3B, 1082.

[25] Janet Nelson, 'The Problematic in the Private', *Social History* 15 (1990), 355–64.

Roman empire in the West was decided in the school-room and on the playing field, by boys who having failed to internalize old Roman values of self-sacrifice and duty to the *patria*, grew up to be generals, and repeatedly set Roman armies against one another for the sake of challenging a rival, often delaying, and even destroying, armies that were urgently needed on the frontier.[26]

It goes without saying that it had never been easy to turn children into Romans. If one looks at the late Republic or early empire, perfect enactment of the 'old values' was always an exception rather than the rule. But the fact remains that from the late fourth century, new pressures seem to have compromised the cultural machinery that had developed over the centuries to remind children and adults of what was expected of them. For every panegyric celebrating the achievements of a general or wishing fertility on a young couple, we have a shrill Christian treatise attacking a Roman magistrate for his adherence to the old religion,[27] or complaining that too many girls are marrying when they really ought to be dedicating themselves to virginity. From the point of view of gender and family history, we can say that these 'culture wars' made it harder for Roman mothers to raise their sons. To do one's duty or die trying is an ideal possessed of powerful magnetism; it is far less powerful if there is uncertainty about where duty actually lies.[28]

Edward Gibbon argued two hundred years ago that Christian asceticism played a key role in bringing down the Roman empire in the West, since 'pusillanimous youth preferred the penance of the monastic to the dangers of a military life'.[29] Of course, it is not quite so simple. We will see, if we train our eyes on the wives and daughters rather than the sons, that the mechanism by which Christian ideals undermined the single-minded will to *imperium* of Roman élites was far more complicated. The problem was not so much that potential generals joined the ascetic movement instead of the army (although the ferocity of some of the monks suggests that this could have been the case). Rather, it was in the erosion of an ancient consensus regarding duty, honour, and the pursuit of the common good. When

---

[26] Bryan Ward-Perkins, *The Fall of Rome and the End of Civilization* (Oxford, 2005), 52.

[27] For discussion of the anonymous *Carmen contra paganos* see Lellia Cracco Ruggini, *Il paganesimo romano tra religione e politica, 384–394 d. C.: per una reinterpretazione del Carmen contra paganos* (Rome, 1979).

[28] I have developed this point more fully in Kate Cooper, 'Gender and the Fall of Rome', in Philip Rousseau, ed., *The Blackwell Companion to Late Antiquity* (Oxford, forthcoming).

[29] Edward Gibbon, *History of the Decline and Fall of the Roman Empire*, 3, cited in Kate Cooper and Conrad Leyser, 'The Gender of Grace: Impotence, Servitude, and Manliness in the Fifth-Century West', *Gender and History* 12 (2000), 536–51, at 536.

crucial military and political decisions hung in the balance – for example, whether to set an army against the enemy or against one's rival – it made a difference if it was obvious that parties agreed on where duty lay. A general who knew that his best men would not follow him was less likely to start – or escalate – a civil war.

The end of empire was also decided household by household, by individual landowners as they faced seemingly small-scale decisions about which local strong-man to back, which taxes to evade, when to impose order on unruly subordinates and when not to bother.[30] The idea behind the present study is that to understand the role played by this undertow of self-interest in the last years of the empire in the West, the fragmentary sources documenting ethical debates among the late Roman householder class need to be better understood, and they need to be understood in light of the wider social context in which the householders in question were expected to act.

With this in mind, the present study concentrates particularly on a series of little-known texts addressed to aristocratic women from the reign of Honorius (395–425) to that of Theoderic the Great (493–526). Many of the recipients are identifiably of senatorial status and probably substantial landowners in their own right, and most are identifiably married (there are a few virgins as well, but at least one of these is herself a senatorial landowner). We cannot always identify the precise standing of the woman's family with certainty, and I have thus tried to be specific where possible about senatorial or curial values, and in other cases limited discussion to a more general 'aristocratic' or 'landowner' point of view, trying always to reflect the emphasis of the sources as I understood them. The same is true for questions of date and authorship. Where they can be deduced, I have tried to be as precise as possible; otherwise, I have tried to indicate what level of generality or uncertainty is required for fair use of the source in argument. The aim has been to construct a tapestry of threads and patches – a composite picture – of the aristocratic household and of the changing role of the *domina* within it. Where the evidence allows us to speak firmly of datable instances and developments, I have tried to do so, and where it does not, I have not.

An important premise has been that late Roman Christianity, as the laity experienced it, was far less 'theological' than centuries of monastic librarianship have made it seem to be. The late Roman laity were interested in

---

[30] On this point, see now Ward-Perkins, *Fall of Rome*, 30, and Peter Heather, *The Fall of the Roman Empire: A New History* (London, 2005), ch. 3, 'The Limits of Empire', 100–42.

ethics, but systematic theology would not be invented for another five or six hundred years, and most of the laity were as baffled by the mysteries of the Trinity as their modern counterparts. This does not make them any less 'Christian'. The evidence suggests that their Christianity was deeply felt, yet concerned mostly with ethics, not theology *per se*. (Theology was the preserve of specialists, in other words of bishops and heretics.) Thus I have made every effort to re-place 'significant' writers like Jerome and Pelagius in the company of 'minor' Latin poets such as Commodian, or the anonymous author of a letter on the right use of riches addressed to the Roman virgin Demetrias, or, *primus inter pares*, the 'Bishop John' to whom is ascribed a curious text known as the *Ad Gregoriam in palatio*, a manual for a married laywoman, to which we shall return more than once below (and a full translation of which is appended to this study).

In describing what I have tried to do with this sometimes intractable source material, I find the words of another, very different, study of the later Roman aristocracy, strangely appropriate:

I have been concerned throughout, not with the abstract but with the concrete – with the actual events of the time, and with the many individual participants whose tastes and activities make up the texture of the book. In approaching the subject in this way, I have encountered great difficulties of structure and organization, above all in the deployment of detailed material.[31]

This study aims to find a pattern to lend meaning to a thousand seemingly unrelated *tesserae* of collected source material, in a way that, it is hoped, will reflect something of the lively specificity that still makes *Western Aristocracies and Imperial Court* so vivid thirty years after it was written. In principle, this seems a reasonable ambition. We shall return frequently, for example, to the figure of the enigmatic Gregoria, the senatorial *domina* for whom *Ad Gregoriam in palatio* was written, in the hope of finding a narrative thread to lead us through the maze of our evidence.

But the fact remains that 'my' individual participants are, as often as not, obscure men (the writers) and women (their subjects), to whom we can often only barely put a century, much less a year or a name. Having drawn the reader away from the 'public men' whose careers were engraved on marble inscriptions and commemorated as matters of public record by the historians of their day, I can make no apology for leading him (her) by the hand through sometimes lengthy *explications de texte* of little-known material about the all-but-forgotten minor players of late Roman history.

[31] John Matthews, *Western Aristocracies and Imperial Court AD 364–425* (Oxford, 1975), xi.

These women and men, as I have come to know them, are far more interesting than one might have suspected. The decisions they make, for the most part, seem to be motivated not by grand political or religious concepts, but by simple, practical, human – sometimes even petty – ambitions. Providing for one's children, getting a better return on a parcel of inherited land, keeping the neighbours from knowing too much about the skeletons in the closet, working out how to get out from under the oppressive weight of what one's parents (or parents-in-law) think one ought to be doing: these, it makes so much sense to discover, are the engines of social change in the last years of the Roman empire in the West.

That said, our hard-won glimpse of these individuals is only that, a glimpse. In writing, I have of course been acutely conscious that in the sources – even first-person sources – the individuals described are always something of a social and literary construct. Where women are concerned, this is in part because we almost always see them at second hand through the distorting lens of other writers, usually male.[32] But the texts by women in our period are so stylized in their representation of gender that it would be misleading to suggest that there is less distortion in their case; there are only different agendas.[33] If the present study does not seem overly concerned with this problem on a theoretical level, it is only because while wrestling with unknown authors writing to unknown addressees in unknown circumstances the temptation to think I was dealing with 'reality' seemed never to present itself.

For the record: where primary sources discussed below are addressed to a named but otherwise unidentifiable person, my assumption has been that a historical person probably did exist to whom the text was addressed. It goes without saying, however, that the source tells us about the views of the author rather than of the recipient. Fortunately, a competent author tends to be careful to 'manage' situations in which he suspects his reader will not like what he has to say – especially in a late Roman context when the addressee of one's text was so often a patron[34] or an ally whose help he needed or knew he

---

[32] Especially important in the secondary literature on this point is Elizabeth A. Clark, 'The Lady Vanishes: Dilemmas of a Feminist Historian after "the Linguistic Turn"', *Church History* 67 (1998), 1–31. My own views on this aspect of the problem are discussed at greater length in Kate Cooper, 'Insinuations of Womanly Influence: An aspect of the Christianization of the Roman Aristocracy', *JRS* 82 (1992), 150–64, and eadem, *The Virgin and the Bride: Idealized Womanhood in Late Antiquity* (Cambridge, Mass., 1996).

[33] See, e.g., Leslie Brubaker, 'Memories of Helena: Patterns of Imperial Female Matronage in the Fourth and Fifth Centuries', in Liz James, ed., *Women, Men and Eunuchs: Gender in Byzantium* (London, 1997), 52–75.

[34] On this point, see Anne Kurdock, '*Demetrias ancilla dei* : The Problem of the Missing Patron', in Kate Cooper and Julia Hillner, eds., *Religion, Dynasty, and Patronage in Early Christian Rome, 300–900* (Cambridge, 2007), 190–224.

might need – and uses rhetorical markers that allow the alert historian perceive that someone is being mollified. Sometimes, of course, there is reason to suspect that an author has got carried away with his rhetorical construction of the 'you' to whom he is writing, and it no longer bears a meaningful relationship to his idea of what his reader wants to hear. Where I think this is happening I have called attention to it. What I wanted to discover was what parameters the sources allow us to imagine for certain kinds of human experience and interaction; this, I think, is possible on the basis of the mental constructs of the sources, however treacherous the sources themselves.

AGAINST LUXURY: COMMODIAN

We turn now to the problems posed by the emergence of a Christian patronage class in the period after Constantine. To begin with, it is worth considering the *Instructions* of Commodian, traditionally believed to be the earliest Christian poet.[35] The date of Commodian's two poems, the *Instructiones* and *Carmen apologeticum*, has been disputed since they were discovered, in the seventeenth and nineteenth century respectively. Both texts engage in a sustained critique of the traditional gods, in language that may reflect a view of paganism as the dominant religion, and invoke the concept of martyrdom in a way that, on the face of it, suggests a third-century date. It is entirely possible, however, that Commodian's diatribe is written from the viewpoint of a fifth-century ascetic, and that his critique of idolatry is in fact directed at Christians whom he suspects of wavering in their commitment to Christian values.[36] We will see that the concept of 'daily martyrdom', so dear to Commodian, was a major theme of the post-Constantinian martyr literature.

These somewhat intractable dating questions are not particularly significant for our purposes, since there is reason to believe that whatever their date, the poems of Commodian were known in Italy during the fifth and sixth

[35] Commodianus does not appear in Jerome, *De viris illustribus*, but he does appear in the sixth-century Decretals of Gelasius, alongside the fourth-century poetess Proba, who will be discussed in the next chapter. *Decretum de libris recipiendis et non recipiendis*, (*TU* 38, 61–2), and in Gennadius, *De viris illustribus* 15 (*TU* 14, 67).

[36] On the date of Commodianus, see Josef Martin, 'Commodianus', *Traditio* 13 (1957), 1–71, at 51–71, arguing for a third-century date, and Pierre Courcelle, 'Commodien et les invasions du Ve siècle', *Revue des Études Latines* 24 (1946), 227–46, suggesting that Commodian could have written as late as the mid fifth century, largely because a passage in his *Carmen apologeticum* seems to know a passage of Orosius describing a persecution of Valerian. A pillar of the third-century dating, his close familiarity with the works of Cyprian, is of course only evidence that he did not write *before* the third century; Cyprian's far-reaching influence on later patristic writers will be discussed in a later chapter.

centuries. More important is the question of the likely readership of the
Instructions. The poet's interest is clearly to address the wider Christian
community, speaking in turn to catechumens, parents, married women,
the rich, clergy, and bishops, among other groups. Commodian has been
seen as a populist poet, perhaps in part because his poetry does not follow
established metrical conventions, and tends to stray from vowel quantity
toward accentuation as a structural principle.[37] Not only does Commodian's
poem fail to show easy fluency with the canons of elite literary expression; it
is pointed in its criticism of the rich. Commodian repeatedly returns to warn
the rich lest their riches tempt them away from Christian values.

But the obsession with the rich can in fact be read as an indication of his
interest in 'reaching' a readership drawn from the Christian patronage
class. Early in his treatment of the problem of riches, Commodian warns
the reader that the fawning of certain other teachers is not to be trusted.[38]

> If certain teachers, while looking for your gifts
> Or fearing your persons, relax individual rules to you,
> I am compelled to speak the truth.[39]

Because they are compromised by the need for patronage, other teachers
attempt to 'soften' the message of Christian teaching, allowing the aristocratic laity to carry on as before:

> You go to vain shows with the crowd of the evil one,
> Where Satan is at work in the crashing of the circus.
> You persuade yourself that everything that shall please you is lawful.[40]

The consequences of this 'softening', however, are that the aristocratic
Christians in turn are in danger of losing the favour of their own higher
patron. By contrast, compassion for the less fortunate is stressed repeatedly
as the cornerstone of virtue.

---

[37] On style, see Barry Baldwin, 'Some aspects of Commodian', *Illinois Classical Studies* 14 (1989),
331–46, at 332.

[38] This is a warning that occurs frequently in texts directed to powerful lay patrons; for discussion, see,
e.g., *Ad Gregoriam* 17 (*CC* 25A, 221): 'Let no one seduce you with vain words: here is what you should
hear . . . which is veiled by no cloud of fawning or eloquence.'

[39] Si quidam doctores, dum exspectant munera vestra,
Aut timent personas, laxant singula vobis;
Et ego non doleo, sed cogor dicere verum . . .
        Commodianus, *Instructiones* 57 (*PL* 5, 244).

[40] Cum caterva mali pergis ad spectacula vanna,
Ubi satanas fragoribus circo operatur.
Licere persuades tibi quodcumque placebit.
        Commodianus, *Instructiones* 57 (*PL* 5, 244).

The brother oppressed with want, nearly languishing away, cries out at the splendidly fed, and with distended belly.
What do you say of the Lord's day?
If he have not placed himself before, call forth a poor man from the crowd, whom you may take to dinner.[41]

Beware of trampling on your inferiors when weighed down with miseries.
Offer yourself as a protector only, and do no hurt.
Lead yourself in a righteous path, unstained by jealousy.
In your riches, make yourself gentle to those who are of little account.
Give of your labour, clothe the naked.[42]

The ethics of the *Instructions* are clearly designed for the powerful, not those at the mercy of others.

The greedy survey of the eyes is never satisfied.
Now, therefore, if you may return and consider, lust is vain . . .
Whence God cries out, You fool, this night you are summoned.
Death rushes after you. Whose, then, shall be those talents?[43]

Death appears here not as something to be feared, but as a sort of joke on the rich: their greed is ultimately pointless.

When Commodian turns to address married women, his advice reflects an aversion to luxury which at first glance may simply be traditional, reaching back through Tertullian to Paul's Letter to the Corinthians:

You wish, O Christian woman, that our matrons should be as the ladies of the world. . . .
You are adorned at the looking-glass with thy curled hair turned back from thy brow.
God is the overlooker, who dives into each heart.

---

[41] Oppressus inopia frater juxta tabescens.
De die dominica quid dicis? si non ante locavit,
Excita de turba pauperem, quem ad prandium ducas.
    Commodianus, *Instructiones* 61 (*PL* 5, 248).

[42] Oppressos miseriis deprimere cave minores.
Tutorem accommoda tantum, et noli nocere.
Tramite vos recto ducite sincereo prae zelo.
In tuis divitiis comem te redde pusillis.
De labore tuo dona, nudum vesti: sic vinces.
    Commodianus, *Instructiones* 63 (*PL* 5, 249).

[43] Oculorum acies numquam satiatur avara.
Nunc ergo si redeas et cogites, vana cupido est.
Unde Deus clamat: Stulte hac nocte vocaris,
Post te mors ruit: cujus erunt ista talenta?
    Commodianus, *Instructiones* 64 (*PL* 5, 249–50).

But these thing are not necessay for modest women.
Pierce your breast with chaste and modest feeling.
The law of God calls upon such habits to depart
From the believing heart; to a wife approved of her husband,
Let it suffice that she is so, not by her dress, but by her good disposition.[44]

The concern is not sex *per se* – it is the ostentatious display of wealth:

Do you good matrons, flee from the adornment of vanity;
Such attire is fitting for women who haunt the brothels
... Show forth all your wealth in giving.[45]

But the point is eventually lost in a lather of condemnation.

Why should I tell of your dresses, or of the whole pomp of the Devil?
You are rejecting the law when you wish to please the world.
You dance in your houses; instead of psalms, you sing love songs.
Although you may be chaste, do not prove thyself so by following evil things
... Be pleasing to the hymned chorus,
And to an appeased Christ with ardent love fervently offer your savour to
  Christ.[46]

Whether Commodian imagined a female readership for his poem is uncertain and perhaps beside the point. The condemnation of female luxury was certainly a commonplace, and no historical woman needed to be in view for a moral writer to get wonderful mileage out of it. But we will see in the chapters that follow that Commodian's themes were of great interest to the devotional literature addressed to females in the fifth and sixth centuries.

---

[44] Matronas vis esse, christiana, ut saeculi domnas,
... Ornaris ad speculum, cincinnos fronte reflexos;
... Est Deus inspector, penetrat qui singula corda;
Ceterum pudicis ista necessaria non sunt.
Casto atque pudico sensu pertundite pectus.
Lex Dei testatur tales abscedere leges
Ex corde qui credit, feminae marito probatae
Sufficiat esse non cultibus, sed bona mente.
  Commodianus, *Instructiones* 59 (*PL* 5, 245–6).

[45] Vos matronae bonae vanitatis fugite decorem.
In feminas congruit cultura lupanas.
... In dando, divitias vestras ostendite totas.
  Commodianus, *Instructiones* 59 (*PL* 5, 246).

[46] Quid memorem vestes, aut totam Zabuli pompam?
Respuitis legem cum vultis mundo placere.
Saltatis in domibus, pro psalmis cantatis amores.
Tu licet sis casta, non te purgas sinistra sequendo:
... Ymnificato choro placitoque Christo placete;
Zelantes fervore Christo offerte odorem.
  Commodianus, *Instructiones* 65 (*PL* 5, 247).

THE *MILES CHRISTI* AS A DEVOTIONAL MODEL
FOR CHRISTIAN WOMEN

We turn now to consider briefly the key devotional texts of the late fourth and early fifth centuries which inspired much of the later conduct literature for women. Perhaps unsurprisingly, an image that would be picked up again and again was that of the Christian – even the teenaged virgin – as a valiant solider on the battlefield, fighting for Christ. The language of spiritual warfare as a means for establishing Christian identity already had a long history by the fourth century.[47] It appears as early as the famous exhortation to eschatological battle in the New Testament's Letter to the Ephesians – 'for we are not contending against flesh and blood, but against the principalities, against the powers … against the spiritual hosts of wickedness in the heavenly places' (Ephesians 6:12)[48] – and in the vivid battle imagery of the Book of Revelation. Origen's third-century allegorical readings of the military books of the Hebrew Bible developed this idea of spiritual battle, but it was in fourth-century ascetic literature that the metaphor found its most compelling application. The famous episode of Saint Antony doing battle with the demons in Athanasius' mid-fourth-century *Life* of the saint was widely influential in ascetic literature, as were Evagrius' contemporary attempts to prepare ascetics for the inevitable battle with temptation,[49] and those of John Cassian a generation later. John Cassian would develop the theme of invisible spiritual battle as more dangerous than the visible battle of military engagement.

By the late fourth century, a specifically female interpretation of this tradition was emerging in the Latin West. Ever one to bring what was most up-to-date to the attention of his aristocratic patronesses in Rome, Saint Jerome gave emphasis to the theme in his 22nd letter, published in Rome in the spring of 384 and addressed to Julia Eustochium, the daughter, in her early teens, of his principal patroness Paula.[50] The letter invites the young virgin to consider the spiritual life in terms of the battle with principalities and powers noted above in Ephesians 6:12. As an ascetic, she must don the breastplate of faith, 'for we are surrounded by great bands of enemies',[51]

---

[47] See, e.g., Adolf Von Harnack, *Militia Christi: The Christian Religion and the Military in the First Three Centuries*, trans. and intr. by David McInnes Gracie (Philadelphia, 1981); Andreas Wang, *Der 'Miles Christianus' im 16. und 17. Jahrhundert und seine mittelalterliche Tradition: ein Beitrag zum Verhältnis von sprachlicher und graphischer Bildlichkeit*, Mikrokosmos 1 (Frankfurt, 1975).
[48] Here and below I have cited the Revised Standard Version of Biblical texts.
[49] Evagrius, *Praktikos* 48 (*SC* 171, 608).   [50] Jerome, *Ep.* 22 (*PL* 22, 394–425).
[51] Jerome, *Ep.* 22.3 (*PL* 22, 396).

a battle which is cast in ascetic terms, as taking place between the flesh and the spirit. The young virgin is invited to remember Jerome's own ascetic struggles[52] and – by extension – those of Antony, and presumably to take heart from the comparison: her own struggle with the flesh at home on the Aventine is mapped onto the heroic battles of the desert itself.[53] Three decades later, the letter of Pelagius to the virgin Demetrias takes up the military theme. Her life is to be a battle for virtue with God as her commander; her assault against the camp of the Devil means that not only must she shun what is evil, she must also actively do what is good. Reflecting a stunning disregard for literary consistency, the meta-phor suddenly turns from the battlefield to the virtues as the 'most precious pearls with which the bride of Christ should be adorned'.[54] This inconsistency may reveal the writer's self-consciousness regarding the gender of his young warrior, but the mixing of masculine and feminine points of identification in texts addressed to women was by no means unusual. Indeed, we will see below that *Ad Gregoriam in palatio* develops and escalates the use of battle language in the text, at the same time as its commitment to the spirituality of marriage and house-holding requires that it substitute chaste, fertile marriage for virginity, and thus reinterpret the battle as primarily with the vices of the heart rather than those of the body.

The *Letter to Eustochium* raises a series of other issues which we will see in the conduct litertature for married women: recourse to the authority of scripture,[55] the difference between being and merely seeming to be spiri-tually expert,[56] the problem of association with those who would under-mine one's spiritual purpose[57] and the related problem of gossip,[58] the dangers of avarice,[59] and the peril of vainglory, present even in the pursuit of perfect humility.[60] Her reward for successful negotiation of

---

[52] Jerome, *Ep.* 22.7 (*PL* 22, 399).
[53] On this point, see Rousseau, *Ascetics, Authority, and the Church in the Age of Jerome and Cassian* (Oxford, 1978), 91–138, and V. Burrus, *The Sex Lives of Saints: An Erotics of Ancient Hagiography* (Philadelphia, 2004), 19–52.
[54] Pelagius, *Ad Demetriadem*, 16.1 (*PL* 30, 30), tr. B. R. Rees, *The Letters of Pelagius and his Followers* (Woodbridge, 1991), 52.
[55] Jerome, *Ep.* 22.10 (*PL* 22, 400), 'innumerabilia sunt de scripturis divina responsa'.
[56] Jerome, *Ep.* 22.15 (*PL* 22, 403), 'explosis igitur et exterminatis his quae nolunt esse virgines, sed videri . . .'
[57] Jerome, *Ep.* 22.16 (*PL* 22, 403), 'nolo habeas consortio matronarum . . .'
[58] Jerome, *Ep.* 22.24 (*PL* 22, 410), 'ne declines aurem tuam in verba malitiae'.
[59] Jerome, *Ep.* 22.31 (*PL* 22, 417).
[60] Jerome, *Ep.* 22.27 (*PL* 22, 412–13), 'Nec satis religiosa velis videri, nec plus humilis quam necesse est, ne gloriam fugiendo quaeras.'

these hazards is figured as an eschatological encounter with a band of female biblical personages, angels, and saints.[61]

Perhaps even more influential than Jerome's *Letter to Eustochium* in establishing the genre of the letter of spiritual instruction of a noble lady is the letter written by Pelagius to the equally young Demetrias, daughter of Anicia Juliana and Anicius Hermoginanus Olybrius and granddaughter of Sextus Petronius Probus, to commemorate her veiling as a virgin in 413. Pelagius begins by declaring that to praise so illustrious a young woman as Demetrias is no difficult task, but by contrast, to presume to offer instruction to one already so wise is as difficult as praising her is easy. He acknowledges that she has already achieved fame for her virtue: 'She wants her conduct to become no less an object of wonder than her conversion has been: already noble in this world, she desires to be even nobler before God and seeks in her moral conduct values as precious as the objects which she spurned in this world.'[62] He goes on to explain the pastoral basis for the Pelagian theology of will which was eventually to lead to his condemnation, though it is easy to see in this context why he felt it was a crucial tool for pastoral work. To put it simply, he wishes the girl never to succumb to discouragement, but rather to understand that it is within her power to do what God asks her to do: 'the best incentive for the mind consists in teaching it that it is possible to do anything which one really wants to do.'[63]

He goes on to argue – an argument strikingly similar to one of Augustine's arguments for Original Sin, though its point is of course the reverse – that there is a natural sanctity in the human mind which causes the instinctive sense of shame which we have at our own wrongdoing. Next comes a summary of the virtues of the Patriarchs even before the giving of the Law to Moses – again a summary not dramatically different in tone from the position taken by Augustine in his *De bono coniugali*, although while there the virtue of the patriarchs is used to argue for the good of the married estate, here it is used to argue for the heroic capacity of human nature. What causes the difficulty of doing good in human beings is, rather than an intrinsic inability, a long habit of doing wrong – but if certain people were able to live holy and righteous lives not only before the coming of Christ but even before the Law, surely 'sin will have no dominion over you, since you are not under the Law but under grace'.[64] This leads to an

---

[61] Jerome, *Ep.* 22.41 (*PL* 22, 424–5).   [62] Pelagius, *Ad Demetriadem* 2 (*PL* 30, 16; tr. Rees, 36).
[63] Pelagius, *Ad Dem* 2.1 (*PL* 30, 16; tr. Rees, 37).
[64] Pelagius, *Ad Dem* 8.4 (*PL* 30, 23; tr. Rees, 45), quoting Romans 6:14.

assertion of the urgency of studying scripture, since to do God's will she has first to know it.

If in choosing virginity she has undertaken to do something even greater than what is commanded, however, she should remember that this is no excuse for neglecting the commandments which even those in a lower spiritual estate are careful to fulfil. The metaphor of the wide and narrow paths is reinvented here: not only ordinary sinners, but ascetics who think that their exemplary virtue in one respect places them above the law in others are among those who throng the broad path to death, while Demetrias is encouraged to think of herself as ready to tread the more difficult path to eternal life, which requires righteousness in all things. This means, of course, spurning the riches of this world in favour of the more permanent riches of the next, and cultivating the immortal honour which is far more important than nobility in the earthly sense. It is the feasts of divine Wisdom which she must crave, and which she will crave ever more, the more she partakes of them.[65]

The next few paragraphs draw repeatedly on references and analogies to the domestic setting with which the virgin is presumed to be well acquainted. She should be as anxious to please God as the married woman is anxious to please her husband, remembering, however, that even a *matrona* burdened by the care of husband and children is responsible to live the life of righteousness: how much more so a virgin who has been released from all the impediments of this world? She should think of herself as a child, whose habit of doing good must be formed and strengthened while it is still young and flexible. She should remember that her mother and grandmother have set their hearts on her as the hope of the family: while previous generations have included men at the pinnacle of the Roman state, none has brought on the *gens* so great an honour as that conferred by a virgin's vow.

But this does not relegate her to the domestic sphere; quite the reverse is the case. Her act of profession is depicted as a matter of public significance equal to the exploits of the great consuls of the *gens*: 'the whole world has become so exultant at your conversion', and again, 'consider now that the faces and eyes of all are turned upon you and that the entire world has settled down to watch the spectacle of your life. Take care not to disappoint so many, if they find in you less than they are looking for.'[66] Having stirred the girl to a rapture of self-consciousness, Pelagius then concedes that God

---

[65] Pelagius, *Ad Dem* 11.2 (*PL* 30, 27; tr. Rees, 49), citing Sirach 24:21.
[66] Pelagius, *Ad Dem* 14.2 and 14.3 (*PL* 30. 29; tr. Rees, 51–2).

himself is the only really important spectator in the struggle that is this life. Her life is to be a battle for virtue with God as her commander; her assault against the camp of the Devil means that not only must she shun what is evil, she must also actively do what is good. This leads to a further reprise of the theme that to God the small commandments are as urgent as the great ones.

Pelagius then turns to argue that even in this world vice has no real attraction over virtue. Only two vices, gluttony and lust, offer any real inducement of even transient pleasure, and these, he notices, do not tend to attract virgins. More dangerous to the virgin because less alluring and more insidious, are the other vices such as envy, hatred, anger, which rather than delight, offer only torment to the mind. In exhorting her to avoid the real peril posed by these lesser vices, he returns to the theme of the girl's honour and nobility. Fasting and abstinence should be adornments to her real virtue, rather than a ploy to cover her vices; she is not only the daughter of an illustrious family but also a daughter of God. There is certainly real pastoral insight behind his encouraging her to cultivate something not far from what a modern would call self-esteem: 'If you wish to guard yourself adequately you must always consider your own honour to be a precious possession, since everyone treats himself with less caution the lower the opinion he has of himself.'[67] But Pelagius is here walking a fine line between his impulse to praise the girl on grounds which are fundamentally those of her family's high standing, and an equal and opposite consciousness that earthly ties of family cannot be the basis for spiritual merit. The parallelism which he repeatedly invokes between her human ancestry and her heritage as a daughter of God is a way of trying to resolve this tension.

Next he gives a list of the lesser vices from which she must refrain. Not only must she refrain from disparaging others, but she must refuse to listen to those who would disparage. She must avoid swearing oaths, and all superfluous speech, cultivating a reputation for circumspection and modesty. She should remember that many vices wear the cloak of virtue, such as the false humility which masks a pride in one's seeming accomplishment; real humility is measured by her endurance when she is misunderstood or even insulted. Flatterers, by contrast, should be feared as enemies, since they lure the listener away from self-knowledge to a dependence on the opinions of men. Finally, her pursuit of the virtues of fasting and abstinence should be moderate, lest, by laying her open to pride, the virtues themselves become the occasion of her downfall.

---

[67] Pelagius, *Ad Dem* 19.1 (*PL* 30, 33; tr. Rees (adapt.) 56).

She should set herself apart for a period in every day for prayer and the study of scripture – not, of course, that any hour of her life should be devoid of spiritual striving. Scripture should serve her as a mirror, in which she may examine the features of her soul, correcting the blemishes and highlighting what is attractive. A mixed diet of scripture, with Old Testament histories, prophets, the Psalms, and the Wisdom of Solomon complemented by the evangelists and apostles, should be mingled alternately with prayer, though always in moderation – even reading can lead to the vice of intemperance. The image of a girl before a mirror is invoked again, as Demetrias is reminded that as a bride of Christ she must be more splendidly adorned than the brides of this world, 'since the greater the one whom one is seeking to please the greater the effort which is required in order to please him'.[68] As an ornament for the head, she needs in place of a diadem only the unguent placed upon her in baptism, but as an ornament for the ears, she should prefer the words of God to the most precious stones; her limbs should be ornamented with the works of holiness. After citing Song of Songs 4:7, 'You are all fair, my love; there is no flaw in you,'[69] Pelagius turns to his final warning against the strategies of Satan, reminding her that the very virtues which make her attractive to God will at the same time serve as a bulwark against the Enemy.

It is the Devil's envy of God which Demetrias most needs to fear. He is the paradigm of the man who rejoices in bringing others down so that he himself may seem less vile. It was envy that caused him to dislodge Eve from her place in paradise. The letters of Peter, James, and Paul are all invoked as warnings against the stratagems of the Devil; she must put on the armour of God (Ephesians 6:13) in order to fight a battle in which even a woman can triumph if she studies the strategies of her opponent assiduously enough, and if she learns to use all the weapons at her disposal. Even self-doubt is revealed as a tool of the Devil: 'a mind may easily be deterred from making progress with a project as it begins to realize how harsh are the first steps involved.'[70] It is important to distinguish between fleeting thoughts which the mind instantly repels, and those on which the mind dwells and to which it offers its internal consent: only the latter should give rise to self-censure.

The final section reprises in turn the points of advice which Pelagius has raised through the treatise, from the necessity of prayer and scriptural study to that of despising riches. The virgin's straining toward her eternal reward

---

[68] Pelagius, *Ad Dem* 24.2 (*PL* 30, 38; tr. Rees, 62).   [69] Pelagius, *Ad Dem* 24. 2 (*PL* 30, 39; tr. Rees, 63).
[70] Pelagius, *Ad Dem* 26.1 (*PL* 30, 40; tr. Rees, 65).

takes on an eschatological dimension as the final judgement is invoked by comparison to the recent sack of Rome: if the destruction of a single human city struck fear in the hearts of all, how much more so the end of the world itself? But the virgin will have nothing to fear on the day of the Lord, for she will fly upwards to the embrace of her Bridegroom, rejoicing with the chorus of the blessed and the throng of holy virgins.

A word must be said, before we take leave of Pelagius, about the role of the Pelagian controversy in the production of literature for the fifth-century laity. Across the twentieth century, scholars were accustomed to assume that any anonymous Christian text addressed to a Christian aristocrat was probably inspired by a Pelagian emphasis on the Stoic virtues of the Roman aristocracy, and ultimately by a corresponding idea of human perfectibility. Although this view is no longer widely held among English-speaking scholars, it still informs a lively tradition of scholarship in France.[71] It may be suggested, however, that a great deal of evidence has been attached to the 'Pelagian movement' that is actually evidence for something very different – the Christianity of normal, if perhaps aristocratic, householders. Many of these seem to have been influenced – or at least those who wrote to them were – more by Augustine than by Pelagius. We will see below that – to the degree that his authorship of surviving texts can be established – Pelagius himself seems to have been more of an 'Augustinian' than has previously been recognized. The reason these texts did not gain wide circulation in the Middle Ages is not, for the most part, that they were understood as having been written by heretics. Rather, it is that they really were not of much interest to later monastic librarians.[72]

FATHERS AND SONS

In picturing Demetrias and her family, it is all too easy to assume that the primary new element in her world was Christianity. Once we begin to think about the social developments bearing on fourth-century aristocratic households, however, it becomes clear that developments in household ethics during our period can usefully be understood not only as reactions to the religious revolution under Constantine (306–37), but also as reactions

[71] See, e.g., Gerald Bonner, *Augustine and Modern Research on Pelagianism* (The Saint Augustine Lecture, 1970) (Villanova, 1972); Jean-Marie Salamito, *Les Virtuoses et la multitude: aspects sociaux de la controverse entre Augustin et les pélagiens* (Grenoble, 2005).
[72] Conrad Leyser, 'Late Antiquity in the Medieval West', in Rousseau, ed., *Companion to Late Antiquity*; this said, the *Liber ad Gregoriam* makes an appearance in the ninth-century catalogue of the library of Wulfad of Bourges. See below, n. 128.

to developments in the administration of the Roman empire from the time of Diocletian (284–305) onward, changes that had little, specifically, to do with Christianity.

The administrative reforms under Diocletian are a case in point. This emperor is best known for establishing the Tetrarchy, the system by which up to four emperors could rule jointly, a visionary solution to the problem of making imperial authority less remote at a time when the power of Rome reached from Hadrian's wall to Arabia. A number of his other reforms reflected a similar impulse to enhance communication between the emperor and the provinces. By establishing regional palaces at strategic points across the empire, where he and his court could settle for months or even years, he demoted Rome from a position of unparalleled privilege; at the same time, in a reorganization of the structures of provincial administration, Italy was demoted to regional status instead of being the beneficiary of the taxes of other provinces.

Accompanying this emphasis on efficient communication was a vigorous programme of centralization. Wherever possible, administrative structures were streamlined in favour of greater control by the imperial 'centre' (which meant, in practice, wherever the court happened to be settled), and wherever possible, the collection of tax was reorganized to enhance the efficient skimming off of surplus income from the regions. In some ways, these developments were the fruit of reforms reaching back to Trajan, who had structured the relationship between the municipalities and the Roman state, so that compulsory state service (*munera*) could be extracted from the *curiales* or members of the city councils.[73] Since the prestige of council membership was high, performance of the corresponding *munera* was understood to be an investment in social standing as well as in the community.

But in the third and fourth centuries, the need to increase revenue in order to pay for an expanding army meant that the benefits of membership in the city councils became fewer. Peter Heather puts it thus:

---

[73] The vivid if somewhat tendentious description of the rise of *munera* in H. P. L'Orange, *Art Forms and Civic Life in the Late Roman Empire* (Princeton, 1965), 3–4, is still valuable; L'Orange concludes: 'The individual no longer lived independently but within the state. He was no longer seen in his natural environment within life's organic groupings, in lively harmony with his surroundings, but as a firmly incorporated immoveable part in the cadre of the state.' See also F. Oertel, 'The Economic Life of the Empire', in S. A. Cook, F. E. Adcock, M. P. Charlesworth and N. H. Baynes, *The Imperial Crisis and Recovery: AD 193–324*, Cambridge Ancient History 12 (Cambridge, 1939), 232–81, at 256, describing 'the replacement of one economic system by the other, and the substitution of a new civilization and attitude toward life'.

Competitive local building in this context was all about winning elections and hence controlling the use of local funds. The confiscation by the state of local endowments and taxes in the third century removed most of the fun from local government. By the fourth, there was little point in spending freely to win power in your hometown, if all you then got to do was run errands for central government.[74]

Senators, however, were exempt from these *munera*, and in late antiquity curial families made every effort to achieve senatorial status in order to gain immunity from curial duties. How they did this was by entering the imperial bureaucracy; eventually those who served in the bureaucracy retired to their home provinces as *honorati*, exempt from the *munera* and with political clout that those who had stayed at home lacked. Not only, then, did the desire to escape curial *munera* drain talent away from the cities; it also removed the motivation for those who stayed home to make the splashy philanthropic gestures – such as the building of civic buildings – on which the cities' prestige and quality of life ultimately depended.

Resentment of taxation, and strategizing to avoid it, was thus a constant among the provincial gentry. Meanwhile, a different set of pressures was felt by those who held – or attained – senatorial status. Here, too, the increased importance of the imperial bureaucracy created both threats and opportunities. The reorganization of the bureaucracy under Diocletian and the removal of the court from Rome, except during visits by the emperor, made for dramatic changes to the role of the senate in the Roman state. Although the senate retained a privileged position, their standing as public men on whom the state depended was under threat. The emperor, his bureaucracy, and the army could both defend and govern with little senatorial input. Across the century and a half from Diocletian to Valentinian III (425–55), senators progressively themselves took up positions within the imperial bureaucracy, until, under Valentinian, the senior positions were virtually the exclusive preserve of senatorial families.[75] A turning-point of this development was the move of the imperial court to Milan in the early 380s; the relative proximity of the court to Rome made for enhanced communication between court and senate, and for greater participation by senators in the imperial administration.

Ironically, despite attempts to enhance communication with (and exploitation of) the provinces, the fourth-century reforms in fact undermined a valuable network of communication among provincial élites. As

---

[74] Heather, *Fall of the Roman Empire*, 116.
[75] Jairus Banaji, *Agrarian Change in Late Antiquity: Gold, Labour, and Aristocratic Dominance* (Oxford, 2001), 130.

the imperial bureacucracy shifted, across the fourth and early fifth centuries, from one that attracted men from diverse geographical and social backgrounds to one in which senators predominated, an important forum ceased to exist, not only of participation in government but also of contact and communication among representatives of the different communities and traditions within the Empire. John Matthews characterized the 'senatorial takeover' of the imperial bureaucracy as the replacement of 'public' by 'private' power – i.e. the giving way of authority derived from institutional standing to power derived from wealth and family standing.[76]

Across the fourth and fifth centuries, the senate was brought more closely into the imperial *militia* through appointment to administrative posts; at the same time, as a result of contribution by distinguished persons, the imperial bureaucracy gained in standing. The relationship between the senatorial aristocracy and the imperial bureaucracies has been the subject of much debate. If the senate had held itself apart from the imperial administration in the third century, in the reign of Diocletian a new 'imperial nobility of service'[77] was formed, and by that of Valentinian III in the fifth century the Western senatorial aristocracy had, as a group, taken over the administrative posts of the imperial bureaucracy. Meanwhile, the senate's membership was in turn reconstituted by imperial adlection and by appointment of *novi homines* to posts which 'carried' the title of *clarissimus*.[78]

The *novi homines* studied by Matthews, whose participation did so much to lend vitality to the imperial bureaucracy even if their absence drained vitality from the localities, were progressively replaced by an even more powerful group of men, who saw the logic of the strategy and decided to use it to reposition themselves within their own social milieu. We will see in Chapter Three that these cash-rich imperial men were a source of anxiety to their communities, both in Italy and the provinces, since they often invested their earnings, and used their political connections, in ways that displaced the landowners who had more continuous commitments in the locality.

In a justly famous review of Matthews' study, Patrick Wormald suggested that it is the acute perception of the social consequences of regional

[76] Matthews, *Western Aristocracies and Imperial Court*, 387–8.
[77] A. H. M. Jones, 'The Social Background of the Struggle between Paganism and Christianity in the Fourth Century', in Arnaldo Momigliano, ed., *Paganism and Christianity in the Fourth Century* (Oxford, 1963), 17–37, at 35, cited in Michele Renee Salzman, *The Making of a Christian Aristocracy: Social and Religious Change in the Western Empire* (Cambridge, 2002), 109.
[78] On the growth of the senate, from c. 600 in the third century to ca. 2,000 in 359, see A. H. M. Jones, *The Later Roman Empire, 284–602: A Social, Economic, and Administrative Survey*, 3 vols. (Oxford, 1964), 142–3 and 527, and Michele Renee Salzman, *The Making of a Christian Aristocracy: Social and Religious Change in the Western Empire* (Cambridge, Mass., 2002), 31.

participation – and exclusion – in government that constitutes its lasting contribution.

M. significantly broadens our conception of the ruling classes of the later Empire: not just the Roman senate, but also a whole range of provincial gentry who, even when they attained the clarissimate by their services to the government, often retired to their native provinces, and continued to associate with those now below them on the social scale. . . . perhaps we should think less of the replacement of a 'public' by a 'private' tradition, than of the reassertion of an Italian, at the expense of a provincial, interest, with serious consequences for provincial loyalties.[79]

From our perspective, what is important about the 'senatorial takeover' or Italianization of the imperial bureaucracy is that it introduced a divisive element into the career strategies of the families at the peak of wealth and inherited standing, in a way similar, *mutatis mutandis*, to that experienced by the curial class.

This brought with it, among other things, a change in the balance of power within Roman families, since sons in service to powerful employers within the imperial bureaucracy were ideally expected to bring social advancement to the family.[80] As a result, the son would sometimes have better information, or better contacts, than his father. A wise father would entrust his son with the authority to act, at least up to a point, on what information he had been able to gather, instead of deferring unthinkingly to the advice of elders who, whatever their wisdom, might on occasion not have all the facts.[81] If the son was at court and the father elsewhere, this independence of judgement could become a habit.

Christianity's great success in this period, and its perniciousness from the traditional point of view, was that it offered an orderly framework of ideas, and incipient institutions, through which the aspirations of sons could be given preference over the wisdom of their fathers. In the history of ideas, this was a first, important step on the long development, culminating in the twelfth century, by which the individual came to be recognized as a free-standing subject, whose moral and existential dimensions were never

---

[79] Patrick Wormald, 'The Decline of the Western Empire and the Survival of its Aristocracy' (review of Matthews, *Western Aristocracies*), *JRS* 66 (1976), 217–26, at 220–1.

[80] On the triangle, already visible in the principate, comprising the emperor, the dominant families, and the families on the rise, see Keith Hopkins, 'Élite Mobility in the Roman Empire', *Past and Present* 32 (1965), 12–26; Ramsay MacMullen, 'Social Mobility and the Theodosian Code', *JRS* 54 (1964), 49–53, explores the mismatch between the emphasis on stasis of the law codes, and the realities of fourth-century social mobility.

[81] Gillett, *Envoys and Political Communication*, 237, discusses the analogous issue of empowering diplomatic envoys to make on-the-spot decisions on the government's behalf based on what they had been able to gather, along with the problem of setting limits to this power.

completely subsumed by the duties and obligations of participation in a social grouping. But the social historian should resist the temptation to view late antiquity as the incipient stage of a process whose later development we foresee. We are prone to impose a twelfth-century logic of the individual on late Roman texts, and thus to miss their late Roman logic, which was always conceived in terms of the human person as participant in a complex social choreography of relationships, obligations, and reciprocities. We must stick firmly to this 'relational' idea of the self if we wish to perceive the intense late Roman excitement – and agitation – over new forms and paradigms of personal obligation.

For the social historian, the new social mobility of both senate and provincial gentry must be understood as a tectonic pulse of instability in a society that had tried, over the centuries, to foster social stasis by instituting the duty and obligation of each son to his *paterfamilias* both through law and through the cultural norms of *pietas*.[82] We see the new idea of the moral independence of sons encapsulated in an incendiary sermon of Augustine, one suppressed from his sermon collection but painstakingly restored from fragments in medieval homiliaries by Raymond Étaix in the 1970s. A hypothetical son addresses his father:

What did God say to me? 'Honour thy father and mother' (Exodus 20:12). I admit that God told me this. But don't be angry if I put Him who said this – only Him – ahead of you. I love, I love indeed, and moreover, I love you. But he who taught me to love you is better than you. So please do not lead me away from Him; love Him as I do, who taught me to love you, but not more than Him.[83]

In fact, this is only one of an ocean of Christian texts proposing that young men – and sometimes women – should listen to their consciences rather than their fathers. From the *Acts of the Martyrs* to the *Lives of the Desert Fathers*, the message that Christians should not always obey those placed in authority was everywhere at the end of antiquity.[84]

---

[82] Richard P. Saller, 'Pietas, Obligation and Authority in the Roman Family', in Peter Kniessl and Volker Losemann, *Alte Geschichte und Wissenschaftsgeschichte: Festschrift für Karl Christ* (Darmstadt, 1988), 393–410.

[83] Raymond Étaix, 'Sermon inédit de saint Augustin sur l'amour des parents', *Revue Bénédictine* 86 (1976), 38–48, lines 150–5, at 45: 'Quid mihi dixit Deus? *Honora patrem tuum et matrem tuam* (Exodus 20: 12). Agnosco, Deus mihi dixit. Tu noli irasci quando eum solum tibi praepono qui hoc dixit. Amo, amo omnino, amo et te. Sed qui me docuit ut amem te, melior te est. Tu tantum noli me trahere contra illum et mecum ama illum qui me docuit ut amem te sed non plus quam illum.'

[84] For discussion of the contribution of early hagiographical sources to this atmosphere of suspicion of authority, see Cooper, *The Virgin and the Bride*, 56–62 and 66–7, and eadem, 'The Voice of the Victim: Gender, Representation, and Early Chrisitan Martyrdom', *Bulletin of the John Rylands Library* 80:3 (1998), 147–57.

The rise of asceticism contributed greatly to the development of a literature which affirmed that children could – and should – defy their parents in matters of conscience. It is beyond the scope of the present study to consider whether the fourth-century interest in asceticism was a reaction to the new social mobility, but the 'fit' between ascetic ideas and the new independence of sons is very striking indeed. One of the reasons ascetic literature found an enthusiastic audience beyond the numerically small community of ascetic practitioners may have been its repeated stress on the moral independence of youth, who must always consider the possibility that their elders' judgement was clouded by the old gods, the demons sent by Satan, or simply moral turpitude.[85]

At the same time, from the late fourth century the literature reassuringly began to suggest that this youthful defiance should always be tempered by obedience to a respected senior man, an abbot or a bishop. One imagines that as it became more institutionally orientated in the late fourth century, the ascetic movement may have both benefited from and contributed to a fourth-century habit of reassigning at least part of the father's authority to an institutional mentor.[86] Structurally, the Christian hierarchies of diocese and *coenobium*, with the focus of each on the authority of a bishop or abbot, echoed the hierarchy of imperial authority in a way that was pleasing to the mind.

But Roman fathers did not take all this lying down, and the clergy sometimes took their side. We will see below that in the fifth century a distinctively paternal – indeed, paternalist – vision of Christianity was emerging, a vision which tried to reconcile the imperatives of Christian ethics with an older ideal of the senatorial *dominus* – or *domina* – as the guarantor of justice for his or her community of dependents. Although unhymned by later centuries, this conservative voice was a force to be reckoned with. It is important to remember that the eventual success of the ascetic movement was far from a foregone conclusion in the fourth and fifth centuries.[87] As late as the sixth century, there is evidence that the movement was still viewed with suspicion in some quarters.

---

[85] Amongst ascetics, grey hair was not in itself necessarily taken as a sign of moral authority; see Cassian, *Collationes* 2.13 (*CSEL* 13, 52–58); Rousseau, *Ascetics, Authority, and the Church*, 189–94, and Conrad Leyser, *Authority and Asceticism from Augustine to Gregory the Great* (Oxford, 2000), 55.

[86] For a vivid tale of rejection of a biological father in favour of a spiritual replacement, see the *Sermo de vita sancti Honorati* as discussed by Conrad Leyser, ' "This Sainted Isle": Panegyric, Nostalgia, and the Invention of "Lerinian Monasticism" ', in William E. Klingshirn and Mark Vessey eds., *The Limits of Ancient Christianity: Essays on Late Antique Thought and Culture in Honor of R. A. Markus* (Ann Arbor, 1999), 188–206.

[87] See Leyser, *Authority and Asceticism*, 33–61.

MILES CHRISTI AND MILES SAECULI

It may be no accident that it is from the imperial city of Milan that our earliest example of a new literary genre, the Christian conduct manual, originates. It has long been noted that the arrival of emperor and court at Milan c. 381 had an unusually disruptive effect on the city and its territory, with the local gentry more or less helpless in their dealings with the incoming personages attached to court and *militia*.[88] (It should be remembered that the term *militia* meant 'administration' and was frequently applied to the imperial bureaucracy.) Roughly between 388 and 390, Ambrose, bishop of Milan, addressed a treatise *On Duties* to his ecclesiastical 'sons', the Milanese clergy, in imitation of the treatise bearing the same name addressed by Cicero to his own son.[89]

There is every reason to think that the implied audience of Ambrose's attempt to define a Christian position on Cicero's territory was in fact an élite lay readership, for whom Cicero's ideas about the responsible exercise of power would have been an inherited point of reference.

If Symmachus and his [pagan] literary friends were to notice one book among the formidable output of their Christian contemporaries, moreover, it would surely have been this attempt to usurp and supersede one of 'their' classics. Indeed, *De officiis* seems written so that only those with a mental concordance to (or their own copy of) Cicero's original could properly appreciate it.[90]

This reading develops an older view, according to which Ambrose's *On Duties* was intended to challenge, or at least appropriate, a philosophical discourse associated with pagan conservatism. Indeed, one of the more eirenic interpreters of Ambrose's intent in writing the treatise has suggested

---

[88] 'The *curiales*, who in other capitals (particularly Antioch in Syria, where they had centuries of civic tradition to sustain them) fought a stiff rearguard action in defence of their political identity and economic interests against the periodic eruptions of the court, remain almost invisible in Ambrose's Milan,' Neil B. McLynn, *Ambrose of Milan: Church and Court in a Christian Capital* (Berkeley, 1994), 222. The crucial study on the displacement of the Milanese gentry (among other things), to which we will return in Chapter Three, is still Lellia Cracco Ruggini, *Economia e società nell' 'Italia annonaria': Rapporti fra agricoltura e commercio dal IV al VI secolo d.c.*, 2nd edn (Bari, 1995).

[89] On the date of *De officiis* see Ivor J. Davidson, 'Ambrose's *De officiis* and the Intellectual Climate of the Late Fourth Century', *Vigiliae Christianae* 49 (1995), 313–33, at 326. On Ambrose's engagement with Cicero's *De officiis*, see Klaus Zelzer, 'Zur Beurteilung der Cicero-Imitatio bei Ambrosius', *Wiener Studien* n.f. 11 (1977), 168–91.

[90] McLynn, *Ambrose of Milan*, 272; with bibliography on the problem of the intended readers of *De officiis* at 255–6. At 272–5, McLynn offers an intriguing reading of *On Duties* as a follow-up to the religious face-off between Ambrose and Symmachus during the Altar of Victory controversy a half-decade earlier, by calling attention to a not-so-veiled criticism of Symmachus' failings as Urban Prefect during a corn shortage in Rome.

that 'Men like Ambrose . . . aspire to reinvest the familiar classical genres with a new profundity . . . [they] naturally turn to classical texts but now find that such texts greatly require an infusion of revealed truth.'[91] If the point of Christianizing the Ciceronian inheritance was essentially to secure its future, the 'requirement' of infusing 'classical texts' with 'revealed truth' may have been not so much intellectual as pastoral.

All parties, whatever their religious affiliation, may have suspected that the old father–son paradigm of socializing élites to accountability in power was too weak to regulate the massive social mobility of the administrative *militia*. The 'infusion of revealed truth', by contrast, carried with it a structure of accountability honed over centuries in the context of a very different *militia*, the *militia Christi*. The accountability of priests and laymen to their bishops was imperfect, but from the third century a robust and vigorous system of penance had evolved to give teeth to the ideal of episcopal oversight. Any shadow of doubt as to whether the Bishop of Milan could bring the emperor's men into line was dispelled in the autumn of 390, when the emperor himself knelt before Ambrose in public penance.[92]

To find a concrete example of Christian conduct literature being addressed to an imperial administrator brought into a community from outside, and reminding him that God and the Church will be watching him, we must jump forward to the early sixth century. We turn now to an unusual and little-known document of the history of the Christian laity, the treatise on good government addressed by the deacon Ferrandus of Carthage, best known as the probable biographer of Fulgentius of Ruspe,[93] to a highly placed Christian military official. Addressed to a certain Reginus, called *dux illustris* in the text,[94] the *Letter to Reginus* has received little scholarly attention, perhaps owing to its absolute lack of interest in doctrinal or ascetic matters. From the point of view of the history of the laity, however, the letter represents a rich resource. Particularly interesting for the present study is its explicit and extended attempt to reconcile the two aspects of Reginus' authority as *miles Christi* and as *miles saeculi*.

---

[91] Davidson, 'Ambrose's *De officiis*', 323.
[92] On Theodosius' penance in Milan after the Massacre of Thessalonica, see McLynn, *Ambrose of Milan*, 315–30, and F. Kolb, 'Der Bussakt von Mailand: Zum Verhältnis von Staat und Kirche in der Spätantike', in H. Boockmann, K. Jürgensen and G. Stottenberg, eds., *Geschichte und Gegenwart: Festschrift für K. D. Erdmann* (Neumünster, 1980), 41–74.
[93] On the arguments for and against Ferrandus as the author of the *Vita Fulgentii*, see Antonio Isola, tr., *Pseudo Ferrando di Cartagine: Vita di San Fulgenzio* (Rome, 1987), 5–8.
[94] Ferrandus, *Ad Reginum Comitem Paraneticum* 1 (*PL* 67, 928).

Reginus himself is a cipher in the historical record. Not only women but also men – even politically important ones – are often only glancingly documented in our period.[95] One other letter to him is preserved, no. 18 in the corpus of Fulgentius, on the incorruptibility of Christ, but it is brief and gives little away.[96] There is reason to think that Ferrandus wrote to Reginus shortly after Belisarius' campaign to re-establish Roman rule in Vandal North Africa between 532 and 534.[97] It is very likely that the text was part of a wider effort to establish an accountable *militia* in the aftermath of conquest. Reginus would have been one of five *duces* and six provincial governors charged with assisting the Praetorian Prefect at Carthage in ruling the seven provinces of Roman Africa, but biographical information about him beyond the slim indications provided by Ferrandus and Fulgentius has not come down to us.

The letter envisions the *dux*'s role not as a commander of forces in battle but as a judge and administrator, the embodiment of imperial authority in the newly reconquered province.[98] Reginus' task is envisaged primarily as one of stewardship. He is urged to bring stability, peace, and fertility to the province, and to ensure that the poor are not crushed by the greed of men more powerful than themselves. This last point had military as well as ethical significance, for Procopius records a vivid speech by Belisarius to his soldiers early in the campaign, chastising them for stealing food from the surrounding fields rather than buying it at a fair price from the local farmers.[99] It was at risk of their own lives and of the invasion's success,

---

[95] *PCBE*, 507–13.

[96] In addition to the letter of Ferrandus, *Letter* 18 in the corpus of Fulgentius is addressed to Reginus (*CC* 91A, 619–24).

[97] *Codex Justinianus* 1.27.1 and 2 (rescript to Belisarius on reorganization of the province, April 534). Denys Pringle, *The Defence of Byzantine Africa from Justinian to the Arab Conquest: An Account of the Military History and Archaeology of the African Provinces in the Sixth and Seventh Centuries*, British Archaeological Reports, Int. Ser. 99 (Oxford, 1981); Charles Diehl, *L'Afrique byzantine: histoire de la domination byzantine en Afrique (533–709)*, 2 vols. (New York, 1959).

[98] For a recent discussion of Roman administration of Africa after the conquest of 533–4, see Jonathan P. Conant, 'Staying Roman: Vandals, Moors, and Byzantines in Late Antique North Africa, 400–700' (unpublished doctoral dissertation, Harvard University, 2004), ch. 4, 'New Rome, New Romans', 235–311. According to Conant (295), each of the five *duces* in post-conquest Africa was assigned a staff of 43 aides, clerks, and subordinate officers. On the wider sixth-century evolution of the role of *dux* from that of a general on active campaign duty to that of a civil administrator, see T. S. Brown, *Gentlemen and Officers: Imperial Administration and Aristocratic Power in Byzantine Italy AD 554–800* (Rome, 1984), 53–56, with literature cited there. He suggests at 54 that at this period 'no clear limits existed between civil and military authority', even in areas such as Italy where civil bureaucracy had enjoyed comparative continuity.

[99] Procopius, *Wars* 3.15.1–5, ed. Haury, repr. with tr., H. B. Dewing, Loeb Classical Library 81 (Cambridge, Mass., 1916), 142, 144.

he reminded them, that they dared to anger the Roman population of the countryside, for the invasion plan had spread forces and resources thinly indeed, relying on the Roman population to support the Byzantine forces as welcome liberators from the yoke of Vandal occupation. Ferrandus' discussion of the ethics of military government drew force from both writer's and reader's awareness that even after the conquest, the military and civil authorities could ill afford to do without the help of the Catholic clergy in cementing the population's loyalty to Constantinople.

Reflecting the Augustinian tradition for which the early sixth-century circle around Fulgentius of Ruspe was known, Ferrandus imagines human authority in terms of responsibility rather than glory. The *dux* must understand his own rule as subordinate to the will of God, while at the same time watching carefully to make sure that none of the lesser men acting on his behalf abuse their position, for it is he who will bear responsibility for the misdeeds of his subordinates. Even his enemies should be brought to love him by the justice of his rule. As a manual of Christian authority the letter to Reginus anticipates in many respects both the *Regula pastoralis* of Pope Gregory the Great and the *Fürstenspiegeln* of the Carolingian period.[100]

The initial proposition of the letter is to consider how the metaphor of the *miles Christi* applies to a military professional. Ferrandus opens the treatise with a rhetorical tour de force, introducing the polar opposition between the *miles Dei* and the *miles saeculi*,[101] only to establish that the opposition is an illusion. The *miles*, in this case the *dux* Reginus himself, has it within his power to choose – without in fact relinquishing his established position and duties – whether to identify himself as belonging to the *saeculum* or as belonging to Christ. His choice will be embodied not in whether he takes up the burden of authority in the *saeculum*, but in how he bears it.

The first section sets out the tension between the *miles Christi* and the *miles saeculi*, a tension echoing that between the authority of Ferrandus as a Christian teacher and that of Reginus as *dux*. The contrast between the *milites Dei* and the *milites saeculi* is underscored by presenting an extended list of oppositions: 'those fight against visible enemies, these against invisible ones. Those, avarice renders cruel (*crudeles*), these, mercy renders

---

[100] Marc Reydellet, *La Royauté dans la littérature latine de Sidoine Apollinaire à Isidore de Seville* (Rome, 1981).

[101] Ferrandus, *Ad Reginum* 1 (*PL* 67, 928): 'Propter hoc apostolus Paulus: "Nemo, ait, militans Deo implicat se negotiis saecularibus" (2 Tim 2:4) ostendens esse milites Dei, sicut sunt etiam milites saeculi. Duplex ergo militia duo genera militum signat: alios militia corporalis laborare cum mundo, secundum voluntatem terreni regis astringit; alios militia spiritalis ad coelestia castra per gratuitam gratiam coelestis imperatoris adducit.'

generous (*benignos*).' This series of oppositions carries the important message, central to the letter, of redefining the distinction between earthly military service and membership in the army of Christ not as a distinction of actual military participation, but rather as a distinction of character and ethical commitments. Such a redefinition allows participation in earthly military affairs to be redefined as compatible with the ethical outlook of a soldier of Christ.

The deacon then invites Reginus to join with him in petitioning God the creator, who, according to the Psalmist, created all things according to his will, that

> We ask Him, who orders the world, that he deign to promote those of his soldiers hidden under the uniform of the secular military, guiding them from within, and sending to others the wisdom to rule, just as he has given it to you, Reginus, *dux illustris.*[102]

Ferrandus goes on to review his occasion for writing to Reginus. Reginus had asked Fulgentius of Ruspe to give him a *regula* for the man occupied with both military and spiritual matters, but Fulgentius having died, Reginus has brought the query to Ferrandus, 'almost to make good a hereditary debt'.[103]

This provides an occasion for Ferrandus to expand on his own unworthiness to offer advice to a man so accomplished as Reginus, much less to stand in the shoes of Fulgentius. 'Woe to me . . . here, held fast by the bonds of the ecclesiastical militia, I am confused by worldly matters, and how should I impose the law of the spiritual *militia* on one who serves in the *saeculum*?'[104] Ferrandus goes on to explain that his task of teaching another could only be accomplished if he himself were to live well, a meditation on his own worthiness that will inform his advice to Reginus on how the *dux* in turn should exert a morally uplifting influence on the men assigned to his command. Ferrandus consoles himself with the thought that it is not human but divine teachings that Reginus wishes to be guided by.

At this point, the author turns to list seven 'rules of integrity (*innocentia*)' by which the soldier of Christ must be guided, a list whose elaboration

---

[102] Ferrandus, *Ad Reginum* 2 (*PL* 67, 929): 'Rogemus . . . eum qui disponit orbem . . . ut videlicet milites suos sub habitu militiae saecularis latentes promovere dignetur ad maximas dignitates: regens eos intus, et regendi alios scientiam tribuens; sicut tibi quoque, dux illustris Regine, jam donasse cognoscitur.'

[103] Ferrandus, *Ad Reginum* 2 (*PL* 67, 929): 'ut me iubeas tanti viri quasi hereditarium debitum solvere'.

[104] Ferrandus, *Ad Reginum* 3 (*PL* 67, 930): 'Vae mihi misero . . . Ecce ego militiae ecclesiasticae vinculis alligatus, curis saecularibus dissipor; et quomodo in saeculo militanti militiae spiritalis audeam legem ostendere?'

will constitute the remainder of the letter. The first rule, to acknowledge the necessity of grace, sets the moral agenda for the treatise: not only does Ferrandus draw explicitly on the Augustinian theology of grace, but he clearly has in mind, as we will see below, Augustine's pastoral instinct that the most insidious spur to discouragement in a community is the *superbia* of its élite. The practical military context which Reginus faces as *dux* is invoked immediately by the biblical exempla which Ferrandus chooses: the book of Judith illustrates the proposition that while no one can protect a city if God himself does not sustain the defence, a small band can triumph with God on their side; the book of Judges provides the authority for the assertion that when the *dux* finds himself embroiled in the difficult business of reconciling factions among his men, he should remember that God himself is the source of all peace.

Ferrandus turns next to exhort Reginus to let his own life be a mirror from which his soldiers can learn morality. The second rule emphasizes Reginus' responsibilities as a judge of his men, but they are redefined to incorporate the Pauline prohibition (Rom 2:1) against judging others lest one be judged. Reginus is exhorted to cultivate the virtues – justice, mercy, patience – which will make him a fair leader and an example to his men. Added to these is the virtue of *continentia*, understood in its classical sense as the self-control which allows a leader to listen to the counsel of the wise, rather than that of flatterers.[105] Our writer now invokes a single New Testament dictum directly pertinent to the correct behaviour of soldiers, Luke 3:14, in which a group of soldiers petition John the Baptist and he replies, 'rob no one by violence or by false accusation, and be content with your wages.' Out of this slim material Ferrandus renders a broad picture of the ruin caused to a province under military rule if the occupying soldiers' instinct for extortion and plunder is not checked by the word and example of a wise leader.[106]

The third rule – 'seek not to be eminent (*praeesse*) but to be useful (*prodesse*)' (935) – develops the theme of the leader's responsibility to contain the behaviour of his men. 'Aside from these things you will be seen to be useful in two ways; if you do not harm anyone, and if, insofar as you

[105] Ferrandus, *Ad Reginum* 5 (*PL* 67, 933). Whether the vocabulary of continence is being invoked here polemically against the sexual definition of *continentia* which prevails among the moral writers of the period, or whether Ferrandus is writing in a milieu where the sexual meaning would simply be a secondary meaning, remains an open question.
[106] See now Christopher Kelly, *Ruling the Later Roman Empire* (Cambridge, Mass., 2004) ch. 4, 'Purchasing Power', 138–85, on the problem of regulating access to justice in provincial government at this period.

can – which is to say insofar as Christ has given you the power – you prohibit those who have the tendency to harm, or wish to, from doing so.'[107]

The *dux* who takes seriously his duty to the civilian population under his dominion will understand that containing the tendency to corruption among his men is at least as important as the more visible exercise of power,[108] and it should be understood that it is the leader's responsibility to seek out such crimes against the powerless rather than imagining that he is not responsible for what he does not know about.[109] 'By this conscientiousness he may acquire such good fame, that even if a superior wants to harm those below him, he can help by his intercession, and easily persuade him to spare those whom he himself would spare.'[110] Indeed, the good *dux* should try to leave rich those whom he found poor, rather than the other way around. It is the man who brings his subjects prosperity, not oppression, who will be remembered.

This leads naturally to the fourth rule, to love the commonwealth (*rempublicam*) as much as oneself. The good general wants to see her tranquil, peaceful, and fertile. He should be guided by this principle and by his conscience. 'So enter there, O best of men, as often as you consider how you have to act in military affairs, enter into the vast sanctuary of your conscience.'[111]

The fifth rule, to put divine things before human ones, offers specific advice for the man who is stationed in areas where the civilian population are Arians. While in matters of ecclesial custom Reginus is encouraged to follow indigenous practice for fear of scandalizing others, he is encouraged

---

[107] Ferrandus, *Ad Reginum* 7 (*PL* 67, 935): 'Praeter haec quoque duobus modis prodesse videberis, si neminem laedas, et illos qui solent aut volunt laedere prohibeas quantum potes, imo quantum posse donaverit Christus.' Note the directly Augustinian pedigree of *praeesse/prodesse*: Augustine, *Civ. dei* 19.19 (*CC* 48, 687), also *Serm.* 340 (*PL* 38, 1484). Augustine's discussion is confined to the character of episcopal authority: in common with other sixth-century readers of Augustine, Ferrandus here broadens the remit: see *Regula Benedicti* 64.8 (*SC* 182, 650) on abbatial authority, and Gregory the Great, *Regula Pastoralis* 2.6 (*SC* 381, 204, with discussion and further references at 47–8) on the *rector*.

[108] Ferrandus, *Ad Reginum* 7 (*PL* 67, 935): 'Tunc autem dux optimus neminem laedet, si in omni praetorio illius non audeat aliquis amicus, cliens, medicus, armiger, aut propter officii publici devotionem lateri ducis semper adiunctus, concessa beneficia vendere. Quid enum miseros juvat, si dux exhibeat continentiam boni ducis, et alius sibi de potestate illius occasionem faciat avaritiae satiandae?'

[109] Ferrandus, *Ad Reginum* 7 (*PL* 67, 935): 'Non potest sapiens dux excusari de ignorantia, quoties forsitan dixerit: Ego nescio, non audivi, nullius ad me querela pervenit.'

[110] Ferrandus, *Ad Reginum* 7 (*PL* 67, 936): 'Potest plane per hanc diligentiam sic acquirere famam bonam, ut etiam si persona superior laedere voluerit subditos, libera intercessione subveniat; et parcendum facile persuadeat, quibus ipse primo pepercerit.' The language here – *libera intercessione* – is that of the tribune of the people, who could annul a decree of the senate by his veto.

[111] Ferrandus, *Ad Reginum* 9 (*PL* 67, 937): 'Ingredere igitur tu, virorum optime, quoties cogitas qualis esse in actibus militaribus debeas, ingredere conscientiae tuae latissima penetralia.'

in matters of doctrine to work on behalf of the Catholic faith, and to act in consultation with the clergy. An extended agricultural metaphor echoes the exhortation to the *dux* as a husbandman of the fertility and prosperity of the territory under his control. While Reginus' task is to sow the seeds of the Catholic faith, it is the task of God to see that the soil is fruitful.

The last two rules exhort Reginus to avoid self-righteousness and to remember that he is a Christian. Since their purpose is not only to exhort but also to draw the letter to a close, it seems appropriate that the last two rules draw the reader's attention from the specific task and circumstance of the *dux*, back to the broader Augustinian point of view with which Ferrandus had framed the treatise initially. Ending on the broad point of principle may also have been an attempt to show respect for Reginus' own judgement and the scope of his authority.

How the letter would have been received is a question for which no evidence survives. Reginus clearly belonged to a class of men the steering of whose judgement required the exercise of great diplomacy. For a deacon such as Ferrandus to address him – even if Ferrandus himself was a person of standing – would have been received less as a gesture of admonition than as a gift, a token of friendship, perhaps an attempt to attract patronage, at the same time as a public and perhaps tactical assessment of the character of Reginus, a gesture of expectation that he was the kind of man to welcome such musings. We will see in the chapters that follow, that although the literature addressing Reginus and other powerful laypersons is only scantily preserved, there is reason to suspect that a wide effort was made to cultivate a lay élite who would both support, and be accountable to, the Christian bishops and their clergy.

POVERTY, OBLIGATION, AND INHERITANCE: TRADITIONALIST SENATORIAL CHRISTIANITY DURING AND AFTER THE BARBARIAN INVASIONS

'A drift into respectable Christianity': thus have modern historians tended to characterize the accommodation reached (or sought) between the lay aristocracy and their spiritual advisers.[112] Unwittingly or otherwise, this

---

[112] P. R. L. Brown, 'Aspects of the Christianization of the Roman Aristocracy', *JRS* 51 (1961), 1–11, at 9; before coining the phrase, however, Brown himself warns, rightly, at 5 that 'the works of Paulinus, Augustine, Pelagius and Palladius [reflected] the impact of an extreme "oriental" form of asceticism . . . a radical departure from the previous Christian traditions of Rome; its leaders were not Romans themselves; its ideals involved a rejection of the social life of the City and, almost inevitably, the abandonment of Rome for the centres of the new devotion – the Holy Places and Egypt.'

view adopts the position of the late Roman ascetic movement in its assault on traditionalist Christians. These traditionalists were branded as foot-draggers by rhetorically gifted polemicists like Jerome, and the accusation has stuck for fifteen centuries. But the scholarly account of Christian *embourgeoisement*, while it captures the dismissive tone of the radical ascetic party, really does not do justice to the moral integrity of those it describes, or the social complexity of their position. The men and women who saw it as their duty to protect the continuity of ancient families were alarmed by what seemed to be an attack on the institutions of property and parental authority. It is perhaps not surprising to discover that in the debate between traditionalists and ascetics we find ourselves, again, faced with the tension between parents and their ambitious children in the century after Diocletian.

But the issue between radicals and traditionalists was not asceticism *per se*. Some traditionalist Christians probably suspected, correctly as it happens, that ascetic values as understood in the late fourth century were not really in line with the teaching of the early Church (we will return to this point in Chapter Four). But other traditionalists were themselves ascetics, and were simply worried by the tendency of radicals within the movement to belittle – and ultimately to undermine – the old ways of holding the rich accountable. The discomfort of traditionalist Christians with the ideal of the renunciation of wealth rested, fundamentally, on widely held late Roman values about the moral obligations of the rich to their dependents.

Ancient families still believed, in the fourth and fifth centuries, that the responsible landowner and *paterfamilias*, despite or even because of his vested interest, was a person who could be relied on to maintain public order. The honest *paterfamilias* was understood to be a steward of wealth and power in whom the community – and indeed the Church – could rightly place their trust. To undermine the role of these men and women – we will see below that the law recognized female landowners as *patresfamilias* where matters of property were concerned – or to discourage them from intimidating others into orderly and sociable behaviour, was a very risky proposition. In the 'honour system' of the aristocracy, compliance was voluntary, even if honour brought with it material rewards. If its critics were right to criticize the fragility of the system, dissuading the honest from participation did little to strengthen it.

These ideas did not die quickly. A recent study by Richard Bartlett, for example, has argued that in the Italy of Theoderic, enthusiastic pursuit of personal poverty was still perceived as a betrayal of senatorial values. For a writer like Ennodius, ascetic virtues were valued, but ascetic aspirations were no excuse for a failure to perform the traditional duties of a senatorial landowner. In any event, personal asceticism did not necessarily involve personal poverty, and poverty was not a virtue if it compromised one's ability to undertake responsibility for the welfare of others. We see this for example in the *Vita* of Epiphanius, Ennodius' predecessor as bishop of Pavia, a text to which we will return in Chapter Five. Ennodius' correspondent Arator (evidently the same Arator who wrote the hexameter *De actibus apostolorum* in the early 540s) seems to have lived as an ascetic while holding public office, for example as *comes rerum privatarum* in 526.[113] If in other milieux a man like Arator would be expected to join a monastery, in early sixth-century Italy he was expected to bring his ascetic aspirations into line with running a household and the performance of traditional duties.[114]

In the fifth century, what we see is in fact a wide spectrum of attitudes and approaches to the problem of wealth. It is clear, on the one hand, that landowners were becoming jumpy about their ability to hold onto wealth in the politically unstable environment of the barbarian invasions. On the other, there was simply disagreement, in the matter of using wealth according to Christian principles, about where duty lay.

The anonymous *Passio Sebastiani* (*BHL* 7543), written in Rome in the fifth or very early sixth century, offers reassurance to the wealthy Christian that he or she may confidently entrust wealth in the institutions of the Church; note that this text considers the problem from the point of view of the self-interested landowner and passes in silence over the question of his responsibility for the welfare of others. In a sustained address to the wives and parents of his young protégés Marcus and Marcellianus, the soon-to-be martyr Sebastian explains that the true Christian should not allow the love of riches to dissuade him from standing up for the faith.

Therefore let it be asked, 'Why were riches given by the Creator if they must be condemned?' Let the riches themselves, made by the creator, address their lovers in this way, saying, 'Thus you love us in the hope that we will never be separated from you. But we are not able to follow you when you die.'[115]

---

[113] On Arator, see Claire Sotinel, 'Arator, un poète au service de la politique du pape Vigile', *MEFRA* 101 (1989), 805–20.

[114] Richard Bartlett, 'Aristocracy and Asceticism: The Letters of Ennodius and the Gallic and Italian Churches', in *Society and Culture in Late Antique Gaul: Revisiting the Sources*, ed. Ralph Mathisen and Danuta Shanzer (Aldershot, 2001), 201–16, at 207–8.

[115] *Passio Sebastiani* 15: 'Interrogatur ergo: Cur a Creatore divitiae datae sunt, si contemnendae sunt? Respondemus: Istae divitiae a Creatore factae, alloquuntur quodammodo amatores suos, dicentes: Sic nos amate, ut a vobis numquam separemur. Sequi vos morientes non possumus; antecedere autem vos viventes possumus: sed si ipsi iubeatis' (*AASS Jan.*, 2, 265–78).

The *Passio*'s author is here steering close to a motif from the sermons of Augustine of Hippo, that the rich should understand the poor as *laturarii* – porters – who are able to carry the baggage of the rich ahead to heaven.[116] The author of the *Passio Sebastiani* offers, in Sebastian's speech, a vision of the rich man's dilemma cast in the vivid imagery of the barbarian invasions.

> Let's say you were crossing through the centre of a battle-line of Barbarians, and came upon a strong man who has always loved you, who had given you a bag of coins, and he said to you, 'Give me the guardianship of the money I gave you, because these barbarians close upon us are threatening to take it from you, and they will steal it from you, killing you with swords.' Would you not, once you had thrown yourself at his feet, ask Him to take them, who were sure would return more than He had received, and even free you from your enemies? From now on you may have Christ as a safe-keeper (*tutor*) for your riches.[117]

How the rich Christian should enact this willingness to trust God as a guardian is not made explicit, but it is worth noticing that this source encourages the rich Christian to entrust his wealth to 'a strong man who has always loved you' – perhaps God himself but also to a bishop, abbot, or other trusted representative – instead of placing the burden of riches directly on the backs of the poor.[118]

Two texts written in the mid-fifth century, the *Adversus avaritiam* of Salvian of Marseilles and the anonymous *De vera humilitate*, addressed to the senatorial virgin Demetrias during her mature years in Rome, grapple with the problem of riches through a very different metaphor, that of the human relationships involved in working an estate. While Salvian encourages the Christian landowner to see him or herself as a *precario tenens* or tenant occupying an estate whose real *dominus* is God himself,[119] *De vera humilitate*, by contrast, figures the earthly *dominus* not as a tenant,

---

[116] Augustine, *Sermo* 18.4 *De eodem versu Psalmi XLIX, Deus manifestus veniet, etc.* (PL 38, 130 and 131); *Sermo* 38.9 *De verbis Ecclesiastici II, 1–5, Fili, accedens ad servitutem Dei, etc. Et de verbis Psalmi XXXVIII, 7, Quanquam in imagine ambulat homo, etc. De continentia et sustinentia*, (PL 38, 235–41, at 240); *Sermo* 60 *De verbis Evangelii, Matthaei, cap. VI, 19–21, Nolite vobis condere thesauros in terra, etc., exhortatorius ad faciendas eleemosynas* (PL 38, 402–9, at 406).

[117] *Passio Sebastiani* 16 (*AASS Jan.*, 2, 265–78).

[118] This would be compatible with the view, which I have put forward elsewhere, that the *Passio Sebastiani* was one of a number of texts designed to encourage lay patronage of the Roman monasteries: Kate Cooper, 'Family, Dynasty, and Conversion in the Roman Gesta Martyrum', in *Hagiographische Überlieferung im Frühmittelalter – Zwischen Niederschrift und Wiederschrift*, ed. M. Diesenberger (Vienna, forthcoming).

[119] Salvian, *Adv. Avaritiam* 1.5 (*CSEL* 8, 231–2): 'Videamus breviter vel a quo sint datae facultates ipsae vel obquid datae, ut cum auctorem et causam datae rei ostenderemus, facilius ad quem referenda et in quem usum conferenda sint approbare possimus. Omnem substantiam mundialem divino cunctis munere dari nullus homo ut reor, ambigit . . . Igitur si omnia omnibus Deus tribuit, nemini

but rather as the *procurator*, the steward who administers an estate on behalf of a *dominus*.

The important point for the author of *De vera humilitate* is the urgent importance of the role of the rich Christian. He or she has a crucial job to do, one central to the enactment of God's justice, and will not be excused for failing to do it.

> Not only are Christ's poor sustained by the resources of those who, in order to follow the Lord with less encumbrance, have divested themselves once and for all of their wealth; the same cause is also served by the property of those who administer their possessions exclusively as the goods of the poor, in a kind of stewardship (*procuratione*) for the Church, each one working according to his resources in order that the household of God may be supplied with what is necessary for food and clothing, and at the same time seeing to it that in their own households all are cherished in kindness and controlled by good discipline under a just and holy management. For as the Apostle says, *If anyone does not take care of his own, and especially of his household, he has denied the faith and is worse than an unbeliever.* (1 Tim 5: 8)[120]

While it might be possible for the owner of an estate to tolerate the substandard performance of a *precario tenens*, delinquency in a *procurator* would pose a direct threat to the interests of his employer that could not be overlooked.

De vera humilitate goes on to make clear that this view of the obligation of the Christian *domina* is by no means an attempt to evade responsibility. The point is to reach a clearer understanding of where the *domina*'s

---

dubium est quod ea quae Dei dono accepimus ad Dei cultum referre debeamus . . . Hoc est enim agnoscere munus Dei . . . ut datis suis illum honores, a quo data ipsa acceperis: quod quidem etiam humanarum rerum exempla docent . . . nonne ingratissimus omnium atque infidelissimus judicetur qui oblitus scilicet hominis benfici ac liberalissimi, spoliare illum jure domini sui velit qui eum ipsum usus possessione ditaverit. Et nos itaque usum tantum earum rerum accepimus quas tenimus . . . *quasi precari possessores sumus.* Denique egredientes e mundo isto velimus nolimus hic cuncta relinquimus.' Cur ergo cum possessores tantum usufructuarii sumus quod nobiscum auferre non possimus avertere a proprietate domini atque alienare tentamus?' The passage is cited in Maria Monachesi, 'Arnobio il Giovane ed una sua possible attività agiografica', *Bolletino di studi storico-religiosi* 1 (1921), 96–109, at 93–4). On late Roman *precaria*, see Jens-Uwe Krause, *Spätantike Patronatsformen im Westen des Römischen Reiches* (Munich, 1987), esp. 254–62.

[120] *Epistula ad Demetriadem de vera humilitate: A Critical Text and Translation with Introduction and Commentary* (Washington, D.C., 1965; CUA Patristic Studies 97) 5, ed. and trans. Sister M. Kathryn Clare Krabbe, 158–9: '. . . non dubium est, et pauperes Christi non eorum tantum facultatibus sustineri qui, ut expeditiores Dominum sequerentur, simul se omnibus suis opibus exuerunt, sed eidem operi etiam illorum substantias deservire qui possessionibus suis non aliter quem rebus pauperum praesunt et ecclesiasticae utilitati sub quaedam procuratione famulantur, elaborantes singuli pro suarum virium portione, ut ad victum atque vestium familiae Dei necessaria conferantur, et simul prospicientes ut in domibus ipsorum sub iusto sanctoque moderamine omnes et benignitas foveat et disciplina contineat, dicente apostolo: Si quis autem suorum, et maxime domesticorum curam non habet, fidem negavit, et est infideli deterior.'

responsibility actually lies. This point is driven home with a sustained meditation on the metaphor of the community as Body of Christ interpreted through the lens of Augustine's *Praeceptum* and the Acts 4:32 tradition (the 'union of hearts' of the Jerusalem community),[121] concluding, 'so great is the peace and concord there that even what belongs to the individual cannot exist unless it belongs to all (*non possit esse nisi omnium quod est singulorum*)'.[122] The Christian landowner, particularly if she is an ascetic, is no less indispensable than her peers living in a monastic community. Rather, she fulfils an office analogous to that of an abbot or abbess, by seeing after the well-being of the dependents of her own establishment. In this text, what we see is not an opposition between 'ascetic' and 'householder' Christianity, but the view that even for the ascetic, service as a Christian householder can be an important office of the Church.

Ad Gregoriam in palatio, an anonymous conduct manual addressed to a senatorial *domina* of the fifth or early sixth century, reprises a number of themes we have already seen. Here is the voice of temptation as it plays on the anxieties of the Christian *domina*, encouraging her to believe that as a property-owner and patron of the Church other Christians will make a play for her money but will not even notice her attempts to live a life of holiness:

All mortals (*omnes homines*), all the mighty and the low, even the bishops of God will venerate you and will be able to honor you only insofar as you have been able to be furnished with money, and not insofar as you have succeeded in being holy. Why do you diminish yourself by wealth (*potestate*) and slip into being prey to your own riches?[123]

In suggesting how she should respond to these taunts, the anonymous author draws on the metaphor of God as a trustworthy guardian which we saw above in the *Passio Sebastiani*.

If the consuls of this world do not fear a vain expenditure of their wealth, to enrich chariot-drivers and actors, and to make brothel-keepers and mimes rich men, but rather glory in these excesses, so long as by this loss of possessions they purchase the favour of the contemptible crowd, why with the praise of all angels do I fear to offer a coin for the relief of the servants of God, which (coin) I trust is to be given back to me a hundredfold by the right hand of my King (*regis mei dextera*)? And if the earth returns a seed more fruitful than when she received it,

---

[121] Leyser, *Authority and Asceticism*, 10–19.   [122] *De vera humilitate* 6 (Krabbe, 158 and 160).
[123] *Ad Gregoriam* 12 (*CC* 25A, 209): 'Te omnes homines, te universi sublimes et humiles, te ipsi antistites dei tantum venerabuntur et praeferre poterunt, quantum nummatus, non quantum sanctus esse potueris. Quid temet ipsum potestate extenuas, et in praedam tuis opibus cedis?'

why should I not believe that it will be returned to me by the Lord Jesus Christ, especially when I have his bond (*chirografum*) of promise and warning: *Amen, Amen, I say unto you, whatever he has done to the least of those who believe in me, he has done to me?*[124]

Our author brings home his point by developing Augustine's motif of the poor as the porters who carry the burden of riches forward to heaven. Again, an internal speech is furnished:

For why should I be afraid to give of my own accord what an idle heir (*otiosus heres*) makes off with against my will (*mihi invito*)? For that reason I make over the things that are mine to Him, because I am not able to take them away with me. I will make altogether my own that which in truth is not my own, and I will show my true love for my riches, when I have sent them ahead of me instead of letting them perish. I must press on to reach the most sacred retinue, from which I will no more be allowed to absent myself; there I will build myself a house; in that place I will build storehouses. And because there are no conveyances or beasts of burden, by which I may convey my riches to the other side, which will have been able to enter there, I will set all of my belongings on the shoulders (*cervicibus*) of the servants of God.[125] With these porters nothing of mine is allowed to perish; it is necessary that those of whom Christ is the teacher, and the holy angels the protectors, be the ones to carry my riches to the heavens. Let the stomachs of the poor, in which Christ witnesses that he both hungers and is filled, be the storehouses for my crops. Why should an heir mock me with a false blessing, and with lying lips wish [me] life while he grumbles in his soul that [my] death comes slowly?[126]

---

[124] *Ad Gregoriam* 12 (*CC* 25A, 209–10): 'Si huius consules mundi, ut aurigas histriones que locupletent, ut que lenones ac mimos divites faciant, non metuunt suarum opum inanem subire iacturam, quin immo in his profusionibus gloriantur, dummodo cum damno rerum favorem contemptibilis vulgi mercentur, ego ad servorum dei requiem cum favore omnium angelorum nummum proferre cur timeam, quem mihi centuplatum regis mei dextera reddendum esse confido? Et si terra uberiora semina quam susceperit reddit, cur ego mihi a domino Iesu Christo reddi non credam, praesertim cum eius chirographum teneam pollicentis atque ita caventis: Amen amen dico vobis, quia qui uni de minimis qui in me credunt fecerit, mihi fecit?' Cf. Matt. 18:5–6, Mark 9:42, Luke 17:2.

[125] A return to the Augustinian theme of the poor as *laturarii*; see footnote 116 above.

[126] *Ad Gregoriam* 12 (*CC* 25A, 210–11): 'Cur enim dare sponte timeam, quod mihi otiosus heres tollit invito? Cui idcirco relinquo quae mea sunt, quia me cum ea auferre non valeo. Faciam plane meum quod vere meum non est, et verum meis opibus amorem ostendam, cum meas me divitias praeire fecero, non perire. Pergendum mihi est ad sacratissimum comitatum, unde me egredi ulterius non licebit; illic mihi domus, illic horrea construam. Et quia illic nulla vehicula, nulla poterint iumenta ingredi, quibus illuc meas possim divitias transmigrare, famulorum Christi cuncta quae mea sunt cervicibus ponam. His laturariis nihil mihi perire permittitur; ipsi opes meas ad caelos perferant necesse est, quorum magister Christus est, et sancti angeli protectores. Sint viscera pauperum horrea frugum mearum, in quibus Christus et esurire se testatur et refici. Cur me heres ficta benedictione inrideat, et cum increpet animo quod tarda mors veniat, labiis mendacibus vitam exoptat?'

But the *laturarii* here are no longer exclusively the poor, they are the 'those of whom Christ is the teacher, and the holy angels the protectors', or again, 'the servants of God'. While Gregoria is encouraged to share her surplus, there is no question of her giving up the estate itself. Rather, the intention of the anonymous author is to encourage her to see her benign performance of the role of Christian *domina* as a crucial contribution to the well-being of the wider Christian community. One of the ways she can do this is to charge 'the servants of God' with the task of finding a use for the surplus which her own establishment does not require.

AD GREGORIAM IN PALATIO: THE SENATORIAL *DOMINA* AS *MILES CHRISTI*

It is worth engaging in a sustained discussion here of *Ad Gregoriam in palatio*. It is a text that we will meet again and again in this study, since it considers, repeatedly and in great depth, the issues that concern us. In a way different to the *Vita Genovefae*, *Ad Gregoriam* offers a cautionary tale for how the instincts of later writers (in this case a modern scholar rather than a medieval librarian) can suppress the usefulness of a source to later readers. *Ad Gregoriam* was first edited at the beginning of the twentieth century by the influential Benedictine, Dom Morin, who made what seems to have made a snap judgement about its date, authorship, and theological significance, and as a result until recently it has been relegated to study within the context of semi-Pelagian monasticism, when its significance, and importance, in fact lie with the study of the late Roman household.[127]

What can be said with certainty about the date, authorship and context of *Ad Gregoriam in palatio* is very little, but enough can be deduced from internal criticism to make it possible to use it, with caution, as a source of advice directed to a senatorial woman, the wife or daughter of a royal or imperial officer of high standing, in the period between Valentinian III

---

[127] Discovery of this text was announced by Germain Morin, 'Un Traité inédit d'Arnobe le Jeune', *RBen* 27 (1910), 153–71. Morin's attribution of the text to Arnobius the Younger was accepted by Klaus Daur in his edition of *Ad Gregoriam* (ed., *Arnobii Iunioris Opera Minora*, CC25A (Turnhout, 1992)); and by Michel Cozic, *Le Liber ad Gregoriam d'Arnobe le Jeune: édition, traduction, étude historique, doctrinale et littéraire* (Villeneuve d'Ascq, 1997). A dissenting view is offered in Kate Cooper, 'The Date and Authorship of the *Liber ad Gregoriam*: A Call for Re-investigation', Appendix A of eadem, *Concord and Martyrdom: Gender, Community, and the Uses of Christian Perfection in Late Antiquity* (Unpublished dissertation, Princeton University, 1993), and eadem, 'The Date and Authorship of *Ad Gregoriam in palatio*: An Open Question' (in preparation). In both studies, I suggest that *Ad Gregoriam* could as easily belong to the sixth century as the fifth.

(425–55) and Theoderic the Great (493–526), and probably in the reign of
Theoderic. The manuscripts identify the author as 'Johannes episcopus
Constantinopolitani', and in three of four cases the text appears alongside
Latin texts attributed pseudonymously to John Chrysostom. Yet since it
makes numerous direct borrowings from Latin sources it was almost
certainly written in Latin. For the sake of convenience we will refer to
the author simply as 'John', as at least one Carolingian library catalogue
did,[128] when repeated reference to 'the anonymous author of *Ad Gregoriam
in palatio*' becomes too cumbersome. This said, there is reason to suspect
that 'John' may have borne a different name altogether, and that he acquired
'John' as part of the process by which he became a pseudo-Chrysostom.

There is no reason, however, to think that the addressee of the text was not
a historical person called Gregoria. No married woman called Gregoria
famous enough to attract pseudonymous literature seems to have existed,
and certainly none in the circle of John Chrysostom.[129] Still, there are two
Latin-speaking historical Gregorias, one certainly and the other probably
married, attested in the period during which *Ad Gregoriam* could reasonably
have been written. One, Gregoria *cubicularia* in the palace at Constantinople
in the last decade of the sixth century, and a correspondent of Gregory
the Great, need not detain us at length. I have explored elsewhere the
case that could be made that she was the addressee of *Ad Gregoriam* and
that its author was a later *Johannes episcopus Constantinopolitani*, John the
Faster, bishop of Constantinople 582–95.[130] I would now argue, however,
that a date after the Gothic Wars is difficult to reconcile with the text's
complacent way of referring to both a king and an emperor without setting
them in opposition.

The second Gregoria is more interesting, because even if she was not the
addressee of the letter she illustrates well the kind of woman who was. This
is Gregoria *illustrissima*, a *materfamilias* of Arles in the late fifth century,
who is remembered with her kinsman Firminus in the *Vita Caesarii* as

---

[128] This is the *Biblia Wulfadi*, the list of books of Wulfad, bishop of Bourges during the reign of
Charles the Bald, which records 'Epistolae Ioannis ad Gregoriam in palatio'; see A. Molinier,
Catalogue des manuscrits de la Bibliothèque Mazarine (Paris, 1885–92) I, 227. For discussion, see
Cooper, 'The Date and Authorship of the *Liber ad Gregoriam*,' in *Concord and Martyrdom*, at
357–83, and eadem, 'The Reichenau *Ad Gregoriam in palatio* (Codex Augiensis 172) and the
Problem of Women as Readers and Book Owners' (in preparation).

[129] By definition none of the three virgins called Gregoria remembered in the literature of the patristic
period (one of the 11,000 virgins associated with Saint Ursula, one of the virgins of Methodius of
Olympus's *Symposium*, and one of the Roman virgins in Gregory the Great's *Dialogues*) would have
attracted a text such as *Ad Gregoriam in palatio*, whether pseudonymously or otherwise.

[130] Cooper, *Concord and Martyrdom*, at 373–83.

having taken the young monk Caesarius in when he arrived in Arles after he was sent away from Lerins as a trouble-maker around 500.[131] It was they who made the introductions which led to his alarmingly swift rise to become bishop in 502.[132] Gregoria and Firminus (also an *illustris*) are often referred to in the secondary literature as a married couple, though what the text in fact says is that Gregoria was the *proxima* of Firminus – which in this case probably means blood kinswoman – and that she is a *materfamilias*, a status which did not necessarily involve being married.[133] Cyprian, Firminus, and Viventius, the authors of the *Vita Caesarii*, seem not to have known exactly how Gregoria was related to Firminus. By calling Gregoria *illustrissima*, the *Vita* suggests that her status was higher than that of Firminus, and that her father or husband had sat in the senate in Rome and had held a high position in the imperial bureaucracy, since after c. 400 *illustris* standing could only be gained by high office or *adlectio*.[134] This is exactly the kind of woman whom the author of *Ad Gregoriam in palatio* set his sights on.

The absolute *termini* for the dating of *Ad Gregorian* are the sack of Rome in 410 and the writing of Isidore of Seville's *De viris illustribus* (which mentions the text) in the early seventh century, but repeated references to siege and invasion, a tendency to speak of royal and imperial authority as if they are not in opposition, and what seems to be a reference to the *Edictum Theoderici* (a text to which we will return) suggest that it was probably written in the kingdom of Theoderic the Great, which included Italy and, after 511, the Visigothic territories in Spain and Gaul. The martyrs of the city of Rome constitute a shared territory of the imagination for both the writer and the intended reader. Special attention is given to three Roman martyrs who were married women: Anastasia, Symphorosa, and Felicitas (each of the three had a shrine in Rome, along with a *passio*); there are also echoes of the *passio* of the Roman martyr Sebastian, a point we have already

---

[131] *Vita Caesarii* 8 (*MGH SRM* 3, 460): 'Erat igitur tempore illo Firminus illustris et timens Deum, et proxima ipsius materfamilias Gregoria, illustrissima feminarum in praedicta urbe Arelatensi, quorum studio et vigilantia curaque circa clerum et monachos, circaque cives et pauperes civitatis, praedicta reddebatur illustrior. Uterque enim proprias opes non consumebant mundana luxuria, sed ad paradisum sibi eas deportatione pauperum transmittebant. Qui praedictum S. Caesarium ad se causa misericordiae receperunt.'

[132] William E. Klingshirn, *Caesarius of Arles: The Making of a Christian Community in Late Antique Gaul* (Cambridge, 1994), 72.

[133] This is a point discussed in Chapter Four, pp. 112–13.

[134] If she was married, her title would have been that of her husband, not her father, since on marriage women's status 'followed' that of their husbands: Bruce W. Frier and Thomas A. McGinn, *A Casebook of Roman Family Law* (Oxford, 2004), 97. On *illustres*, Chris Wickham, *Framing the Middle Ages: Europe and the Mediterranean, 400–800* (Oxford, 2005), 152.

seen. Anastasia, whose shrine was on the southern slope of the Palatine Hill, receives the most attention. Her palatine location resonates with four of the five known manuscripts' address to Gregoria *in palatio*, although unlike the other two saints, Anastasia had a church in Ravenna as well as Rome. The historical Gregoria could have been at court in Ravenna, or elsewhere, even if it is tempting to think of her in the old Palace at Rome. It can be said with certainty, in any case, that John wished to call attention to Gregoria's links to court. In addition to the *in palatio* of the title, he refers to her as having taken up the standards of Christ's army *intra palatium*.[135]

The senatorial *domina*'s responsibility as a Christian to treat those under her authority with the justice she herself would expect from God is stressed, along with her responsibility to offer her own conduct as an *exemplum*.[136] This exhortation to responsible stewardship of God's justice reflects the importance of the authority of the senatorial *domina*, who was expected to supervise a complex and economically substantial establishment, as we will see in Chapter Three. The closing section of *Ad Gregoriam* reviews the requirements of the Christian life, and stresses the urgency of safeguarding the divine precepts by assiduous searching and observance (*inquirere et servare*).[137] To an imagined objection that it is not the place of the married to excel in the Christian life, our author replies that the *caritas* of marriage is itself a vehicle of grace.

Ad Gregoriam opens with an extended description of what it imagines as Gregoria's own musings about the spiritual status of a woman who finds herself bound by the married estate despite her yearning for an unencumbered spiritual life. The traditional rhetorical gesture of invoking a patron's real or imaginary request[138] acquires pastoral urgency here. The lady reader is pictured as asking the author to 'give a ruling on what place a wife will be able to find before God, or to clarify to what extent she should pay compensation for the licence of the marital state'.[139] She is troubled by her awareness that the estates of widowhood and virginity are accorded a higher status than that of marriage, and the writer's task is to allay her concern. (The treatise strongly implies that Gregoria and her husband have not abandoned marital relations, a point to which we will return in Chapter Four.)

[135] *Ad Gregoriam* 10 (*CC* 25A, 206). [136] See especially *Ad Gregoriam* 18–19 (*CC* 25A, 224–33).
[137] *Ad Gregoriam* 22–4 (*CC* 25A, 237–44); here *Ad Gregoriam* 24 (*CC* 25A, 241).
[138] Tore Janson, *Latin Prose Prefaces: Studies in Literary Conventions*, Studia Latina Stockholmensia 13 (Stockholm, 1964).
[139] In the preface, the author characterizes Gregoria's request to him as follows: 'ut quem locum uxor apud deum invenire poterit digneris dare responsum', *Liber ad Gregoriam, Praef.* (*CC* 25A, 191).

This preface dispenses with the protestations of reluctance on the part of the writer which are common in the treatises addressed to noble women. We are led to believe that our author takes it as a given that his approach to the noble Gregoria will not be seen as self-serving, although it is difficult to judge whether this reflects his own status, a secure existing relationship with the lady in question, or simply rhetorical bravura. Nonetheless, he presents himself as making a straightforward and vivid approach to what he expects his readers to acknowledge as a pressing pastoral problem. It is of course impossible to judge whether Gregoria or any other married woman of the patronage class really *was* disturbed by the high status accorded to widowhood and virginity, but our author was by no means the only male writer of his day to imply that they were or ought to be.[140]

The first chapter establishes a central theme of the treatise, that life on this earth is to be understood as a period of spiritual testing, and that endurance of these tests will lead to eternal rejoicing. That 'the human race is to be tested' is a prominent theme in the writings of John Chrysostom, and this may be one of the reasons why a reader like Isidore of Seville perceived the text as a Latin translation of one of Chrysostom's writings.[141] Gregoria should know that God will reward her steadfastness, and it is not God but the Devil who torments her with his tribulations. This is because her right-eous conduct so offends him: 'And not without cause is the Devil tormented by the affliction of his own envy, when he laments that you have done a rare thing among married women, having taken up arms against him.'[142]

John develops here a metaphor which he will sustain throughout the treatise: that of Gregoria as a soldier of Christ. 'The King of Vices grieves that you are fighting boldly against his own soldiers, that is, against the battalions of sins, and he fears that unsheathed, the sword of your faith menaces the necks of his generals.'[143] He goes on to try to convince her that every difficulty encountered during her married life has been an attempt by the Devil to win her away from the cause of God.

For already at the very beginning of [your] marriage, because the Enemy saw you handed over after the training of your parents to the embraces of a most Christian

---

[140] For a discussion of the sources, see Cooper, *The Virgin and the Bride*, 116–43.

[141] Kate Cooper, 'Annianus of Celeda and the Latin Readers of John Chrysostom', *Studia Patristica* 27 (1993), 249–55, on the context of fifth-century translations of the works of Chrysostom.

[142] *Ad Gregoriam* 1 (*CC* 25A, 192) 'Nec inmerito suae dolore torquetur invidiae, cum te inter matronae, quod rarum est, contra se corripuisse arma diabolus ingemescit.'

[143] *Ad Gregoriam* 1 (*CC* 25A, 192): 'rex vitiorum contra milites suos, contra omnem scilicet numerum peccatorum, dolet fortiter dimicantem, evaginatumque tuae fidei gladium suorum expavescit ducum cervicibus inminere.'

man, in whom no disgrace of concubines, no immodest conceit of female friends, was able to prevail, in whose heart purity of morals holds sway as if in its own dominion; then, I say, the author of all crime presaged that you would be his assassin. Nor from any other motive did he attempt either at first to incite quarrelling between you, or afterwards to plant the seed of various instances of discord except in order that he – the Devil – might separate those joining together against him and wishing to live in the love of Christ.[144]

Marital quarrelling is here understood as an expression of Satan's temporary victory over two soliders of Christ whom he seeks to turn against one another instead of himself. If Gregoria has bestirred the enemy by choosing to follow in the footsteps of Christ, so now she must hasten to follow him, protecting herself from the Devil's arrows by a shield of forbearance.

In keeping with much of the advice literature of the period, *Ad Gregoriam* opens with praise and encouragement. 'I marvel greatly, esteemed daughter, that you have turned toward the Holy Spirit, having left behind the fleshly concerns of a legitimate bond.' Like many Latin prose prefaces, John points to a request from his addressee as the genesis for his work. Next comes an equally conventional gesture, a description of the lady's request for guidance, which spurred the writing of the text, in itself an irreproachably conventional gesture. In chapter Two, Gregoria is urged to go to the High King for protection, 'Use the *officium* of your nobility, claim *imperium*, bring the apostles as counsel.'[145] She is exhorted to petition him, 'Constantly demand deliverance', and to present herself in the court of God as the daughter of the High King 'unlawfully dishonoured by the daughter of a captive barbarian'.[146] This agonistic language is unusually strong for the devotional manuals and sermons of the period.[147] It takes on added significance from the *altercatio* in chapters 11–15, which is

---

[144] *Ad Gregoriam* 1 (*CC* 25A, 192–3).

[145] *Ad Gregoriam* 2 (*CC* 25A, 194): 'Tunc, inquam, exclama in fortitudine et noli parcere; utere tuae nobilitatis officio, vindica tibi praerogativam imperii, adplica advocatos apostolos, martyrum quoque candidatum excercitum, parentes quoque tuos, o anima, sanctos angelos pulsa: insiste, exequere, et omnino vindictam exposce.'

[146] *Ad Gregoriam* 1 (*CC* 25A, 193–4): 'Defende, ergo, nobilitatem generis tui, et cum te tenere voluerit diaboli filia, omnis procul dubio delectatio cuiuscumque peccati, aut occasio cuiuscumque facinoris, tunc te exclama summi regis filiam a captivi barbari filia exhonoratam iniuste. Tunc, inquam, exclama in fortitudine et noli parcere; utere tuae nobilitatis officio, vindica tibi praerogativam imperii, adplica advocatos apostolos, martyrum quoque candidatum excercitum, parentes quoque tuos, o anima, sanctos angelos pulsa: insiste, exequere, et omnino vindictam exposce.'

[147] *Ad Gregoriam* 1 (*CC* 25A, 198): 'In acie se adserit contra hostem fortiter pugnaturum, qui intra castra positus acies contremiut mediantes; et qui hinnientem equum ferre non potuit, quomodo leonis fremitum non timebit? quomodo varietatem tolerabit barbarorum, qui civem vociferantem expavit?'

set out as a metaphorical battle between the forces of God and the forces of the Devil warring over the soul.

The literary form of *Ad Gregoriam* is highly unusual, ambitious to the point of being rather confusing. The text is structured in two main parts. The first, a conduct manual outlining the trials which a married Christian woman should expect to encounter, begins and ends the text,[148] while the second, a visionary meditation in which Gregoria is invited to ascend to the high tower of wisdom,[149] and to view, arrayed below her, the allegorical battle between the *miles Christi* and a succession of personified vices, is tipped in, rather disruptively, half way through (chapters 11–15).[150] The visionary segment takes the form of an *altercatio*, a dialogue between the vices and virtues as they face each other in battle, and in this respect *Ad Gregoriam* constitutes one of the earliest attestations, building on Prudentius' *Psychomachia* some decades earlier, of an important medieval literary genre.[151]

Of course at one level this metaphor, the psychomachy of vices and the virtues, is simply a splendid literary pretence, an opportunity to call up imagery from Prudentius' fourth-century poem, and from even more distant Christian literature such as the second-century *Shepherd of Hermas*, whose allegorical ladies stood arrayed for the soul's edification. Yet while the *admonitio* expresses inherited concerns about nobility, high status, and respect of persons, they are inflected with unusually vivid urgency and there are clues that Gregoria's fear of her earthly circumstances is no mere literary convention.

If the text is a product of Italy during or shortly after the civil wars of the late fifth century, the siege metaphor had a sharper contemporary meaning. Gregoria and her adviser are likely to have been too young to inherit more than a legendary awareness of the sieges of Alaric and the sack of Rome in 410, but by the late fifth century, besiegement had become a regular

---

[148] We will return to discuss this section in detail in Chapters Three and Four.

[149] *Ad Gregoriam* 10 (*CC* 25A, 207) for the *turris sapientiae*. We will discuss this section in detail in Chapter Five.

[150] The hinge between the two elements is the assertion (ch. 10 (*CC* 25A, 207)) that the Christian wife should not believe that gender or the vocation to marriage will exempt her from service in the spiritual battle-lines. This assertion serves to introduce the *conflictus*; the section ends (ch. 16 (*CC* 25A, 218–20)) with an excursus on endurance (*patientia*) as the root of all virtues.

[151] Morton W. Bloomfield, *The Seven Deadly Sins: An Introduction to the History of a Religious Concept, with Special Reference to Medieval English Literature* (Michigan State College Press, 1952). In general, see the classic A. Katzenellenbogen, *Allegories of the Virtues and Vices in Mediaeval Art from Early Christian Times to the Thirteenth Century*, tr. A. J. P. Crick (London, 1939); and now R. Newhauser, ed., *In the Garden of Evil: The Vices and Culture in the Middle Ages*, Papers in Mediaeval Studies 18 (Toronto, 2005).

occurrence in the Western empire, even in Rome itself. After Attila and Bleda's successful besiegement of Naissus and Viminacium in 442,[152] the Romans could no longer be confident that their fortified cities were impregnable. Rome was sacked again by Geiseric in 455, and besieged in 471, during the stand-off between Ricimer and Majorian. In the sixth century, Rome was besieged repeatedly, by Belisarius in 535, by Witiges in 537, and by Totila in 546–7 and 555, but these episodes were probably not known to the author of *Ad Gregoriam*, who seems to have written before 526.

Ad Gregoriam offers us an opportunity to perceive how the repeated danger and expectation of siege during this period came to influence the Roman literary imagination. Scholars have long been aware of the sixth-century Roman Church's efforts to develop a liturgical framework for fortifying the Roman faithful. One writer, characterizing the prayers written by Pope Vigilius for the Mass during Witiges' siege of Rome in 537, has suggested that they 'indicate the fear and the sufferings of the Romans; the fear of the Goths roaming around the walls, destroying the cemeteries, and the sufferings from the plague and the shortage of food'.[153] But little scholarly attention has been dedicated to the problem of how the earlier military crises of Italy were registered in the imaginations of the faithful.[154]

Arching over *Ad Gregoriam* is the metaphor of a lady watching from a tower on the ramparts as the fate of her city is decided in battle by opposing armies below. Sometimes she watches from above, while sometimes she is pictured as fighting among the defenders of the city. This mixed positioning of the implied reader reflects what might be called an 'ethics of participation', in which the female householder is invited to see her own lot as not differing in the essentials from that of the martyr in the arena, the ascetic in the desert, or the soldier in the battlefield. To be sure, the text is addressed to a reader whose gender implied that her experience of the battlefield would ideally be at second hand, but this is all the more reason to encourage her to find a meaningful link between her own experience and the persistent sense of military alert. This was especially important if her pursuit of righteousness was believed, as we saw in the case of Genovefa and her *matronae*, to make her able to call down the powers of heaven should they be needed.

---

[152] Heather, *Fall of the Roman Empire*, 302.
[153] Peter Llewelyn *Rome in the Dark Ages* (London, 1970), 66, citing A. Chavasse, 'Messes du pape Vigile dans le Sacramentaire léonien', *EL* 64 (1950), 161–213, and 66 (1952), 145–215.
[154] Ralph W. Mathisen's vivid study of fifth-century Gaul, *Roman Aristocrats in Barbarian Gaul: Strategies for Survival in an Age of Transition* (Austin, 1993) offers a valuable model.

When Gregoria is invited to ascend the Tower of Wisdom, and to view the battle arrayed before her, we are perhaps right to see her as one of a long line of women, real and imagined, who stood on ramparts, at windows, and even on specially constructed wooden platforms, to witness the battles of European literature. But the intent of the author is not to relegate her to a passive role in the grand drama of the soul's salvation, or, indeed, in that of Ostrogothic Italy. John uses two complementary strategies to exploit the metaphor of the psychomachy, and Gregoria's level of engagement differs dramatically between the two. While in the *psychomachia*, the noble lady watches the battle from the comparative security of her tower, repeatedly at other points in the text she is pictured as fighting herself among the defenders of the city. Even as she stands watching the battlefield, it is an aspect of herself – her soul's own virtue – which takes up arms against vice.

Perhaps the most striking passage in the opening section offers the image of Gregoria racing to follow the leader of her own army, Christ the King, while the arrows of the Devil hail down upon her, and her shield of tolerance protects her as she runs. What *Ad Gregoriam* represents here is a situation in which the commander – Christ – has already signalled a tactical retreat, perhaps back to within the walls of the city itself – but members of his army, who should be following him as swiftly as they can in retreat, are being harried by the members of the opposing army, who wish to make the most of their temporary advantage. John encourages Gregoria not to stop to defend herself: 'for if you slow down to engage in any skirmish, the one you are fleeing from will draw closer, while the distance between you and the one you were following will grow ever greater.'[155]

John seems throughout to be trying to take the by then traditional theme of the *psychomachia* and give it added concreteness and urgency. Here are the words supplied for Gregoria to address the Devil, as he encourages her to slow down:

Listen to the lover (masc.) of patience [responding] to this. 'Oh, most misguided (*inperitissime*),[156] nay, most deceitful (*dolosissime*) persuader to madness! I flee Impatience with her father, the Devil, and I follow Endurance, the daughter of the highest God. I flee the impious barbarian and you direct me to linger; as I follow

---

[155] *Ad Gregoriam* 1 (*CC* 25A, 193): 'quem fugis fuge et quem sequeris sequere: gradum penitus in totum non figas, nulla te damna rerum, nullae retineant sermonum iniuriae. Si enim te stare fecerit suo quocumque certamine, ille adproximat quem fugiebas, et ille quem sequebaris elongat.'

[156] The vocabulary of *peritia* and *imperitia* (connected to that of *patientia* and *impatientia*) appears in Gregory and Cassian; it can describe both the inexperienced, vulnerable practitioner of the Christian life, and the false adviser (whose lack of *peritia* causes him to dispense misleading advice). See Leyser, *Authority and Asceticism*, 54–55, 162–77.

the pious King, you prevail upon me to stop, so that the One whom I am following may pull farther ahead, and the one whom I am fleeing may draw closer ... I will not forsake Endurance, until I reach my most victorious King. It is endurance herself who will offer me the safety of the city; let her bring me forward[157] in the presence of the King whom I long for.'[158]

Here and elsewhere, *Ad Gregoriam* finds the connection between the metaphor of military engagement and inherited concerns about nobility, high status, and respect of persons, inflected with unusually vivid urgency.

THE *DOMINA* AT THE GATE

We have already seen that, whatever the situation of the historical Gregoria, the lady in her tower was a figure in a Christian literary tradition which we meet also, in a variant form, in the *Life of Genovefa*. We should be aware, however, that there existed also a negative version of this literary figure of the Christian *materfamilias* in the besieged city. Ancient historians recorded that during the long siege of Rome by Alaric's Goths, a lady of the highest Roman nobility had decided to open the gates of the city and simply invite the barbarians in.[159] Whether she was moved by pity for the sufferers of famine and plague within the walls or by some more suspicious motive is unclear. In fact, historians were uncertain even about the identity of the lady. Zosimus, writing in the reign of Anastasius (498–518), suggested that the *augusta* Serena, widow of the generalissimo Stilicho, had intended to open the gates to Alaric in 408, before she was executed by order of the senate,[160] while Procopius asserted that it was Anicia Faltonia Proba, the grandmother of the virgin Demetrias.[161]

Though the status of the apocryphal story is dubious, it is significant that, despite their many differences, Serena and Proba were both matriarchs of dynasties at the pinnacle of Roman society, members of the group

---

[157] For *repraesento*: Ludwig Schnorr von Carolsfeld, 'Repraesentatio und Institutio: Zwei Untersuchungen über den Gebrauch dieser Ausdrücke in der römischen Literatur', in Max Kaser, Hans Kreller and Wolfgang Kunkel, eds., *Festschrift Paul Koschaker* (Weimar, 1939), 103–16; the article was prepared from the schedae of the *TLL* to which Schnorr von Carolsfeld had access.

[158] *Ad Gregoriam* 1 (*CC* 25A, 193): 'immo imperitissime, immo dolosissime huius persuasor insaniae! Inpatientiam cum suo patre id est diabolo fugio et sequor patientiam filiam summi die. Barbarum impium fugio, et tu me stare iubes; regem pium sequor, et tu gradum figere persuades, ut is quem sequor elonget, et ille quem fugio adpropinquet ... ego ad regem meum victoriosissimum quousque perveniam, patientiam non dimittam: ipsa mihi ostendet securitas urbem, ipsa me regis quem desidero representet aspectibus.'

[159] Procopius, *Wars* 1.2.27. Further discussion of this episode, and of Serena's career, can be found in Cooper, 'Gender and the Fall of Rome'.

[160] Zosimus, *Historia nova* 5.38.   [161] Procopius, *Wars* 1.2.27.

standing guard over the *mores* and values that defined what it was to be Roman. Serena was the niece and adopted daughter of Theodosius the Great, while Proba was the matriarch of the senate's most distinguished dynasty. Both women were known to be patronesses of the ascetic movement, with Proba the grandmother of the celebrated virgin Demetrias, and Serena the protector of the wealthy eccentric Melania the Younger.[162] Even assuming the story was not true, it was alarming enough to consider the mere idea that a noble Roman *materfamilias*, or an *augusta* like Serena, could be moved to undertake an act so contrary to the Roman values of solidarity, ferocity, and stoic endurance.

One wonders whether the literary figure of Gregoria, by contrast, was a warning, not only to women but to the whole senatorial class. By calling attention to how the apparently inconsequential moral dangers of the quotidian could offer purchase to the Devil's armies, John sought to make vivid how easy it was to fall away from the path that led to the starry heights. He also seems to have perceived, however, how dangerous it was, socially, to allow an indispensable class of persons to believe that they must choose between Christian values and maintaining the fabric of society. The popularity of ascetic literature seems to have created a ripple effect of anxiety in writers like the author of *Ad Gregoriam in palatio*, who saw that ancient Roman habits and institutions of the family and household needed to be rearticulated if they were to have staying power in the new moral climate. Their reaction was to set out terms of participation for a Christian élite who would be indispensable precisely in their capactiy as householders and *domini*.

Ironically, the social vision of the ascetic movement was structurally surprisingly similar to the bureaucratic 'updraft' that had sapped talent away from the localities at the curial level, and at the senatorial level made ancient families more dependent on the whim of an emperor or king. Both asceticism and bureaucracy threatened the older, more embedded way of doing things. By ancient tradition, the household was the crucial social and economic unit, ruled by a *paterfamilias* who in Roman law was paradigmatically both the biological father of sons and the owner of substantial property. Paternal authority was the bedrock of property relations and thus of society. From the time of Diocletian onwards, both bureaucrats and

---

[162] On Melania's troubles, see Kate Cooper, 'The Household and the Desert: Monastic and Biological Communities in the *Lives* of Melania the Younger', in Anneke Mulder-Bakker and Jocelyn Wogan-Browne, eds., *Household, Women, and Christianities in Late Antiquity and the Middle Ages* (Leiden, 2005), 11–35.

bishops would conspire to undermine the father's authority over his sons and married daughters. How wives and daughters fared, under both the old regime and the new, is one of the problems that will concern us in this study. We will see, also, that attention to their part of the story will help us to expose the mechanics of social change in the Roman household, and the role of the household in the last years of the Roman empire.

CHAPTER 2

'The obscurity of eloquence'

In the early sixth century, the monk-priest Eugippius of Lucullanum made a compendium of extracts from the work of Augustine of Hippo, thus making accessible for future generations a body of work so voluminous that, according to another early medieval handbook, only a liar could claim to have read it all.[1] Eugippius dedicated his collection, the *Excerpta Augustini*, to an aristocratic lady, the virgin Proba, with the modest reflection that even if in the vast abundance of her book collection she could engage directly with Augustine's writings, she might nonetheless find pleasure in having the extracts. Scholars have long suggested that it was probably from Proba's library in Rome, near St Peter's, that Eugippius worked, since the wording of the sentence in which he contrasts the 'complete' works in her collection with the exiguity of his extracts implies that the extracts were made on the basis of her codices.[2] The daughter of Quintus Aurelius Memmius Symmachus (consul in 485) and the sister-in-law of Boethius, the virgin Proba was a personage of standing, and there is every reason to believe that her library was exceptionally well-appointed, since she came from a line of women writers and literary patronesses going back nearly two centuries.[3]

Sadly, however, Eugippius' extracts are all that remain of Proba's library. We will see below that some literary codices bearing traces of senatorial ownership do survive from early sixth-century Rome, but only a handful. These manuscripts would originally have been held in the great family collections; as objects of great prestige and economic value, those that have

---

[1] See James J. O'Donnell, *Augustine, Sinner and Saint: A New Biography* (London, 2005), 135.

[2] Eugippius, *Excerpta Augustini praef.* (*CSEL* 9.1, 1): 'bibliothecae vestrae copia multiplex integra de quibus pauca decerpsi contineat opera.' For comment, see e.g. Michael M. Gorman, 'Marginalia in the Oldest Manuscripts of St. Augustine's *De Genesi ad litteram*', *Scriptorium* 37 (1984), 71–7, at 72.

[3] On Proba, see *PLRE* 2, 907 (Proba 1), and Anne N. Kurdock, *The Anician Women: Patronage and Dynastic Strategy in a Late Roman* domus, *350 CE–600 CE* (PhD Dissertation, University of Manchester, 2003), 229.

survived must eventually have been given or left to a monastery. We know this because only monastic collections were blessed with the combination of institutional continuity, good fortune, and ambitious librarianship that allowed parchment codices to be protected continuously for fifteen centuries from the rapid decomposition that can be triggered by being stored next to a damp wall.[4] If manuscripts belonging to Proba have survived, they do not bear identifying marks recognizable to the modern eye. To be sure, we can make calculations about which texts she could have known. But we can no longer know her as an aristocrat, as a senatorial daughter and granddaughter, as the young (and then older) woman who bore the name of a celebrated Christian poetess remembered as being among her ancestors, as a book-collector whose copies of Augustine may – it is not too far-fetched to believe – have come down to her from yet another Proba in the family, to whom more than one of Augustine's letters had originally been addressed.

We have dwelt on this point because the world of the senatorial aristocracy in late antiquity was a world of books.[5] To begin with, trying to understand these individuals without knowing what they read, and what they wrote about, is an unreasonable aspiration. At the same time, it was a also a world in which the handing-down of traditions and treasures was a matter of family and lineage. The men (and a very few women) who addressed the sons and daughters of these noble houses did so knowing that except among a shrill minority, the claims of family were viewed with reverence. But as we will see below, it is to the shrill minority that we owe all we know about ancient society.

When trying to acquaint ourselves with the senatorial Christians of Proba's day, we also have to contend with a paradox made famous nearly a half-century ago by the monastic historian Jean Leclercq. In *The Love of Learning and the Desire for God*, Leclercq made an arresting comparison of two influential senatorial Christians of the early sixth century, Magnus

---

[4] Claudia Villa, 'Cultura e scrittura nell'Italia longobarda. Renovatio e translatio: centri amministrativi ed eredità culturale', in Walter Pohl and Peter Erhardt, eds., *Die Langobarden: Herrschaft und Identität* (Vienna, 2005), 502–23. Much scholarly ink has been spilt on the problem of whether the library of Vivarium, the monastery founded by Proba's contemporary Cassiodorus, survived; a compendium of references can be found in Arnaldo Momigliano, 'Cassiodorus and the Italian Culture of his Time', in his *Secondo contributo alla storia degli studi classici* (Rome, 1960), 191–229, at 194. More recently, see the attempt to identify Vivarium codices by Fabio Troncarelli, 'I codici di Cassiodoro: le testimonianze più antiche', *Scrittura e civiltà* 12 (1988), 47–99, and idem, *Vivarium, i libri, il destino*, Instrumenta patristica 33 (Brepols, 1988), met with a degree of scepticism by E. Condello, *Una scrittura e un territorio. L'onciale dei secoli V–VIII nell'Italia meridionale* (Spoleto, 1994), 65–79.

[5] *Pace* Caesarius, *Sermones* 2 (*CC* 103, 18–19) on book collections that are never used. See Conrad Leyser, *Authority and Asceticism from Augustine to Gregory the Great* (Oxford, 2000), 95.

Aurelius Cassiodorus and his contemporary, the mysterious author of the *Rule of Saint Benedict*.[6] Why, Leclercq asked, does Benedict (d. c. 540) occupy such a dominant position in the collective memory of European monasticism, remembered not only as an authority, but as an insightfully humane spiritual teacher – when in fact know very little is known about him, and his one surviving text, the *Rule*, is a spare, almost skeletal document, while at the same time Cassiodorus, one of our most copious and valuable sources, and who was arguably far more influential at the time, is remembered as a worthy but far less magnetic figure? The answer, of course, lies in the afterlife of the sixth-century monastic tradition, with Benedict the subject first of a vivid biography by Gregory the Great toward the end of the sixth century,[7] and then of a mounting interest by the eighth-century monastic reformers.[8] But this is not the whole story. Leclercq's paradox is that we know not too little about Benedict, but too much about Cassiodorus.

Lerclercq argued that the process by which Benedict was remembered, and Cassiodorus neglected, was not entirely arbitrary; it began in the literary output of the men themselves. Cassiodorus left a copious testament of his participation in both the civic and religious affairs of his day, writing across a wide variety of genres. But where specifically religious matters were concerned, his effort was directed at fulfilling the expectations and very specific literary interests of Vivarium, the community on his estate. Benedict, by contrast, minimized what was specific about the monastic communities known to him when he came to write the *Rule*. This meant that his text could be held up as a mirror to almost any community engaged on the coenobitic life, and in which each could find itself reflected. This universal quality, Leclercq argued, was the secret of the *Rule*'s ability to seem 'fresh' to successive generations. Cassiodorus, by contrast, had spoken, eloquently, in the idiom of his own place and time. Thus, his work was revered, and copied, but as a relic of an earlier generation, rather than as the mirror of an enduring spiritual 'present'.

We will find that Lelercq's paradox holds equally true for the other senatorial Christians. Late Roman literate discourse was a game played by esoteric rules, and one's command of those rules marked one's place within the discursive community. It goes without saying that rules of this kind change over time, and the majority of modern readers will find that the

---

[6] Jean Leclercq, *The Love of Learning and the Desire for God*, tr. K. Misrahi (New York, 1961), 21.
[7] See Leyser, *Authority and Asceticism*, 102, 181–4.
[8] The 'making of St Benedict' awaits its historian. In the interim, see Ian Wood, *The Missionary Life: Saints and the Evangelisation of Europe, 400–1050* (Harlow, 2001), esp. 64–73, 108–11, 145–62.

mannerisms that made a fifth- or sixth-century text seem vivid and com-pelling at the time now mark it as distractingly stylized. Of this off-putting quality, there are few better examples than the *Ad Gregoriam*, as we will see below. The achievement of its author is to make Cassiodorus' texts look positively Benedictine in their capacity to speak across the ages. The value of the text, then, is that it represents a lost chapter in the development of senatorial Christianity. The sociology of late Roman liter-acy was naturally hierarchical, and within the charmed circle of the literate classes, professional and social standing were reflected by different levels of engagement with the written and spoken word. We can conveniently imagine three sub-groupings of decreasing size. The vast majority of the literate were aspiring state bureaucrats whose parents, usually members of the provincial gentry like those of the young Augustine, had saved to make sure of their chance at gaining advancement through a post requiring literate skill, and perhaps eventual promotion to the clarissimate, the lowest rung of the senatorial order.[9] A more restricted group was that of their teachers.[10] These men, from a similar background to that of their pupils, found that their gifts at grammar, rhetoric, or both, meant that their best ambition was to secure a distinguished teaching post. To the gifted few, this route, too, could confer dazzling advancement. In the late fourth century, for example, the grammarian Ausonius of Bordeaux, tutor to the emperor Gratian, held a series of increasingly prestigious imperial offices, becoming praetorian prefect in 378.[11]

The smallest population was that of the senatorial élite, men and women whose need to command the cultural territory of *romanitas* was less a matter of professional necessity than of self-image – although from the mid-fourth century these families increasingly found it useful to place their sons in competition with their social inferiors for the more desirable administrative posts. Even within the senate, there was a steeply raked hierarchy, and office could be a means of advancement for those at the lower rungs, and of retaining privilege for those at the higher. But for men

---

[9] Peter Heather, 'Literacy and Power in the Migration Period', in Alan K. Bowman and Greg Woolf, eds., *Literacy and Power in the Ancient World* (Cambridge, 1994), 177–97, at 185: 'the fact that this shared articificial literacy was the key to rewarding careers, both gave mastery of it an extra functional point, and meant that the landed classes had every interest in involving themselves actively in the state.'

[10] Robert A. Kaster, *Guardians of Language: The Grammarian and Society in Late Antiquity* (Berkeley, 1988), 104–9.

[11] John Matthews, *Western Aristocracies and Imperial Court, AD 364–425* (Oxford, 1975), 51–4 and 69–74 on the career of Ausonius from c. 367, when he was called from the chair of rhetoric at Bordeaux to become tutor to Gratian, to the death of Gratian in 383.

and women at this level of society, cultured leisure played an important role in establishing moral title to the immense wealth at their disposal. For the senatorial families, authorship, literary patronage, and connoisseurship of valuable book collections all contributed to the projection of an identity as the *pars melior humani generis*,[12] the benevolent guardians of all that was best about Rome. There is reason, then, to look for a specifically senatorial ethos in late Roman literature, since it was the group at the pinnacle, the patronage class, whom the others, by and large, sought to please.

There is, however, an important caveat here. Christian writers affiliated with the ascetic movement often sought, when addressing this group, to establish their moral independence, and often did so by revealing ambivalence – and even outright hostility – toward the old values of family and paternalism. Scholars have tended to confuse the later dominance of this group with their position in the fifth century. Men like Jerome remained the clients of those whom they sought to attack and perhaps to amuse, with the unadorned form and radical content of their speech. To his modern readers, however, Jerome appears like a Church Father, not a literary lapdog. After fifteen centuries of transmission by ascetically minded librarians, the sources which remain to us have been bleached of the deep hues of a world that would be destroyed by the Gothic Wars. During the fifth and early sixth centuries, the political conditions that favoured the stability of the literate hierarchy – the existence of a state strong enough to sponsor schools and greedy for literate young recruits to its bureaucracy – were still in place across much of the West, and a good proportion of the then celebrated Christian literature was imagined along lines consonant with the old senatorial ethos. But after the Gothic Wars, a shift of balance took place. The ability of the Church to muster a polity for social organization, whose effectiveness was increasingly independent of the health – or even the existence – of a properly functioning state, ceased to be a matter of curiosity and became an indispensable political fact.

As a result, an anachronistic paradigm of the Church as a fully developed organization, with coherent ascetic and episcopal institutions, is often projected back into the fifth and fourth centuries. At the same time, the role of the aristocratic laity, the men and women whose opinions and resources had been indispensable during the improvisational period of the fourth and fifth centuries, tends to be brushed out. Thus the ancient sources reflecting the older ethos, which sought harmony between

---

[12] Quintus Aurelius Symmachus to Vettius Agorius Praetextatus (Symmachus, *Ep.* 1.52 (*MGH AA* 6/1, 26).

Christian ideas and the old Roman values of tradition, family, and property, are often dismissed as 'nominally Christian' or 'Pelagian'. (We will
return to discuss the latter label in Chapter Five.) It is also very difficult not
to view the senatorial Christians through the eyes of their ascetic critics,
since the great ascetic writers were so beloved by later monk-librarians, and
are thus disproportionately well represented in the sources that have come
down to us. But we must try to do so, because otherwise we cannot
understand developments that were in fact by no means inevitable.

Family life and even marriage itself, we will see in a later chapter, came
to be reimagined during the fifth and sixth centuries, in a process leading
eventually to the emergence, in Francia for example, of a new court
culture, in which the voices of churchmen were *de iure* accorded a
privileged status among powerful laity. No need, any longer, to sound
shrill.[13] To understand this shared culture, and the privileged position
accorded to ordained and monastic voices within it, we must first attempt
to understand the exuberant senatorial Christianity which it replaced, and
the negotiations by which late Roman élites, accustomed by ancient
tradition to act as custodian of the empire's religious institutions, were
persuaded to defer to a new kind of religious leadership, drawn in large
part from among their social inferiors.

THE 'JEWELLED STYLE' AND THE *CENTO* OF PROBA

Latin literacy was always, first of all, about Virgil. It is important to
recognize that the central role played by poetry in cultivating a sense of
identity and belonging held true for Christians as well as pagans. Virgil was
the fundamental point of reference, and Christian writers did not 'shake
off' the deep engagement with him that their teachers had worked so hard
to instill.[14] One of the great cultural projects of the fourth century was to
cast the spiritual traditions of Christianity in a language more pleasing than
that of the Gospels to ears steeped in the rhythms of Homer and Virgil.[15]
These efforts merit attention as reflecting a sensibility distinctively easy in
its attitude to the problem of reconciling Athens with Jerusalem,[16] perhaps

---

[13] 'a Merovingian court culture shared by laymen and ecclesiastics': Heather, 'Literacy and Power', 197,
citing Ian Wood, 'Administration, Law, and Culture in Merovingian Gaul', in Rosamond
McKitterick, ed., *The Uses of Literacy in Early Medieval Europe* (Cambridge, 1990), 63–81.
[14] Sabine MacCormack, *The Shadows of Poetry: Vergil in the Mind of Augustine* (Berkeley, 1998).
[15] Michael Roberts, *Biblical Epic and Rhetorical Paraphrase in Late Antiquity* (Liverpool, 1985).
[16] See now Charles W. Hedrick, *History and Silence: Purge and Rehabilitation of Memory in Late
Antiquity* (Austin, 2000) on professed Christians cherishing the memory of their pagan ancestors.

in part because, as Jerome's *De viris illustribus* records, the early authors and patrons of Christian Latin poetry tended to be men and women of high standing.[17] New strategies of reading were emerging as well: at the end of the fourth century, Augustine of Hippo expressed his delight and relief at finding a new depth in the frustratingly humble Christian sources thanks to the techniques and traditions of allegorical reading made known to the West by Ambrose; we will return to these in a later chapter. Here our interest is in the products of the Christian literary élite, though we will pay more attention to pastoral ideas conveyed by the texts than to their specifically literary properties.

A generation ago, it was common to think of late Roman poetry as decadent, since its sensibility differs so dramatically from that of Virgil and Horace, the very writers whom the late Roman poets revered. But the mid-twentieth century brought a revolution in literary scholarship, with scholars beginning to appreciate the fact that the stylized effect of late Roman poetry was the reflection of a new cultural sensibility, not of declining skill among late Roman poets.[18] We are now in a position to delineate the aesthetic and something of the social register of the *literatus* who ran the salons to which Jerome hoped to gain entry. This aesthetic was distinct from that of classical antiquity on the one hand, and on the other from the medieval monastic future.

The 'jewelled style' of late Roman poetry found its champion in a 1989 monograph by Michael Roberts,[19] who argued that every distinctive aspect of late Roman sculpture and mosaic art could find its parallel in literary expression. Roberts drew liberally on the idea of the Norwegian archaeologist H. P. L'Orange, that the administrative reforms of Diocletian and his successors had been reflected in a 'block style'. For L'Orange, the picture plane of late Roman bas-relief or mosaic had evolved into a visual geometry, in which each component took a place calculated according not to concerns of naturalistic representation, but according to the need to visualize hierarchical relationships. Thus, for example, an emperor would stand at the centre of the composition, while geometrically calculated rows of dignitaries would be represented in bands below and beside him. The

---

[17] e.g. Jerome, *De viris illustribus* 84 (Juvencus), 111 (Acilius Severus) (*TU* 14, 44 and 50).

[18] Jean-Louis Charlet, 'Aesthetic Trends in Late Latin Poetry (325–410)', *Philologus* 132 (1988), 74–85; Jacques Fontaine, 'Unité et diversité du mélange des genres et des tons chez quelques écrivains latins de la fin du IVe siècle: Ausone, Ambroise, Ammien', in *Christianisme et formes littéraires de l'antiquité tardive en Occident*, Fondation Hardt, Entretiens sur l'antiquité classique 33 (Geneva, 1976), 438–46; idem, 'Comment doit-on appliquer la notion de genre littéraire à la littérature latine chrétienne du IVe siècle?', *Philologus* 132 (1988), 53–73.

[19] Michael Roberts, *The Jeweled Style: Poetry and Poetics in Late Antiquity* (Ithaca, 1989).

needs of visual hierarchy won out over those of realism, so that the emperor's image could be twice the size of that of his attendants, even when they were represented as standing next to one another. Here is L'Orange on the changing social and political reality of late antiquity, which he saw reflected in the new aesthetic:

> The everyday life of the average man – his whole political, economic, and social life – was transformed during late antiquity. The free and natural forms of the early Empire, the multiplicity and the variation of life under a decentralized administration, was replaced by homogeneity and uniformity under an ever-present and increasingly more centralized hierarchy of officials. Characteristic of the earliest period of the Principate was the infinite variety in the modes of life on the local level, the vigorous natural growth of the towns, the provinces, and the land districts of the enormous Empire, the self-development and natural rounding-off of civic life in individual urban communities (*municipia*), each with its own municipal government and administration. Late Antiquity leveled and regulated these forms of free growth, the community organizations were absorbed into the compact, all-powerful state.[20]

For L'Orange, the increasing importance of the *militiae* in late antiquity – we have seen above that the term *militia* refers both to the military and to the imperial bureaucracy – meant that organic and naturalistic forms of representation had to give way to what he calls 'block formations'.

> The contrast between the military and the civil orders is just the contrast between mechanical coordination and organic grouping, between the natural formations in free life and a massive alignment in rank and square, between individual, natural motions and movements *en bloc*. Both in community life and in art the large block formations and mass movements now appeared ever more clearly behind the continually thinning veil of traditional antique forms.[21]

This displacement of realism by abstraction would have important implications not only for the geometrical relationship among compositional elements but in a new way of articulating the surface. The aesthetic of the 'block style' brought with it an equal and opposite tendency toward visual fragmentation evident, for example, in late Roman mosaics.

Michael Roberts argued that the poetry of the same period developed similarly toward abstraction, reflecting the same mutation in cultural and aesthetic sensibility, the same underlying 'style'. In a wonderfully confusing paragraph Roberts transposes L'Orange's description of an early medieval wall mosaic into a verbal idiom, to show how apposite a description

---

[20] H. P. L'Orange, *Art Forms and Civic Life in the Late Roman Empire* (Princeton, 1965), 3.
[21] L'Orange, *Art Forms and Civic Life*, 8.

results of the style of late Roman poetry. (Where Roberts has made a substitution from L'Orange's original, he offers the original wording within brackets alongside):

In contrast to the classical poems (mosaics) . . . the entire structure (surface) is now broken up into a myriad of single, chromatically separated words (stones); the countless units (tesserae) glitter and scintillate with reflected light and color. Here the individual brilliant words (stones), which the poets (artists) of antiquity tried to subdue and control, are deliberately brought out to full effect. Instead of disappearing from view in a realistic description (an imitation of plastic form), each word (stone) retains its own sparkling qualities of light and color.[22]

Instead of seeking always to subordinate individual elements of language into a seamlessly integrated whole, as was the custom among writers of the Augustan age, the late Roman writers had gloried in the attention-grabbing qualities of discrete elements:

The reader is distracted by the brilliance of individual words or subsidiary compositional units, the brilliance of the unit in isolation and its relationship to other equivalent units, to the extent that in the most extreme cases the meaning of a sentence is only with difficulty perceived amid the disconcerting impression of verbal dazzle.[23]

We will see below that in prose writing, a similar phenomenon can be discovered, though at the level of clause and sentence rather than of word and phrase.

At the same time, another aspect of the 'jewelled style', the breaking down of narrative structure into a chain of roughly equal units, aligned to capture a balance between repetition and variation, is equally important in prose; it is a strategy used similarly, as we will see below, in Prudentius' *Psychomachia* and *Ad Gregoriam in palatio*. Roberts suggests that the changing approach to narrative in fact reflects a changing relationship to meaning.

In late antiquity what seems to have happened is that the referential function of language/art lost some of its preeminence; signifier asserts itself at the expense of signified. In the arts this means a vagueness in the outline and interrelationships of plastic form; in literature it means a tendency for constituents to break loose from syntactic structure and to 'wander,' demanding attention disproportionate to or at odds with their logical role in the economy of the sentence.[24]

---

[22] Roberts, *The Jeweled Style*, 71, citing H. P. L'Orange and P. J. Nordhagen, *Mosaics*, tr. Ann E. Keep (London, 1966), 9.
[23] Roberts, *The Jeweled Style*, 75.   [24] Roberts, *The Jeweled Style*, 72.

Instead of being harnessed into a secure position within an overarching structure, components become more autonomous, and the reader is required to dedicate ever-greater attention to the problem of their relationship.

When late Roman writers came to engage with poetry, another mechanism was at work in addition. What Roberts called 'the fragmenting exegetical techniques of the grammatical schools' led late ancient readers of Virgil and Horace to focus their study on narrow textual soundings rather than on 'the larger, characteristic qualities of symmetry and design',[25] with the result that the influence exerted by the earlier poets on their later successors was channelled very narrowly to the level of phrase, line, and stanza rather than to the architecture of narrative elements building toward a unified whole.

Nowhere is this channelling more visible than in the late Roman enthusiasm for the curious genre known as the cento, a form based on patterned borrowing, in which a new narrative is constructed from lines, or part-lines, drawn entirely from a previous poet. The fourth-century biblical epic of the aristocratic poetess Proba, one of the earliest substantial Christian poems to have survived, uses just this technique. We will see below that Proba also offers a valuable witness to a distinctively senatorial way of thinking about Christian values.

Though uncomfortably stylized from a modern viewpoint, the cento format offered a dazzlingly direct medium for reconciling ancient language and *mores* with Christian ethics and narrative.[26] This is certainly true in Proba's case. Pieced together entirely from borrowed lines and phrases from Virgil's *Aeneid*, *Eclogues*, and *Georgics*, the 694 lines of Proba's poem offer a flying summary of biblical history from the Creation to the post-resurrection appearance to the disciples of Jesus, and his ascension to heaven. Men and women for whom the *Aeneid* was the crucial point of reference may have bristled at points where the borrowings were fused together infelicitously, but the project itself – the re-clothing of biblical epic in the harmonious and familiar dialect of cultural prestige – would have reached a group of readers who flinched at the rough diction of the Gospels, whether in the original Greek or in the old Latin translation, the *Vetus Latina*.

It has been suggested that the *Cento Probae* was designed as an introduction to Christian ideas for schoolchildren, possibly in the aftermath of

[25] Roberts, *The Jeweled Style*, 68, citing Michael Roberts, 'The Treatment of Narrative in Late Antique Literature: Ammianus Marcellinus (16.10), Rutilius Namatianus, and Paulinus of Pella', *Philologus* 132 (1988), 181–95, at 190–1.
[26] Filippo Ermini, *Il centone di Proba e la poesia centonari latina* (Rome, 1909), esp 142–61.

Julian the Apostate's edict against Christians practising as teachers in 362. The logic here is that Christian parents would have felt ambivalent exposing their children to pagan lore, at the same time as they wished them to benefit from the shared literary culture of their peers.[27] It is clear that in Proba's view Christianity was a legacy to be handed down within families, rather than a call to abandon family life. A dedication to Proba's own *dulcis coniunx* is proposed in the closing lines of the poem: 'This observance do you keep, O husband sweet, and if we do win merit through our piety, then pure in heart may our children's children keep the faith.'[28] If Proba is not thinking of a readership of children, she is at the very least thinking of a readership of parents.

Again and again, the emphasis in Proba's poem is on bringing Christian values close to those of the early Romans. The bonds of family, including conjugal affection, are stressed repeatedly. In the case of the story of the rich young man, for example, it is striking that Jesus does not tell him to 'go, sell all you have, and give it to the poor' as in Matthew 19:21; rather, the young man is told to keep a chaste household – 'casta pudicitiam servet domus' – (line 526) and live a spartan lifestyle, a recommendation much closer to the old Roman values of a frugal warrior aristocracy than to the ascetic traditions built on Matthew's story.[29] A suspicion that *domus casta* refers to an ascetic household would be ill-founded; as we will see in Chapter Four, the meaning of *castus* at this period is linked to fertility, not asceticism. For example, in a dedicatory inscription (*CIL* 6.1755, discussed below), the son and daughter-in-law of Anicia Faltonia Proba celebrate her as *servandae ac docendae castitatis exemplum* directly before they mention that she is both daughter and mother of consuls. The renunciation of wealth *per se* is certainly not in view in Proba's treatment of the rich young man.

Equally, Proba seems untroubled by the ascetic currents which had begun to converge on the relationship between Mary, Jesus, and Joseph. For Proba, Mary is a heroic Roman *materfamilias*, exemplary in her devotion to her child. Great emphasis is given to the mother's efforts to

---

[27] Elizabeth A. Clark and Diane F. Hatch, *The Golden Bough, The Oaken Cross: The Vergilian Cento of Faltonia Betitia Proba*, American Academy of Religion Texts and Translations Series 5 (Chico, Ca., 1981), 99–100.

[28] *Probae Cento*, lines 692–4 (*CSEL* 16, 609, tr. Clark and Hatch, 95): 'Hunc ipse teneto/ o dulcis coniunx, et si pietatis meremur/ hac casti maneant in religione nepotes.' In addition, the poem bears a dedication to a Roman emperor, seemingly composed by a scribe, which envisages the use of the poem as a schoolbook for children of the imperial dynasty: see Clark and Hatch, *The Golden Bough, The Oaken Cross*, 106.

[29] See e.g. Augustine, *Confessions* 8.6.14–15 (*CC* 27, 121–3), referring to Athanasius, *Vita Antonii* 2.

protect the child from King Herod during the Massacre of the Innocents. In the context of a town seized by *magnis terroribus*, Mary emerges as a figure of bravery and intelligence. Certainly, Proba is aware that the child's father is not Joseph, but this fact is taken as an occasion to celebrate the brilliant *nomen* of the child's true father rather than the sexual history of the mother.[30]

At the same time, Proba seems carefully to have 'carried across' ideas of harmonious family life from the original setting of her borrowed texts. Elizabeth Clark and Diane Hatch have shown that in her choice of passages from Virgil, Proba drew particularly on scenes of conjugal devotion – for example those involving Creusa and Andromache – and of filial piety, especially the relationship between Aeneas and Anchises.[31] Although these passages are put to new use, such as describing the bond of loyalty between Jesus and his disciples, Proba seems to have understood the Christian relationships as reflecting rather than subverting the bonds of loyalty evoked by the earlier poet.

Proba's identity has been disputed. The brief description of her by Jerome makes it clear that she was a fourth-century matriarch of the *gens Anicia*, a senatorial dynasty to which we will have occasion to return more than once in the course of our discussion, but it is impossible to be more specific with confidence.[32] The intricacies of the debate need not concern us here.[33] Internal evidence would support ascription either to Faltonia Betitia Proba, wife of Clodius Celsinus Adelfius (urban prefect in 351), or to her younger kinswoman, Anicia Faltonia Proba, wife of Sextus Claudius Petronius Probus, (consul of 371). Anicia Faltonia Proba's copious attestation in the epigraphic record shows that it was a family that prized both accomplishment and visibility in its women-folk.[34] In addition to the well-known funerary inscription dedicated by this Proba to her husband shortly

[30] *Probae Cento*, lines 354/5 (*CSEL* 16, 590): 'tum vero manifesta fides clarumque paternae/ nomen erat virtutis.'

[31] Clark and Hatch, *The Golden Bough, The Oaken Cross*, 110–18.

[32] A. H. M. Jones, 'The Social Background of the Struggle between Paganism and Christianity in the Fourth Century', in Arnaldo Momigliano, ed., *Paganism and Christianity in the Fourth Century* (Oxford, 1963).

[33] Useful starting-points are Danuta Shanzer, 'The Anonymous *Carmen contra paganos* and the Date and Identity of the Centonist Proba', *Revue des Études Augustiniennes* 32 (1986), 232–48; John Matthews, 'The Poetess Proba and Fourth-Century Rome: Questions of Interpretation', in Michel Christol *et al.*, eds., *Institutions, société et vie politique dans l'empire romain au IVe siècle ap. J.-C.: Actes de la table ronde autour de l'oeuvre d'André Chastagnol (Paris, 20–21 janvier 1989)* (Paris, 1992), 277–304; Hagith Sivan, 'Anician Women, the Cento of Proba, and Aristocratic Conversion in the Fourth Century', *Vigiliae Christianae* 47 (1993), 140–57.

[34] This is a point made well by Sivan, 'Anician Women', 153–4.

after his death c. 390, a number of inscriptions celebrating her virtue as wife and mother are preserved. One dedicated by her son and daughter-in-law (Anicia Juliana, mother of the celebrated virgin Demetrias) celebrated her as 'Anicia Faltonia Proba, trustee of the ancient *nobilitas*, pride of the Anician family, a model of the preservation and teaching of wifely virtue, descendant of consuls, mother of consuls'.[35]

For our purposes, what is important is that as late as the early seventh century a Proba was remembered as having written a cento, and that the sixth-century Anicians almost certainly knew enough about her to claim a relationship.[36] Indeed, the very name of the early sixth-century Proba almost certainly reflects a conscious attempt by her parents to claim a place for her in the line of distinguished ancestresses bearing the name. Her patronage of the *Excerpta Augustini* suggests, in addition, that this was a badge of honour which she sought to live up to.

PRUDENTIUS

More directly influential for the confluence of patristic and Roman traditions that we will see in the late fifth and early sixth centuries, however, was Prudentius, the Christian poet for whom we have the best evidence of an enthusiastic sixth-century readership. Prudentius was best known as the author of two influential poems on devotional themes, the *Peristephanon* celebrating the spiritual victory of the martyrs, and the *Psychomachia* describing the battle between the vices and the virtues. That we still posesss in autograph the annotations to his *Peristephanon* made in 527 by Vettius Agorius Basilius Mavortius attests to the high regard in which his writings were held, as well, of course, as to the economic value of the books.[37]

The *Psychomachia* – sometimes translated as 'The Soul-Battle'[38] – stands as a monument to the élite Roman Christians whose sensibilities required literary and philosophical polish. Its use of iambic verse makes for an

---

[35] *CIL* 6.1755, tr. Brian Croke and Jill Harries, *Religious Conflict in Fourth-Century Rome: A Documentary Study* (Sydney, 1982), 116, amended. Other inscriptions to this Proba are *CIL* 6.1754 and 1756; her epitaph to Sextus Petronius Probus appears in *CIL* 6, unnumbered, directly after 1756; see discussion in Kate Cooper, *The Virgin and the Bride: Idealized Womanhood in Late Antiquity* (Cambridge, Mass., 1996), 103–4.

[36] Leslie Brubaker, 'Memories of Helena: Patterns of Imperial Female Matronage in the Fourth and Fifth Centuries' in James, ed., *Women, Men and Eunuchs*, 52–75.

[37] Paris, Bibl. Nat. Lat. 8084 (fols. 1–155), saec. VI in. For discussion of the manuscript, see E. A. Lowe, *Codices latini antiquiores* 5 (Oxford, 1950), 16.

[38] E.g. Susanna Morton Braund, *Latin Literature* (London, 2002), 235.

engagement with Virgil far more subtle than Proba's. Where Proba had borrowed from Virgil in order to piece together an eccentric patchwork – this is the literal meaning of *cento* – Prudentius made his own fluent use of the inherited idiom, evoking the epic tradition and establishing new terms of reference. The balance of critique and appropriation of the classical tradition in his work remains a point for debate. Recent scholarship has seen in the *Psychomachia* both a straightforward attempt to imitate Latin epic in Christian terms, and alternately as a Christian attack on paganism through a critique of Vergilian epic, a debate which we will not attempt to resolve here.

Important for the present study is the poet's contribution to the development of Christian allegory. Prudentius played an important role in what can only be understood as an allegorical revolution at the end of antiquity. As we will see in the next chapter, allegorical exegesis of inherited texts had been used by pagans, Jews, and Christians for half a millennium to protect elements of the Greek and Hebrew cultural inheritance which had come under attack, whether because of the convergence of conflicting cultural traditions in the cosmopolitan milieu of a great city such as Alexandria,[39] or because of changing sensibilities within a single tradition, such as those which led Neoplatonic interpreters of Homer to read the *Iliad* as an allegory of conflict within the human psyche. The emergence of Christian Latin poetry reflects the same impulse, and it is not coincidental that the most influential of late Latin poets was the author of the *Psychomachia*.[40] From being primarily a strategy for appropriating existing material, allegory became, in the course of the fourth century, a formal language which could be used constructively to persuade a reader of a point by describing a debate between personified ideas.

Personification allegory would become one of the most influential genres of Christian devotional writing. Around the turn of the sixth century we see it in a number of guises, both in texts of moral instruction such as Ennodius of Pavia's *Paranaesis didascalia*,[41] and in writers such as Boethius, to whom we will return below. Some students of the *Psychomachia* have placed emphasis on the aptness of the *altercatio* format

---

[39] David Dawson, *Allegorical Readers and Cultural Revision in Ancient Alexandria* (Berkeley, 1992), esp. 74–82, 219–34.

[40] Robert Lamberton, *Homer the Theologian: Neoplatonist Allegorical Reading and the Growth of the Epic Tradition* (Berkeley, 1986), ch. 4, 'The Interaction of Allegorical Interpretation and Deliberate Allegory', discusses the place of Prudentius in the transition from allegorical interpretation of existing material to material conceived explicitly in terms of allegorical personification (pp. 145ff.).

[41] Ennodius, *Paranaesis didascalia* (*MGH AA* 7, 310–15).

for expressing social tension and competitiveness, and this may help us to understand the use of allegorical dialogue in *Ad Gregoriam*.

It is not necessary here to describe the *Psychomachia* in detail, but a brief discussion will be useful, since the poem serves as a point of reference for later literature on the vices and virtues, including *Ad Gregoriam*. The poem opens with an excursus on the faithful patriarch, Abraham, 'who first showed the way of believing',[42] suggesting that in his willingness to sacrifice his own son, Abraham showed that none of our works ('children') is pleasing to God unless we have first overcome the vices of the enslaved heart. Only then will the Spirit, 'embracing in holy marriage the soul that has long been childless ... make her fertile by the seed eternal'.[43]

The poem turns to celebrate the Virtues which Christ has furnished to aid his followers, and the reader is admonished to 'mark at close quarters the very features of the Virtues and of the monsters that close with them in deadly struggle'.[44] This is the starting-point for an extended description of battle, with each of the Virtues brought forward to fight against its opposite vice, each taking the field in a way that reveals something of its character.

Faith comes forward first, to fight against Worship-of-the-old-Gods. She is accompanied by a host of martyrs who have fought to the death on her behalf, whom she clothes in flowers and imperial purple. Modesty then takes the field against Lust. She argues that she can follow the example of Judith, but adds that the Virgin Mary has already destroyed Lust: 'Because of Mary all flesh is divine now, and sordid Lust cannot violate my authority.'[45]

Prudentius offers a more fulsome description of the battle between Endurance (*Patientia*) and Anger. The poet repeatedly specifies the weapons and armour in use: Endurance wears a *thoraca* of impenetrable mail, her *lorica* deflects Anger's *pinus*; Anger's *iaculum* – here probably both a spear and a barbed insult – cannot move her. Endurance brings forward Job, the biblical exemplar of trustful endurance in the face of adversity, to show what is possible to human beings with her aid. Endurance, the poet argues, developing on an old theme of Christian stoicism visible in the writings of Cyprian and Tertullian, is the single indispensable virtue.

---

[42] Prudentius, *Psychomachia*, preface, line 1: 'senex fidelis prima credendi via', (ed. Thomson, 274).

[43] Prudentius, *Psychomachia*, lines 64–6: 'Animam deinde Spiritus conplexibus/ pie maritam, prolis expertem diu,/ faciet perenni fertilem de semine ...' (ed. Thomson, 278).

[44] Prudentius, *Psychomachia*, lines 18–20: 'ipsas /Virtutum facies et conluctantia contra/viribus infestis liceat notare ' (ed. Thomson, 280).

[45] Prudentius, *Psychomachia*, lines 87–8: 'dona haec sunt, quod victa iaces, lutulenta Libido,/ nec me post Mariam potis es perfringere iura' (ed. Thomson, 284).

Although Prudentius offers a vivid sketch of Humility's battle to the death with Pride, it is not given precedence over other battles. We will see below that this assessment was not taken up by later treatises on the vices and virtues. Where they specify a most dangerous vice it tends to be pride, probably under the influence of Augustine's *City of God*, a text written after Prudentius had completed his poem. *Ad Gregoriam*, however, will follow and develop upon Prudentius in the precedence accorded to the virtue of Endurance. The psychomachy section of *Ad Gregoriam* is virtually a hymn to endurance – *Patientia* – while the Augustinian problem of pride – *Superbia* – does not even merit a mention.[46]

It is also worth mentioning Prudentius' battle between Luxury and Sobriety. Luxury glides in on her chariot, strewing violets and rose petals, a Lady Bountiful raised above the company by her rich vehicle. Sobriety recognizes instantly that with all her charm, Luxury will be a far more dangerous rival than the more overtly frightening vices such as Anger. Indeed, the Virtues are swayed by Luxury's charms. Sobriety gives a rousing speech, but to little avail:

What blinding madness is vexing your disordered minds? Where are you rushing, to whom do you bow your neck? What bonds – for shame – are these that you want to bear on arms that were meant for weapons, these yellow garlands strewn with bright lilies, these wreaths with red flowers? Is it to chains like these that you will give hands trained to war?[47]

In the end, Sobriety's most powerful weapon is not words but the Cross, which she holds up as a shield against Luxury's on-coming chariot. Luxury tumbles out, and Sobriety is able to subdue her in hand-to-hand battle.

After numerous further skirmishes, Peace is able to banish War, and Concord gives the signal to take the victorious standards back to the tents. Discord has stolen in among the ranks, however, and with a concealed dagger attempts to wound Concord. Discord is revealed to be the disguise of heresy, so Concord gives a speech against the heresies of the day. Then the gathered virtues build a New Temple, and Wisdom is installed on her throne.

---

[46] *Ad Gregoriam*, while in many ways deeply 'augustinian', sidesteps the African bishop's view of the sin of Pride. On other, contemporary, attempts to draw down the authority of Augustine while specifically avoiding his teaching on pride, see the discussions of Pomerius and Caesarius in Leyser, *Authority and Asceticism*, 69–76, 90–4; and of Eugippius in O' Donnell, *Augustine*, 309–10.

[47] Prudentius, *Psychomachia*, lines 351–7: 'Quis furor insanas agitat caligine mentes? /Quo ruitis? cui colla datis? Quae vincula tandem,/ pro pudor, armigeris amor est perferre lacertis,/ lilia luteolis interlucentia sertis/ et ferrugineo vernantes flore coronas?/ His placet adsuetas bello iam tradere palmas /nexibus' (ed. Thomson, 302).

We will return in Chapter Five to consider how the heady mix of verbal argument and military engagement made vivid in the *Psychomachia* was adopted in a variety of different genres at the end of antiquity, developing the Christian motif of the invisible battle between the vices and the virtues. Below we will consider a single case, the allegorical battle segment of *Ad Gregoriam in palatio*, in which we can watch a Christian writer struggling to bridge the gap between the literate idiom which might appeal to a senatorial reader, and the gladiatorial truths of the Christian desert.

THE ARISTOCRATIC LAITY AND THE 'OSTROGOTHIC RENAISSANCE'

Arnaldo Momigliano has captured the sense of moral urgency behind the Hellenism of the Ostrogothic renaissance:

These antiquarians were not frivolous. They were aware that their attempt to combine Christian devotion with pagan tradition could succeed only if it was supported by the strength of Greek thought and by the continuity of imperial tradition. They looked to the East where exciting things seemed to be happening. In Constantinople Priscian was opening new vistas to Latin grammatical studies. In Alexandria the school of Ammonius was making a new effort to harmonize Plato, Aristotle, and Porphyrius and to reconcile all with Christianity. These were intellectual events giving hope to men whose hearts never turned away from the classical past of Greece and Rome.[48]

But the senatorial tradition was not without its critics. The distinction between the uninstructed and those steeped in pagan literature was not, *a priori*, a distinction between clergy and laity or between monks and the married; rather, it was a distinction of class, and its imposition was sometimes met with bitterness. Of course, the tension between literary education and Christian values was a long-standing concern, from Tertullian's 'what has Athens to do with Jerusalem?'[49] to Jerome's feverish worry that he was 'more a Ciceronian than a Christian'[50] and Augustine's reassurance that learning from the pagan classics could be seen as a form of 'spoiling the Egyptians'.[51] In the fifth century, we see a writer like Salvian of

---

[48] Momigliano, 'Cassiodorus', 198–9.
[49] Tertullian, *De praescriptione haereticorum* 7.9 (*CC* 1, 193), with discussion by Robert Markus, *The End of Ancient Christianity* (Cambridge, 1990), 27–32.
[50] Jerome, *Ep.* 22.30 (*PL* 22, 416).   [51] Augustine, *De doctrina christiana* 2.40 (*CSEL* 80, 75–6).

Marseilles beginning to invoke a distinction between *laici* and *religiosi* as readers.[52] Ascetic and clerical writers who did not share the literary education of a Sidonius or a Jerome increasingly found it possible to accuse aristocratic writers of being overly committed to 'worldly literature' (*saecularis litteratura*).

In the early sixth century, we find Eugippius attempting to drive a wedge between 'lay' and 'religious' readers and writers precisely in terms of this issue of 'cultural literacy'.[53] Eugippius himself was no stranger to the Roman aristocracy – indeed, we have seen above his relationship to the senatorial virgin Proba.[54] But he captures the sense of unease that could sometimes accompany the social mobility of men of the Church, especially when those of humbler backgrounds found themselves dealing with the aristocratic *litterati*.

Prefixed to Eugippius' memoir on the life of Severinus of Noricum, completed c. 511, is a dedicatory epistle addressed to Paschasius, deacon of the church of Rome. Eugippius tells of how a noble layman (*laicus nobilis*) had approached him, asking for a short sketch of the life of Severinus. Eugippius knew the man's earlier work, evidently a fussy verse biography – now lost – of the monk Bassus, and he was dejected at the thought that only through such a writer should the virtues of Severinus be known.

> While you are alive [he wrote to Paschasius] it seemed unfair to ask a *laicus* to do the job, someone whose judgement about the style and tone of the piece it would be difficult to correct without seeming presumptious, lest, having been trained only in secular literature (*saeculari tantum litteratura politus*), he should write the life in such language (*tali sermone*) ... that the long-hidden virtues [of Severinus] would not be able to pierce the obscurity of [the writer's] eloquence, at least for us who are ignorant of the liberal arts.[55]

---

[52] David Lambert, *History and Community in the Works of Salvian of Marseille* (DPhil, Oxford, 2003), 75–8.

[53] Eugippius' date of birth is unknown; he came with Severinus' body to Lucullanum during the pontificate of Gelasius (492–6); he was abbott in 511, and died in 536. Cassiodorus was born c. 485 and died c. 585 (while the dates are uncertain he is recorded as having lived into his mid-nineties at least).

[54] See Kate Cooper, 'The Widow as impresario: Gender, Legendary Afterlives, and Documentary Evidence in Eugippius' *Vita Severini*', in *Eugippius und Severin: Der Autor, der Text, und der Heilige*, ed. Walter Pohl and Maximilian Diesenberger (Vienna, 2001) 53–63, for further discussion of this letter of Eugippius.

[55] *Vita Severini* 2 (SC 374, 148): 'Hac ergo protinus oblatione compulsus commemoratorium ... composui, non sine magno maerore animi, iniustum scilicet reputans, ut te superstite laicus a nobis hoc opus efficere rogetur, cui et modus et color operis non sine praesumptione quadam possit iniungi, ne forsitan saeculari tantum literatura politus tali vitam sermone conscriberet, in quo multorum plurimum laboraret inscitia et res mirabiles, quae diu quadam silentii nocte latuerant, quantum ad nos attinet ignaros liberalium litterarum, obscura disertitudine non lucerent.'

It is not difficult to see why a figure such as Eugippius would perceive the 'insider language' of the *litterati* as a barrier to open-hearted communication across the social spectrum of the Christian faithful, but this is no reason to dismiss the spiritual discourse of these men and women as insufficiently Christian. Put simply, when the Christian *litterati* thought and wrote as Christians, they did so in their own idiom.

Eugippius clearly meant to serve a warning that aristocratic literary culture was a 'closed' discourse. His paradox, 'the obscurity of eloquence', cited above, encapsulates an idea of language as a boundary-marker, fostering solidarity among those who fall within its ambit, and imposing exclusion on those beyond.[58] To the uninitiated, eloquence could only be a stumbling-block. It is probably this exclusionary quality that led works like the lost *Life of Bassus* to be given lesser priority for conservation and copying by the monk-librarians of the early Middle Ages, as they worked to preserve what now survives of ancient literature.

The monumental literary figures of the late fifth and early sixth centuries, such as Boethius and Martianus Capella, were by no means isolated. That these men are only the best-remembered of a thriving senatorial literary culture is evident from the work of other writers such as Fabius Planciades Fulgentius, author of the less well-known *Mythologies* and the *Exposition of the Content of Virgil*,[56] or Ennodius, priest of Milan and later bishop of Pavia, whose *Paraenesis didascalia*[57] offers a guide to the literary circles of Italy at the period.

Fortunately, a number of luxury codices from the early sixth-century 'Ostrogothic renaissance' have come down to us. The codices bear signed scholarly glosses and thus offer an alternative witness to the learned pursuits of Italian senatorial *litterati* whose letters and other writings have not been preserved. One of the best-known of these is the subscription by Aurelius Memmius Symmachus – the father-in-law of Boethius and probable father of Proba – and Macrobius Plotinus Eudoxius, *vir clarissimus*, to a manuscript of Macrobius' commentary on Cicero's *Somnium Scipionis*.

---

[56] It has long been debated whether the works of Fulgentius the Mythographer could have been written by Fulgentius, bishop of Ruspe in the early sixth century; Pierre Langlois, 'Les Oeuvres de Fulgence le mythographe et le problème des deux Fulgence', *Jahrbucch für Antike und Christentum* 7 (1964), 94–105, argues for a single Fulgentius but admits at 94 that 'le problème en est à ce point que celui qui veut être convaincu dans un sens ou dans l'autre peut l'être, parce que personne n'a des preuves décisives à apporter.'

[57] Ennodius, *Paraenesis didascalia* (MGH AA 7, 314–15), cf. Pierre Riché, *Education et culture dans l'Occident barbare, VIe–VIIIe siècles* (Paris, 4th edn, 1995), 26–7.

[58] On shared literary culture as a force binding fifth-century élites, see Ralph W. Mathisen, *Roman Aristocrats in Barbarian Gaul: Strategies for Survival in an Age of Transition* (Austin, 1993), 105–18.

Both descendents of the pagan symposiasts whom Macrobius had commemorated in his *Saturnalia*, Symmachus and Macrobius clearly intended to
commemorate their own families at the same time as they sought to
preserve ancient literature, and the motivation of family honour would
have been well understood by their contemporaries.[59]

It is difficult to assess whether these men and women perceived themselves as the proponents of a distinctively senatorial brand of Christianity,
since the scholars often seem to have ignored distinctions of religion
altogether when they were not writing for a specifically polemical purpose.
Pietas for one's ancestors blended easily with Christian values. Another
figure from the same senatorial circle, Vettius Agorius Basilius Mavortius,
consul in 527 and a descendent of the famously pagan Vettius Agorius
Praetextatus, tended to the texts of both Horace and Prudentius.[60] The
ownership and care of learned manuscripts had not only a strongly aristocratic connotation, but also one of progression toward a heightened
sensibility of things spiritual.[61] An example of the cosmopolitan religious
sensibility of the Roman élite is reflected in the subscription made by the
Christian Securus Memor Felix to his emended text of Martianus Capella's
De nuptiis Philologiae et Mercurii:

I, Securus Memor Felix, *vir spectabilis*, count of the consistory, rhetor of the city of
Rome, have emended this manuscript from very corrupt copies, with my scholarly
pupil Deutherius cross-checking the text, in Rome by the Porta Capena, under the
consulship of Paulinus, *vir clarissimus*, on the seventh day of March, with the aid
of Christ.[62]

Here the iconic text of 'aggressive paganism', the pride of the careful
scholar, and the aid of Christ stand easily alongside each other, revealing
a congenial familiarity between ancient traditions.

The date here – the consulship of Paulinus was in 534[63] – is also striking.
We are on the threshold of the Gothic Wars, and thus of the destruction of

---

[59] O. Jahn, 'Über die Subscriptionen in den Handschriften römischer Classiker', *Berichte über die
Verhandlungen der Königl.-Sächsischen Gesellschaft der Wissenschaften, Philologisch-Historische Klasse* 3
(Leipzig, 1851), 327–73, at 347. On the fourth-century forebears, see Alan Cameron, 'The Date and
Identity of Macrobius', *JRS* 56 (1966), 25–38.

[60] Jahn, 'Über die Subscriptionen', 353; discussion in Momigliano, 'Cassiodorus', 198.

[61] On the 'sciences "éveilleuses"' of the scholar, see H.-I. Marrou, *Saint Augustin et la fin de la culture
antique*, Bulletin de l'École Française de Rome 145) (Paris, 1938), 304ff.

[62] Cited in Helen Kirkby, 'The Scholar and his Public', in Margaret Gibson, ed., *Boethius: His Life,
Thought, and Influence* (Oxford, 1981), 44–69 (here, 51), whose translation I have cited. The
subscription is discussed in Jahn, 'Über die Subscriptionen', 353.

[63] *Comes consistorianus*; the consulship (of Paulinus) during which he edited Martianus Capella 'was
presumably 534 rather than 498' (*PLRE* 3A, 481).

the infrastructure of Roman society in the Italian peninsula. Yet we should not conclude that the Roman senators were fiddling while their cities burned. Scholarship was seen as a morally urgent business, a custodial service to the cultural patrimony which in turn stood as the justification for empire. T. S. Brown reminds us that later in the century, when Naples was besieged by the Lombards in 581, not only did the bishop direct monks to continue correcting manuscripts, but the circumstances were commemorated in the texts themselves, one of which – an exemplar of Eugippius' *Excerpta Augustini* – is still preserved.[64] The urgency of scholarship as an enterprise, even in life-and-death circumstances, was acknowledged by all parties.

In turn, the association of eloquence with earthly nobility by no means disqualified it as a worthy vehicle for spiritual power. The recitation of poetry would often have been a public event in which more than one social class participated, though this by no means undermined the association of eloquence with élite culture. The public recitation in April and May of 540 of Arator's *De actibus apostolorum* held in the Roman church of St Peter ad Vincula illustrates a number of these points simultaneously. The writing of the poem had fulfilled a vow made by the aristocrat Arator, deacon of the Roman church, while imprisoned during Witigis' Roman siege of 537–8.[65] Surgerius, *primicerius* of the school of notaries, had been instructed to place *De actibus apostolorum* in the church archives, but then Pope Vigilius gave instructions for the public reading, which had to be interrupted a number of times because of the chaos prevailing in the city.

Aristocratic women played an especially active and visible role in constructing the terms of Christian identity. This meant that elite christianity was coloured more vividly by feminine interest than that lower down the social scale. A figure like the poetess Proba, for example, proposed ideas dramatically different to those of the better-known male ascetic writers of her day. We will see below, therefore, that to understand the imaginative landscape against which aristocratic readers and their literary protegés considered the ethics of Christian participation, one must also understand the class-specific instincts about gender.

---

[64] The manuscript (Paris, Bill. Nat. Lat. 11642) is a ninth-century copy preserving a late sixth-century subscription, from which we learn that corrections were made to Eugippius' *Excerpta Augustini* on the orders of Bishop Redux during a siege of the city by the Lombards in 581. For the text of the subscription, see Knöll, *CSEL* 9/1, xxv–xxvi. As observed by T. S. Brown, *Gentlemen and Officers: Imperial Administration and Aristocratic Power in Byzantine Italy AD 554–800* (Rome, 1984), 19, Naples in this period was unusually strong as a centre of high culture.

[65] Claire Sotinel, 'Arator, un poète au service de la politique du pape Vigile?', *MEFRA* 101 (1989), 805–20.

Sidonius Apollinaris' well-known late fifth-century description of the library of Tonnantius Ferreolus in his villa near Nîmes implies that men and women differed in their reading habits:

The books which had their place among the chairs for the ladies were found to be of a religious style, while those by the seats of the heads of household (*patrum familias*) were ennobled by the high style of Latin eloquence.[66]

But we should mot be misled into thinking that it was only women who were deeply engaged with Christian matters, or that only men knew their Virgil and Horace. A Christian *materfamilias* like the poetess Proba would have been found sitting complacently on what Sidonius would have thought of as the men's side of the room.

Sidonius goes on to account for how learned men would gather to discuss the Christian inheritance in light of its relationship to the Latin classics. Considerably less elliptical than his original is a résumé by Jill Harries, worth citing at length:

Their aim was to compare the Christian writers with pagan predecessors closely associated with them; thus Augustine, who had attacked Varro in the *City of God*, was considered in parallel with him, and Prudentius was analysed in the light of his use of Horace. This method of study, despite its informal context, was part of a continuing process of learning, using, and building on methods acquired at the school of the *rhetor*, and underlay Sidonius' own use of past writings, both the pagan classics and the Bible, in the service of Christianity.[67]

To the degree that there was a tension between the *stilus religiosus* of a Eugippius and the *cothurnus latialis eloquii* of a Proba, it was a tension between two strategies for managing the shared cultural inheritance.

BOETHIUS, CASSIODORUS, BENEDICT, GREGORY

To understand the relationship between literary education and lay spirituality, we will consider the case of two senatorial laymen of early sixth-century Italy, Anicius Manlius Severinus Boethius (c. 480?–525/6) and Flavius

---

[66] Sidonius, *Ep.* 2.9 to Donidius (*MGH AA* 8, 30): 'Sic tamen quod qui inter matronarum cathedras codices erant, stylus iis religiosus inveniebatur: qui vero sub sellia patrum familias, ii cothurno latialis eloquii nobilitabatur. Licet quaepiam volumina quorumpiam auctorum servarent in causis disparibus dicendi parilitatem. Nam similis scientiae viri, hinc Augustinus, hinc Varro; hinc Horatius, hinc Prudentius lecitabantur. Quos inter Adamantius Origenes, Turranio Rufino interpretatus, sedulo fidei nostrae lectoribus inspiciebatur.' In translating the passage, I have borrowed Jill Harries' vivid phrasing of the last clause, see Jill Harries, *Sidonius Apolloninaris and the Fall of Rome* (Oxford, 1994), 106.

[67] Harries, *Sidonius Apolloninaris*, 107.

Magnus Aurelius Cassiodorus Senator (c. 485–c. 585). Further to Leclercq, we can ask – why is Boethius remembered and Cassiodorus, again, the bridesmaid? Both were holders of public office at the highest level – Boethius consul in 510, *magister officiorum* from September 522 and his sons joint consuls in the same year;[68] Cassiodorus *quaestor palatii* from c. 506/7 to 511, consul in 514, Boethius' successor as *magister officiorum* 523–7, and praetorian prefect of Italy 533–8.[69] The two were probably kinsmen, since Cassiodorus refers to the virgin Proba as his *parens*, and she is elsewhere referred to as the sister of Galla, Boethius' sister-in-law.[70] Each left a literary corpus reflecting a representative idea of the relationship between 'Christian' and 'senatorial' identities, and thus can help us to understand the distinctive landscape of male senatorial Christianity.

Though he was the younger and longer-lived of the two men, we will consider Cassiodorus first. Like many sixth-century men of letters, he involved himself in civic and ecclesiastical affairs, but maintained a distinction between two periods of activity. This is reflected particularly in his writings, which fall, he suggests in his *Institutes*, into two distinct periods, one 'secular' and the other 'Christian'.[71] During a long and distinguished civic career in office under the Ostrogothic monarchs, Cassiodorus established a literary profile for himself very much along the ancient lines of civic oratory, along with historical writings on Roman history, the history of the Goths, and the *Ordo generis Cassiodorum*. The *Variae*, covering the period 506–37, represent his carefully selected letter-book of diplomatic correspondence written first on behalf of the Ostrogothic crown, and then, in an additional book appended after publication, of his writings while praetorian prefect after 533.[72] But if Cassiodorus' literary career at this point was

---

[68] John Matthews, 'Anicius Manlius Severinus Boethius', in Gibson, ed., *Boethius*, 25–31.
[69] *PLRE* 2, 'Fl. Magnus Aurelius Cassiodorus Senator 4', 265–9; Arnaldo Momigliano, 'Cassiodorus and the Italian Culture of his Time', in idem, *Studies in Historiography* (London, 1966), 181–210; James O'Donnell, *Cassiodorus* (Berkeley, 1979); Averil Cameron, 'Cassiodorus Deflated', *JRS* 71 (1981), 183–6.
[70] Cassiodorus, *Institutiones* 1.23 (ed. Mynors, 62): 'ad parentem nostram Probam, virginem sacram'. On Boethius, his father-in-law Symmachus, and the Cassiodori, see Cassiodorus' *Ordo generis Cassiodori* (*Anecdoton Holderii, MGH AA* 12, v–vi).
[71] On the division, Mark Vessey, 'Introduction', in Cassiodorus, *Institutions of Divine and Secular Learning: On the Soul*, tr. James W. Halporn (Liverpool, 2004), 3–101, at 18.
[72] Excellent commentary can be found in S. J. B. Barnish, *The Variae of Magnus Aurelius Cassiodorus Senator* (Liverpool, 1992). On the *Variae* as 'a monument to its author and his peers, rather than their masters', as commemoration, instruction, and encouragement for the administrative élite rather than 'Ostrogothic propaganda', see Andrew Gillett, 'The Purposes of Cassiodorus' *Variae*', in Alexander Callander Murray, ed., *After Rome's Fall: Narrators and Sources of Early Medieval History; Essays Presented to Walter Goffart* (Toronto, 1998), 37–50. (Arnaldo Momigliano, 'Gli Anicii e la storiografia latina del VI sec. D.C.', *Secondo contributo alla storia degli studi classici*

focused on administrative affairs, his sphere of activity was by no means exclusively outside the Church.

The 'secular' Cassiodorus was in fact active as a Christian patron acting in concert with the Roman clergy.[73] This is most visibile in his own account of an attempt made, in concert with the Roman bishop Agapetus (535–6), to found a Christian academy in the city. 'I was deeply grieved, I admit', he muses in the introduction to his *Institutes of Divine Learning*, 'that Holy Scripture should so lack in public teachers, whereas secular authors certainly flourish in widespread teaching.' The project was destroyed by Belisarius' invasion of Italy in 535: 'But since I could not accomplish this task', Cassiodorus lamented, 'because of raging wars and violent struggles in the Kingdom of Italy, for a peaceful endeavour has no place in a time of unrest, I was moved by divine love to devise for you [the monks on his estate at Scyllacium], with God's help, these introductory books to take the place of a teacher.'[74]

Cassiodorus did of course continue to write during the Gothic Wars, both his diplomatic correspondence and, at some point during the period between 536 and 554, a treatise on the seven liberal arts 'intended for a readership of courtly, aristocratic Italians who were opposed to Byzantine rule and whose tastes ran to philosophical-pedagogical texts in elegant formats'.[75] Here, Cassiodorus attempted to bridge the gap between the two cultural 'systems' by offering a summary outline of 'secular letters', first as an independent treatise and then, in a revised edition, as the second part of his *Institutes of Divine and Secular Learning*. Recent scholarship has shown that this treatise was published as a free-standing effort to begin with, while the later version was specifically designed to assist monks in coping with an unfamiliar literary culture.[76]

Cassiodorus' summary became important to later generations as the cornerstone on which the medieval curriculum of the liberal arts was built.[77] For our purposes, it is worth briefly considering his summary of 'secular letters' as a starting-point for understanding the cultural landscape of the Italian senatorial aristocracy, though we will reserve a fuller

---

(Rome, 1960), 191–229, is still valuable on Cassiodorus' different motivations at different points in the evolving triangular relationship among Roman elites, Ostrogothic monarchs, and the emperors in Constantinople.)

[73] His first Christian writing, the *Explanation of the Psalms*, is seen to date 'traditionally if none too securely' from c. 538: see Vessey, *Institutions* 16, 35.

[74] Cassiodorus, *Institutiones praef.* (ed. Mynors 3, tr. Halporn, 105).   [75] Vessey, 'Introduction', 40.

[76] Fabio Troncarelli, *Vivarium, i libri, il destino*, Instrumenta patristica 33 (Turnhout, 1998), 12–21, 30–1 ; and Vessey, 'Introduction', 39–42.

[77] Ilsetraut Hadot, *Arts libéraux et philosophie dans la pensée antique* (Paris, 1984).

discussion of Cassiodorus until later in this chapter. He begins with what would become the *trivium* – grammar, rhetoric, and dialectic – and proceeds to arithmetic, music, geometry, and astronomy, the subjects of the *quadrivium*. Most of what is important for the present discussion falls within his first category, grammar, defined as 'the skill of speaking stylishly, gathered from famous poets and writers; its function is to compose prose and verse without fault; its purpose is to please by the impeccable skill of polished speech or writing'.[78] The *artes grammaticae* included textual criticism (*emendatio*) and cultural-historical exegesis (*enarratio*).[79] At the same time, probably around 538, Cassiodorus began his *Explanation of the Psalms*, his first foray into Christian literature.[80] During the 540s he seems to have moved to Constantinople, possibly when the Ostrogothic king Witiges, taken captive by imperial forces, was sent there as prisoner.[81]

It was after peace was finally established in 554 that Cassiodorus retreated to his estate at Scyllacium (now Squillace), in the south Italian province of Bruttium, and established a monastery there, which he called Vivarium for its fish-ponds. During this period of Christian *otium*, Cassiodorus produced the *Institutes*, a guide to the traditions of Christian and secular learning self-consciously offered as a testament for future generations to remember the world that had been destroyed. For Cassiodorus, engagement as a Christian patron was compatible with a public career at the highest level, but the channelling of his pedagogic aims into written form seems to have been synonymous with retirement from Italian civic life. The story he constructs is one of nostalgia for a lost world, and of lost faith in the future.[82] His *Institutes* would serve as one of the 'core texts' of the monastic curriculum across the Middle Ages.[83]

If the opacity of Cassiodorus is partly caused by his intense engagement with a specific time and place, it is not the whole story. Cassiodorus, in fact, took a very particular line of interpretation on how the 'Christian' and 'civic' identities of the senatorial class should be dovetailed. Certainly, the Gothic Wars created a caesura. It was the restoration of property effected

[78] Cassiodorus, *Institutiones* 2.1.1 (ed. Mynors, 94; tr. Halporn, 175).
[79] But James Zetzel, *Latin Textual Criticism in Antiquity* (New York, 1981), cautions against a too enthusiastic assessment of their role; see also Zetzel's list of inscriptions.
[80] See Vessey, 'Introduction', 35, and literature cited there. [81] Momigliano, 'Cassiodorus', 210.
[82] Markus, *End of Ancient Christianity*, 217–24.
[83] James J. O'Donnell, *Avatars of the Word: From Papyrus to Cyberspace* (Cambridge, Mass., 1998), 190–6, developing on his *Cassiodorus*, rejects the idea of Cassiodorus as 'saviour of western civilization', a deduction which later generations extracted from his own rhetoric: see R. R. Bolgar, *The Classical Heritage and its Beneficiaries* (Cambridge, 1958), 36–7, with discussion in Vessey, *Institutions*, 5.

by Justinian's Pragmatic Sanction of 554, which occurred sometime around his seventieth birthday, that allowed Cassiodorus to retire to his estate at Scyllacium. Since the time of Augustine and Paulinus of Nola, one way of making the link between asceticism and the venerable ancient traditions had been to see conversion to the ascetic life as a fulfilment of the senatorial craving for *otium*.

Boethius, by contrast, represents an entirely different way of drawing the line between senatorial and Christian literary spheres. There is no dramatic 'watershed' moment in his career. This may of course be accounted for by the fact that he was young, probably in his mid-forties, when he died. But Augustine had been ten years younger when he made his retreat to Cassiciacum. It is more likely that like many lay *literati* Boethius simply observed no distinction between the 'sacred' and 'secular' aspects of his contribution to society. His early writings include both academic treatises and theological writings in a way that suggests that the two identities of lay intellectual and Christian theologian could be engaged upon simultaneously and to mutual benefit. His idea of *otium*, however, was firmly classical: *otium* was what he had given up, when he had been tempted, inspired by 'Platonic notions' of the philosopher-ruler,[84] to take up office as *magister officiorum*.[85]

The *Consolation of Philosophy*, his final testament written at Pavia where he was held after being charged with treason by Theoderic in 524, and where he was later executed,[86] adopts a brand of Neoplatonic philosophy imbued with Stoicism but showing little explicit Christian influence.[87] Students of the *Consolation* have always been aware of the importance in this period of the *ascensus*, the uplifting to spiritual heights associated with apocalyptic literature and Neoplatonic philosophy, but a tendency to characterize it as 'a non-Christian work written by a Christian' has prevailed.[88] The tendency to impute a lack of Christian engagement[89] to Boethius is in some ways understandable. Certainly, he was not above

---

[84] Boethius, *De consolatione philosophiae* 1.4, 5 (*CC* 94, 7).

[85] Henry Chadwick, *Boethius: The Consolations of Music, Logic, Theology, and Philosophy* (Oxford, 1981), 47.

[86] Chadwick, *Boethius*, 55, 'there is some probability favouring 525; but 524 or early 526 remains possible.'

[87] Chadwick, *Boethius*, 23.   [88] Chadwick, *Boethius*, 247–53, at 249.

[89] Momigliano's view was that he ceased being a Christian, whether he noticed or not; but this assumes a rigid boundary between paganism and Christianity, a view challenged by Alan Cameron, 'Paganism and Literature in Late Fourth Century Rome', in *Christianisme et formes littéraires de l'antiquité tardive en occident*, Fondation Hardt pour l'Étude de l'Antiquité Classique, Entretiens 22 (Geneva, 1977), 1–30.

speaking of the clergy with patent disrespect – most famously in his account of the 'entirely incomprehensible' debate at a council of Roman clergy and senators some time after 513, which he attended along with his father-in-law Symmachus.[90]

But Boethius clearly meant his comment to be understood ironically, as a dismissive criticism of the unseemly conduct and nonsensical preoccupations of the clergy, rather than as a confession of his own incompetence. We should not confuse his anti-clericalism with a lack of Christian feeling. His ambivalence was not without precedent. The ecclesiastical historian and lawyer Socrates, writing in the 440s, had taken the view that ecclesiastical affairs were ill-served by the pointless quarrelling and jockeying for power of churchmen, and required the judicious and authoritative stewardship of the divinely appointed imperial family.[91] We know equally, from the sniping of Eugippius against the aristocratic author of the *Life of Bassus*, that the distaste was mutual. Many churchmen found the rarified discourse of senatorial laymen equally off-putting.

To suggest that the traditionalist idiom of *De consolatione philosophiae* was 'non-Christian' is to miss the point. Different groups understood Christianity differently. Lay aristocrats played an important role in ecclesiastical affairs across the end of the Roman empire, attending – and often presiding at – Church councils until the late sixth century.[92] Another contemporary, Liberius the Patrician, moved back and forth easily between roles, presiding at the Council of Orange in 529, and coming out of retirement to lead Justinian's military expedition to Sicily in 550.[93] The self-made Senarius, appointed *comes patrimonii* and elevated to the senate in September 509, acted as legate for the Ostrogothic crown in over two dozen embassies, meanwhile corresponding with the Roman deacon John (who probably became Pope John I) over the liturgical practice necessary for admitting Arian converts into the Roman Church.[94]

---

[90] Chadwick, *Boethius*, 181. The text is the preface of the fifth tractate of *opuscula sacra* (*Contra Eutychen et Nestorium*).

[91] On this tendency in Socrates, see Kate Cooper, 'Empress and *Theotokos*: Gender and Patronage in the Christological Controversy', in R. N. Swanson, ed., *The Church and Mary* (Woodbridge, 2004), 39–51; on the date of his history, see Hartmut Leppin, *Von Constantin dem Grossen zu Theodosius II: Das christliche Kaisertum bei den Kirchenhistorikern Socrates, Sozomenus und Theodoret* (Göttingen, 1996), 274–79 (suggesting a date between 444 and 446), Theresa Urbainczyk, *Socrates of Constantinople: Historian of Church and State* (Ann Arbor, 1997), 34, arguing for the early 440s, and Martin Wallraff, *Der Kirchenhistoriker Socrates: Untersuchungen zu Geschichtsdarstellung, Methode und Person* (Göttingen, 1997), 210–12, arguing for a date before 443.

[92] Mathisen, *Roman Aristocrats*, 183 on laymen at Church councils.

[93] James. J. O'Donnell, 'Liberius the Patrician', *Traditio* 37 (1981), 31–72.

[94] On Senarius, see now Andrew Gillett, *Envoys and Political Communication in the Late Antique West, 411–533* (Cambridge, 2003), ch. 5, 'Cassiodorus and Senarius', 172–219.

It has been argued that Menippean satire, the prose-poetic genre in which Boethius cast *De consolatione philosophiae*,[95] carried strong religious connotations in the late fifth and early sixth centuries. In an important study of Martianus Capella's *De nuptiis Philologiae et Mercurii*, Danuta Shanzer called attention to the theme of the heavenly voyage as one of the characteristic elements of the genre in this period. Shanzer suggested that while the genre tends to irony and even parody, this does not mean that the religious sentiment expressed therein should be understood as insincere – *De nuptiis*, she argued, should be understood as a work of 'aggressive paganism'.[96] In a 1993 study of Menippean satire across antiquity Joseph Relihan developed Shanzer's suggestion, proposing that the late Latin revival of the genre served to express – and to some degree to reconcile – the tension between Christian faith and classical culture made famous by the polemical pronouncements of earlier writers such as Tertullian and Jerome. If Relihan's argument is correct, it is wrong to isolate the highly literate writings of a text like *De consolatione philosophiae* from the devotional literature of the period. One might look, instead, for a continuity of Neoplatonic ascent motifs across religious boundaries, and across levels of literacy within Christianity.

A third likely kinsman of the *gens Anicia*,[97] the son of Boethius' contemporary Gordianus, also became famous for his efforts to offer a Christian philosophy for the literate laity, but his own career followed a distinctly different trajectory to that of Boethius and Cassiodorus. This son of the Italian senate, Gregorius, was appointed *praefectus urbi* – the official who presided over meetings of the Roman senate – in 573; this was still a symbolically important office toward the end of the sixth century though it was in decline, and is last attested in 599.

Soon after his tenure as *praefectus urbi* Gregory decided to establish a monastery on one of his family's properties, located on the Caelian Hill across from the library intended for the failed Christian university which

[95] Danuta Shanzer, *A Philosophical and Literary Commentary on Martianus Capella's De Nuptiis Philologiae et Mercurii Book 1*, University of California Publications: Classical Studies 32 (Berkeley, 1986), 33.

[96] Shanzer, *A Philosophical and Literary Commentary*, 43.

[97] A notoriously controverted matter. Contrast the scepticism of H.-I. Marrou, 'Autour de la bibliothèque du pape Agapit', *MEFRA* 48 (1931), 124–69, with the recent enthusiasm of E. Giuliani, and C. Pavolini, 'La 'Bibloteca di Agapito' e la Basilica di S. Agnese', in *The Transformations of* Urbs Roma *in Late Antiquity*, ed. W. Harris, *JRA* Supp. Ser. 33 (1999), 85–107. Robert Markus, *Gregory the Great and his World* (Cambridge, 1997), 8, rejects the claim of Gregory of Tours that Gregory the Great was born into 'one of the foremost senatorial families' (*Decem libri historiarum* 10.1), but admits a distant link to the *Anicii*, although with a cautionary reference to Seeck's 'Anicius' article in *RE*, which warns of the 'ubiquity' of claims to relationship with this *gens*.

his kinsman Pope Agapetus had attempted to establish with Cassiodorus. With famous reluctance, Gregory then accepted ordination as a deacon of the Roman Church, and was appointed *apocrisarius* to the imperial city, Constantinople, from c. 579 to 586 by Pope Pelagius. It was as *apocrisarius* during the early 580s that Gregory addressed a series of sermons on the sufferings of Job to the Latin-speaking laity in the Eastern capital, among them a number of Italian senatorial exiles. In his *Moralia in Iob*, the written-up text of these sermons, the theme of consolation appears again through a sustained meditation on Job as the *exemplum* of the just man faced with inexplicable suffering, followed by unexpected good fortune. The motif of ascent here is linked explicitly to the soul's progress in virtue, figured as a series of steps on the 'via Dei',[98] a mountainous path from which the Christian may look down to view what he has left below.[99]

Gregory suceeded Pelagius as pope in 590, but he did not lose touch with his friends in Constantinople.[100] Among the audience of the original sermons on Job in Constantionople would have been the Roman exiles based there with whom he corresponded on his return to Italy, such as Rusticiana – probably the granddaughter of Boethius – and others associated with the imperial family: Domnica, Rusticiana's daughter Eusebia, and Gregoria, a *cubicularia augustae* or lady-in-waiting, probably of the empress Constantina (the wife of Maurice) and quite possibly a younger relative of the addressee of *Ad Gregoriam in palatio*. These women seem to have assisted him both with his business at court and materially with his pastoral projects during and after the Lombard invasion, while he offered

---

[98] Gregory the Great, *Moralia* 5.16. (*CC* 143, 240–1): 'Quattuor quippe gradibus vitam beati Iob virtutes enumerando distinxit dum et timori fortitudinem, et fortitudini patientiam, et patientiae perfectionem iunxit. In via etenim Dei a timore (241) incipitur ut ad fortitudinem veniatur.'

[99] Gregory the Great, *Moralia* 31.47.96 (*CC* 143B, 1616): 'Hoc namque esse speciale specimen electorum solet, quod sic sciunt praesentis vitae viam carpere, ut per spei certitudinem noverint iam se ad alta pervenisse, quatenus cuncta quae praeterfluunt sub se esse videant, atque omne quod in hunc mundum eminet amore aeternitatis calcent ... Quasi quaedam inferiora terrae sunt, damna, contumeliae, egestas, abiectio, quae ipsi quoque dilectores saeculi dum per latae viae planitiem ambulant, vitando calcare non cessant ... At si semel cor in caelestibus figitur, mox quam abiecta sint cernitur quae alta videbantur. Nam sicut cum quisque montem conscendit eo paulisper cetera subter iacentia despicit, quo ad altiora amplius gressum tendit, ita qui in summis intentionem figere nititur, dum annisu ipso nullam praesentius vitae gloriam esse deprehendit, super terrae altitudines elevatur; et quod prius in imis desideriis positus super se credidit, post ascendendo proficiens sibi subesse cognoscit.' The motif is one of a number in the *Moralia* that is anticipated in *Ad Gregoriam in palatio*; on the relationship between the two texts, see Cooper, *The Virgin and the Bride*, 135–9.

[100] Markus, *Gregory the Great and his World*, 11–12, 83–96, and the wide-ranging study of Lellia Cracco Ruggini, 'Gregorio magno e il mondo mediterraneo', in *Gregorio Magno nel XIV centenario della morte: convegno internazionale, Roma, 22–25 ottobre 2003*, Atti dei Convegni Lincei 209 (Rome, 2004), 11–87.

them encouragement with matters spiritual. To Gregoria, Gregory addressed a short letter on the remission of sin, along with at least one other, lost letter.[101] In June 603, shortly after he heard of the murder of the Emperor Maurice, Gregory addressed a brief note to Eusebia, Rusticiana's daughter, advising her to concentrate her mind on spiritual matters despite – or indeed because of – the troubles besetting both city and empire.

Gregory, of course, went on to be remembered as Gregory the Great,[102] not least because his pastoral vision was perceived as luminously, compellingly straightforward by successive generations.[103] But this later vision makes it difficult to perceive him in his sixth-century context. Rather than the inheritor or even founder of a fully established ecclesiastical institution, Gregory must be seen as an impresario of contingency, an aristocrat able and willing to make use of whatever resources his powerful friends could put at his disposal to support his various projects. In this respect, little had changed between his days as *praefectus urbi* and his later career as bishop of Rome.

CHRISTIAN PROSE AND THE 'JEWELLED STYLE'

We return now to *Ad Gregoriam in palatio*, to consider how a clerical writer in sympathy with the ideals of senatorial Christianity might try to bring the old paternalism into harmony with ideas drawn from the ascetic writers, offering his pastoral advice in prose designed to invoke the visual play of contemporary poetry. As we saw in Chapter One, the senatorial *domina* to whom *Ad Gregoriam* was addressed probably came from the same Italian milieu as the despicable author of the *Life of Bassus*. John's advice to Gregoria speaks at a number of levels. It is meant to be read both as an entertainment and as a serious warning of what is expected of the Christian *domina*. John is not trying to turn Gregoria into an ascetic, or anything other than what she is. It is precisely as a *domina*, a householder and owner of estates, that he wishes to reach her. There is in fact an ethical urgency behind *Ad Gregoriam*'s literary aspirations: what we have here is an ethics of

---

[101] Gregory the Great, *Ep.* 7.22 (*MGH Epp.* 1, 464–5) on the remission of sin refers to another letter which has not been preserved.

[102] From the late Carolingian period onward: see John the Deacon, *Vita Gregorii* 4.63 (*PL* 75, 213), and for discussion and further references, P. Lehmann, 'Mittelalterliche Beinahmen und Ehrentitel', *Historisches Jahrbuch* 49 (1929), 215–39, and now, Conrad Leyser, 'Late Antiquity in the Medieval West', in Philip Rousseau, ed., *Companion to Late Antiquity* (Oxford, forthcoming).

[103] Leyser, *Authority and Asceticism*, 185–7; Peter Brown, *The Rise of Western Christendom: Triumph and Diversity, AD 200–1000*, 2nd edn (Oxford, 2003), 190–215, 236–7, 249–57.

participation, in which no member of society is allowed the excuse of standing beyond the reach of the Christian message.

A significant proportion of *ad Gregoriam*'s length is dedicated to an *altercatio*, a battlefield scene conceived as a verbal contest. Gregoria is invited to view the battle from the 'tower of contemplation', a tower built in the walls of her city. The *altercatio* is a substantial scene, nearly 3,000 words in length, with six sub-scenes dedicated sequentially to six different battles, each taking place at the foot of the city walls, which the lady is invited to view from her tower. Gregoria's tower of contemplation would call to mind a wide variety of parallels, and to different readers different parallels would seem most obvious. The most direct parallel is to the *Psychomachia* of Prudentius. But equally obvious to an ancient eye would have been the ancient motif of *teichoskopia* reaching back to book three of the *Iliad*, in which Helen and Priam view the Greek heroes from the walls of Troy.[104] The tower itself also evokes monastic connotations, marking a relationship to the tower of John Cassian,[105] and anticipating that of Benedict of Nursia as commemorated a generation later in Gregory the Great's *Dialogues*.[106] In his *Homilies on Ezekiel* Gregory accords to the *speculator*, the man who views from above, a panoptical authority strongly identified with that of the bishop, though he views ordained and lay authority as resting on the same foundations.[107] (Already in the *Regula pastoralis*, Gregory had recommended contemplation as an integral part of rulership, a form of authority which he specifies as open to the lay *materfamilias*.[108])

The intent of John's *altercatio* in *Ad Gregoriam in palatio* is slightly different to that of Prudentius. As with Prudentius, the contestants are the vices and virtues between whom the soul is torn; here, the virtues are Truth, Benevolence, Contempt for Worldliness, Fasting, Chastity, and Endurance. As with Prudentius, great effort is expended in making the battle-scenes seem vivid and realistic, with description of the armour and battle-formations used. But John's point seems to be to assimilate the aristocratic *psychomachia* with a genre of spiritual writing borrowed from the desert fathers, the

[104] A brief overview of *teichoskopia* from Homer to Boccaccio is given by Paolo Mantovanelli, 'In difesa di Romilda: Innamoramento classico e supplizio barbarico in Paolo Diacono, Boccaccio, Niccolò Canussio', in *Integrazione mescolanza rifiuto: Incontri di popoli, lingue e culture in Europa dall'Antichità all'Umanesimo: Atti del convegno internazionale, Cividale del Friuli, 21–23 settembre 2000* (Rome, 2001), 337–54, at 341–2.
[105] Cassian, *Coll.* 9.2 (*CSEL* 13, 251).
[106] Gregory the Great, *Dialogues* 2.35 (*SC* 260, 236–42 and nn.1–7).
[107] On the *speculator* tradition, see Leyser, *Authority and Asceticism*, 28–31 and 160–3.
[108] Gregory the Great, *Reg. past.* 2.5 (*SC* 381, 196–202).

manual of advice for handling the assaults by which the Devil struggles to halt the ascetic's progress in the virtues.[109] In his second *Conference*, John Cassian, following Evagrius,[110] had explained that the invisible struggle with the vices would place the ascetic in danger of perdition unless he found a reliable guide to these secret matters:

For [the ascetic's] enemies are not visible but invisible and merciless; the daily and nightly encounter is a spiritual battle not against one or two, but against innumerable companies, whose destructive power is all the more dangerous, insofar as the enemy is the more hostile, and the contest the more hidden.[111]

The *altercatio* of *ad Gregoriam* represents an attempt to take this advice and to render it vivid for a literate lay readership.

At the same time, it seems plausible to read *Ad Gregoriam*'s mingling of allegorical dialogue with spiritual instruction as a commentary on the social dangers of its reader's milieu. The agonistic frame reflects the constant rivalry and one-upmanship that Gregoria can expect to encounter, even – or perhaps especially – if she seeks to withdraw from 'worldly' concerns. Our reader is repeatedly warned not to be impressed by the self-important rambling of other *dominae*. More often than not, she is told, these airs and graces have no real substance – they represent nothing more than the Devil's attempts to ensnare her through the sin of envy. But it is significant that debate and interpretation – watching the virtues closely to discover if they are real or sham, discerning the difference between spiritual discourse and the snares of the Enemy – are the techniques of spiritual progress in which the reader must school herself. If we know one thing about the enigmatic Gregoria, it is that John saw her as a *salonière* – a person of not inconsiderable learning, and one who moved in circles known, if not for intellectual fireworks, then at least for an appreciation of fine talk and literary accomplishment.

If *Ad Gregoriam* invites its reader to imagine herself as sharing in the life of the desert fathers or of the militia defending her city, its image of the lady reader is also that of an aristocratic literary patron. We have seen above that textual criticism – and preservation of the precious manuscripts within

---

[109] We meet it, for example, in *De diversis malignis cogitationibus* (*PG* 79, 1200–33) and *De octo vitiosis cogitationibus* (*PG* 40, 1272–8), both of Evagrius Ponticus. Monks were not the only recipients of this kind of instruction, as the *Liber* itself attests, but they were certainly its stereotypical recipients.

[110] Evagrius, *Praktikos* 48 (*SC* 171, 608).

[111] Cassian, *Coll.* 2.11 (*CSEL* 13, 52): 'Habet enim non adversus visibiles, sed invisibiles atque inmites hostes diurnum nocturnumque conflictum nec contra unum seu duos, sed contra innumerabiles catervas spiritale certamen, cuius casus tanto perniciosior cunctis, quanto et infestior inimicus et congressus occultior.'

which the texts themselves were copied – was understood as an act of *pietas* among the men of Gregoria's social sphere. *Ad Gregoriam* provides an intriguing glimpse into the relationship to books of women of the patronage class, at a period earlier than that for which there is substantial evidence. There is evidence enough at this period for female scribes in the context of monastic scriptoria,[112] and for the use of commercial scribes by property-owning women in sixth-century Italy,[113] but there is little direct evidence for the engagement of laywomen with prestige literary manuscripts before the Carolingian period. (In fact, the earliest surviving manuscript of the *Ad Gregoriam* itself bears signs of female ownership, but the manuscript comes from the ninth century.)

If we look within the text of *Ad Gregoriam* for evidence of the intended reader's relationship to the book itself, however, we find what may be a trace of familiarity with illustrated Prudentius manuscripts.[114] The *altercatio*, the debate between the vices and virtues, builds a markedly visual metaphor for contemplation through the repeated use of *ecphrasis*. The image which the *Liber* invokes of its author guiding the aristocratic *domina*'s eye as she views the battlefield may also operate at a second level, at which both narrator and reader join in admiring a precious manuscript. This section is peppered with second-person exhortations from the narrator to the reader – 'Look at the swords, the spears, the pikes, the bows, the arrows and quivers . . . direct your attention to the very King of Vices himself, how he drives the vigorous soldiers . . .'[115] These direct instructions could well refer to the act of reading an illustrated manuscript of the kind which survive of the *Psychomachia*, or of the battle-scenes of the book of Psalms, the biblical text to which *Ad Gregoriam* refers more than to any other.[116] This would confirm what we know about the contemplative intent of early medieval manuscript

---

[112] Kim Haines-Eitzen, *Guardians of letters: Literacy, Power, and the Transmitters of Early Christian Literature* (Oxford, 2000).

[113] J. O. Tjäder, *Die nichtliterarischen lateinischen Papyri Italiens aus der Zeit 445–700*, 3 vols. (Lund, 1954–5).

[114] For a valuable treatment of the *miles Christi* in early medieval manuscript illumination, see Elizabeth Sears, 'Louis the Pious as *Miles Christi*: The Dedicatory Image in Hrabanus Maurus' *De laudibus sanctae crucis*', in Peter Godman and Roger Collins, *Charlemagne's Heir: New Perspectives on the Reign of Louis the Pious (814–840)* (Oxford, 1990), 605–28, and literature cited there, especially Richard Stettiner, *Die illustrierten Prudentiushandschriften* (Berlin, 1895/1905); H. Woodruff, 'The Illustrated Manuscripts of Prudentius', *Art Studies* 7 (1929), 33–79; and Adolf Katzenellenbogen, *Allegories of the Virtues and Vices in Mediaeval Art from Early Christian Times to the Thirteenth Century*, tr. A. J. P. Crick (London, 1939).

[115] *Ad Gregoriam in Palatio* 10 (*CC* 25A, 207).

[116] On early medieval illustrated psalters, see Jacobus H. Engelbrecht, *Het Utrechts Psalterium: een eeuw wetenschappelijke bestudering (1860–1960)* (Utrecht, 1965).

illumination. The metaphor reaches out to encompass the reader of the *admonitio*, not only Gregoria herself but perhaps another *domina*, to whom Gregoria is offered as an *exemplum* for imitation.

We have suggested above that the literary airs of a text like *Ad Gregoriam in palatio* pose an obstacle for the modern reader. The kind of allegorical dialogue around which it is built has been out of fashion for centuries, and the plaintive urgency of more simplistic texts sits more easily with modern notions of Christian pastoral writing than does *Ad Gregoriam*'s attempt to steer a very specific reader by means of flattery, mannered Latin, and the threat of humiliation. But for a reader in Ostrogothic Italy, the very characteristics we find off-putting would have advertised the interest of what the reader could expect to find upon entering the world of the text.

The writing of *Ad Gregoriam* constituted a passionate intervention in a long chain of debate about how best to understand the struggles of the Christian life, and about whether the struggles of monks and clerics were somehow different from those of other men and women. Our writer has clearly read widely in the classics of patristic wisdom, and he clearly wants to find a language through which he can convey this patristic legacy across the great divide between lay and clerical élites. At the same time, the text represents an attempt to sustain a wide sphere for clerical moralizing, to include and engage with a class of matriarch who had become the mainstay of the Church's engagement with civic life, but who might have a tendency to perceive themselves as beyond the reach of Christian instruction.

It is worth dwelling briefly on Boethius as an intriguing foil for the enigmatic Gregoria, who may well have been his kinswoman and almost certainly travelled in the same senatorial circles during the period of Ostrogothic rule in Italy. While we know Gregoria only as the object of consideration by a man of the Church, we have numerous first-person narratives from Boethius, and we see in him the discomfort of senatorial men with the clerical brand of Christianity. We will see in Chapter Four that in the fifth and sixth centuries advice to married householders did not tend to come from ascetics *per se*, but rather from bishops and deacons, men in positions of institutional responsibility for the *cura animarum*, the care of souls. Of course, some writers belonged to both ascetic and clerical orders at the same time, and as we have seen above, a writer like Eugippius of Lucullanum, himself both a monk and a cleric,[117] could obfuscate the

---

[117] Cassiodorus refers to him as 'the priest Eugippius whom I myself saw – a man indeed not well educated in secular letters, but well read in Divine Scripture' (*Inst.* 1.23, ed. Mynors, 61–2, Halporn, 154).

distinction between clerical and monastic approaches to the laity, attempting to present a united front of 'men of the Church' when dealing with
'men of the world'.

A number of the themes of Boethius' *Consolation* find echo in
Ad Gregoriam. Each takes up the theme of *consolatio* in the form of an
allegorical dialogue. Boethius offers a first-person account in which Lady
Philosophy visits his prison cell to guide him as he faces imprisonment and
execution. Most importantly for our purposes, Boethius was the most
important of a number of writers who appropriated the Stoic theme of
consolatio from a Christian senatorial perspective.[118] His *De consolatione
philosophiae* is unusual, in that the person being consoled is the narrator
himself, with the task of consolation taken on by none other than the
hypostasized Lady Philosophy.

Faced not with the destruction of an entire society – Boethius did not
live to see the Gothic Wars which left such a decisive imprint on the
contribution of Cassiodorus – but with the narrower if still daunting
prospect of his own individual death, Boethius reached instinctively for a
Roman tradition cherished by men of his kind since republican times. In
the *Consolation*, Boethius draws directly on Cicero, Seneca, and Plotinus; it
is almost as if Tertullian and Cyprian had not, in the second and third
centuries, effected a fusion of the Stoic to the Christian world-view, and
Augustine and others had not done the same for Christianity and
Neoplatonism in the fourth.[119] The author of *Ad Gregoriam in palatio*, by
contrast, takes up the theme of *consolatio* with repeated, almost driving
reference to a host of Christian writers of previous generations, some of
them cited *verbatim*. It is as if, while Boethius wished somehow to
stand free of a Christian literature with which he was almost certainly
perfectly familiar, the author of *Ad Gregoriam* sought to consolidate
an existing patrimony of Christian thinking for a new pastoral situation,
and possibly to showcase his own command of a Christian literary
inheritance.

John differs from Boethius, however, in how he adduces the allegorical
element. He establishes a triangle in which the male spiritual director turns
back and forth between addressing the lady reader and describing an
allegorical dialogue, in which successive vices attack the Christian soul.

---

[118] Peter von Moos, *Consolatio: Studien zur mittellateinischen Trostliteratur über den Tod und zum
Problem der christlichen Trauer* (Munich, 1971).
[119] Although Boethius' deep engagement with Augustine is in fact well documented (Chadwick,
Boethius, 213).

The linguistic register of the text is closer than that of Boethius to the 'plain style' preferred by Eugippius for works of spiritual instruction, but like Boethius, the author is able and willing to showcase a fully periodic style, by no means limiting himself to the repetitive parataxis of contemporary sermon literature. (Where repetition is used, it is clearly used for effect, in accordance with the sensibilities of the 'jewelled style'.)

Where philosophical ideas are concerned there is a similar sensibility at work: the writer seems both to want to show a full awareness of the Christian Stoic and Neoplatonic traditions, and at the same time to communicate with readers who are not *au courant* to the same degree. Thus the Christian Stoic vocabulary established by Tertullian and Cyprian is adopted, but the meaning of the text does not depend on a reader's ability to recognize the allusions. Neoplatonic ideas appear in an easily accessible guise, with the ability to show forth virtue understood, for example, in mystical terms as a swelling of light through the body: 'For the Lord has shown his light in you for the good of many. And as that light spreads through your members He separates you from the shadows of this world, and makes you show forth varying powers (*virtutes*) to all.'[120] Similarly, the treatise ends with the theme of heavenly ascent, with the lady reader ascending the path toward heaven, looking neither to left nor to right.

The metaphor of the viewing-tower allows John to invoke the ideal of the *miles Christi* while at the same time interposing an imaginary distance. The *matrona* is asked to *view* the *altercatio* rather than fighting – even though it is her own soul that must do battle with the forces of evil. It can be argued that she is assigned a passive role as a spectator, but the situation is more complex than this would suggest. In the main body of the text her own actions in daily life are viewed as a form of direct engagement in spiritual warfare, and this spills across to colour the interpretation of the sequences in which the virtues – *her* virtues – are at war with the vices. Across the text as a whole Gregoria is both soldier and spectator.

If the modern reader fails to perceive the text's moral urgency, it is because our writer is reaching in an unexpected direction to find his spiritually disadvantaged quarry among the mannered *literati* of his day. This gesture of inclusion would cast a long shadow, for *Ad Gregoriam* was being circulated in court circles in the Carolingian period.[121] On a more

---

[120] Ad Gregoriam 25 (*CC* 25A, 243).
[121] On the earliest manuscript of *Ad Gregoriam*, see Kate Cooper, 'The Reichenau *Ad Gregoriam in palatio* (Codex Augiensis 172) and the Problem of Early Medieval Women as Readers and Book Owners', in preparation.

modest level than the *Excerpta Augustini* or the *Institutes* of Cassiodorus, *Ad Gregoriam* is a sixth-century time-capsule, a compendium of everything its writer thought relevant to a lay householder, with 'high' literary allusions crammed in alongside snatches of both great and insignificant works of Christian instruction. That it has not received the attention it deserves is due in part to its writer's fierce commitment to writing in the idiom of his generation. Equally, what the writer of *Ad Gregoriam* saw as most precious in the late Roman pastoral inheritance was a cluster of ideas that have fallen out of favour in recent centuries, although they were tremendously influential across the Middle Ages. We will return to these ideas – of daily martyrdom, allegorical battle, and the imitation of Christ and the saints – in Chapter Five.

CHAPTER 3

Household and empire

The cultural landscape explored in the previous chapter should not allow us to forget that the champions of *romanitas* were not exclusively men and women of leisure. More often than they wished to admit, they were engaged in running the productive concerns on which their wealth depended, and their management of these concerns was decisive for the well-being of their dependents, often numbering in the hundreds and sometimes thousands. Agricultural wealth was the basis on which cultured leisure rested, and for all the rhetoric of *otium*, the men and women of this class had to manage numerous agricultural holdings – or more precisely to direct the work of overseers in doing so. A pyramid of human effort depended on their will, involving slaves, tenants, and paid labourers. In addition, for the large landowners, there were periodic negotiations with their estate managers and with *conductores*, the large-scale tenants who leased whole estates; landowners might also themselves act as *conductores*, taking on parcels of imperial land or land belonging to other *domini*. In all of these negotiations, a balance had to be found between the financial interest of the *domini* and the ability of those below them in the pyramid to bear the weight of their leisure.

Otium and commerce were so closely yoked in the rural life of the *dominus* that it is often hard for the historian to tell them apart. *Otium* included most of the activitity that we moderns would class as 'business'; it represented respite not from commercial business but from the political concerns and duties of the public man.[1] The pose of senatorial disregard for trade did not actually reflect a lack of involvement in it; already from the time of Cicero the rhetoric of *otium* as cultured leisure could be used as a pretext to justify a man's absence from Rome when he needed to get home to see to business interests.

[1] Jean-Marie André, *L'Otium dans la vie morale et intellectuelle romaine: des origines à l'époque augustéenne* (Paris, 1966), 282–3.

When senators left Rome for their estates, it was to attend to the source – or sources – of their livelihood. Thus, for example, when Cicero complained that P. Sestius failed to return to Rome from his villa near Cosa, what kept him in Tuscany was probably not poetry. Sestius' substantial business at the Tuscan villa can be documented.[2] The wine from his vineyards there was loaded into amphorae produced in his own terracotta factory, onto trade ships which he owned, perhaps as quietly as possible, in partnership with men who were not his social equals. Only the shipwreck of one of these vessels, recovered in the waters off Marseilles in 1952, has allowed historians to connect the literary and political figure Sestius known from Cicero's letters with the terracotta manufacturer whose mark SEST was embossed on over 1,000 amphorae found in the wreck, and again with the trade 'footprint' left by dozens of other amphorae recovered across the western Mediterranean from Spain to Greece, all bearing the same stamp.[3] Although men and women of the upper classes tended to dissimulate about their involvement in generating income, proper management of one's estates and other interests was both a demanding task and a point of honour.[4] *Otium*, then, was something of a euphemism.

At the same time, when we consider the Roman *domina*, we are dealing with a class of person whose role was by no means merely decorative. Her pose of leisure, like that of her menfolk, was a calculated performance, and a large dose of rhetoric is present in the sources describing her role within the household. This is better understood for other historical periods than for the late empire. Historians of the antebellum South, for example, have debated contrasting interpretations of the seeming 'helplessness' which many sources attribute to the aristocratic plantation mistress. Initially, feminist history tended to minimize the economic centrality of women as owners and managers – so, for example, Elizabeth Fox-Genovese's *Within the Plantation Household: Black and White Women of the Old South* proposed that nineteenth-century plantation mistresses had 'little involvement' in the running of the agricultural or other business

---

[2] John D'Arms, *Commerce and Social Standing in Ancient Rome* (Cambridge, Mass., 1981), esp. ch. 3, 'Senators and Commerce', 49–71, with discussion of Sestius at 55–62.

[3] E. L. Will, 'Les Amphores de Sestius', *Revue Archéologique de l'Est et du Centre-Est* 7 (1956), 224ff., with Daniele Manacorda, 'The *Ager Cosanus* and the Production of the Amphorae of Sestius: New Evidence and a Reassessment', *JRS* 68 (1978), 122–31, cited with discussion in D'Arms, *Commerce and Social Standing*, 56 and 57, respectively.

[4] Peter Garnsey, 'The Land', in Alan K. Bowman, Peter Garnsey and Dominic Rathbone, eds., *Cambridge Ancient History* 12, *The High Empire, AD 70–192* (Cambridge, 2000), 679–709, for an overview; see Pieter Wim de Neeve, 'A Roman Landowner and his Estates: Pliny', *Athenaeum* 78 (1990), 363–42 on our best source for the management situation of an individual *dominus*.

in which their households were engaged.[5] Indeed, Fox-Genovese suspected that her subjects had little understanding of the work done by their subordinates even close at hand within the 'big house', and took references to 'management' in the primary sources to be a euphemistic way of referring to self-important posturing by a person uninvolved in the labour on which her leisure was based.

A second generation of scholars, however, have made it clear that the helplessness of the plantation mistress was a social performance calculated to secure a household's place within the class hierarchy, and in turn to stabilize the hierarchy itself. On the one hand the mistress was depicted as a conspicuous consumer of the labour of others, a figure whose seeming leisure underlined the wealth of her household; on the other hand, she was perceived as a tempering influence on the harder form of authority exercised by men. In both cases she magnified her family's power in the eyes of others, while simultaneously making it seem more bearable.[6]

The nineteenth-century plantation mistress as she is recorded in the sources was to some degree, then, a social fiction. Real historical women probably contributed, both intentionally and inadvertently, to the fiction by their words and actions; as readers and writers of texts they were both subjects and objects of rhetorical manoeuvring. Southern women's legal position was in many ways less autonomous than that of their Roman counterparts, but even so the mistress regularly exercised the role of 'master' in the plantation household. Her position seems to have changed in the years from the American Revolution to the Civil War, but the change may be partly a change in rhetoric. The progressive textual repositioning of the image of the plantation mistress away from autonomous authority and toward an image of helpless innocence may have reflected less a change in women's scope for agency than a new way of manipulating her rhetorical visibility in a 'culture war' among élites: in a nation polarized over the issue of slave-holding in the aftermath of the Fugitive Slave Act of 1830, Southern writers increasingly sought to avoid calling attention to the 'mastery' of the 'mistress', preferring to portray her as a bearer of sweetness and light.

There is ample reason to suspect that an analogous 'culture war' was at play in the later Roman empire. Ironically, rather than the issue of

[5] Elizabeth Fox-Genovese's *Within the Plantation Household: Black and White Women of the Old South* (Chapel Hill, 1988). Such a generalization would not be offered today without strong supporting evidence. A nuanced view of developments in the field, arguing for the economic centrality of plantation mistresses, is found in Kirsten E. Wood, *Masterful Women: Slaveholding Widows from the American Revolution through the Civil War* (Chapel Hill, 2004), e.g. 8–11.

[6] See, e.g., Stephanie McCurry, *Masters of Small Worlds: Yeoman Households, Gender Relations, and the Political Culture of the Antebellum South Carolina Low Country* (New York, 1995), 16–19.

bondage, the trigger for disagreement may have been the expansion of wage labour alongside the more paternalistic forms of slave labour and tenancy. In the discussion that follows we will see that the *domina*'s role as manager of the senatorial household of the fifth and early sixth centuries was the subject of lively debate, centred on the question of how the household's relations of power and ownership should reflect Christian social ideals. By contrast to the better-known ascetic texts of the same period, the conduct literature addressed to senatorial Christian *dominae* makes every effort to find a Christian context for the old aristocratic idea of the moral burden of authority. In a text like *Ad Gregoriam in palatio*, or the fragmentary Bobbio letter which will be introduced below, we see the early stirrings of a Christian paternalism which, on the face of it, would not be out of place in a nineteenth-century novel. But we should not be beguiled by the over-familiarity of certain motifs and turns of phrase. The surviving household manuals bear witness, as we will see shortly, to a domestic balance of power entirely unlike that of the nineteenth century.

They also bear witness to a reorientation in late antiquity of the biological triangle involving the *domina*, her father, and her husband. Just as we saw the erosion of the father's authority over his son in Chapter One, so in Chapter Five we will see the erosion of his authority over his son-in-law. We will also see that the Christian texts find a new balance of emphasis where the authority of the female head of household is concerned, attempting to steer her toward a new attitude of dependence on her husband.

To understand the power of the Roman *domina* we need to unlearn an old habit of imagining women and children in a parallel universe independent of the economic and political problems that coloured the world of adult males. The great senatorial estates were crucial to the Roman economy, but they were also Roman households. The household or *domus*, the primary Roman unit of cohabitation and economic production, could involve vast numbers and multiple sites in the case of the great landowning families. Roman law did not distinguish between residential and commercial property, and this meant that the *domus* in its wider sense was the venue for production and exchange in the late Roman economy.[7] This had important consequences for the participation of women.

Here, too, a comparative approach can help us to understand the balance of power within and beyond the household. In the merchant

---

[7] On the consequences for the ancient economy of the failure to distinguish between personal and business wealth, see M. I. Finley, *The Ancient Economy* (London, 1973), 114–17. See also Kate Cooper, 'Closely Watched Households: Visibility, Exposure, and Private Power in the Roman *Domus*', *Past & Present* 197 (forthcoming, 2007), on the reach of the *domus* into the spheres of business and politics.

economies of Leiden and Cologne in the late medieval period, Martha Howell suggested some years ago, decline of the household as the primary unit of production and the corresponding erosion of powerful kinship-based economic networks caused the erosion of women's position as owners and high-status workers;[8] in the Roman period, by contrast, we will see that women played a central role and that their share of ownership was surprisingly high. We will find that Howell's idea of a 'household economy' is very useful in thinking about the place of the Roman household in social and economic networks, with special reference to the symbolic and practical role played by the *materfamilias*.

The *domus*, then, was by no means a sphere standing in isolation from the commercial and productive life of the ancient city. Rather, it was a central arena for the social, economic, and even political negotiations in which its members participated. A household at the top of the Roman social pyramid was as complex in its staff and holdings as a modern corporation.[9] Indeed, in the early 1970s, the papyrologist Roger Rémondon suggested that the great estates were poised, Janus-like, between their private function as an economic interest, and a potential public function, as an institution charged by the state with aspects of the maintenance of public order such as imprisonment of criminals.[10]

The progressive eastward 'drift' of imperial favour meant that in the long term, senators based in Italy were net 'losers' in the transformation of the fifth and early sixth centuries – indeed many senatorial families relocated to Constantinople after the Gothic Wars – but this would have been difficult to foresee in the fifth century. Up to the Gothic Wars many senators were still multi-regional landowners, even if in their aftermath it seems to have become impossible to keep hold of estates outside Italy and Sicily.[11] Although Theodosius II relaxed to some degree the ancient requirement that senators maintain a residence in Rome (or Constantinople) and be

---

[8] Martha C. Howell, *Women, Production and Patriarchy in Late Medieval Cities* (Chicago, 1988).
[9] Carla Sfameni, 'Residential Villas in Late Antiquity: Continuity and Change', in Will Bowden, Luke Lavan, and Carlos Machado, eds., *Recent Research on the Late Anitique Countryside* (Leiden, 2003), 335–75, at 348. On the estates of Melania the Younger, see Paul Allard, 'Une grande fortune romaine au cinquième siècle', *Revue des questions historiques* 81 (1907), 5–30.
[10] Roger Rémondon, 'Situation présente de la papyrologie Byzantine', in Emil Kiessling and Hans-Albert Rupprecht, eds., *Akten des XIII internationalen Papyruskongresses, Marburg/Lahn, 2.–6. August 1971* (Munich, 1974), 366–72, at 72. Jean Gascou, 'Les Grandes Domaines, la cité et l'état en Égypte byzantine', *Travaux et mémoires* 9 (1985), 1–90. On domestic imprisonment see Jens-Uwe Krause, *Gefängnisse im römischen Reich* (Stuttgart, 1996), 187, and now Julia Hillner, 'Monastic Imprisonment in Justinian's *Novels*', *Journal of Early Christian Studies* 15 (2007), 205–37.
[11] Chris Wickham, *Framing the Early Middle Ages: Europe and the Mediterranean, 400–800* (Oxford, 2005), 167: Church holdings 'were better able to survive the political localization which destroyed the

physically present when the Senate was in session – unless public business required their absence or an imperial dispensation authorized it – there is little evidence to indicate a diminished senatorial presence in Rome in the fifth and sixth centuries. Indeed, it has recently been argued that the city was the focus not only of senatorial, but of much imperial (and after 476 royal) interest.[12]

The fact that Italy was no longer the centre of an empire would have been felt, in Rome itself, in the diminished tax income and the decline of the *annona*.[13] But the crises of the mid and late fifth century, and even the military victories by which Odoacer and Theoderic won the right to establish Italy as a client kingdom after 476,[14] did not completely disrupt 'the civilized and thoroughly civilian society of Italy's Roman inhabitants'.[15] For our purposes, the Ostrogothic kingdom of Italy up to the death of Theoderic in 526 can be seen as 'late Roman'. Although 'radically different versions of Theoderic's constitutional position were circulating, and . . . his government was coy about giving it precise expression', imperial titles were frequently used in addressing or describing him, and his *de facto* status seems to have been as the (decidedly junior) Western emperor.[16] An intense effort was clearly made on all fronts to establish the Amal dynasty as the guardians of a *civilitas* that was recognizably Roman.[17] The public offices of the *cursus honorum* were still in operation, and it is fair to say that a senator before the death of Theoderic 'still imagined himself as living within an *unbroken* Roman Empire, one whose ultimate sovereign reigned at Constantinople'.[18] Every effort seems to have been made to minimize tensions between Gothic and

greater senatorial families: by 600, they must have been the largest private estates left anywhere in the Mediterranean. But, though they had a staying-power that lay landowners did not have, it was not infinite.'

[12] Mark Humphries, 'From Emperor to Pope? Ceremonial, Space, and Authority at Rome from Constantine to Gregory the Great', in Kate Cooper and Julia Hillner, eds., *Religion, Dynasty, and Patronage in a Christian Capital: Rome, 300–900* (Cambridge, 2007); see also Andrew Gillett, 'Rome, Ravenna, and the Last Western Emperors', *Papers of the British School at Rome* 69 (2001), 131–67.

[13] Wickham, *Framing the Early Middle Ages*, 34: '. . . the loss of Africa hit Italy hard, and particularly Rome, which, as a result of the ending of the African taxation which fed the city, experienced its sharpest population fall in precisely this period. Demographic decline in the city of Rome was indeed probably the most important structural change in Italy between 400 and 535.'

[14] Cf. Brian Croke, 'AD 476: The Manufacture of a Turning Point', *Chiron* 13 (1983), 81–119; and Arnaldo Momigliano, 'La caduta senza rumore di un impero', *Sesto contributo alla storia degli studi classici* (Rome, 1980), 159–79.

[15] T. S. Brown, *Gentlemen and Officers: Imperial Administration and Aristocratic Power in Byzantine Italy AD 554–800* (Rome, 1984), 1–2.

[16] John Moorhead, *Theoderic in Italy* (Oxford, 1992), 39–51, with citation at 51.

[17] Moorhead, *Theoderic in Italy*, 75–80.

[18] Patrick Amory, *People and Identity in Ostrogothic Italy, 489–554* (Cambridge, 1997), 133.

Roman élites. The marying of Amal warrior virtue with the moral language of aristocratic Christianity allowed for some fluidity in the application of ideas of aristocratic virtue across ethnic lines – so, for example, Cassiodorus' praise of queen Amalasuintha, as 'one who has made the Danube Roman again'.[19] Romans and Goths were governed discretely, each under their respective traditional laws, with Roman law continuing in force in all the territories governed by Theoderic, including Italy and after 511 the Visigothic kingdom of his nephew Amalaric, extending as far as Spain until 526, and afterward to the east bank of the Rhône. We will see below that where the household was concerned, the presence or absence of a Gothic *rex-princeps* was less significant than the economic pressures passed down from Constantinople.

We should consider the possibility, too, that the 'Christianization' of the household was the result of social engineering, yet another instance of the cooperation of episcopal authority with the state. One of the roles of the Church, from the point of view of a fifth- or sixth-century emperor or king, was to establish an axis of participation, conformity, and patronage for lay élites. At the same time as bishops progressively took over civic functions previously carried out by lay magistrates, their advice and moral exhortation often served as an attempt to conscript and 'place' the lay élites with whom they found themselves in contact. Thus in the 480s Remigius of Rheims could address the Frankish king Clovis as a Roman administrator, offering him suitable advice on how to attain harmony in his province, despite the fact that Clovis was neither a Catholic nor in service to the emperor.[20]

It is not difficult to imagine that the emergence of Christian senatorial conduct literature such as *Ad Gregoriam* was part of a campaign, whether calculated or instinctive, to re-establish the authority of the senatorial class on a new and firmly Christian footing, and we have seen above that in the 530s men, too, were addressed with exhortations along similar lines. From the second century onward, at least some Christian writers had been concerned to defend the idea that their household polity was conducive to the socialization of a law-abiding citizenry,[21] but the ideals of the Christian household came to have new meaning once they applied to the ruling class. This was all the more the case in the first quarter of the

---

[19] Cassiodorus, *Variae* 11.1.10 (*MGH AA* 12, 329).
[20] Ralph W. Mathisen, *Roman Aristocrats in Barbarian Gaul: Strategies for Survival in an Age of Transition* (Austin, 1993), 121.
[21] Margaret MacDonald, *Early Christianity and Public Opinion: The Problem of the Hysterical Woman* (Cambridge, 1996), esp. 240–8.

sixth century, when the senate's claim to moral leadership of the Roman people seems to have begun to erode. The emergence of 'a poorly-documented stratum of non-senatorial magnates with powerful local interests who were already taking over the role of the senators'[22] meant that embeddedness in the ideas and networks of the Church was increasingly valuable in lending stability and legitimacy to senatorial power. The real crisis of the senate in Italy did not occur until the Gothic wars,[23] and even after their conclusion in the 550s some vestiges of senatorial office persisted in Byzantine Italy. The rule of law was reasonably secure in Italy up to the death of Theoderic – which is really only to say that each successive phase of civil war eventually gave way to a re-establishment of order under the latest victor.

This chapter will consider three conduct manuals for senatorial householders produced between the reign of Honorius and the beginning of the Gothic Wars. One, *Ad Gregoriam in Palatio*, we have already seen; the other two, the Acephalous Bobbio Letter and Ferrandus of Carthage's *Ad Reginum*, are addressed to figures similar to Gregoria in many respects, and for whom, similarly, there is no corroborating biographical evidence external to the text itself. Thus, the study of these texts can shed only uncertain light on the changing role of the senatorial aristocracy in the fifth and early sixth centuries. Still, that change – however it is eventually defined – is the context against which our sources must be measured. Why, one might ask, was it only after the death of Theodosius that such manuals seem to have been produced?

The answer may be a question of survival rather than of production. If comparable pagan materials were produced in the West – and the survival of Simplicius' *Enchiridion* suggests that they could have been – they were simply not of sufficient interest to the monastic librarians of the Merovingian and Carolingian periods to ensure their survival. (Indeed, the transmission history of the three surviving *Christian* manuals, which survive as unique examplars or in tenuously small numbers, seems to reflect ambivalence on the part of librarians about diverting library resources away from more ascetically minded materials.)

It is also possible, however, that in the fifth and early sixth centuries traditional householding itself needed to be defended, or at least given shape

---

[22] Brown, *Gentlemen and Officers*, 36.
[23] 'The destruction of the Senate was the price for the destruction of the Goths': Marinus A. Wes, *Das Ende des Kaisertums in Westen des römischen Reiches* (The Hague, 1967), 193, cited in Brown, *Gentlemen and Officers*, 32.

as a legitimate vocation for committed Christians, in the aftermath of both the 'senatorial take-over' of the imperial bureaucracy and the ascetic revolution. Certainly, numerous voices such as that of Jerome were contending, from the late fourth century, that the hallmark of the truly spiritual person was a complete refusal to fulfil the expectations both of his superiors and of those further down the chain of command, whether children or low-status persons within and beyond the household, who depended on him or her for protection and guidance. But not nearly enough attention has been paid to the efforts of a 'silent majority' of late fourth- and fifth-century writers – including Julian of Eclanum, Augustine, John Chrysostom, Pelagius, Jovianian, and the anonymous authors of important but little-understood fifth-century texts such as the *Epistula ad Demetriadem de vera humilitate* discussed in Chapter One – who repeatedly suggested that fulfilment of the traditional obligations of the Roman *paterfamilias* or *materfamilias* constituted a wholesome goal for even the most spiritually ambitious. These voices of caution made strange bedfellows, and it is in many ways unfortunate that theological misunderstandings set men such as Augustine and Julian, who in many respects were natural allies, against one another, a point to which we will return in Chapter Four.

It is tempting to imagine that the Christian household manuals are among other things an *apologia* for an old-style senatorial ideal of accountable, face-to-face estate management, revived in Christian guise to counter a rising trend of absentee ownership, in which even the pretence of accountability could be abandoned. One of the most arresting aspects of the texts addressed to Christian women is the way they dwell on the *domina* as a mistress of slaves. Great emphasis is placed on the element of obligation in the relationship. The idea seems to be that the senatorial aristocracy is central to the social order precisely because its members are able benevolently to shoulder responsibility for the well-being of others, and that it is a matter of urgency for senators to fulfil these ancient expectations.

THE STRUCTURE OF THE LATE ROMAN ESTATE

The Latin term *domus* could refer both to the extended network of the human household and to physical space, whether a single dwelling or the extended estate controlled by a property-owner on the grand scale. This would include both agricultural holdings and any other business interests. I say 'controlled by' rather than 'owned', because much of the Roman land under cultivation was owned by the imperial fisc and let out on long leases. The propertied men and women whom we will be discussing are usually referred to by scholars as *possessores*, the holders of *possessio* of estates whether as owners or leaseholders; Roman *possessio* differs from English 'title' in that it refers to control rather than outright owner-ship. Many *possessores* also belonged to the overlapping but distinct group of the *domini*, the outright owners who held title (*dominium*) to the property in question. The sources also use *dominus* and *domina* in a relational sense among human beings; this is in part because slaves, while human, were property as well. (In the slave–master relationship the master held *dominium* over the slave.) In addressing a social superior as *dominus* or *domina* one implied, very generally, that he was the owner of property.

The social reality of the fifth- and early sixth-century estate probably bore little relationship to the ancient ideal of the resident *paterfamilias* dispensing justice to his or her dependants. For one thing, during this period the rich were getting richer – at least in relative terms – and the poor were getting poorer. Jairus Banaji has recently argued that in Egypt, where the best documentation survives, monetary expansion in the period from Constantine to Justinian based on the introduction of the gold *solidus* made it easier for the beneficiaries of imperial patronage to convert their ascendancy into ever-more-extensive land-holdings. *Domini* who collected and reinvested cash surpluses, whether gained through office-holding, through more exploitative management of agricultural holdings, or both, could benefit from the fluid economic situation.[24] Building on the earlier work of A. H. M. Jones and Roger Rémondon, Banaji suggested that up to the late fourth century, 'the countryside had been firmly in the grip of families connected with the town councils',[25] but that in the middle of the fifth century mega-estates emerged whose *possessores* had no real connection to the social fabric of the rural towns and villages.[26] The 'essential feature' of this aristocracy was that it 'fused the

[24] Jairus Banaji, *Agrarian Change in Late Antiquity: Gold, Labour, and Aristocratic Dominance* (Oxford, 2001), with useful review by Chris Wickham (*Journal of Agrarian Change* 3 [2003], 434–6); see also Peter Sarris, 'Rehabilitating the Great Estate: Aristocratic Property and Economic Growth in the Late Antique East', in Will Bowden, Luke Lavan, and Carlos Machado, eds., *Recent Research on the Late Roman Countryside*, Late Antique Archaeology 2 (Leiden, 2003), 55–71, at 60–3, for succinct but lucid discussion. Peter Brown, 'The Later Roman Empire' (review of Jones, *Later Roman Empire*), *The Economic History Review* n.s. 20 (1967), 327–43, is no longer read as regularly as it ought to be; see also Brent D. Shaw's review (*BMCR*, 24 Feb. 2002) of E. Lo Cascio and D. W. Rathbone, eds., *Production and Public Powers in Classical Antiquity*, Cambridge Philological Society, suppl. vol. 26 (Cambridge, 2000).

[25] Banaji, *Agrarian Change*, 132.

[26] Peter Sarris, *Economy and Society in the Age of Justinian* (Cambridge, 2006), 181–91, considers late fourth-century legislation attempting to contain land-grabbing by the emerging 'great estates'; his study also offers valuable exploration of the best source for this type of enterprise, the Oxyrhyncus archive of the Apion household. On the Apions, see also Roberta Mazza, *L'archivio degli Apioni: terra, lavoro, e proprietà senatoria nell'Egitto tardoantico* (Bari, 2001).

power of high-ranking officials with the affluence of big landowners in a combination characteristic of the late empire'. In 'the important middle decades of the fifth century', the loyalties of the super-rich were prised from their geographical moorings.[27]

There is no convincing evidence that the same buoyant conditions obtained in the West, but there is good reason to believe that a similar process took place by which a small proportion of families, by combining ancient wealth with the profits derived from imperial office-holding, were able to use liquid capital to buy up the estates of lesser landowners. Lellia Cracco Ruggini has shown, for example, that the arrival of the imperial capital at Milan set off a chain of bankruptcy sales, with cash-rich *potentes* buying up the farms of small and medium landowners as they successively failed to meet obligations to the fisc or to their creditors.[28]

When a senator like Boethius complained (in 523) about bribing and patronage among court officials, what he probably had in mind was the fee-collection used by the imperial administration to attract the ambitious to imperial service.[29] This system is now well understood for the Eastern Empire thanks to a lively study by Christopher Kelly.[30] There is reason to think that palatine roles were somewhat more fluid under Theoderic,[31] although there is no equivalent in his kingdom to John Lydus as a source for the 'professional, middle-level bureaucrat'.[32]

Across the empire, the emergence of the super-rich made for jostling between 'old' and 'new' money, and 'new' money – or at least the money of those playing the new game – had the advantage. It was of course a point of

---

[27] Banaji, *Agrarian Change*, 130, citing Roger Rémondon, 'L'Égypte au 5e siècle de notre ère: les sources papyrologiques et leurs problèmes', *Atti dell'XI Congresso Internazionale di Papirologia, Milano 2–8 Settembre 1965* (Milan, 1966), 135–48. At 130–1 Banaji also makes the connection between this process and the restructuring of senatorial honours between 450 and 530 studied by Jones (*Later Roman Empire* I, 529), which restricted numerous privileges to *illustres*, thus excluding *clarissimi* and *spectabiles*, as a result of the expansion of the clarissimate.

[28] Lellia Cracco Ruggini, *Economia e società nell' 'Italia annonaria': rapporti fra agricoltura e commercio dal IV al VI secolo d. C.*, 2nd edn (Bari, 1995), 25–6.

[29] Amory, *People and Identity*, 133–5. Men in the Ostrogothic royal service were almost certainly understood, technically speaking, as servants in the imperial bureaucracy, if Theoderic was acting implicitly as the junior, Western emperor; on his status, see Moorhead, *Theoderic in Italy*, 75–80.

[30] Christopher Kelly, *Ruling the Later Roman Empire* (Cambridge, Mass., 2004), offers a vivid analysis of the mechanics of wealth accumulation among office-holders.

[31] Andrew Gillett, *Envoys and Political Communication in the Late Antique West, 411–533* (Cambridge, 2003), 202–3.

[32] The phrase is from Andrew Gillett, 'The Purposes of Cassiodorus' *Variae*', in Alexander Callander Murray, ed., *After Rome's Fall: Narrators and Sources of Early Medieval History: Essays Presented to Walter Goffart* (Toronto, 1998), 35–50, at 39 n. 3, with secondary literature comparing Cassiodorus and John Lydus.

resentment that the liquidity of the very rich allowed them to gain ever greater advantage. Even in agriculture they had the edge, since they could hold back produce from their estates, waiting out the market and eventually selling at a higher price than could others who needed to sell as quickly as possible whatever the price. Here is Banaji on L. Aurelius Avianus Symmachus, father of the celebrated orator:

> In Ammianus' description Symmachus' father was a 'paradigm of learning and moderation'. But these were personal qualities and it seemed insufficient not to mention the fact that his *domus* across the Tiber had been burned down because (it was alleged) he had said 'he would rather use his own wine for quenching lime-kilns than sell it at the price which the people hoped for' – an incident emblematic of his position as a large producer.[33]

Even the quintessential 'public men' were known to give priority to the private interests on which their fortunes depended, and they were widely resented for doing so.

The economic situation of the western provinces – and thus of Rome itself – was somewhat paradoxical. Fifth- and sixth-century sources complained that Roman taxes were high, with little return to the citizenry, and it is true that funding an unremitting series of wars, along with tribute payments to barbarian warlords, represented a financial drain which emperors passed down to their subjects.[34] As a result, *possessores* in the fifth and sixth centuries felt considerable pressure to realize a maximum return from their land. This was achieved by attempting to sell at the most advantageous point in the price cycle wherever possible, and also by estate management strategies geared to producing more or spending less to produce it. We may be confident that every attempt was made to hand the cost down again, to the labour force.

The terms on which labourers were employed on late Roman estates are not well understood. Slaves worked alongside free hired workers on the estates managed directly by a *possessor* or his agents, while *coloni* (tenant-farmers) were legally bound to the land, and could either pay an agreed rent or, as share-croppers, a proportion of their harvest.[35] The evidence suggests

---

[33] Banaji, *Agrarian Change*, 84, citing Ammianus, 27.3.3–4 in Rolfe's translation.

[34] A lucid introduction to the key issues can be found in Federico Marazzi, 'The Destinies of the Late Antique Italies: Politico-Economic Developments of the Sixth Century', in Richard Hodges and William Bowden, eds., *The Sixth Century: Production, Distribution and Demand* (Leiden, 1998), 119–59.

[35] In a field of inquiry that has seen intense debate recently, the very lucid explanation of tied and free tenancies by Jones is still a useful starting-point: *Later Roman Empire*, 796–9. Valuable guides to the more recent literature are Chris Wickham, *Framing the Middle Ages*, 520–7 and Domenico Vera, 'Le

that were variations of practice from region to region, and that within regions different crops tended to favour different kinds of labour, but there seems to have been enough flexibility in the system that a *dominus* could try a different mode of labour if he was unhappy with the surplus he or she was getting.[36] Banaji suggests that wage labour rather than tenancy was a characteristic of the mega-estates of the fifth and early sixth centuries, and that this 'commercial agriculture' was scientific in its extraction of maximum surplus.[37] Direct management should not be necessarily be confused with accountability on the part of the *dominus*, however. In fact slave labour and even tenancy seem to have been perceived as carrying with them a heightened accountability on the part of the *possessor*, who would face both shame and economic loss if the hunger of his dependents tipped over into starvation. Free wage labour, by contrast, was a form of exploitation allowing the *possessor* to bear little or no responsibility for the year-round or long-term well-being of those in his or her employ.

By a shift to a greater proportion of wage labour, it has been suggested, *possessores* found a way to reduce their responsibilities attached to production without significantly increasing their liabilities.[38] The only added liability of wage labour from the landlord's point of view would be in instances where the potential work-force was insufficient to meet demand, but there seems to be no evidence that this was the case in later antiquity. To be sure, the *possessor* shouldered other risks and burdens, such as the possibility of a failed harvest, but these risks were no greater than those he or she faced if the land was worked by tenants or slaves.

In many of the surviving landlord–tenant contracts, the above-mentioned risks would be undertaken by the landlord precisely because it was in his long-term interest that his tenants continue to be able to survive year after year at very close to subsistence level. From the landlord's point of view, the maximum surplus could be realized where tenants did not themselves try to build up a base of capital, but rather relied on the landlord to provide machinery, and often seed, as necessary. A similar balance seems

forme del lavoro rurale: Aspetti della trasformazione dell'Europa romana fra tarda antichità e alto medioevo', in *Morfologie sociali e culturali in Europa fra tarda antichità e alto medioevo*, Settimane di studio sull' alto medioevo 45 (Spoleto, 1998), 293–338, along with idem, 'Padroni, Contadini, Contratti: *realia* del colonato tardoantico', in Elio Lo Cascio, ed., *Terre, proprietá e contadini dell'impero romano: dall'affitto agrario al colonato tardoantico* (Rome, 1997), 185–224.

[36] De Neeve, 'A Roman Landowner and his Estates', offers an overview of the factors considered by Pliny centuries earlier.

[37] Banaji, *Agrarian Change*, 132. This would have been an alarming departure from the Roman consensus described by Finley, *The Ancient Economy*, 115–22, in which social pressures and an idea of 'amenity', rather than an economic calculation, governed estate management.

[38] Banaji, *Agrarian Change*, 181–5.

to have been found where the spread of risk was concerned. Lin Foxhall has suggested that the sample Roman leases preserved in the *Digest*, in which the tenant would bear responsibility for routine hazards such as spoilage while the landlord covered 'extraordinary' hazards such as damage by landslides or plundering armies, reflect an attempt to make use of the landlord's greater liquidity while under normal circumstances offering him or her a maximum return.[39]

Wage labour was a comparatively 'faceless' form of labour management, and thus may have dovetailed smoothly with the ever greater absenteeism of the great landowners. At the same time, the very size of late Roman estates could create the kind of 'facelessness' which our sources critique. The archaeological record for rural Italy from the fourth to early sixth centuries reveals a picture of increasing differentiation between well-resourced estates and others whose buildings reflect an absence of élite occupation. In the 1970s and 1980s Andrea Carandini's excavation of the rich villa at Settefinestre[40] near Cosa, not far from where Sestius had his vineyards and factory, was crucial in bringing to Italy a stratigraphic archaeology, able to chart how the use of buildings changed over time. The resulting explosion of stratigraphic analysis of rural sites in Italy has made it possible to begin to understand the 'rationalization' of rural holdings by powerful landowners by showing the stages through which an individual property could be 'repositioned' within a larger portfolio.[41]

Some of their estates, it stands to reason, would be relegated to a second- or third-tier role, serving strictly for production rather than for the mix of production, display, and leisure encapsulated in the concept of *otium*.[42] From the fourth century up to the Gothic Wars, fewer (and at least in the fourth century, richer) 'residential villas' are visible in the landscape, at the

---

[39] Lin Foxhall, 'The Dependant Tenant: Land Leasing and Labour in Italy and Greece', *Journal of Roman Studies* 80 (1990), 97–114.

[40] Andrea Carandini, *Settefinestre: una villa schiavistica nell' Etruria Romana*, 3 vols. (Modena, 1985) See also J. T. Smith, 'The Social Structure of Roman Villas', *Oxford Journal of Archaeology* 6 (1987), 243–55.

[41] A weakness of the debate over 'contintuity' and 'catastrophe' as models for the developments of the fifth and sixth century seems to be inadequate attention to the place of an individual property in a portfolio of holdings. Thus Tamara Lewit, '"Vanishing villas": what happened to élite rural habitation in the West in the 5th–6th c?', *JRA* 16 (2003), 260–74, argues that the changes in residential standards were 'cultural'; implicit seems to be an assumption that a single *possessor* could not maintain different properties in his or her portfolio to different standards, depending on whether the owner expected to visit regularly. On 'continuitists' and 'catastrophists' see B. Ward-Perkins, 'Continuitists, Catastrophists and the Towns of Post-Roman Northern Italy', *PBSR* 65 (1997), 157–76, and Kim Bowes and Adam Gutteridge, 'Rethinking the Later Roman Landscape', *JRA* 18 (2005), 405–13.

[42] De Neeve, 'A Roman Landowner and his Estates', 397; see also Alexandra Chavarría Arnau, 'Villas in Hispania during the Fourth and Fifth Centuries', in Kim Bowes and Michael Kulikowski, eds., *Hispania in Late Antiquity: Current Perspectives* (Leiden, 2005), 519–55.

same time as the focal buildings on other properties seem to have been demoted to less exalted purposes, serving for storage, housing for workers, or as the base for non-élite managers in the employ of the *dominus*.[43] Even though the urban *domus* and rural *villa* seem to have become if anything more important as a location for the self-presentation of the great landowners,[44] men and women who possessed dozens of holdings would not have expected personally to visit each of them, and physical absence made it easier for a *dominus* to disregard the human consequences of profit-seeking.[45]

Already in the time of Ambrose and John Chrysostom, Christian bishops took up the task of browbeating the *possessores* whose treatment of their tenants was unworthy of their status as honourable men and women.[46] When we turn to consider the Christian household literature, we will try to capture the climate of moral expectation within which these men and women dealt with their dependents. We will see below that the Christian texts on household management go into some detail about the obligations not of the *servus* to the *dominus* – after all, these would have been obvious – but about those of the *dominus* to the *servus*. It is possible that this emphasis on reciprocity of obligation reflects a contemporary critique of profit strategies such as the hiring of paid seasonal labourers for whom the *dominus* could avoid taking responsibility during the slow season. For this reason it is noticeable that *Ad Gregoriam in palatio*, which bears traces of having been addressed to a *domina* from a family closely allied to the imperial bureacracy, places such a strong emphasis on the *domina* as the mistress of *vernaculi*, slaves raised from birth on her own estate. The *domina* is clearly being held up to an old-fashioned standard of senatorial womanhood. We will return below to consider what effect the author meant to achieve by casting her in this light.

DOMUS AND FAMILIA

We turn now to consider the Roman *domus* as a social rather than an economic institution. We will begin with an overview of the legal situation under the empire. While in Chapter Four we will consider the changes to

[43] Neil Christie, *From Constantine to Charlemagne: An Archaeology of Italy 300–800* (Aldershot, 2006), 429.
[44] Sarah Scott, 'Elites, Exhibitionism and the Society of the Late Roman Villa', in Neil Christie, ed., *Landscapes of Change: Rural Evolutions in Late Antiquity and the Early Middle Ages* (Aldershot, 2004), 39–65.
[45] Sfameni, 'Residential Villas', 365.
[46] Cracco Ruggini, *Economia e società nell' 'Italia annonaria'*, e.g. 26, 87.

family law in late antiquity, the present discussion will introduce ground-rules that remained relatively stable from the time of Augustus to Justinian. For moderns, there are some surprises in the balance of power in the Roman household. The fundamental point to be borne in mind is that property ownership and biological parenthood were deeply interconnected in Roman thinking. We will see below that legitimate authority was understood through the metaphor of a benevolent father and landowner, a person whose paternity could not really be distinguished from his *dominium*. This was the *paterfamilias*, the queen bee around whom the Roman hive was built.

Starting with the *paterfamilias* makes it easier to understand the difference between the two Roman conceptions of the family group, *domus* and *familia*. Both terms could refer either to property or to human kin.[47] But the two had strikingly different meanings. *Familia*, in essence a legal term, cannot be understood apart from the institution of *patria potestas*. The first, and most juridically precise, meaning of *familia* was that of the persons who fell under the *potestas* of the *paterfamilias*. This included both slaves and legitimate children or grandchildren, though in common usage it is also attested as referring to other non-biological dependents or agnatic kin not *in potestate*.[48] It did not include children born outside marriage, unless those children belonged to the *familia* as slaves. This aspect of *familia* as the institution articulating *potestas* was crucial. Indeed, there are instances in which the term refers to the slave *familia* to the exclusion of the biological relatives.[49] Semantic analysis suggests that *familia* assimilates kin to the servile dependency of the *famulus*, rather than the other way round.

Domus meant something rather different. It could mean either a man's wife, children, and domestic slaves, or the extended kindred of which the nuclear group was understood as the core.[50] The *domus* stood as an important symbol within Roman thinking. Unlike *familia*, it could be

---

[47] The Roman jurist Ulpian opens his discussion of the term 'familia' with a citation from the Twelve Tables on patrimony, a restricted legal meaning: Saller, 'Familia, Domus, and the Roman Conception of the Family', 347. By the Empire, *familia* tended to refer to people rather than inanimate property (337–8).

[48] Saller, 'Familia, Domus, and the Roman Conception of the Family', *Phoenix* 38 (1984), 336–55, at 339 and 341. At 341 Saller discusses three exceptions (e.g. Cicero's reference in the *Pro Scauro* to the dignity of Scaurus' *familia*, *gens*, and *nomen*). At 337 he notes that the *Thesaurus Linguae Latinae*, Lewis and Short, and the *Oxford Latin Dictionary* do not distinguish between the cognatic and agnatic situation.

[49] *Familia* could mean either mean kin and slaves or just slaves: Richard P. Saller, *Patriarchy, Property, and Death in the Roman Family* (Cambridge, 1994), 83. *Familia* could be used to denote the slave household specifically – i.e. exclusive of the free biological kin of the *paterfamilias* (Saller, 'Familia, Domus', the Family, 344).

[50] Saller, 'Familia, Domus', 342–3.

used specifically to refer to the free kinship group not including slaves and other dependents. Beginning from its meaning as a physical house or those who reside within it, *domus* could also have an expanded sense of the broad kinship group including cognates as well as agnates.[51]

In its sense as a family group, the *domus* was organized along two principal axes of reciprocal obligation, distinct from the relations of the *familia*. The hierarchy of obligations is summarized by Cicero in *On Duties*: 'First comes the husband–wife bond, then the parent–child, and third the bond of those within the *domus*.'[52] The husband–wife relationship served as the symbolic core of *domus* in its human sense. Even the physical *domus* bore a symbolic link to the *coniuges* or husband–wife pair. Legally, the *coniuges* would establish a principal residence, 'the place where they established the *lar* for the marriage'.[53] The second axis of obligation was that between parents and children. The historians recorded with praise instances of exceptional *pietas* for or loyalty to a parent.[54] Both fathers and mothers took responsibility for educating the child. Punishment of the child was intended as having an educative function, and excessive humiliation of the *filius* could undermine the socialization for which the parents were responsible.[55]

The different aspects of *familia* can be seen in the lineage terminology of consanguinity (*cognatio* and *agnatio* – though the latter in a jural rather than a biological way) and affinity, or kinship by marriage (*adfinitas*).[56] The elaboration of the legal concept *familia* was driven by a concern for the rights of the *paterfamilias* and his legitimate heirs, especially in cases of

---

[51] Saller, '*Familia, Domus*', 342.
[52] Cicero *De officiis* 1.58; for discussion, see Saller, '*Familia, Domus*', 344.
[53] On the location of *lar* and account books as criterion for principal residence, see Saller, *Patriarchy, Property, and Death*, 81.
[54] Saller, '*Pietas*, Obligation and Authority', 399–401.
[55] Saller, '*Pietas*, Obligation and Authority', 404–5 (discipline of sons by fathers), Saller, *Patriarchy, Property, and Death*, 73 (distinction between treatment of children and that of slaves), and Saller, '*Familia, Domus*', 343 (citing Seneca *De ira* 3.35.1): 'Seneca castigates the man who complains of the loss of *libertas* in the *res publica*, but then destroys it in his own *domus* by forbidding his slave, freedman, wife, or client to talk back to him.'
[56] Roman *cognatio* and *agnatio* were asymmetrical. *Cognatio* was the general term for blood kinship, referring to kin whether through the paternal or maternal line, and whether they were members of the same *familia* or not. Its binary opposite was *adfinitas*, kinship through marriage. *Agnatio*, by contrast, referred to the specific jural relationship that existed between a *paterfamilias* and his children born from a legitimate marriage, or other dependents introduced through adoption or *coemptio*. *Agnatio* was recognized through seven degrees (including both lineal degrees upwards or downwards, and lateral through siblings who shared the same father). Definitions of *agnatio* and *cognatio* as the Romans understood them are found in Gaius, *Institutes*, 1.156; see Suzanne Dixon, 'The Marriage Alliance in the Roman Élite', *Journal of Family History* 10 (1985), 353–78, at 361–2 and 372.

intestate succession.[57] The value of contiguity, the bond of reciprocal obligation based on cohabitation, was not reflected in a specific legal concept.[58] But the importance of contiguity is clear when we turn to consider the term *domus*. While *familia* refers to male lineage and to ownership, two relational aspects of the position of the *paterfamilias*, *domus* represented the alternate relation of cohabitation and contiguity. But in general the reciprocal bond of cohabitation seems to have been subsumed within the wider Roman concern for reciprocity, or within the notion of *pietas* where family members were concerned. *Domus* meant 'house' or 'household' both in the sense of a building and of the people within it, in both concrete and symbolic terms. In contrast to *familia*, *domus* represented the household as a lived social reality, and it was in fact the crucial unit in the pyramid of social order.

A household was ideally headed by a married couple. Where Roman sources wished to specify what we would call the nuclear unit they would refer to a man's wife and children, his *coniunx liberique*. Richard Saller and Brent Shaw argued two decades ago that the *coniunx liberique* formed the basis of Roman cohabitation.[59] In other words, the Romans did not always live in the extended kinship groups imagined by an earlier generation of scholars, although the additional presence of servile and other non-kin dependents could lead to large numbers nonetheless.[60]

---

[57] Even where there was a will, children could argue that it was impious if it did not leave them the 'share of piety' – at least one fourth of what would come to them if the estate were divided equally among surviving offspring. See Saller, '*Pietas*, Obligation and Authority', 401.

[58] On the repercussions of contiguity for the slave *familia*, see Marleen Boudreau Flory, 'Family in *familia*: Kinship and Community in Slavery', *American Journal of Ancient History* 3 (1978), 78–95. It is clear that this bond was recognized, reflected for example in the fact that Roman law exerted more stringent control over a master's treatment of the *vernaculus*, or slave born within his own *domus*, than over one who entered the *familia* after birth.

[59] Richard P. Saller and Brent Shaw, 'Tombstones and Roman Family Relations in the Principate: Civilians, Soliders, and Slaves', *JRS* 74 (1984), 124–56. The methodology employed in this study has recently been challenged by Dale B. Martin, 'The Construction of the Ancient Family: Methodological Considerations', *JRS* 86 (1996) 40–60.

[60] The most useful studies on this subject tend to derive from the earlier empire. Bruce W. Frier, 'Demography', in Alan K. Bowman, Peter Garnsey, and Dominic Rathbone, eds., *Cambridge Ancient History* 12, *The High Empire, AD 70–192*, (Cambridge, 2000), 787–816, at 807: 'The egyptian census returns provide the only secure evidence as to the ordinary household size and structure in the early empire. In complete or nearly complete returns the average household was smaller than might be anticipated: about 4.3 family members.' See, however, Andrew Wallace-Hadrill, 'Houses and Households: Sampling Pompei and Herculaneum', in Beryl Rawson, ed., *Marriage, Divorce, and Children in Ancient Rome* (Canberra and Oxford, 1991), 191–227, at 197, with an interesting discussion at 217 of the others – lodgers, guests, freedmen and clients – envisaged by the legal sources as part of the domestic establishment.

The lack of inter-generational cohabitation was in part the result of demography – Saller has estimated that only a quarter of Roman men would have a living father by the time they married around age 25, the average male age of marriage – and in part the result of a tendency among aristocrats to fund independent residences for mature sons even when the father was still living.[61] Important here is the institution of *emancipatio*, through which an adult child could be granted status *sui iuris*, as a legal person in his or her own right, rather than *in potestate*, a legal dependent of the *paterfamilias*. Until the age of 25, emancipated or fatherless adult children would be subject to guardianship (*tutela*) by a paternal relative appointed by the *paterfamilias* either at the time of emancipation or through his will.[62] Even children *in potestate* could be assigned a *peculium* which allowed them to live more or less independently.

THE *DOMINA* AS FEMALE *PATERFAMILIAS*

The habit of the 'neutral masculine' in Roman legal thought – as in the Latin language – meant that the position of women was sometimes not explicitly thought out. This is particularly true where the definition of the role of the *materfamilias* is concerned. Indeed, as Richard Saller has shown, the term *paterfamilias* itself in many legal sources clearly refers to a property-owning head of household who was not only not necessarily a father, but also not necessarily a man.[63] At her father's death or after *emancipatio*, a woman would, like her brothers, be *sui iuris* and able to hold property in her own right.[64]

The legal sources clearly understand the independent female landowner as implicitly accorded many of the rights defining the powers of the *paterfamilias*.[65] Given the two aspects of the position of the *paterfamilias*, ownership and male lineage, magistrates were expected to be – and almost

---

[61] Richard P. Saller, '*Patria Potestas* and the Stereotype of the Roman Family,' *Continuity and Change* 1 (1986), 7–22, at 13 and 17. Since Saller's numbers are derived largely from epigraphic sources, they are probably most directly relevant to the prosperous end of the property-owning classes, which is to say the same 'normative' but limited group envisioned in the law codes.

[62] From the third century, the age of majority was 25, but 'after 324 boys aged 20 and girls of 18 were allowed to request *venia aetatis*, that is, a personally granted majority (*CTh* 2.17.1)', Arjava, *Women and Law*, 117.

[63] Richard P. Saller, '*Pater familias, Mater familias*, and the Gendered Semantics of the Roman Household', *Classical Philology* 94 (1999), 182–97, on how in common parlance 'paterfamilias' actually meant 'landowner'; see also Antti Arjava, 'Paternal Power in Late Antiquity', *Journal of Roman Studies* 88 (1998), 147–65.

[64] See Arjava, 'Paternal Power', 161–3 on *emancipatio*.

[65] Saller, '*Pater familias, Mater familias*', 182–97.

certainly were – able without difficulty to apply a gender-neutral definition of *paterfamilias* where ownership was concerned, with a gender-specific definition where lineage was involved.

There is no distinct term for the wife of a *paterfamilias* who was not a *paterfamilias* in her own right, although this may have been the original meaning of *materfamilias*. Pauli Festus gives marriage to a *paterfamilias* as the defining characteristic of a *materfamilias*, but Ulpian followed a broader definition, concentrating on the honour and moral stature signified by the term.

> We ought to take *materfamilias* to mean a woman who does not live dishonourably; it is morals which distinguish and separate the *materfamilias* from all other women. So it will make no difference whether she is married or widowed or divorced, free-born or freedwoman: for it is not marriage or birth which makes a *materfamilias* but good morals.[66]

Thus *materfamilias* must be distinguished from the term *matrona* which, by contrast, referred exclusively to a woman established in an honourable marriage.[67]

Roman law distinguished between three distinct corpora of property in the household. The first corpus of property was that of the male head of household or *paterfamilias*. The second was that of the *materfamilias*, which remained in her own or her father's power throughout the marriage, or in some instances under that of a guardian (*tutor*) who by law could not be her husband.[68] The third corpus was the wife's *dos* or dowry, of which the husband had usufruct for the duration of the marriage, but which was returned at the end of the marriage to the wife, her father, or her heirs (as specified in the nuptial contract).

Since each corpus of property could in theory include any configuration of land, buildings, slaves, and moveable goods, the balance of authority and responsibility between the *paterfamilias* and *materfamilias* in a household where both were present would depend on the terms on which each entered the union. The *materfamilias* could and did administer her own estate, which might include business interests and agency as *patronus* to a retinue

---

[66] 'Matrem familias accipere debemus eam, quae non inhoneste vixit: matrem enim familias a ceteris feminis mores discernunt atque separant. Proinde nihil intererit, nupta sit an vidua, ingenua sit an libertina: nam neque nuptiae neque natales faciunt matrem familias, sed boni mores' (*Digest* 50.16.46.1, *lix ad edictum*); see discussion in Susan Treggiari, *Roman Marriage: Iusti Coniuges from the Time of Cicero to the Time of Ulpian* (Oxford, 1991), 280.

[67] Treggiari, *Roman Marriage*, 279.

[68] Arjava, *Women and Law*, 114–18, argues that by the mid-third century *tutela* of women had largely disappeared; while both male and female minors would normally be under *tutela* to age 25.

of clients. Estimates on female property ownership in late antiquity differ dramatically, from one sixth of the total of privately held property to nearly a half.[69] In theory, there is no reason the higher figure could not be correct, since Roman inheritance law did not privilege sons over daughters, but in practice men had fuller access to the institutions and informal opportunities through which wealth could be accumulated.[70] The *materfamilias* was typically the sole representative of her own *familia* in the husband's *domus*, and this fact may be one reason why substantial legal rights were accorded to women as property-owners.

There was a strong moral expectation that the husband should provide a home for his wife,[71] and indeed *deductio in domum*, the physical removal of the bride from her father's house to that of her husband, was a symbolically central aspect of the Roman marriage ritual.[72] But among the very rich more than one residence was always in play, and not all belonged to the husband. There seems to have been no rule about how the households of *materfamilias* and *paterfamilias* should be merged in practical terms – decisions about whose house(s) to occupy, and whose slaves should perform what function, seem to have been made on the basis of individual preference and, perhaps more importantly, the balance of power between the two families. Normally, the husband and wife were united in marriage *sine manu*, which is to say that it did not follow the republican custom of transferring the bride to her husband's *familia*. Generally the *materfamilias* was either *sui iuris* (if her father were dead or she had been emancipated) or under her father's (or grandfather's) *potestas*. Either a man or woman could

---

[69] Roger S. Bagnall suggests that women owned 'somewhere between one-sixth and one-quarter' of land in Egypt (*Egypt in Late Antiquity* (Princeton, 1993), 130–3), while Arjava, *Women and Law*, 71, suggests that 'somewhere between 30 and 45 per cent of the total is possible and any figure under 25 per cent seems unlikely'. However, Arjava notes that his figure applies only to the upper classes, and accepts Bagnall's estimate for the villages. For an earlier period, Janne Pölönen, 'The Division of Wealth between Men and Women in Roman Succession (ca. 50 BC–AD 250)', in Päivi Setälä *et al.*, *Women, Wealth, and Power in the Roman Empire* (Rome, 2002), 147–79, suggests (at 178) that under the Principate, women inherited ca. 40 per cent of the total value of recorded bequests. She cites Päivi Setälä, *Private Domini in Roman Brick Stamps of the Empire* (Rome, 1977) as arguing that in Rome itself a third of landowners were female, rising to 50 per cent under the reign of Antoninus Pius. In her contrbution, 'Women and Brick Production – Some New Aspects', to Setälä *et al.*, *Women, Wealth, and Power*, 181–201, Setälä demonstrates that a proportion of female wealth was accumulated through the success of female-owned businesses rather than through inheritance.

[70] On the repercussions for women of the law of Roman inheritance, see Arjava, *Women and Law*, 62–75, esp. 70.

[71] Treggiari, *Roman Marriage*, 332–40.

[72] A useful overview of Roman *deductio* is included in Philip Lyndon Reynolds, *Marriage in the Western Church: The Christianization of Marriage during the Patristic and Early Medieval Periods* (Leiden, 1994), 32–4.

act as sole head of household if *sui iuris*, and indeed more than one head of household could be accommodated in a marriage structure where the estates of husband and wife were kept distinct.

We have already seen that both *paterfamilias* and *materfamilias* could own estates in their own right, and that in its meaning as a property-owner the term *paterfamilias* referred not to a biological father but to an individual who could be male or female and might or might not in fact have children. The 'neutral masculine' reflected the Roman assumption that the normative property-owner was both male and the father of legitimate children, and we may suspect that the power of property-owners who were also fathers benefited as result. But when we think of the Roman *domina* on whom Christian writers set their sights, we must think of her as a formidable personage, the daughter of a powerful father, and the mistress, in her own right, of a handsome patrimony. Otherwise, we will misunderstand the efforts of others to guide her in exercising her power.

OBLIGATION AND RECIPROCITY: THE BOBBIO *DOMINA*

Along with the letter to the enigmatic Gregoria, another text addressed to a Christian *domina* survives, an anonymous manual of instruction for a Roman *matrona* preserved in Bobbio. This text offers a similar vision to that of *Ad Gregoriam*, although couched in less studied language. Both texts shed light on the *ethos* of the senatorial *domina*, and on obligations to slave and free dependents, offering an insight into social expections of the Christian landowner instead of the more practical advice on managing crops and livestock to be found in better-known texts on estate management such as the roughly contemporary fifth-century *Opus agriculturae* of Palladius.[73] Indeed, the texts do not make it clear whether we are meant to imagine the *domina* in her urban *domus* or on her rural estate, although a *domina* of the kind to whom the texts were addressed would certainly have possessed both.

In the idealistic proposals for the relationship between a *domina* and her subordinates, we can see the outlines of a way of thinking about the relationship between power and obligation. The Christian manuals make frequent use of the term 'servus' – slave – and other terms, 'vernaculus',

---

[73] It is worth noting that Palladius himself steers clear of the issue of labour management, on the grounds that regional and crop variations would require different approaches to the problem. See Domenico Vera, 'Dalla "Villa perfecta" alla villa di Palladio: sulle trasformazioni del sistema agrario in Italia fra Principato e Dominato', *Athenaeum* 83 (1995), 189–211 and 331–56.

'ancilla', associated with slavery. We will see below that the emphasis on the *domina* surrounded by slaves may in fact be an attempt to call up a tableau of traditional senatorial femininity.

The old Roman tradition had maintained fairly uniform views on the subject of aristocratic conduct with regard to dependents. Whether individual persons lived up to the ideal or not – and one must assume that they often did not – it is important to understand what was *perceived* as ideal nonetheless, since differing ideas of perfection had differing social consequences. Central to this tradition was the buttressing of aristocratic privilege by a balanced system of reciprocal obligations. These lines of reciprocity strengthened the 'vertical' relationships within the hierarchy, fostering cross-class loyalty and cohesion.

Most men and women in power were well aware that there was an 'invisible line' beyond which the systematic skimming off of the surplus generated by those beneath them in the social hierarchy would backfire. This was Roman *aequitas* as defined by the philosophers and in the law codes; the sense that the pressure put on subordinates by their superiors must be orderly, even if it was hard to bear.[74] We should not forget the importance of *aequitas* in a society whose hierarchy was as steeply raked as that of late antiquity, for it was one of the supports on which the claim to legitimate authority was based. While no one would argue that the Roman slave system did not involve cruelty – indeed Keith Hopkins has suggested that cruelty to slaves was so completely accepted as to go virtually unnoticed[75] – there were nonetheless limits. If a slave believed himself to be mistreated by a senatorial *dominus*, for example, he could bring his case to the Urban Prefect of Rome, the magistrate who had responsibility for domestic complaints against senators.[76] When Christian writers pointedly called attention to the obligations of masters to slaves, they were among other things reminding their listeners of the public shame awaiting those who went too far.

---

[74] Saller, *Patriarchy, Property, and Death*, 73; see also Richard P. Saller, 'The Hierarchical Household in Roman Society: A Study of Domestic Slavery', in Michael Bush, ed., *Serfdom and Slavery: Studies in Legal Bondage* (London, 1996), 112–29, and idem, 'Corporal Punishment, Authority, and Obedience in the Roman Household', in Beryl Rawson, ed., *Marriage, Divorce, and Children in Ancient Rome* (Oxford, 1991), 124–56.

[75] Keith Hopkins, "Novel Evidence for Roman Slavery', *Past and Present* 138 (1993), 3–27.

[76] André Chastagnol, *La Préfecture urbaine à Rome sous le Bas-Empire* (Paris, 1960), 111 n. 3 discusses the cases in which a slave can appeal to the urban prefect if mistreated by his master. See also Peter Birks, 'The Roman Law Concept of Dominium and the Idea of Absolute Ownership', *Acta Juridica* (1985), 1–37, at 18, on the right of mistreated slaves to seek sanctuary at a temple or statue of the emperor.

We are safe in imagining that the author of *Ad Gregoriam in palatio* and others like him had noticed more than one troubling shadow cast across the senatorial ethos of their day, by writers who thought that 'real' Christians should cultivate a distance from 'worldliness'. An alarming number of sources, for example, had contrived to speak well of the brazen scion of the Valerii, Pinian, a man who had defied his own family and even the *praefectus urbi* in the matter of responsible estate management. Pinian had flaunted his lack of *pietas* for his forebears, and his contempt for his moral obligation as a *dominus*, by attempting to sell off the inherited slaves serving in at least one major establishment without offering first refusal to a relative who would see to their protection and employ them in the way to which they were accustomed.[77] On that occasion, Pinian's brother Severus resolved the impasse by buying the slaves with a promise to fulfil their expectations, but we have to reconstruct the brother's actions from a hostile source, the *Life* of Pinian's wife Melania the Younger, which naturally takes Pinian's side. The *Life of Melania* celebrates Pinian's contempt for worldly responsibility, although it nonetheless furnishes enough detail to see why his slaves and relatives might be inclined to criticize.[78] Even his admirers did not claim that Pinian had much sympathy for the dependents who stood as an obstacle to his unworldliness.

I have suggested in Chapter One that from a traditional point of view, it would have seemed obvious that the new ascetic ideals of 'unworldliness' involved something like hypocrisy when practised by the very rich.[79] The defenders of Christian paternalism may or may not have believed that there was a grain of truth in the ascetic critique of private property. But they believed that owners were bound by duty to place the well-being of the dependents of an estate ahead of their own desire to be free of responsibility.

The discussion of obligation to dependents which we find in the household manuals may thus represent an attempt to defend the traditional

[77] For penetrating discussion of the obligations to which Pinian's slaves called attention, see the Claude Lepelley, 'Mélanie la Jeune entre Rome, la Sicilia, et l'Afrique: les effets socialement pernicieux d'une forme extrême de l'ascétisme', in *Atti del IX congresso internazionale di studi sulla Sicilia antica* (*Kokalos* 43–4, 1997–8) 1.1, 15–32. Also valuable are Andrea Giardina, 'Carità eversiva: le donazioni di Melania la giovane e gli equilibri della società tardoromana', *Studi storici* 29 (1988), 127–42, and G. A. Cecconi, 'Un evergete mancato: Piniano a Ippona', *Athenaeum* 66 (1988), 371–89.

[78] Kate Cooper, 'The Household and the Desert: Monastic and Biological Communities in the *Lives* of Melania the Younger', in Anneke Mulder-Bakker and Jocelyn Wogan-Browne, eds., *Household, Women, and Christianities in Late Antiquity and the Middle Ages* (Leiden, 2005), 91–107.

[79] See also Kate Cooper, 'Poverty, Obligation, and Inheritance: Roman Heiresses and the Varieties of Senatorial Christianity in Fifth-century Rome', in Kate Cooper and Julia Hillner, eds., *Religion, Dynasty, and Patronage in Early Christian Rome, 300–900* (Cambridge, 2007), 165–89.

domina from attack on two fronts. On the one hand, it was important to make the case for estate management as a worthy, and even an indispensable Christian vocation, since the ascetic movement threatened to dissuade exactly the kind of men and women who would bring honour to the role from wishing to take it on. At the same time, there were always more than enough aspiring landlords waiting for their opportunity to grab what others were reluctant to keep. From the point of view of the slaves and tenants, it was no cause for rejoicing if the Christian scions of old families, concerned that there was little spiritual merit in ruling their estates justly, decided to sell them on to the kind of people who were looking to buy rather than to sell. Even if the proceeds were given to a good cause, for those attached to the land it was out of the frying pan and into the fire.

To gain a sense of the viewpoint of Pinian's critics, we will turn to one of our conduct manuals for Christian *dominae*, the now fragmentary treatise on the governance of the household preserved in a manuscript held at Bobbio until the early modern period, when it was divided between Vienna and Milan.[80] The two parts were identified in the early 1990s as deriving from the same exemplar.[81] Although the first page is still missing and the text is therefore anonymous, it can be dated to the reign of Honorius thanks to a reference to a consular year and indiction in the explicit.[82] Unlike the more literary *Ad Gregoriam in palatio*, which survives in a handful of medieval copies, the text contained in the Bobbio manuscript is not otherwise attested.

It is worth considering what we know about this manuscript's production and survival in some detail, because it illustrates the perilous transmission history of texts that were not perceived as being of ascetic, literary, or administrative importance. Its survival in a damaged state serves as a chilling illustration of how much was left to chance in the transmission of ancient sources. The format of the exemplar itself is of interest, in that it has

---

[80] Germain Morin, 'Fragments pélagiens inédits du manuscrit 954 de Vienne', *RBen* 3 (1922), 265–75.

[81] Mirella Ferrari, 'In margine ai Codices latini antiquiores: spigolature ambrosiane del sec. VIII', in A. Lehner and W. Berschin, eds., *Lateinische Kultur im VIII. Jahrhundert: Traube Gedenkschrift* (St Ottilien, 1990), 59–78. The text of the restored letter was subsequently edited by Yves-Marie Duval, 'La Lettre de direction (acéphale) à une mere de famille du MS 954 de Vienne (CPL) 755: édition des divers fragments dans leur ordre original', in Michel Soetard, ed., *Valeurs dans le stoïcisme: du Portique à nos jours* (Lille, 1993), 203–43.

[82] 'Die XIII mensis aprilis Honorio III Lu III indictione XIIII'. This reference does not 'line up' properly with the surviving consular lists, although it is safe to assign the text to the reign of Honorius (395–423 AD). A third consulate is attested for Honorius in 396, but his colleague in that year was his brother Arcadius. Although a Lucius is attested as consul in the early fifth century, no official whose name began with *Lu* is recorded as having held the office at the same time as Honorius. See Roger S. Bagnall, Alan Cameron, and Seth R. Schwartz, eds., *Consuls of the later Roman Empire* (Atlanta, 1987), s.v. 396

survived in an unbound quaternion which has, since the early modern period, been kept in a parchment envelope. Copied in an eighth-century minuscule hand in northern Italy, possibly but not certainly at Bobbio where its existence can first be traced, the surviving manuscript cannot be precisely dated, but it nonetheless stands as an important link in the chain establishing continuity from the fifth- and sixth-century treatises for the laity through to the revival of the genre in the Carolingian period.[83] To be sure, its importance lies partly in its illustration of why our evidence for lay élites is so slim, and how a multitude of other texts of a similar nature could have been written, yet failed to survive.

The fact that the acephalous Bobbio letter's known transmission has been as an independent pamphlet is in itself significant, and raises the very interesting, though speculative, possibility that the eighth-century exemplar was copied specifically for use by a householder, perhaps a laywoman of a station comparable to that of the original addressee. Since shorter texts were normally either copied directly into compilation volumes or (if copied individually) bound in with other texts to make up a more substantial volume, it seems reasonable to suspect that the free-standing pamphlet copy may have been made so that a larger volume, now lost, was not out of circulation for the sake of a single short text, if that text were to be lent or given to (or indeed, had been commissioned by) a lay householder. Another point of interest concerns the parchment onto which the text is copied. The eighth-century minuscule is written over a scraped fifth- or sixth-century uncial text of Proverbs. Given the high cost of writing materials, it seems fitting that an exemplar designed for lay use should have been consigned to palimpsested parchment. The social status of such an exemplar would of course have differed substantially from the illuminated books of hours which are associated with noblewomen in the later Middle Ages, but in the early medieval context even a manuscript of comparatively plain materials and workmanship would have been recognized as an object of prestige.

The acephalous Bobbio letter brings together the concerns of a manual of spiritual instruction with those of a treatise on household management, so that the reader's own spiritual progress is presented as inseparable from the well-being of those whose earthly life takes place within the sphere of

---

[83] There is a logic to the letter's having found its way into the collection at Bobbio, since it is one of the few monasteries for which we can document substantial testation of book collections by lay donors in the early Middle Ages; see Claudia Villa, 'Cultura e scrittura nell'Italia longobarda. Renovatio e translatio: centri amministrativi ed eredità culturale', in Walter Pohl and Peter Erhardt, eds. *Die Langobarden: Herrschaft und Identität* (Vienna, 2005), 502–23, at 510–11.

her authority. It is clear that its anonymous author means both to defend marriage and the biological household, and to offer a critique of the most shrill proponents of asceticism.

The letter begins with a meditation on the distinction between real and sham virtue, warning that it is far better to be virtuous without seeming to, than to seem virtuous without being so. Next comes the importance of moderation in one's ascetic practice – not only is there the danger of not being able to sustain a pattern of fasting which is too arduous, but there is also the danger that over-ambitious practices will attract a kind of admiration which threatens the reader's spiritual progress. Since the intended reader is explicitly a wife and mother, and there is no reference to a vow of continence, we are safe in assuming that the anonymous author wanted to propose at least limited ascetic practice as an ideal for sexually active married householders. Fasting and abstinence are praised as a means toward cooling the heat of an immoderate *libido*, but it is *pietas*, not fasting and abstinence, which 'holds the promise of present and future life'.[84]

The writer then goes on to encourage the reader to think not of how intense a fast she can sustain, but rather of seeing that those who have too little to eat are given nourishment.[85] This contrast introduces a substantial section on the care of the poor. Those who devote themselves to the service of the needy, he reminds her, will hear Christ's blessing, 'I was hungry and you gave me to eat' (Matthew 25: 35), while those who have merely looked to their own fasting and abstinence will be denied it: 'for God does not delight so much in our own fasting as in seeing us offer nourishment to those who fast from necessity.'[86] She is reminded that if she fasts with moderation, she will be able to carry on with prayer, abstinence, reading, and chanting the psalter, rather than diminishing her accomplishments to a single action which is itself imperilled by excess: this is a far cry from the spirituality of the desert, and much closer to Augustine's admonition that the married woman may successfully imitate the wife-martyr Crispina, even while the virgin, who sets her sights on the more splendid example of the arch-virgin Thecla, encounters a failure brought on by her own arrogance.[87]

The Bobbio *domina* is encouraged to occupy herself so entirely with doing good, that there is simply no opportunity for doing evil. Similarly,

---

[84] *Acephalous Bobbio letter*, section 3 (Duval, 217).
[85] Cf. Isaiah 58, Conrad Leyser, *Authority and Asceticism from Augustine to Gregory the Great* (Oxford, 2000), 169 n. 36.
[86] *Acephalous Bobbio letter*, section 4 (Duval, 219).
[87] Augustine, *De sancta virginitate* 45 (*CSEL* 41, 290).

she should teach her tongue the habit of speaking only of the good, in order that there is no danger of speaking evil. She should know that her thoughts are more patent to God than her actions are to other people, so there is no use in thinking that evil thoughts are acceptable as long as they do not lead to evil actions. On the other hand, it is also important that she make certain that her good intentions are known through good actions. The pagans should not be given a pretext for slandering the Christians on account of her behaviour. Certainly, virtue can expect to encounter slander from those who envy it. But ideally, she should live so irreproachably, that anyone who speaks ill of her finds that no one believes him.

This leads to a section on backbiting. Our writer notes that it is common among men, and even more so among women: 'they believe that they are calling attention to their own virtue if they denigrate that of another,'[88] and the truly virtuous are seen as an object for scorn rather than as an example from which to learn. The true Christian will not engage in this kind of discussion even by listening. She may take consolation that, in refusing to listen, she is made noble not only by her human lineage but also by the reflection of her soul's divine origin. She does no harm, by contrast, if she believes good that has wrongly been said of another, so it is better to err in believing the vicious virtuous than the virtuous vicious.

When we come to the treatment of children and slaves, we see that the responsibility to them is not dissimilar. For children, it is important to remember that the greatest legacy to them is not riches, but the life of justice. The mother is the example on whom their character will be formed. For slaves, she must remember that affection, not rigour, is crucial to her task. As *materfamilias* she should be as a mother to all in the household – a mother rather than a mistress (*domina*). Her authority is encompassed by a greater Christian purpose, since it is God who is master of both slave and owner. Since a true Christian causes no harm even to the helpless, the government of slaves is the ultimate test of her progress in virtue.

The Bobbio *domina*'s dignity is invoked repeatedly in the sections which follow. She should refuse to swear an oath, preferring rather to live so patently honest a life that none should dare to ask her to do so. Only where there is mistrust is an oath relevant. Similarly, when she avoids the vices of hate, of jealousy, of speaking evil and mendacity, she should remember that it is not Christianity which bans them but *honestas ipsa*, the virtue of the aristocrat whether pagan or Christian. Yet it was for this that Jesus himself came to earth. Our writer cites the words of 1 Peter, 'Christ suffered for

---

[88] *Acephalous Bobbio letter*, section 8 (Duval, 223).

you; he left you an example, so that you could follow in his footsteps, he who committed no sin and in whose mouth no evil word was found . . .'[89] Just as the mother provides an example to the child, so Christ himself, in his suffering, offers an example to the mother; following this example is the price of being a Christian in deed and not merely in name. This identity with the suffering Christ is not, however, seen in opposition to the aristocratic values of honour and glory. Rather, the two streams have flowed into one: the reader is asked to remember that she is now a daughter of God, and must live in such a way as to bring honour to his lineage.

Our writer turns next to Matthew's metaphor of the Two Ways. The route toward immortality and incorruptibility is narrow and arduous, but this, rather than the wide and easy path to eternal death, is the path which must be trod. No one is more in danger of failing to reach the reward of eternal life than the rich and illustrious; the fact that they are accustomed to glory will make their fall all the harder. To make his point all the clearer, he poses the hypothetical question, if you were told that half of your life would be in suffering and poverty, and the other half in joy and plenty, would you not choose to endure the difficult half first, knowing the contrast would make the second half all the sweeter? This, of course, is the basis on which she should look to secure her position in the afterlife rather than the present world. This means not only ridding herself of vice, but establishing virtue in its place: she is reminded that the Psalmist says not only 'turn away from evil,' but 'turn away from evil, and do good.'[90]

In the final sections, our writer addresses the question of how his reader can be sure of renouncing evil successfully, and of finding herself able really to do good. His answer is that she should harness the force of habit. If she cultivates in herself a hatred of vice, a day will come when not only does she not wish to do evil, but she simply cannot do it. Similarly, if she takes up the habit of doing good, she will find that what seemed difficult has now become easy. Thus the steep and narrow path to virtue will seem less and less arduous. He closes with a few words of flattery for his addressee, and asks her forgiveness for offering counsel which is less advanced than the life which she is already leading.

A number of things can be said about the advice given to the Bobbio *domina*. The first is that it represents an attempt to consider seriously the obligations of a *domina* toward those who depend on her, by contrast to other letters of spiritual advice which focus more narrowly on the spiritual

---

[89] *Acephalous Bobbio letter*, section 14 (Duval, 231), citing 1 Peter 2: 21–4.
[90] *Acephalous Bobbio letter*, section 20 (Duval, 241), citing Psalm 36: 27.

well-being of the addressee. It is intriguing to think that the text was written during the reign of Honorius, roughly a decade before the incident between Pinian and his brother over the fate of Pinian's slaves. One imagines that the author of the acephalous Bobbio leter would have stood firmly in the camp of Pinian's critics; while there is no way of knowing his identity, or that of the *domina* whom he addressed, it is reasonably safe to pencil them in on the side of his more conservative brother Severus.

We should also take note of the Bobbio letter's seeming Augustinianism – the emphasis on moderation and the force of habit, and on the greater value of certain commitment to modest aims than of extravagant gestures that do not really amount to anything. These ideas would become commonplaces in the Christian literature for the laity, although at the turn of the fifth century when the Bobbio manual was written, they were perhaps less familiar. We will see below that *Ad Gregoriam* develops many of the same themes.

SLAVES AND MASTERS: *AD GREGORIAM IN PALATIO*

In turning to *Ad Gregoriam*, we should not be misled by its operatic quality into overestimating its originality. Where it differs from the acephalous Bobbio letter written roughly a century earlier is primarily in its cultural register, rather than the nature of the advice given. This said, its repeated use of the personages and rituals of a great court as the basis for its metaphorical scheme suggests a readership of wives and daughters of men well established in the imperial *militia*, and this, too, is significant. We are squarely, now, in the territory of the families whose power expanded, rather than waned, during the fifth century.

Advice on the *domina*'s relationsihp with dependents is concentrated in two substantial chapters, 18 and 19, on the management of slaves. These chapters reflect the balancing act of the *domina*'s position with striking clarity. On the one hand, she looks to God in expectation of mercy and in fear of judgement. On the other she looks to those who depend on her, and is expected to offer to them the same justice and clemency which she herself hopes for from God.[91] As an opening gambit in his discussion on the *domina*'s duty with regard to her slaves, John reminds Gregoria that as she

---

[91] *Ad Gregoriam* 19 (*CC* 25A, 228–9) evokes the passage in the Lord's Prayer where God is asked to 'forgive your debts as you forgive your slave's'.

sits at her wool-work with her handmaids, the Devil hovers nearby, waiting for his opportunity to catch her if she forgets herself.

For that age-old snake is artful in undermining the mercy by which God sees fit to protect us from the great temptations, and he goads you with the slightest provocations, by which, God forbid, you may be induced to violate God's laws. And directly, if you open well the ears of your discretion, you will hear him thus stirring up against you a dispute before God: 'Why do you take this one (fem) away from my dominion, and add her to the number of holy women? You attach to the company of your attendants one whom you see slighting your teachings on account of a single thread (*per unum filum*), whom the cares of the mortal more than of the divine life concern, whose hands the crafting of human attire occupies more than the study of the holy writings (*lectio divina*).'[92]

Tucked discretely within the reference to the Garden of Eden here are three electrifying words, *per unum filum*, which raise a spectre to chill the blood of a Roman *materfamilias*. For what John means to do, very cautiously, is to invoke the iconic tableau of the Republican *materfamilias* surrounded by her handmaids with spindle and distaff as the standard against which the *domina*'s failings will be judged.[93] Not only, he warns, may Gregoria fail to exhibit the valour of a Lucretia; the moral failure that awaits her may be impossibly, pathetically trivial. But it will not go unnoticed.

Throughout the chapters on slave management, John reflects and develops the metaphor of both household and divine authority modelled on the pattern of biological parenthood. The mistress acts as a *mater* to her slaves, mirroring the fact that God plays the role of *pater* where she herself is concerned. This of course reflects a long tradition of interpreting hierarchical relationships in this way. By comparison with the Bobbio letter above, we notice in *Ad Gregoriam* a glaring lack of emphasis on biological children, a striking omission given that the assimilation of marriage and reproduction in Roman thought was so complete.[94] But the metaphor of maternal authority prevails nonetheless.

This section of the text follows directly after John's analysis of the relation between wives and husbands – a discussion to which we will return in the next chapter – but the husband is noticeably absent here. Gregoria is

---

[92] *Ad Gregoriam* 18 (*CC* 25A, 224–5). See Jacques Rousse, '*Lectio divina* et lecture spirituelle', *DSp* 9 (1976), 470–510.

[93] On the ideological charge of representations of women and wool-working, see Kristina Milnor, *Gender, Domesticity, and the Age of Augustus: Inventing Private Life* (Oxford, 2005), 29–30.

[94] The only reference to children is in the final chapter: 'Finally – before all else – Christ has in you a handmaid, the Church a worshipper, [your] husband a sweetheart, [your] children a teacher', *Ad Gregoriam* 25 (*CC* 25A, 243).

clearly understood first of all in these chapters as heiress and *domina*, rather than as a wife. Similarly, when John considers what obligations may be pulling her away from Christian duties, it is the *maiores* – the *domina*'s ancestors – who are invoked. In keeping with an important stream of Christian tradition, the *maiores* are to be honoured only within limits – or only according to a specific, inflected interpretation of *pietas*.[95]

We should not underestimate the *potestas* that such a person as Gregoria could exercise, not only over slaves, but also over a retinue of dependents and clients at different levels of the social scale. If she was rich enough, her will could be felt by nations. We need only think of Theudis, Theoderic's regent in the Visigothic kingdom after 511, who if we can believe Procopius was able in the 530s to make a successful bid for the kingship in large part because his anonymous wife, a Roman heiress, was able to raise a personal army of 2,000 men from her estates.[96] Understandably, every attempt was made by kings and churchmen to guide the hand of such powerful *dominae*, and there is no particular reason to think that the women themselves were docile about being guided. Less exceptional than the wife of Theudis would have been the the Gothic noblewoman Theodegunda, *possessor* of vast Italian holdings. A letter of 511 from Theoderic addressed to her, preserved in the *Variae* of Cassiodorus, warns that her care of her dependents (*curam subiectorum*) was seen to reflect on the crown.[97] In the context of Roman and Gothic cohabitation in the Italian peninsula the proper management of *servi* was a matter of public concern, and that the conduct of female *possessores* in this respect was no less closely watched than that of their men-folk.

---

[95] *Ad Gregoriam* 19 (CC 25A, 232–3): 'For our forbears are weighed down, when we persist in their deeds against the divine precepts'; 'Behold, the crackling of the eternal fire and the strength of flames gain momentum: you reckon for me the nobility of your *prosapiae*, and you will begin to follow after the *mores* of your ancestors.'

[96] Procopius, *Wars* 5.12.50–4; discussion in Guy Halsall, *Barbarian Migrations and the Roman West* (Cambridge, 2007), 341.

[97] Cassiodorus, *Variae* 4.37 (*MGH AA* 12, 130): 'Decet prudentiae vestrae curam subiectorum negotiis adhibere custodiam, quia vobis ordinantibus illa fieri debent quae regiam possunt demonstrare praesentiam. Sic enim credimus, quia memor natalium tuorum a te abicias omne vitiosum et illa sola diligere possis, quae et nos amare cognoscis. Proavorum forsitan oblitterentur exempla, si longi generis minus facta recolantur: similes autem filii patrum praeconia mox sequuntur. Renatus itaque flebili nobis aditione conquestus est vobis delegantibus cognitores iudicatum se contra Inquilinam nomine post longa temporis intervalla meruisse et excubiis damnisque confecto vestram tandem prospexisse iustitiam: nec tamen litigatoris improbam cessare calumniam, dum redivivis litibus tenuitatem insequitur supplicantis, ut non tam vincendi votum quam adversarii videatur quaesisse detrimentum. Quapropter si vobis iubentibus iudicata cognoscitis nec constat adversarium provocasse legaliter, finitum iure negotium in sua manere facite firmitate, ne longa quaestio litigantium non tam augeat patrimonia, sed evertat et quod fit ambitu lucri, causa videatur esse dispendii.' Discussion in Amory, *People and Identity*, 420.

The *domina*'s relationship to those in her power is clearly seen here as an important thread in the social fabric. Her authority over slaves is not only divinely sanctioned, it is an office to which she has been called. The responsibility for slaves is not simply a matter of ownership (*potestas*); rather, in God's eyes it is a matter of custody (*cura*) of the *imago Dei*.

Take care, I beseech you, Lady, lest anyone see filthy limbs (*squalentia*) among the rags of any of your home-born slaves (*vernaculorum tuorum*), lest any one belonging to you should freeze in the cold of winter on account of poverty; let none suffer hunger, none be wearied by starvation, none by beatings, for there is not one of your slaves – male or female – for whom you may believe that you will not have to give account before God. For to this end mortals were made masters over other mortals, that they might receive the care of the image of God during its sojourn in this world, and might keep safe the riches destined for souls, which daily the plunderer of all that is good bestirs himself to snatch away.[98]

It is precisely in order to fight the Enemy – Satan – on behalf of these souls that *potestas* was granted to a *domina* in the first place. With this in mind, it is striking that God's requirement of the *domina* vis-à-vis the *servus* in *Ad Gregoriam* is expressed in the language of royal favour. At first, the link between authority, property, and biological kinship is emphasized, with Christ and the mother Church as *paterfamilias* and *materfamilias*: 'You will enter the *salutatorium* of the mother Church in the same way as [your slave] does: father Christ speaks to you and to him/her [the slave] with the same voice.' It quickly becomes clear, however, that the *salutatorium* is not just the reception hall of an aristocratic villa such as Gregoria herself would have had at her disposal. It is a royal audience chamber: '[Your slave] was conceived by the same heat of the divine seed as you were, and was born by the same birth of the mother Church: he (she) enters as guest to the King's presence together with you, he (she) – a friend – implores together with you.' *Domina* and slave are now noble kindred approaching the King together. This means that she should only ask of her slave what she would be content to have asked of herself: 'The second birth has made this person, whom the human condition made your slave, to be your sibling . . . Why do you exact [from others] what you are not strong enough yourself to endure, and impose a burden which you yourself cannot bear?'[99]

Instead of trusting that the pursuit of honour will guide the *domina* toward responsible management of her slaves, *Ad Gregoriam* reminds her that it is not only in the eyes of her peers but in the eyes of the Deity that

---

[98] *Ad Gregoriam* 18 (*CC* 25A, 226).   [99] *Ad Gregoriam* 19 (*CC* 25A, 229).

her conduct will be judged. The reader is invited to eavesdrop on the voice
of Satan as he makes the case to God that Gregoria has crossed the line and
left the company of holy women to join his own entourage. The *salutato-*
rium is now nothing less than the court of the Lord at the Day of
Judgement. Satan will take every opportunity to bring forward
Gregoria's negligence as a mistress (*domina*) as evidence against her with
chilling logic:

How can you suffer her with impunity to disregard what is sacred to you, and with
impunity not to know [your commandments], and, not knowing, not at all to do?
Or is it from some other cause that one of her handmaids, weighed down by a
burden, importunes you, [and] resorts to tears [when she is] condemned (*addicta*)?
Or is it not on this account that one [of her household] is hungry, that one is
naked, that one goes about ragged, because she entirely neglected the doing of
those things which your justice (*aequitas*) wished to be known and fulfilled?[100]

Both God and Satan know that she is expected to treat the household as a
training ground for the Christian virtues. Again, her failure to do so offers
ammunition for Satan's case: 'What slave of her household (*familiae*
servum) did she ever bring up for you out of her own means? Which of
her little maids (*ancillulis*) has she dedicated to your service? When has she
enforced a rule of your discipline which had been neglected by her slaves
(although to be sure she never passed over an instance of herself having
been taken lightly)?' John warns her that she must anticipate this judgement by carefully considering the effect of her actions on her subordinates
within the *domus*.

So then be a model (*forma*) for all your slaves: let them see you boldly standing
guard over the riches of truth in your mouth, and of the riches of purity (*castitas*)
with respect to your body, of reverence (*pietas*) in your breast, of innocence in your
hands, of integrity in your expression. Let them see your eyes continually lifted to
the heavens, let them see that the jewels of your ears can in no way be snatched
away by the verbal piracy (*piraticis sermonibus*) of your detractors, nor the
boundaries of your charity be violated by a deceitful garrulity (*loquacitate*). By
this model (*exemplum*) you will secure your own salvation and that of those
[women] over whom you have been worthy to rule.[101]

We will see in the next chapter that Gregoria is expected to exert an equally
edifying influence on other members of the household; the point here is
that slaves should benefit along with the others.

   Since Gregoria is in charge of a substantial establishment, the virtues
required of her are those of *aequitas*, justice: 'Conscientiously inspect and

---

[100] *Ad Gregoriam* 18 (*CC* 25A, 225).   [101] *Ad Gregoriam* 18 (*CC* 25A, 226).

examine your own justice (*aequitas*) concerning your slaves (*servulos*) . . .'[102]
But the *domina* is asked to go beyond mere *aequitas*. We have seen that
aequitas for the Romans was the virtue appropriate to the governance of
slaves as opposed to children, a relationship whose basis was understood as
intrinsically exploitative, rather than as intrinsically educative.[103] But John
wants to push against this distinction, to argue that the *domina* has been
entrusted with a moral obligation to care for the souls in her power.

Here we see John's active use of the metaphor of the mistress as a
mother and teacher. The *domina* bears the responsibility for the behaviour of her slaves; it is a matter of her own honour and accountability that
their conduct should reflect proper training. It is she who must instill
iustitia in her slaves as she educates them; if she does so when they are
young she will find that they do not need to be punished when they grow
older.

Why in your household should the childishness of the younger slaves (*servulorum*)
abound with unruly behavior, and yet in the older ones you seek what you
disdained in the younger? Institute in those of tender years what may later make
you blessed, and may it make you find a crown with the Lord, and in the present
allow you to be tranquil. With difficulty will you exact righteousness (*justitiam*)
from them, who do not have it within themselves at all; and yet, they would have
it, if they had received it when they were small.

There is no excuse for the mistress to be indignant, if it is she who has had
responsibility for the training of those who serve her. Reflected here is a
strong sense of the force of habit:

Do you see, pray, that the fault is ours, if in the time for learning we do not teach
good to those, whose faults, entrenched by long habit, we punish? There is no
other remedy left, except that we conquer the bad with goodness, and prevail over
the impious with piety. For it is impetuousness (*animositas*), rather than justice
(*aequitas*), which has the habit of exacting revenge, allowing each individual to
suffer what he (she) has earned.[104]

Aequitas and *disciplina* are seen here as the more narrow-minded modes of
exerting power that arise from anger and self-importance rather than from
benevolent authority. The practice of *iustitia*, by contrast, along with
pietas, is what is required by Christian virtue. Gregoria is reminded here
that each of her inferiors shares her own status in the eyes of God.

[102] *Ad Gregoriam* 19 (*CC* 25A, 228).
[103] See also Peter Garnsey, *Ideas of Slavery from Aristotle to Augustine* (Cambridge, 1996).
[104] *Ad Gregoriam* 19 (*CC* 25A, 230).

Or perhaps God loves mercy (*pietas*) where you are concerned, yet embraces justice (*aequitas*) with respect to your slave? And if you wish adequately to teach that God loves justice (*aequitas*), why do you teach and at the same time refuse to be taught? For anger (*animus*) is brought forth – veiled in the blasphemous darkness of wrath – and proclaims itself the champion of righteousness (*iustitiae*), at the same time as it has expelled that very righteousness (*iustitiam*) from its mind.[105]

To Gregoria's imagined objections, John replies with a reminder to consider her own faults rather than those of others.

'But God loves discipline (*disciplina*)', you will say. I think you should be careful more on your own account than on that of your slave: for to the degree that your stomach is filled with better food, your body dressed in more expensive clothes, so much more does your soul demand to be adorned by better works of discipline, and to be furnished abundantly with rich and magnificent gifts. Most often, then, show your slaves your compassion (*indulgentiam*), and most often grant forgiveness of their misdeeds (*peccatorum*).[106]

The passage develops in a direction surprisingly critical of hypocrisy in the *domina*:

Because your Lord Himself took care that you know by His own witness: that just as you yourself have judged, so you will be judged, and just as you yourself have measured, so it will be measured to you. O mortal, if you received this saying of the Lord with a whole faith, you would never distress your young slaves (*servulos*) with different types of blows when they err. As a result it happens that that one is wearied with blows, that one cast down, that one driven out, that one expelled, that one banished entirely from your presence, that one handed over to a heavier yoke of servitude. And after this – cursing yourself – you yourself ask your Lord to forgive your debts by the same terms as [those by which] you have forgiven [the debts] of your slave?[107]

Naturally John turns next from criticism to encouragement.

Therefore let us hasten (*festinemus*) to be the friends of mercy (*misericordiae*), nor – for all that – should we so check the reins of justice (*iustitiae*) that we never allow her to run at all, but let us allow her so to run that mercy (*pietas*) may overtake her. And let the former take care justly (*iuste*) to reward the good, and the latter mercifully (*pie*) to raise up the evil, the former to punish offences, and the latter to free those perishing from their guilt (*a reatu pereuntes*), the former to punish the guilty one together with the crime, the latter to rescue the criminal after the crime has been punished. And so let each be allowed to fulfil her own office, so that for the sake of salvation there may be as much the indignation of justice (*iustitiae*) as

[105] *Ad Gregoriam* 19 (*CC* 25A, 230).   [106] *Ad Gregoriam* 19 (*CC* 25A, 231).
[107] *Ad Gregoriam* 19 (*CC* 25A, 231).

the gentle soothing of mercy (*misericordiae*); while one is angry at the wrongdoer, the other sustains the petitioner.[108]

How much John owes here to a specifically Christian view of the duty of the powerful here, and how much to a more ancient Roman ethical tradition, is very difficult to judge. But this is part of his point: where the issue of obligation to dependents is concerned, the two traditions speak with one voice.

One aspect of *Ad Gregoriam*'s use of slave governance is as a metaphor for the relationship between Gregoria and God. Here we find a reference to the legal situation of female slaves with respect to a husband. (The term is *maritum*, although the bond in question can not be the institution of *iustum matrimonium* which necessarily involved free citizens[109].)

> Surely your handmaid (*ancilla*) takes a husband (*maritum accipit*) with this understanding, that both of them should serve you with their servitude, and if perhaps he whom she takes as a husband be born to free status, marriage [nevertheless] bring him under your rule. And is it not unspeakable if through your handmaid you should obtain as a slave one who owed you nothing, while through you – His handmaid – God loses His servant, whom he has bought by His own precious blood?[110]

In Roman law up to the reign of Valentinian III, the enslavement of the 'husband' referred to here would have sounded like nonsense. To begin with, an *ancilla* was not eligible to marry. Further, it went without saying that if a free woman entered the union of *contubernium* with a slave man, she would become the property of her husband's master, but if the woman were a slave and the man were free, she would simply be his concubine, a well-established practice.[111] If she were not his own slave he could be expected to buy her unless he were very poor indeed. A long-standing *contubernium* could lead to manumission of the female partner, and perhaps marriage, unless the male partner were a senator, in which case such a marriage was forbidden.[112]

The context for this reference to the male partner coming under the power of the female partner's owner is almost certainly Gregoria's standing

---

[108] *Ad Gregoriam* 19 (*CC* 25A, 231–2).   [109] Treggiari, *Roman Marriage*, 43.

[110] *Ad Gregoriam* 8 (*CC* 25A, 204): 'Certe hac condicione tua maritum accipit ancilla, ut utrique suo tibi serviant famulatu, et si fore is quem maritum accipit ingenua, sit si sorte progenitus, sui copula tuo illum inclinat imperio. Et nefas non est ut tu per ancillam suam suum deus famulam perdat, quem pretioso suo sanguine conparavit?'

[111] Judith Evans Grubbs, 'Marriage More Shameful than Adultery: Slave–Mistress Relationships, "Mixed Marriages", and Late Roman Law', *Phoenix* 47 (1993), 125–54.

[112] Discussion at Arjava, *Women and Law*, 206–9. We will return in Chapter Four to developments in the legislation regarding concubinage.

within a class of landowner among whose *servi* refugees could be hidden. As early as July 318, Constantine had acknowledged that some men of the curial class, in an attempt to flee the duties to which they were bound by law, had fled 'into the laps of very powerful houses', and by setting up housekeeping with a female slave of the estate had attempted to blend in with the crowd on an estate, without the knowledge of the estate's steward.[113] Under Constantine, the problem seems to have been that when the presence of the 'husband' was discovered, instead of reporting him the landowner would confiscate his property, in exchange for protection, without taking up his curial burden. Constantine's punishment is for the decurion to be deported, his property (including his own slaves) to be returned to the city whose obligations he had attempted to evade, and both the woman, and the steward if he knew of and failed to report the crime, to be condemned to the mines. 'What is at issue is the decurion's abdication from his financial responsibilities to his municipality, and the illegal transfer of curial property to a rural landowner. That is why the abandoned city is to receive the delinquent decurion's property, unless he has left children or other relatives who can take over his obligations.'[114] Even at the height of Roman public justice individuals could slip in and out of communities, and it was one of the functions of law to try to impose order on their movements.[115]

A *Novel* of Valentinian published in 451 attempted to resolve similar complications arising in the case of bound tenants, although this time, greater deference was paid to the claims of the landowner with whom the vagrant sought refuge. Novel 31, issued on 31 January 451 and posted in the Forum of Trajan on 3 February, attempted to establish a statute of limitations for the rights of masters of *coloni vagi*, bound tenant farmers (male or female) who had fled from the estate to which their labour was bound.[116] If the master were able to locate the *colonus* or *colona* within thirty years, he could claim him or her back; otherwise, he or she would now be obligated to the estate to which he or she had fled. The point here was both to make sure that the *colonus* did not expect to go free at the end of thirty years, and to make sure that landowners saw no real incentive in

---

[113] *CTh*. 12. 1. 6 (1 July 318); for discussion of this law and its date, see Evans Grubbs, *Law and Family*, 278–81.

[114] Evans Grubbs, *Law and Family*, 279.

[115] Wickham, *Framing the Early Middle Ages*, 524: 'This [the tying of *coloni*] seems simply to have been linked to the general desire of the state to tie people of all kinds to their professions and localities, *curiales* as much as *coloni*.'

[116] Note that in the apposite passage, *Ad Gregoriam* refers not to a *colona* but to an *ancilla*, a slave.

'poaching' one another's bound labour, since only after thirty years did the new landowner attain rights to the labour. Stipulations were laid down so that husbands, wives, and children should be kept together if the vagrant had established a family, with a substitute being offered in compensation for a wife given to her husband's master, or children given to the mother's.

These provisions do not really alter the sexual balance of established Roman law, but section five of the same *novel* brings in a new element which further erodes the asymmetry of treatment between male and female bound labourers on an estate. Section five of *Novel* 31 deals with freeborn *advenae*, strangers not bound to service, who offer themselves as itinerant labourers. If he should establish a relationship with one of the estate's *colonae* this would put both the woman and the estate in a vulnerable position: 'When satiety overtakes them, they leave; they depart without considering their former status, the association of marriage, the affection of children, since no law prohibits them.'[117] Valentinian's solution to the problems caused by mixing bound and itinerant labour was to require that the *advena* bind himself to the estate, although without losing his free-born status, if he took a lover.

Therefore, if a person who is obligated to no municipality in any manner should join himself to the rustic or urban landed estate of any person and should wish to be united with a woman who is obligated [i.e. as a *colona*[118]], he shall state in the municipal records his intention to reside where he has chosen, in order that, since this bond precedes, he may not desert the habitation which he has chosen and may not break off the union with the woman.[119]

Novel 31 seems to represent an attempt to acknowledge the interests of both landowners in this case.

A Gothic law code of disputed origin, the *Edictum Theoderici*, dated to the mid-fifth or early sixth century, develops the protection of the land-owner further. Here the woman in question can be either an *ancilla*, a female slave, or an *originaria* (another term for a *colona*), so the parallel to *Ad Gregoriam* is more precise than that in the Novel of Valentinian.[120]

---

[117] *Nov. Val.* 31.5, tr. Pharr, 541.   [118] The context is in a discussion of *coloni*, not *servi*.

[119] *Nov. Val.* 31.5, tr. Pharr, 541

[120] 'LXIIII Ancillam alienam uirginem uel originariam cuiuslibet aetatis, quisquis ingenuus, nulli tamen quolibet modo obnoxius ciuitati, corripuerit, si dominus uoluerit, aut corruptor ipse rogauerit, et apud gesta professus fuerit, mansurus in domini mulieris potestate, eius quam uitiuit contubernium non relinquat, nec, eadem mortua, discedendi habeat facultatem. Quod si dominus ancillae non consenserit, aut ille profiteri noluerit, tunc aut huius meriti duo mancipia domino tradat, eius iuri profutura, si eius substantia patiatur' (*Edictum Theoderici* 64, ed. J. Baviera, *Fontes iuris romani anteiustiniani* 2 (Florence, 1940)).

The *Edictum Theoderici* is variously assigned to the reign of the Visigoth king Theoderic II (453–66) and to that of Theoderic the Great (493–526). Detlef Liebs has argued convincingly for the latter.[121] If, as it seems, the *Edictum* is extending the earlier Roman provision to afford additional protection to the landowner, it may reflect a perception that political instability offered ever greater openings to vagrants and to those who wished to avoid obligation to a *dominus*. The cohabitation of two populations, Roman and Gothic, may have added new tensions to the social dynamics among landowners, and to the sexual politics of slave ownership.[122]

A curious symmetry governs the metaphor of the *ancilla* who wins legal possession of her lover for the *domina* who owns her. On the strength of other passages in *Ad Gregoriam* one would expect that the parallel, where Gregoria's relationship to God is invoked, would be that Gregoria should win her own husband to the dominion of God. In this instance the metaphor folds back on itself. The main point of the digression on slave marriage in Chapter 19 is that if the *ancilla* triggers a fit of anger in her mistress Gregoria, the *ancilla* herself will have lost a slave (Gregoria) for God rather than winning one on His behalf.[123] We will see in the following chapter that John takes a more positive line with respect to Gregoria's possible effect on her husband than to the *ancilla*'s effect on her mistress.

Turning to the significance of this passage for situating *Ad Gregoriam* in its proper social context, a number of things can be said. First, that Gregoria is understood to be the *domina* of an estate of the magnitude to attract refugees, whose experience of estate management is hands-on enough to allow her to benefit from a passing reference to the laws governing *contubernium* of migrant workers with the servile population of an estate. This is compatible with the senatorial rank suggested elsewhere in the text, since

---

[121] Detlef Liebs, *Die Jurisprudenz im spätantiken Italien (260–640 n.Chr.)*, Freiburger Rechtsgeschichtliche Abhandlungen, n.f. 8 (Berlin, 1987), 120–6, and 191–4; this said, the *Reallexikon für germansiche Altertumswissenschaft*, s.v. Edictum Theoderici, presents the debate as still open.

[122] Two further references to the enslavement of a freeborn man who cohabits with a female slave have been identified by Antti Arjava. The first, a passing reference in a Greek sermon of unknown date spuriously transmitted under the name of John Chrysostom, sheds no real light on the present discussion. The second, a reference in the register of Gregory the Great, implies that in the late sixth century the practice was still known but that exemptions had been established, for example where the slave partner belonged to the Church. Arjava, *Women and Law in Late Antiquity*, 207 n. 51: 'There is a mysterious reference to it in a sermon of unknown date, Ps. Joh. Chrys. *De legisl.* 3 PG 56.401. For Byzantine Italy, see Gregory the Great, *Ep.* 9.84 (*MGH Epp.* 2, 99): the husband of a slave belonging to the Roman church obviously remains free.'

[123] *Ad Gregoriam* 19 (*CC* 25A, 228–33).

the larger her holdings, the more likely she would be to have experience with legal provisions involving her *ancillae* and *servi*. (It may also imply that migrant labour of *ingenui* was frequent enough for this particular provision to be well-known.)

It is worth remembering that at roughly this period, landowners are 'noticeable by their absence' in many hagiographical sources, while holy men such as Symeon Stylites take their place as the 'hinge men' who act as patrons on behalf of a dispossessed peasantry.[124] In a recent article on the great estates of the eastern empire, Peter Sarris has argued that the presentation of a rural landscape in which holy men, rather than *domini*, see to the need for patronage of the rural population made it possible for ecclesiastical writers gently to threaten landowners with the fact that religious leaders were doing a much better job than they. But if the *dominus* is 'written out' in certain hagiographical narratives, in the household manuals, by contrast, the *domina* is emphatically 'written in'.

To portray the Christian *domina* in a face-to-face relationship with slaves involved in wool production was surely a conscious choice. Naturally the choice had literary overtones, since from the *Odyssey* onward both Greek and Roman literature had prized the figure of the constant wife sitting diligently at her wool-work. The tableau of domestic wool-working in *Ad Gregoriam* seems to reflect an intention to portray the *domina* as a slave-holder rather than as a manager of other kinds of labour; the old-fashioned image of the mistress with her house slaves finds support in the advice to Gregoria that her *vernacula* should not be seen dressed neglectfully in dirty rags.[125] The reference here to the particular obligation of the *domina* toward a *verna*, or house-born slave, demonstrates that John does want to bring forward a traditional ideal of Roman paternalism. We have seen above that in the case of the marriage of a female *ancilla* to a man from beyond the household, while the *Novel* of Valentinian specifies a *colona*, our source specifies an *ancilla* – a slave rather than a bound tenant. (Perhaps this is because the author of *Ad Gregoriam* knows the version of the law in the *Edictum Theoderici*, where *ancilla* is used.) John's use of the term *ancilla* in this passage should probably not be dismissed as an inadvertent slip, and we may imagine that Gregoria's paternalism is meant to extend beyond the hearth and out to the slaves in the fields.

---

[124] Peter Brown, 'The Rise and Function of the Holy Man in Late Antiquity', *JRS* 61 (1971), 80–101.
[125] *Ad Gregoriam* 18 (*CC* 25A, 226); Sarris, 'Rehabilitating the Great Estate', 57–8.

GREGORIA AND REGINUS: *SPIELREGELN* FOR A CHRISTIAN
ARISTOCRACY?

If we think back from Gregoria's handbook to Ferrandus of Carthage's *Letter to Reginus* discussed in Chapter One, it will help us to consider the scope of the *domina*'s authority and agency in a wider social and economic context. The virtues toward which Gregoria is urged to reach are not only those of a wife who has her eye fixed on her husband, but also those of the aristocrat who acts as arbiter of the fate of others. Though reference to her gender pervades the manual it is far from offering a simple exhortation to wifely obedience. On balance, it is noticeable that the virtues proposed are geared to containing the abuses of the powerful, rather than to submission by the weak. Gregoria is clearly understood here primarily as a female *patronus*. If we understand the *domus* as a unit involving the estates of a *dominus* or *domina* in addition to the more strictly domestic environment in the modern sense of the word, we can see that to rule the *domus* with justice was a crucial task within the pyramid of the Roman social order.

Like Ferrandus, the anonymous author of *Ad Gregoriam* warns virulently against the neglect that would allow a Christian to claim ignorance as an excuse for an abuse of authority. While in the case of Ferrandus it is the commander whose men are extorting from the civilian population behind his back, in *Ad Gregoriam* it is the *domina* who has been convinced by ascetic Christians that her role holds no scope for acts of Christian excellence.

Ad Gregoriam's initially surprising emphasis on the *miles Christi* as a metaphor for the spiritual life of a Christian *domina* in fact reflects a literary milieu in which advice to aristocratic laywomen and men drew on shared models for the responsible exercise of Christian authority. The metaphorical nature of her identity as *miles Christi* is understandably stressed where the *domina* is concerned, but in fact the metaphor sits no more easily with the real-life *miles Reginus*, who is first of all an administrator charged with maintaining peaceful relations within his province. Taken together, the two texts offer a window onto the development of a warrior laity who looked to their God as the ultimate guarantor of what justice the *saeculum* afforded.

Ad Gregoriam and the letter to Reginus share an approach to the moral instruction of the powerful laity. When each is asked to think of the effect of his or her actions, the *dux* is invited to imagine it in terms of the civilian population of his province, while the *domina* is invited to think in the diverse terms of husband, slaves, and other dependents. Still, Gregoria's position as mistress of a late Roman *domus* was in fact an office of considerable authority.

The two treatises draw, it may be argued, on what seems to have been a shared tradition of pastoral advice for the aristocratic laity, applicable to both men and women. This conceptual link has far-reaching repercussions. For example, the conduct manuals for women surviving from late antiquity in Merovingian and Carolingian copies may have had an influence on the development of conduct literature as a genre for men in the Carolingian period, a significance wholly ignored by Anton in his discussion of the development of the *Fürstenspiegel* genre.[126]

Household and province represented two of the most important hierarchical layers in the organization of society. It makes sense that their management was seen in similar terms. At the same time, both institutions were seen to be under threat in the early sixth century. The contest among Vandal, Ostrogothic, and Byzantine powers attempting to establish dominion in Italy and North Africa meant that the lack of a stable framework of rulership in which political and social institutions could find their footing was deeply felt. This instability formed the context for the effort by Christian writers to ground the responsible exercise of lay authority in a network of Christian values and institutions, whose force might persist through changes of political dispensation. It is likely, too, that lay *domini* looked to the Church to confirm their authority, and that establishing relationships of *amicitia* with men known for their spiritual prowess could help them to attract the loyalty of those beneath them in the hierarchy. Both *dux* amd *domina* are secured within a hierarchy, with one eye cast below, to those whom they govern, and one cast fearfully above. The perilous balance applies to both.

THE COMING JUDGEMENT

Some time in the fifth or sixth century, an anonymous Christian man wrote a letter of consolation to his 'sister' – whether the lady was his kinswoman by blood or in Christ is unclear – to substitute for a long-wished-for visit.[127] The two had been kept from visiting one another by an unnamed third party. Our writer excuses himself for a long absence, 'I have often

[126] Hans Hubert Anton, *Fürstenspiegel und Herrscherethos in der Karolingerzeit*, Bonner historische Forschungen 32 (Bonn, 1968). This is a point I explore further in 'The Reichenau *Ad Gregoriam in palatio*'.

[127] *Epistula sancti Severi presbyteri ad Claudiam sororem suam de ultimo iudicio* (PL 20, 223–37; CSEL 1, 219–23; CPL 746); English translation and brief introduction in B. R. Rees, *The Letters of Pelagius and his Followers* (Woodbridge, 1991).

wanted to visit you, only to be prevented up to now by the one who is wont to prevent us.'[128] It is unclear whether the human obstacle was the abbot of the author's monastery, the lady's father, alarmed by signs of intimacy in her relationship with a male ascetic teacher, or her husband, mistrustful of her continued intimacy with one of her blood kinsmen. The implication seems to be that the lady was dependent on a boorish male guardian who neither understood nor appreciated her fine spiritual aspirations, but we have no way of knowing if this was the lady's own view of her situation, or if it was simply the hopeful idea of an admirer, wishing to impress her with a flattering and somewhat melodramatic vision of herself. The lady could, in fact, have been perfectly happy in her domestic arrangements, and have seen her spiritual 'brother' as something of a nuisance. As with so many of the ladies to whom anonymous Christian devotional texts were addressed, we know her only through the eyes of a man whose picture of her may have been distorted by his own agenda.

Perhaps impatient with this situation, later copyists of this text decided that the woman's name was Claudia, and that its author was none other than Sulpicius Severus, biographer of Saint Martin. Sulpicius was known to have written 'many letters' to 'his sister' – this, according to Gennadius of Marseilles in his late fifth-century continuation of Jerome's *De viris illustribus*.[129] In our only surviving copy of this letter, a twelfth-century manuscript from Canterbury, Gennadius' notice for Sulpicius precedes the text, which is given the title 'Epistola S Severi presb, ad Claudiam sororem suam de ultimo iuditio'.[130] This attribution to Sulpicius was retained in the early modern editions of the text, but rejected out of hand by Sulpicius' late nineteenth-century editor, primarily on stylistic grounds.[131] While our intention is not at all to reopen the case for Sulpician authorship, the early modern scholarship on the text established a link to Gaul. In his edition of 1678, Etienne Baluze noted a series of borrowings made from the

---

[128]   *Ad Claudiam* 1 (*CSEL* 1, 219, tr. Rees, 315), 'persaepe ad vos venire volui, sed usque adhuc impeditus sum, obsistente eo qui consuevit obsistere.'

[129]   Gennadius of Marseilles, *De viris illustribus* 19 (*TU* 14, 69).

[130]   Trinity College Cambridge MS 78, fol. 151b; description in Montague Rhodes James, *The Western Manuscripts in the Library of Trinity College Cambridge: A Descriptive Catalogue* (Cambridge, 1900), 98–9. The presence of Latin Chrysostomica in this manuscript (and in the related MS 79, also from Canterbury) is worth noting.

[131]   See Halm, *CSEL* 1, xi–xii; followed by e.g. Johannes Quasten, *Patrology* p 4, ed. Angelo di Berardino, tr. Placid Solari, *The Golden Age of Latin Patristic Literature from the Council of Nicea to the Council of Chalcedon* (Allen, Texas, 1986), 538, where the attribution to Sulpicius of the *Ad Claudiam* is dismissed as 'apocryphal'.

Ad Claudiam by Ruricius of Limoges.[132] *Ad Claudiam*, suggests Ruricius' recent English translator, may have been composed in Ruricius' 'own literary circle'.[133]

In addressing his 'sister', the writer sought to conform to the requirements of the ancient philosophical genre of *consolatio*, a genre that met with something of a revival from the end of the fourth century onward. Jerome had engaged with it in a well-known letter consoling Pammachius on the death of his wife,[134] and, as we have seen, the genre would be given new life by Boethius toward the end of the reign of Theoderic the Great. *Ad Claudiam* engages with the genre only rather loosely, but it is part of the horizon of expectation which the writer wants to invoke.

The text offers a complicated *captatio benevolentiae* about the balance of wisdom between the writer and the reader. The writer is acutely aware, he tells her, that there is no real use in his continuing to offer her the spiritual instruction ('precepts to guide your life and faith') which she has requested in her letters, for he has little left to say which he has not already said before, and she has attained a level of perfection in the faith where such instruction is really superfluous. He does go on to offer a single admonition, although it is framed, face-savingly, as an exhortation not to undermine the progress she has already made by looking back at what she has left behind. The Enemy stands, he warns her, ready to take advantage of even a momentary lapse. The rest of the text is, perhaps appropriately, a set piece on the day of judgement which has very little do with the addressee herself, except insofar as it encourges her to look with pity rather than scorn on those 'wise men of this world' (4) who are judged wanting by the Lord.

The so-called *Ad Claudiam* offers a wonderfully useful comparison to *Ad Gregoriam in Palatio*, because the two texts are closely related, overlapping *verbatim* in a number of places. Yet the relationship between the two texts is enigmatic. While *Ad Gregoriam* is lengthy, overwrought, and ambitious, *Ad Claudiam* is much shorter and far more straightforward in its structure. *Ad Claudiam* could have borrowed from the longer and more ambitious *Ad Gregoriam*, but it is more probable that the author of *Ad Gregoriam* took a number of short passages from *Ad Claudiam* as inspiration for sections of his longer text. The idea of *Ad Gregoriam*'s author

---

[132] *Stepani Baluzii Miscellaneorum liber primus, hoc est, collectio veterum monumentorum quae hactenus latuerant in variis codicibus et bibliothecis* (Paris, 1678), *praef.* iii–v.

[133] Ralph Mathisen, *Ruricius of Limoges and Friends: A Collection of Letters from Visigothic Gaul* (Liverpool, 1999), 54.

[134] Jerome, *Ad Pammachium* (*PL* 22, 639–47).

spinning a Baroque fantasy on the brief sketches in *Ad Claudiam* makes more sense than that of *Ad Claudiam*'s writer borrowing short passages from the longer piece while ignoring many of its well-developed themes. In addition, we know from his borrowings from other, identifiably earlier writers such as Tertullian that for John constructing a bricolage of borrowings was a characteristic *modus operandi*.

Ad Gregoriam gives moral complexity to *Ad Claudiam*'s fairly simplistic ideas about God's justice. While the *domina* Gregoria is understood as an illustrious personage, much to be feared by her many subordinates, 'Claudia' is envisaged as a plucky but fundamentally powerless romantic heroine, caught in an impossible situation. Her correspondent offers the remarkable consolation that, whatever the injustice of her circumstances, they will be swept away when Christ comes in judgement at the end of time. Meditation on the Day of Judgement becomes a covert way of criticizing 'the one who is wont to prevent us', the man in charge of 'Claudia's' domestic arrangements. Her oppression is in fact engineered by the Hidden Enemy of all virtue, although the writer does not go so far as to state explicitly that his rival is in league with the Devil. But whatever his intentions, the role of the anonymous *paterfamilias* in this story is as the oppressor of virtue, while the lady stands for the virtue thus oppressed. Only the coming Judgement can resolve the situation, and it is to be yearned for, because of Christ's promise that the mighty will be brought down and the downtrodden receive their reward. 'O, how happy will be that departure of ours, when Christ on his throne receives us, purged from sin's stain by living a better life.'[135]

The writer has already exhorted 'Claudia' to see herself as engaged in a spiritual battle:

Our enemy stands ready against us, hoping speedily to strike the man stripped of his shield of faith. So let us not cast our shield aside, lest our flank be exposed; let us not put away our sword, lest the enemy begin to lose his fear of us; when he sees an armed man, he will go away. Nor are we ignorant of the fact that it is hard and difficult to struggle daily against the flesh and the world; but if you think of eternity, if you consider the kindgom of heaven which the Lord will undoubtedly deign to bestow on us even if we are sinners, what suffering (*quae passio*) is worthy, I ask you, to make us deserve such rewards?[136]

---

[135] *Ad Claudiam* 3 (*CSEL* 1, 229, tr. Rees, 316, amended), 'O quam felix ille noster excessus, cum a labe peccati melioris vitae conversatione purgatos sede suo nos Christus excipiet.'

[136] *Ad Claudiam* 2 (*CSEL* 1, 220, tr. Rees, 316), 'Stat enim adversum nos paratus inimicus, ut nudatum fidei umbonem mox feriat. Non abiciendus est itaque clipeus, ne latus pateat: non remittendus est gladius, ne hostis incipiat non timere: porro cum armatum viderit, abibit. Nec ignoramus durum

The battle, then, is also a *passio*, a martyrdom: indeed, meditation on the saints, whose *passiones* are offered as a guide, is one of the techniques by which the Christian must prepare herself for battle.

At the same time as he warns Claudia to prepare herself, the writer glories in the helplessness that the powerful will be exposed to in the coming Judgement:

> What shall these wretches say in their own defence? 'We did not know you, Lord, we did not see that you were in the world, you did not send the prophets, you did not give the law to this world; we did not see the patriarchs, we did not read the examples of the saints … we fell through ignorance, not knowing what we did!'[137]

But among the mighty it is those who claim to have been unaware of the lore of Christian ethics who will be brought down. The writer here sets out the pointed contrast of those who will be welcomed at the Judgement by Christ, the apostles and the martyrs, as against the fate of those who will attempt to excuse themselves on grounds of ignorance, that they did not know what the Lord required of them. Here an exculpatory speech is put into their mouths:

> 'There were no martyrs whose examples (*exempla*) we might follow, no one foretold the coming Judgement, no one instructed us to clothe the poor, no one enjoined us to prohibit lust, no one persuaded us to fight against greed.'[138]

How could the powerful in a Christian society be unaware, the reader is asked, of the teaching that the rich must fight against greed and take responsibility for the well-being of those beneath them in the hierarchy? The implausibility of the claim is both an accusation of dishonesty against the unperturbed rich, and at the same time a challenge to the Christian collectivity to work tirelessly to spread the teaching of Christian ethics. 'No one instructed us' should never be able to be a fair excuse for neglect of the poor and the powerless.[139] Each of the passages cited above will be

---

esse atque difficile adversus carnem et saeculum cotidie dimicare, sed si aeternitatem cogites, si caelorum regna consideres, quae utique nobis Dominus licet peccatoribus praestare dignabitur, quae tandem condigna passio est, qua tanta mereamur?' Cf. *Ad Gregoriam* 9 (*CC* 25A, 206).

[137] *Ad Claudiam* 3 (*CSEL* 1, 220–1), 'Quid miseri pro sua defensione dicturi sunt? "nescimus te, Domine, te in mundo esse non uidimus: prophetas non misisti, legem saeculo non dedisti: patriarchas non uidimus, sancotrum non legimus exempla … inscientia lapsi sumus, quae fecimus nescientes."' Cf. *Ad Gregoriam* 20 (*CC* 25A, 234–5).

[138] *Ad Claudiam* 3 (*CSEL* 1, 221, tr. Rees, 316, amended), 'martyres non fuerunt quorum exempla sequeremur: futurum iudicium tuum nemo praedixit, vestire pauperem nemo mandavit, prohibere libidinem nemo praecepit, repugnari auaritiae nemo persuasit'.

[139] Along similar lines, a treatise from the so-called Caspari Corpus of Pelagian writings preserves an invented speech in which the apostles attempt to defend themselves against the charge that their failure to offer adequate instruction is the cause of so much backsliding among Christians (*Epistula de malis doctoribus et operis fidei et de ivdicio fututo* (*PLS* 1, 1415–57), especially sections 19–22 of the text).

borrowed *verbatim* by the writer of *Ad Gregoriam*, but we will see below that they are put to a distinctly different use in the later text.

Ad Claudiam continues with first-person speeches from the heroes of the Hebrew Bible – Noah, Abraham, Moses, David, Isaiah – offering a summary of the faith of the patriarchs, citing and situating biblical passages in Genesis, Deuteronomy, Exodus, Leviticus, Psalms, and Isaiah to give an account of the contribution of each to God's unfolding covenant with the faithful. Each in turn argues that God's wishes have been made clear and that only wrongful intent could explain the failure to follow them. The text ends by bringing forward Jesus himself to discourse very briefly on the ethical import of the New Testament, and the reassurance that at the Judgement those who have honestly sought the Lord 'shall lack no good thing'.[140] This means that there is no need to fear either the coming Judgement or mistreatment by the powerful here on earth: 'Therefore, my sister, though these men mock us, though they declare us to be foolish and miserable, let us rejoice all the more at their abuse, for by it glory is heaped up on us and punishment on them.'[141] Once the evangelist Matthew has reminded us of the outer darkness, the weeping and gnashing of teeth which await the unhappy souls who have failed to heed God's messengers, our writer reverts to his own voice to console his reader that if such men mock her, it is she who will be safe in the end, rejoicing while they grieve.

With its focus on the Christian laity's need to prepare for the coming Judgement by faithful study of scripture and faithful attempts to live by the ethical code derived from both Old and New Testaments, *Ad Claudiam* in many ways anticipates *Ad Gregoriam*. Yet in its straightforwardness and simplicity it also provides a striking contrast with the later and longer text. *Ad Claudiam* was classified as a Pelagian text by earlier scholars because of its strong interest the lay practice of Christian ethics, but it in fact resembles nothing more than the *narratio* described by Augustine in his *de cate-chizandis rudibus*. For Augustine, the *narratio* was a first summary of the faith which Christian teachers should offer to men and women seeking to join the Church, and it gave emphasis to the coming Judgement. He suggested that the Christian teacher should open his instruction to the inquirer by congratulating him or her on having been wise enough to seek safety in the face of the world's impending end, and should continue by offering an easy and lucid summary of the main points of Old and New Testaments bearing on the Christian life. Whoever the author of *Ad*

---

[140] *Ad Claudiam* 7 (*CSEL* 1, 223, tr. Rees, 319), quoting Ps. 34: 10.
[141] *Ad Claudiam* 7 (*CSEL* 1, 223, tr. Rees, 319).

Claudiam may have been, it is clear that he meant to offer something similar for his spiritual sister, a compendium of biblical *exempla* from whom she could learn the requirements of Christian ethics while meditating on the coming Judgement. In all likelihood he also meant it for the use of other Christian teachers – such as the author of *Ad Gregoriam* – who might have an occasion to instruct the faithful.

Although *Ad Gregoriam* draws on the earlier text and develops a number of its themes, it is marked by a decidedly different sensibility. Where the author of *Ad Claudiam* had sought clarity and simplicity, the author of *Ad Gregoriam* reaches for the connections between his material and the stylized sensibilities of the senatorial patronage class. Thus the idea that the Christian life is a battle against the vices becomes the seed from which a prose *Psychomachia* is made to spring. Equally, the idea that Gregoria's situation as a married Christian woman merits sympathy becomes the occasion for a *consolatio* weaving together the Christian tradition of Tertullian and Cyprian with the more self-consciously classical inheritance represented by Boethius.

From *Ad Claudiam* to *Ad Gregoriam*, the implicit object of the writer's critical eye has shifted dramatically. Where the earlier writer consoles his reader in her powerlessness, the later writer sees his reader as exercising decisive agency both within and beyond the scope of the Christian household. For example, *Ad Claudiam*'s speech of the powerful before the court of the Lord, excusing themselves as having failed out of ignorance rather than evil intent, is reused by the author of *Ad Gregoriam*, but the humiliation is turned against Gregoria herself, as a warning of the lies she herself may have to tell to defend her own conduct at the Judgement Day. The powerful *matrona* herself will have, if she is not careful, to claim ignorance of God's will. Our writer softens the blow by including himself in the danger, so that it is 'we' and not 'you' who stand in need of correction, but the danger itself is now in the first person.

I believe we will have to say, 'Lord, we did not know that you existed, You did not send prophets, You did not give the Law to the world, we saw no patriarchs, we read no Lives of the saints, Your Son was never on Earth, Peter remained silent, Paul refused to preach, no evangelist taught, there were no martyrs whose example we might follow, no one foretold your coming Judgement, no one commanded that the poor be clothed, no one urged that lust be checked. We fell by lack of awareness and we sinned by ignorance; for those sins which we committed knowing no better, we deserve mercy.'[142]

---

[142] *Ad Gregoriam* 20 (*CC* 25A, 234–5), 'Credo nos dicturos fore: Nescimus te, domine, esse: prophetas non misisti, legem saeculo non dedisti, patriarchas non vidimus, sanctorum exempla non legimus, filius tuus in terris non fuit, Petrus tacuit, Paulus noluit praedicare, evangelista non docuit, martyres

We are no longer standing with the downtrodden as they watch the fall of the mighty, but rather among the mighty themselves as they discover that their situation is more precipitous than they knew. The self-justification of the subordinate giving an awkward account to a superior for his wayward behaviour furnishes comic relief while simultaneously serving a serious warning to the reader.

Gregoria must prepare herself for the coming reversal, for she is among the mighty who will be called to account. The implied reader of *Ad Gregoriam* may be worried that her situation is not heroic, but in the eyes of her spiritual director, her most serious problem is rather that she holds an exalted position in the eyes of the world, and must be held accountable if she presides over injustice, than that she is likely to suffer injustice at the hands of others. We will see, however, in the chapter that follows, that in the fifth and sixth centuries Christian writers were less and less likely to perceive the *materfamilias* as a personage to be feared.

non fuerunt, quorum exempla sequeremur, futurum iudicium tuum nemo praedixit, uestiri pauperem nemo mandauit, cohiberi libidinem nemo persuasit: inscientia lapsi sumus, ignoratione peccavimus, meremur ueniam pro his quae peccavimus nescientes.'

CHAPTER 4

'Such trustful partnership': the marriage bond in Latin conduct literature

You have been bought, o *matrona*, and purchased by the contracts of your dowry agreement (*instrumentis dotalibus*), bound by as many ties as [you have] limbs; nor to be sure have you known your husband carnally (*ingressa es ad maritum*) unless also with the result that you would not be able to have authority (*potestas*) over your body itself, given that even the apostolic authority [1 Cor. 7:4] witnesses, that where her husband is concerned a wife should not have power over her body. You may perhaps respond that the apostle determined as well, that a husband as well does not have authority (*potestas*) over his own body before his spouse.[1]

This disturbing passage drawn from *Ad Gregoriam in palatio* develops a metaphor borrowed from Augustine of Hippo as a tool for thinking out the legacy of early Christian literature for the husband–wife relationship. In Augustine's sermons, we find the repeated suggestion that the contract of Christian marriage involved, among other things, nothing less than the outright purchase of a wife by a husband, much as one would purchase a slave. A famous passage in Augustine's *Confessions*, in which Monnica explains to her friends how she bore with the mistreatment of an abusive husband, picks up the same metaphor.[2] We will see below that the theme of the marriage as a 'sale' of the wife to the husband was not the only idea of Augustine's on the subject of marriage to attract the attention of later writers.

Like a modern pre-nuptial contract, the *tabellae matrimonales* served as an instrument by which Roman families could agree on the disposition of property between husband and wife, and bore important points in common with other contracts, including contracts of sale.[3] When the author of

---

[1] *Ad Gregoriam* 7 (*CC* 25A, 202).
[2] Augustine's famous discussion of his mother's forbearance with regard to his father is at *Confessions* 9.9 (*CC* 27, 145).
[3] This is a point developed by David G. Hunter in an evocative article, 'Augustine and the Making of Marriage in Roman North Africa', *JECS* 11 (2003), 63–85, updated and expanded as 'Marriage and the

Ad Gregoriam takes up the metaphor of the dowry agreement, it is worth noting that the term which he uses for the husband's power over the wife – *potestas* – is the term for paternal authority within the Roman *familia*, both over children and over slaves. We will see below that, at one level, the choice of word was entirely tendentious, since it was well known by all that under Roman law *potestas* over a free woman was held by a woman's father, not her husband, if it was held by anyone at all.[4] But at another level, this passage, and a number of related passages in Latin conduct literature of the fifth and sixth centuries, reflect a sea-change in late Roman thinking about marriage. There is reason to believe that the husband's position was becoming stronger with respect to the wife's in the period from Diocletian to Justinian. What, if anything, this change had to do with Christianity will be the subject of the present chapter.

The Christianization of the senatorial aristocracy in the late fourth century reached out to transform the habitual *ethos* of Rome's great families in many ways that are still not entirely understood. Much attention has been paid to the rising popularity of asceticism at this period, yet a quieter but equally far-reaching development was taking place involving the ancient institution of marriage. At the same time that Christian ascetics were encouraging the faithful to stop reproducing, Christian bishops were asking women to reassign their domestic allegiance from father to husband. This may have been an attempt to give force to New Testament ideals about the indissolubility of marriage. But the aspects of this development which can be assigned directly to Christian influence were accompanied by a number which cannot. Across our period, Roman quaestors tried successively to find legal language to cope with a situation in which the traditional form of Roman marriage, requiring neither ritual nor contract, left couples unable to establish whether they were married or not if they lost contact, through death or social mobility, with the kin or neighbours who could witness the terms on which they had begun to live together. It was also becoming harder to obtain a contested divorce, which meant that women were increasingly vulnerable if they married badly, and men could not quite so easily discard an unwanted wife.

The relationship between Christian custom and Roman law came under increasing pressure during this period. The early Christian communities

Tabulae Nuptiales in Roman North Africa from Tertullian to Augustine', in Philip L. Reynolds and John Witte, Jr., eds., *To Have and to Hold: Marrying and its Documentation in Western Christendom, 400–1600* (Cambridge, 2007), 95–113.

[4] It will be remembered from Chapter Three that a living father could free both male and female children from *potestas* by emancipating them.

had been free to follow customs that marked them off as a group apart – and indeed, various Christian communities had sustained local traditions without any need to impose conformity. Once imperial patronage was involved, however, Christian norms regarding marriage had to be rationalized and even reinvented. They would now come under scrutiny by men who had to consider their relevance to families drawn from different levels of the social order, committed to a dazzling mosaic of local traditions across the empire.[5] Whether the 'social engineering' of marriage undertaken by the emperors of our period was a reaction to Christian ideals is still an open question. In some cases it almost certainly was; in others, however, the more likely motive was a need to 'streamline' family law so that the courts – and the families themselves – were not immobilized by time-consuming lawsuits over property.[6] Confusion over what the law allowed meant that both families and magistrates often had to improvise, and there was reason to suspect that in this situation of flux, the rightful claims of the weak would be swept away by the more persuasive claims of the powerful.

Christian norms were even less securely established than Roman law. The evidence suggests that where marriage norms were concerned, bishops were prone to improvisation. We will see below that if the letter-book of Pope Leo the Great is anything to go by, we must accept that the bishops themselves were sometimes uncertain about the Christian ground rules regarding matters such as concubinage, divorce, and bigamy.[7] The gap between Christian teaching and Roman law meant that those who chose not to follow a bishop's advice would often have the law behind them. They might face ecclesiastical discipline, but this did not make their chosen arrangements invalid.[8] In the West, the added complication of the failure of Roman rule meant that husbands, wives, and bishops were often in all honesty unclear about who had jurisdiction and what rules applied to a given union. Perhaps because of this uncertainty over what norms were valid, marriage contracts became increasingly important across our period. Indeed, in 538, Justinian ruled that 'everyone except those of "abject life" had to have a document attesting their marriage registered with church authorities'.[9]

[5] Gillian Clark, *Women in Late Antiquity: Pagan and Christian Lifestyles* (Oxford, 1993).
[6] Judith Evans Grubbs, *Law and Family in Late Antquity: The Emperor Constantine's Marriage Legislation* (Oxford, 1995), 118–21.
[7] Philip Lyndon Reynolds, *Marriage in the Western Church: The Christianization of Marriage during the Patristic and Early Medieval Periods* (Leiden, 1994), 162–72.
[8] Reynolds, *Marriage in the Western Church*, e.g. 132.
[9] Judith Evans Grubbs, 'Marrying and its Documentation in Later Roman Law', in Reynolds and Witte, Jr., eds., *To Have and to Hold*: 43–94, at 93, citing Justinian, *Novel* 74.4 of 538. A law of 542, however, *Novel* 117.2–6, softened the requirement, restriciting it to *illustres*.

The few marriage contracts surviving or described in ancient sources have recently been the subject of exciting new studies.[10] To the degree that actual marriage tablets survive from late antiquity – and the evidence is limited to a very small number of papyri and wooden tablets – they contain nothing like the 'sale' of the wife implied by the passage above and by the passages in Augustine.[11] Rather, the focus is on 'marital intent' – i.e. establishing that the couple intend that the union should produce legitimate children – and on property arrangements. The marriage agreement drawn up for Gemina Januarilla and Julianus during the reign of the Vandal King Gunthamund (484–96) and preserved among the Albertini Tablets, for example, contains the traditional Roman assertion that the couple are marrying for the sake of begetting children, along with an agreement regarding the dowry, which is very much what we would expect.[12] There is no evidence that Roman marriage contracts involved subordination of the woman to the man in the way we have seen above.[13]

Indeed, Roman women did not, strictly speaking, come under the authority of the husband upon marriage. Legally, Roman women after the age of Augustus remained under the authority of their own *familia* when they married, rather than that of the husband. A tradition of Christian exegesis had seen the punishment of Eve as the beginning of a history of wifely subjugation[14] consolidated by the so-called 'Household tables' of the New Testament.[15] But there is no substantial evidence before 400 that these ideas were taken seriously by Roman wives of the upper

---

[10] Evans Grubbs and Hunter, as notes 2 and 9; see also Marcello Marin, 'Le *Tabulae matrimoniales* in S. Agostino', *Siculorum gymnasium* 29 (1976), 307–21.

[11] Evans Grubbs, 'Marrying and its Documentation', 74–85, and eadem, *Women and the Law in the Roman Empire: A Sourcebook on Marriage, Divorce, and Widowhood* (London, 2002), 122–35. On Augustine, see Brent Shaw, 'The Family in Late Antiquity: The Experience of Augustine', *Past and Present* 115 (1983), 3–51, citing Augustine *Serm.* 332.4 (*PL* 38, 1463), '"You are the master, she is the slave," those are the terms of the *tabellae matrimoniales*', with discussion at Michelle Renes Salzman, *Making of a Christian Aristocracy: Social and Religious Change in the Western Empire* (Cambridge, 2002), 148, along with other instances in Augustine's sermons adduced by Hunter, 'Marriage and the *Tabulae Nuptiales*'.

[12] For discussion, see Evans Grubbs, 'Marrying and its Documentation', 86–7.

[13] Antti Arjava, *Women and Law in Late Antiquity* (Oxford, 1996), notes at 130 that early medieval *formulae* for the marriage contract 'list only property items, neglecting all other aspects of married life'. It may be worth noting that one model will contains the phrase 'ego ancilla tua', addressed by the wife to the husband; see K. Zeumer, ed., *Formulae Merowingici et Karolini Aevi* (*MGH Leges* 5 (Hanover, 1866), 2.17).

[14] See, e.g., Elizabeth A. Clark, '"Adam's only companion": Augustine and the Early Christian Debate on Marriage', in R. R. Edwards and S. Spector, eds., *The Olde Daunce: Love, Friendship and Marriage in the Medieval World* (New York, 1991), 15–31 with notes at 240–54.

[15] Larry O. Yarborough, *Not Like the Gentiles: Marriage Rules in the Letters of Paul* (Atlanta, 1985).

classes, who inherited strong traditions of personal honour and obligation to their own blood kin. As we turn to consider late Roman law and custom on the relationship among members of the aristocratic household, we will see that Augustine's idea of the marriage contract as a contract of servitude was far from being widely accepted.

Augustine's point, to be sure, was that a Christian wife was best served by expecting less, rather than more, honour than she was likely to receive from her husband. In other words, he is not arguing that women *should* be subordinated in this way, but rather his intent is to ease the psychological burden of a subordination which he views as inevitable. There is certainly a great deal of evidence to support the view that married women, even women of property, were in a vulnerable position if the husband was not a man to be trusted.[16] However, Augustine's idea that the Christian wife is sold into slavery by the marriage contract is not widely attested beyond his own writings. This means that when we find the author of *Ad Gregoriam* returning to these ideas repeatedly, it is fair to believe that it reflects his self-conscious choice to invoke the spirit of Augustine. It is also reasonable to suspect that he means to alarm his reader, although to what purpose has to be determined.

ROMAN MARRIAGE IN LATE ANTIQUITY

There are a number of things we need to understand about the Roman institution of marriage in order to appreciate the difficulty, faced by late Roman jurists and churchmen, of reconciling the Roman and Christian traditions. To begin with, Roman marriage – *iustum matrimonium* – was not understood as conferring a permanent or irreversible bond between two persons. Even Justinian, the emperor most given to engaging with Christian teaching as a source for Roman law, was firm on this point. According to one modern historian, 'Justinian's "guiding thought" in the matter of divorce was the principle which he expressed in *Novel* 22: namely, that "of those things that occur between human beings, whatever is bound is soluble".'[17]

At the same time, Christian writers were developing an idea of the 'marital bond' as a permanent and irreversible union of two individuals. It was an idea wholly alien to Roman law, and innovative even from the

---

[16] Patricia Clark, 'Women, Slaves, and the Hierarchies of Domestic Violence: The family of St Augustine', in Sandra R. Joshel and Sheila Murnaghan, eds., *Women and Slaves in Greco-Roman Culture: Differential Equations* (London and New York, 1998), 109–29.

[17] Reynolds, *Marriage in the Western Church*, 63, citing John Noonan, 'Marital Affection', *Studia Gratiana* 12 (1967), 479–509; the reference is to Justinian's *Novel* 22 of 536.

point of view of a New Testament tradition that saw divorce as undesirable, but deferred to Torah or Roman law where validity was concerned. By contrast to the view of Justinian cited above, 'The guiding thought of men like Augustine was the premise that marriage not merely should not but *cannot* be dissolved: to leave one spouse and to marry another was to be guilty of adultery or bigamy, and therefore the new marriage was not valid.'[18] This was an entirely different conception, and one whose implications would not be fully felt by Latin Christians until the time when Roman law was no longer in force. Although emperors from Constantine to Justinian intervened repeatedly in fine-tuning the terms of Roman marriage, trying to clarify provisions that were subject to abuse, they did not alter its fundamental nature.

Under the Roman empire, *matrimonium* was essentially a reproductive contract between two kin groups, the contract by which the son of one family could 'borrow' the reproductive power of another man's daughter in order to continue his father's line. The wife did not 'join' the family of the husband. Up to the first century BC, so-called *manus* marriage had been the norm, and this form of marriage had involved transfer of the bride to the *familia* of the groom. But *manus* marriage had ceased to be the norm in the mid-first century BC.[19]

This means that under the empire, the Roman *familia* did not normally include the female head of the household. The *materfamilias* of course played an important role in her husband's *familia* both by bearing children and by assisting those of her children who belonged to it – especially by including them in her will – but juridically she stood apart.[20] It was as a member of her own father's *familia* that the *materfamilias* contracted to bear children for her husband's line. This point is more important than it sounds to a modern ear, because it means that a wife did not fall within the sphere of her husband's authority as *paterfamilias*. While her children from the marriage would belong to the *familia* of her husband, she herself would remain as part of her father's *familia* throughout her life. She might or might not be married to a *paterfamilias*, a male head of household; indeed, a *materfamilias* could find herself married to a *filiusfamilias* if the husband were the son of a still-living

[18] Reynolds, *Marriage in the Western Church*, 63.

[19] The erosion of *manus* marriage was not caused by the emergence of Augustus as *princeps*, although his legislation built in the same direction.

[20] Richard P. Saller, '*Pietas*, Obligation and Authority in the Roman Family', in Peter Kniessl and Volker Losemann, *Alte Geschichte und Wissnschaftsgeschichte: Festschrift für Karl Christ* (Darmstadt, 1988), 393–410, discusses at 408–10 the *paterfamilias* whose ambitions for his children by a rich wife depended on currying her favour.

father, and had not received *emancipatio*. In financial terms, her husband's establishment might be smaller or larger than her own according to the fortune each brought to the marriage. As with legal standing, so with wealth: the conjugal unit could be asymmetrical in favour of either husband or wife.

Ironically, the fact that the Romans placed such importance on the male line was by no means unfortunate from the point of view of the bride. Since the wife was also someone's daughter, the rights and protections accorded to her father and his line were in fact accorded to her. A Roman bride was valued as the hinge-figure in an important pact between two men – her own father and his son-in-law.

Marriage was a coalition by which the husband gained not one but a number of important relationships. Foremost, of course, with possible future sons. But first, with the older and often more powerful man who was the bride's father. If a young man married a woman of his own standing or higher, he was acquiring the patronage of a man who, if not richer than his son-in-law, was at least closer to the height of his powers. As we saw in Chapter One, there is evidence to suggest that this pattern changed in the fourth century, as young men began to marry 'down' rather than seeking to contract with families equal to or more powerful than their own. But before considering these changes, we must try to understand the starting-point from which they developed.

From the time of Augustus, the contract between husband and wife was understood as a mutually beneficial union between two discrete bloodlines. Its terms were designed to preserve the balance of wealth and power among families within each social class. Marriage was, fundamentally, a partnership for the purposes of reproduction. Naturally it involved various obligations and prohibitions, such as the prohibition of gifts between spouses and the obligation of the husband to provide residential accommodation for the wife, but it did not involve communal property or a legal union of the marriage pair. Once conception of legitimate children had taken place, the contract could be revoked by death or divorce without damage to the legitimacy of the offspring. Even if their birth postdated its rupture, as long as they were conceived while it was in force, the children of a marriage were deemed legitimate members of the father's *familia*.

Continued marriage between the spouses was seen as eminently desirable, not least because it protected the children from the ill-will of step-parents and the eventual claims of half-siblings, but the life-long union of marriage partners was a fragile ideal and by no means a legal requirement. Despite the narrowness of marriage in the legal sense, the ideal was certainly that husband and wife should live in harmony with one another. A high value had always been placed on marriages where husband and wife showed great loyalty to one another. The *Laudatio Turiae* praising a wife's loyalty to her husband during the civil wars of the first century BC is the classic example, but similar sentiments are copiously attested in texts and inscriptions up to the late empire.[21] Indeed, we shall see below that *consensus* between husband and wife was central to the definition of marriage, and the presence of marital *affectio* was the criterion dividing *concubinatus* from *matrimonium*.[22]

The establishment of the *materfamilias* and that of her husband were distinct; and the husband did not control that of the wife. There is in late Roman law no equivalent of the passing of *mundium* from father to husband, attested, for example, among the Lombards.[23] We saw in Chapter Three that when a daughter married, a dowry would pass from her father to her husband, to be administered by him on her behalf. But the wife retained ownership and the dowry was kept distinct from the individual property of both partners, to be returned to the wife or her father in the event of divorce or widowhood. The husband had *de facto* responsibility and authority in the *domus*, but the wife remained independent of him juridically. She managed her own property and if she was accountable, it was to her father or guardian, not to her husband. Reciprocal *pietas* between children and parents, not the union of the conjugal pair, stood at the centre of the Roman institution of the *familia*.

Roman thought assimilated biological parenthood and property ownership, and both were important markers of status, especially for men. The Roman *domus* had always served as an important context for élite men's efforts to display – and to claim – status.[24] At the same time, the

---

[21] On the sources for loyal (and disloyal) wives during the proscriptions of 43 BC see Susan Treggiari, *Roman Marriage: Iusti Coniuges from the Time of Cicero to the Time of Ulpian* (Oxford, 1991), 431–2. See also Plutarch, *Conjugal Precepts*, discussed in Kate Cooper, 'Insinuations of Womanly Influence: An Aspect of the Christianization of the Roman Aristocracy', *JRS* 82 (1992), 150–64, at 153–5. For late antiquity, the *locus classicus* of conjugal unity is the funerary inscription of Fabia Aconia Paulina to Vettius Agorius Praetextatus (*ILS* 1259; *CIL* 6:1, 1779), discussed in Kate Cooper, *The Virgin and the Bride: Idealized Womanhood in Late Antiquity* (Cambridge, Mass., 1996), 97–103; on this inscription see Maijastina Kahlos, 'Fabia Aconia Paulina and the Death of Praetextatus – Rhetoric and Ideals in Late Antiquity (CIL VI 1779)' *Arctos* 28 (1994), 13–25.

[22] Treggiari, *Roman Marriage*, 54–57.

[23] *Munt* or *mundium* was traditionally believed to be central to 'Germanic' marriage practice, but is not well documented except in the Lombard Kingdom; see now Ruth Mazo Karras, 'The History of Marriage and the Myth of Friedelehe', *Early Medieval Europe* 14 (2006), 119–51, who suggests at 130 that it is possible that the Lombards in fact adopted *mundium* not from ancient 'Germanic' practice but from Roman *manus* as described in Gaius' *Institutes*, a fifth- or sixth-century copy of which still survives from Northern Italy.

[24] Kate Cooper, 'Closely Watched Households: Visibility, Exposure, and Private Power in the Roman Household' (*Past and Present* 197, forthcoming 2007).

rituals of kinship served as a vehicle for establishing alliances and trying to make them stick. Historians of late antiquity and the early medieval period have yet fully to absorb the results of recent scholarship on Roman men, which has focused on the negotiation of authority. The position of the political male at every level of Roman society was perilous and needed to be repeatedly reconfirmed through competition and alliance building.[25] Traditionally, both pagan and Christian communities had seen the biological household as a testing-ground for male authority. Since the household was the key economic unit, Greek thought had, since the time of Plato, seen a man's loyalty to his own household as both a building-block of civic identity, and at the same time, a source of temptation to put the interests of his own kin ahead of the common good.[26] The household was not only a microcosm of the city; it was also a potential source of disloyalty to the city, in that a man would always be tempted to give priority to the interests of his own family over those of the common good. This is why his accountability in household governance was understood to be an effective measure of a man's political trustworthiness.

Marriage – the act by which one *familia* coopted the resources of another to establish a new household – was a perilous moment in the life-cycle of a Roman lineage, but equally perilous for the Roman city, since it was in the common interest that no single family succeed too completely in annexing resources at the expense of other families. As each new generation of men within a Roman *familia* negotiated their own standing and that of the new households which they established, they would be well aware of the social visibility of their domestic arrangements. Whom a man married, and on what terms, played an important role in consolidating a husband's social and political position. By achieving a semblance of domestic harmony with a respectable bride and then broadcasting the domestic virtues of his household, a man could both advertise and consolidate an important 'domestic advantage' in how he was viewed by other men.

---

[25] Carlin A. Barton, *Roman Honor: The Fire in the Bones* (Berkeley, 2001); J. E. Lendon, *Empire of Honour: The Art of Government in the Roman World* (Oxford, 1997).

[26] Cooper, 'Insinuations of Womanly Influence'; Kathy L. Gaca, *The Making of Fornication: Eros, Ethics, and Political Reform in Greek Philosophy and Early Christianity* (Berkeley, 2003), 28–55; Kate Cooper, 'Approaching the Holy Household', *Journal of Early Christian Studies* 15 (2007), 131–42.

FROM DIOCLETIAN TO JUSTINIAN: THE CHANGING BALANCE OF POWER IN THE LATE ROMAN HOUSEHOLD

It has been noted that from the early fourth century onward ambitious men were less likely than their ancestors to seek brides from families equal or superior to their own. It is a development which has only recently begun to attract the attention it deserves, and it is by no means fully understood. David Hunter has recently suggested that the changing rhetoric of Latin Christianity, like the changing concerns of Roman marriage legislation, constituted a response to this development,[27] and this evocative suggestion merits sustained inquiry.

The strengthening of the position of the husband in marriage appears in a number of contexts. On the one hand, from the early fourth century, we see the weakening of *tutela mulierum* – legal guardianship of women after emancipation or the death of their fathers – in Roman law.[28] At the same time, we will see below that an increasing emphasis on wifely obedience characterizes the fifth- and sixth-century Christian conduct literature addressed to Roman *dominae*.

The causal relations here are uncertain, and to establish them securely would lie beyond the scope of the present study. Our evidence, however, is compatible with the hypothesis, discussed in Chapter One, that by creating a situation in which power was leached away from the local communities toward the imperial bureaucracy, Diocletian had set in motion a 'domino effect' of social consequences favouring the young man who left home to seek his fortune at the appropriate level of the expanded bureaucracy over his contemporary who married a suitable bride and established himself as a pillar of his local community. This could have held true even if his 'local community' was the senate of Rome, since at each social level the same

---

[27] Hunter, 'Marrying and the *Tabulae Nuptiales* in Roman North Africa', 113, responding to Evans Grubbs, 'Marrying and its Documentation', 91–4.

[28] This form of *tutela* is to be distinguished from the role of the *tutor impuberis*, the guardian assigned to young men and women not *in potestate*. According to Arjava, *Women and Law*, 115–17, up to the third century the age of majority for girls was twelve and for boys fourteen, and a woman could normally be expected to obtain freedom from guardianship through the *ius trium liberorum*, so the additional protection of a *tutor mulierum* after the age of majority was necessitated by the vulnerable age of a young woman during her early married life. Changes to the system of wardship in the early third century, however, meant that a *curator minoris* had responsibility for both women and men up to the age of 25 if they were not *in potestate*, with the ward having the opportunity after 324 to request *venia aetatis*, an early majority (at 20 for boys and 18 for girls). Arjava suggests that the waning of *cura mulierum* in the fourth century was probably due to the later age of majority. A useful discussion of the legal sources can be found in Evans Grubbs, *Women and the Law in the Roman Empire*, 43–6.

phenomenon of social advancement through office-holding may have operated, *mutatis mutandis.*

In an environment where ambitious young men discover that the wealth and standing to be gained by seeking their fortune are more valuable than those to be gained by following the traditions of their elders, social upheaval is the natural consequence.[29] One of the consequences is often an unwillingness to follow the advice of elders who wish to steer the young man into marriage alliances which fulfill long-held local ambitions; the young men – and even the ambitious parent – can often see that once his fortunes have been made, the son will be able to attract a more powerful alliance. On the other hand, as we shall see below, he might be better served by in-laws of lesser standing. In either case, his best interest is no longer served by what his family might have chosen for him in a more stable environment.

One result of this instability might be sequential marriages, but since non-consensual divorce had been made far more difficult by Constantine, it was far better to defer marriage altogether. It was still possible, however, for a young man to establish a 'temporary' household, since *matrimonium* was only one of a number of kinds of stable sexual relationship sanctioned by Roman law and custom. *Matrimonium* was the contract necessary when citizens wished to produce children to whom the wealth and honour of both houses could pass.[30] Both men and women could in theory engage in citizen marriage sequentially, with legitimate offspring from each union. But men could also be involved sequentially in different *kinds* of reproductive relationship, beginning with *concubinatus* with a *concubina* of servile or lower status, whose children did not belong to his *familia*, and progressing later to *matrimonium* with a citizen whose children would be his rightful heirs. Even where *conubium* (the legal right to marry one another) was present, it was theoretically possible that marital intent was absent.[31]

---

[29] Here and below I owe a great deal to Mary Douglas, and to R. I. Moore's discussion of John Middleton's *Lugbara Religion: Ritual and Authority among an East African People* (London, 1960), in his 'Family, Community and Cult on the Eve of the Gregorian Reform', *Transactions of the Royal Historical Society*, 5th series 30 (1980), 49–69, at 64–5.

[30] Roman marriage necessarily involved two free citizens, a fact that would make for alarming consequences at the end of antiquity. During the barbarian invasions, Roman citizens taken captive were by definition no longer eligible to remain united in *matrimonium*. Justinian ruled in 536 that the marriage should be allowed to continue for as long as the captive was known to be alive, but it was a clear violation of the legal principle that marriage was an institution relevant only to the free citizenry. *Novel* 22 (AD 536); discussion in Reynolds, *Marriage in the Western Church*, 55–7.

[31] Treggiari, *Roman Marriage*, 43–9, discusses the rules of *conubium*, and at 54–7 the legal discussion surrounding *maritalis affectio* and *mens matrimonii*. Treggiari translates *maritalis affectio*, the key

In the fourth and fifth centuries many men followed this strategy, including at least some Christians, both priests and laity. The best-known instance of graduation from *concubinatus* to betrothal with a wealthy citizen is the long cohabitation of the young Augustine of Hippo with an unnamed concubine that produced his son Adeodatus, a relationship that ended when Augustine's mother arranged an advantageous citizen marriage with a Milanese heiress. Like Augustine's mother, many Roman parents may have seen concubinage as an orderly way to defer an ambitious son's entry onto the marriage market until he had reached his peak of attractiveness as a candidate. For the fourth-century men who used their individual gifts to take advantage of the social mobility resulting from favour and patronage with respect to imperially sponsored offices, this was a reasonable strategy. (Not long after his advantageous betrothal, for example, Augustine was appointed to the chair of Rhetoric at Milan through the patronage of Quintus Aurelius Symmachus, the eminent pagan senator, whose African connections were well exploited by Augustine's mother. In fact, Augustine did not go through with the marriage, but this does not change the fact that the betrothal was an important landmark in the dazzling career of a minor provincial from Thagaste.)

The progression from one type of sexual union to another, even by the ordained clergy, was accepted by the church hierarchy as a matter of course, and it may well have been viewed as offering a valuable 'loophole' in the marriage system by men, even pious Christians, who were made uneasy by the decreasing availability of unilateral divorce. For example, Rusticus, bishop of Narbonne, wrote to Pope Leo the Great in the 450s to discover whether the daughter of one of his priests could marry a man who had children by a slave concubine. The Roman bishop replied that, since the relationship with a *concubina* was not a marriage contract, it could be disssolved without legal action and presented no impediment to *matrimonium*. Leo did raise the possibility that if he wished for legitimate heirs the

term in the jurists, as 'literally a "marital attiude"' (54). She notes at 56 that it is particularly the intention of the man that is decisive in distinguishing *conubium* from *matrimonium*, although reciprocal intent was required to make a marriage; this said, in the early third-century *Digest* 'the cohabitation of a man and a woman would normally be assumed to be marriage unless there was evidence to the contrary'. Where there was a striking disparity of class, considerations of honour, or the preference that the woman be eligible to receive gifts (which were prohibited between husband and wife) from her partner, could make *concubinatus* the better option. Evans Grubbs, *Law and Family*, 295–6, notes, however, that under Constantine the ability to give gifts to a concubine was dramatically restricted.

man could manumit his concubine and, once she was a free citizen, could marry her, but this was merely a possibility, not a requirement.[32]

Ironically, the jockeying for position made possible by the reforms of Diocletian and Constantine seems to have encouraged men of high standing to consider acquiring a wife whose social standing did little to enhance his own. 'Marrying down' seems to have been a phenomenon associated with office-holding. Susan Treggiari has noted, for example, that in the Italian epigraphic evidence for the principate, 'the most striking feature of the men living in *concubinatus* is the number of those involved in the imperial cult and local government.'[33] If we accept the progressive dependence of increasingly senior men on imperial office for advancement, as discussed in Chapter One, it is not surprising to see them adopting a marriage strategy different to those of their less ambitious peers.

In an equal marriage, when a man married he gained an important alliance with an older man of his own social class, the father-in-law; the latter relationship would continue as long as the marriage endured and the father-in-law remained alive. But a man also gained something if he chose to marry a woman whose family could do nothing for him.[34] What such a family failed to offer by way of assistance, it made up for in deference. A man who married a woman well below his own standing could expect that his parents-in-law would do little to help him, but unlike their betters they would also do little to hold him back if he found an opportunity to pull himself up into a sphere of greater opportunity. This could be by commercial success, by a happy progression from appointment to appointment in the ladder of imperially sponsored offices, or by a deft combination of both strategies for advancement.

There is a paradox in the decreasing independence of Roman wives that resulted from this social climbing. The greater the wife's dependence on the husband, the less value the marriage alliance was likely to have in the husband's eyes. With the decline of *tutela mulierum*, the wife in theory gained greater independence after the death of her father, but both husband and wife lost something valuable. For the wife, what was lost was, quite simply, a powerful claim on her kin-group, the services of a male protector who could offer help of various kinds, especially should the husband prove

---

[32] Leo, *Epistula* 167 (*PL* 54, 1204–5), discussion in Reynolds, *Marriage in the Western Church*, 39 and 163–4, with Evans Grubbs, *Law and Family*, 309–16, and Arjava, *Women and Law*, 209, who suggests that it was unusual for a churchman to propose marrying the concubine in such an instance, citing Maximus of Turin, *Sermon* 88.5 (*CC* 23, 362) as 'rare advice'.

[33] Susan Treggiari, 'Concubinae', *Papers of the British School at Rome* 49 (1981), 59–81, at 68.

[34] Again, I am grateful to Mary Douglas for an eye-opening discussion on this point.

difficult.[35] For the husband, the disappearance of the wife's tutor seems at first sight to be a plus rather than a minus: it meant that once his father-in-law had died, his accountability to his wife's kin was greatly diminished. But in a balanced system of reciprocity, an obligation carries within it the right to make a claim. If the husband was accountable to the wife's father for treatment of the wife, he also could look to the father-in-law for assistance. Thus, the increased dependence of the wife proposed by Christian writers would not be as advantageous to the husband as it seems at first glance, *unless* the husband saw little or no value in the alliance with the wife's father.

Emperors and their quaestors repeatedly tried to bring order to the confusion caused by the rise of dual-status marriages. Efforts were made, for example, to discourage unequal unions, especially where this led to uncertainty about whether the children were legitimate. Confusion could arise as to whether a low-status mother was in fact a wife or a concubine; it was even possible that the spouses themselves had not achieved unanimity concerning the status of the union. Naturally, difficulties could arise as to the status of a couple's children when it hung on a legal criterion – the presence of 'marital intent' on the man's part – that might not be known even to the man himself. Judith Evans Grubbs has noted that late third- and early fourth-century emperors tried to resolve this ambiguity. While a fourth-century source, the *Historia Augusta*, suggests that Aurelian (270–75) had forbidden men outright to take free-born women as concubines, a fifth-century constitution of the emperor Zeno (474–91)[36] cites a law of Constantine, now lost, which seems to have laid out attractive terms for changing illegitimate children into legitimate heirs if the father married their free-born mother after their birth.[37]

---

[35] Up until the reign of Claudius, a woman's guardian had automatically been her agnatic next of kin; afterwards, the role could be assigned either through the father's will or through election by the woman herself, and her agnates seem to have had the right to refuse to serve. According to a law of Justinian (*CJ* 5.30.2), Constantine had re-established the agnatic guardianship, although possibly only for women up to the age of 12 (Arjava, *Women and Law*, 117). Constantin St. Tomolescu, 'Léon Ier et le droit privé', *Accademia Romanistica Constantiniana* 5 (Perugia, 1983), 59–69, argues at 65 that Constantine's law in fact offered women the right to coopt a male agnate to act as guardian; for him the point of the constitution was to prohibit the man thus called from declining to serve. Tomolescu sees guardianship as a benefit which women would have sought, while Arjava (114) sees it as a condition women would want to escape. At 115, Arjava notes, however, that women whose transactions are documented in the papyri often mention a male accompanying them even where they specify that they are acting in their own right owing to the *ius trium liberorum*.

[36] *CJ* 5.27.5 (477).

[37] In classical Roman law, the mother's status at the time of the child's birth was decisive for the child's status: Treggiari, *Roman Marriage*, 57. Where the mother was a free-born concubine this gave the father a number of months between conception and birth to consider his position with regard to both mother and child.

Constantine had made it clear, however, that this applied only to men who had already entered such unions; his aim seems to have been to discourage in future such ambiguous unions among those who ought simply to be married in the first place.[38] Taken with a surviving constitution of Constantine of 336 to the praetorian prefect Gregorius, which extends the Augustan restriction against the marriage of senators with freed-women to include provincial and local dignitaries, and threatens severe sanctions against 'men of rank who persisted in keeping as concubines the women whom they had been forbidden to marry', it suggests that Constantine was trying to limit the range of partnerships available to men of *dignitas* while at the same time encouraging the production of acceptable heirs. Evans Grubbs has shown through prosopographical study of Constantinian appointees such as Ablabius, praetorian prefect from 329 to 337 and Optatus, consul in 334, that wives of dubious origin seem to have been a problem even at the highest reaches of Constantine's government.[39]

Theodosius II ruled in 428 that when a union was not 'between equals' there must be a document for the union to be accepted as a marriage, and this may reflect an acknowledgement that it was not possible to prohibit such marriages altogether.[40] In 454, responding to a query from his praetorian prefect, the emperor Marcian clarified that the language of Constantine's constitution should not be taken as prohibiting the marriage between men of rank and the respectable poor; the phrase *humilis vel abiecta* ('lowly or degraded') referred not to *humiliores* in general but rather to the women in disreputable occupations, such as tavern-keeping, prosti-tution, and the theatre, which had been explicitly specified in the con-stitution itself.[41] It is well known that in the early 520s Justin repealed the Augustan legislation banning marriage between senators and actresses so that Justinian could marry Theodora. It now seems likely that the greater emphasis on documentation in the fifth and sixth centuries was an attempt to resolve problems caused by the increasing tendency of powerful men to marry down.[42] The changing class balance may explain why Christian

---

[38] Evans Grubbs, *Law and Family*, 298.
[39] The constitution in question is *CTh* 4.6.3 (21 July 336); I have attempted here to summarize very briefly the most salient points in the valuable discussion of this constitution in Evans Grubbs, *Law and Family*, 284–94 (esp. 286–7).
[40] *CTh* 3.7.3 (February 428); for discussion, see Evans Grubbs, 'Marrying and its Documentation', 88.
[41] (Marcian, *Novel* 4.4; April 454); discussion in Evans Grubbs, *Law And Family*, 292–3, who suggests that this reading of the earlier constitution was probably correct.
[42] *CJ* 5.4.23 (of 520–3), discussed in Evans Grubbs, 'Marrying and its Documentation', 92.

writers so often saw non-consensual divorce as an ethical issue, at least where the repudiation of a wife was concerned.[43]

Much scholarly discussion has centred on the problem of divorce in the period after Constantine. It has long been assumed that once a Christian emperor was in command, Christian families would have had no reason not to put into practice a 'literalist' reading of the passage in Matthew in which Jesus says, 'What God has joined, let no man put asunder' (Matt. 19:6). But this view of fourth-century ethics does not fit the evidence. In any age, of course, not all Christians are biblical literalists, but there is also the more strictly historical question of when and how the ideal of 'indissoluble marriage' became one which civil and ecclesiastical authorities embraced, and wished to – or believed they could – enforce. The short answer is that the development lies beyond our period. Up to the time of Justinian, Roman law allowed for divorce without difficulty where both parties wished it. But where the divorce was contested, emperors across the period from Constantine to Justinian tried successively to find fair terms on which to limit the power of spouses to repudiate a partner, if the partner wished to remain in the union.[44] It was once believed that Christianity was the reason for these changes to divorce law, but this view has now fallen out of favour.[45] In part, this is because of an increasing recognition that the view of marriage in the late Roman Church was 'less dogmatic and less theological' than that which came to predominate in the Latin Church of the High Middle Ages.[46] It is also more likely that the changes reflect an increasing perception that an older system of face-to-face negotiations between equally matched kin groups was no longer working, if it ever had. A rescript of the emperor Probus (276–82) to a certain Fortunatus regarding nuptial documentation, preserved in the *Codex Justinianus*, reflects the older view that the local memory of kin and neighbours

---

[43] Reynolds, *Marriage in the Western Church*, 128, summarizes a passage from Ambrose's *Commentary on Luke* (*CSEL*, 32.4, 393–4) that reflects a wider trend in fourth- and fifth-century preaching: 'Divorce offends charity, and divorcing a woman in the fragility of her youth leaves her prone to danger, while leaving a woman destitute in her old age shows a lack of *pietas*. If the emperor respects and takes care of his veterans, and if a responsible farmer does not turn out the farm labourer who has grown too old to work, how much more should a man keep faith with his wife, who is not his subject but his equal?' On the wider trend of bishops to preach against divorcing husbands, see Arjava, 'Divorce in Later Roman Law', *Arctos* 22 (1988), 5–21, at 10–12.

[44] A valuable summary of fluctuations in divorce legislation, with representative texts, is offered in Evans Grubbs, *Women and the Law*, 202–10.

[45] Roger Bagnall, 'Church, State, and Divorce in Late Roman Egypt', in R. E. Somerville and K.-L. Selig, eds., *Florilegium Columbianum: Essays in Honor of Paul Oskar Kristeller* (New York, 1987), 41–61; Arjava, *Women and Law*, 184, with summary of the more recent secondary literature; Evans Grubbs, *Law and Family in Late Antiquity*, 253–60.

[46] Reynolds, *Marriage in the Western Church*, 64.

could be relied upon to safeguard against abuses. Responding to Fortunatus' worry that his children will not be acknowledged as legitimate, the emperor reassures him: 'If you have had a wife in your home for the sake of begetting children (*liberorum procreandorum causa*) and your neighbours or others knew this, and a daughter from the marriage has been acknowledged (*suscepta*), then although neither a nuptial document not a document pertaining to the birth of your daughter have been drawn up, your marriage and your daughter are legitimate nonetheless.'[47] The passage offers a concrete illustration of the mechanisms of a face-to-face society, in that Probus' neighbours were clearly expected to have brought him into line had he been deceiving the mother of his children as to whether the relationship was one of 'marital intent'; their witness means that the relationship was accorded legal standing despite the lack of documentation. Equally, they could be expected to protect his widow's claims if he died intestate and other relatives set their sights on his estate. It was this kind of self-regulation that could no longer be counted on in the fifth century.

In a striking article of 1987, Roger Bagnall argued for the fourth and fifth centuries that in Egypt, where civil and canon law can be 'tested' against the documentary evidence of divorce contracts and affidavits, a picture emerges of 'a pastoral church with limited authority over its members', a Church without, in other words, any power to impose its norms.[48] Christian bishops seem to have played an important role in supporting Christian families, for example by advising in cases of marital conflict, but they do not seem to have been in a position to require that their advice be followed. Discussing the attempts by married women to gain protection from violent husbands preserved in *P. Oxy* VI 903 and *P. Oxy* L 3581, respectively a fourth-century affadavit and a petition dated to the fourth or fifth century, Bagnall noted that 'there is not in either document any indication of any disciplinary attempts or coercion by the clergy; rather, so far as we can see, these texts are evidence for a reconciling pastoral role.'[49] Even in cases where Christian social norms were supported by Roman law, such as these attempts to prohibit aggravated assault, the

---

[47] *CJ* 5.4.9, cited in Reynolds, *Marriage in the Western Church*, 17; I cite his translation, although Reynolds uses the passage in support of a different point.

[48] Bagnall, 'Church, State, and Divorce', 61.

[49] Bagnall, 'Church, State, and Divorce', 59. Compare also the discussion of *P. Oxy* VI 903 in Patricia Clark, 'Women, Slaves, and the Hierarchies of Domestic Violence: The family of St Augustine', in Sandra R. Joshel and Sheila Murnaghan, eds., *Women and Slaves in Greco-Roman Culture: Differential Equations* (London and New York, 1998), 109–29, with Cooper, 'Closely Watched Households'.

bishops seem to have worked in cooperation with civil magistrates, but themselves to have exercised little real authority. How much less, then, could they enforce Christian ideals that were at variance with the law. Such ideals (such as strictures on divorce) had to be explained very persuasively. We will see below that bishops such as Augustine and Fulgentius of Ruspe did receive queries from pious families who wished to receive guidance about Christian norms above and beyond those of Roman law, but there is no evidence as to whether the advice, once received, was followed.

THE EARLY CHRISTIAN LEGACY

The 'Christianization' of marriage represented a self-conscious attempt on the part of ecclesiastical writers to establish the husband–wife relationship as a newly central axis of loyalty and reciprocity during a period of social and political upheaval. By comparison to traditional Roman and barbarian forms of marriage, which allowed for divorce, polygamy, or both, Christian writers attempted to make the bond of affinity (*adfinitas*) as binding as other forms of kinship, at the same time as it was elective – a man could choose his affines in a way he could not choose his consanguine kin. In this respect, Christian marriage was not entirely unlike the 'elective kinship' of early Christian communities.[50] The promotion of the conjugal bond was yet another means by which Christian teaching sought to undermine the Roman emphasis on consanguinity.

A number of common misunderstandings about early Chrisitan marriage must be dispelled if we wish to understand how Christian ideas came to influence Roman custom in the fourth and fifth centuries. The first is that early Christian teaching was 'procreationist', i.e. that it was believed that sex between married partners could only be justified by an intent to conceive children. (By the second century, this view had taken hold, but it is no means implied by the New Testament sources.) The second misapprehension is that early Christian bishops agreed that divorce and remarriage among Christians was unacceptable. The third involves confusion about whether early Christian writers approved of marriage in the first place.

We will start with the problem of the early Christian ambivalence about marriage as an institution. A trend of scholarship over the past two decades has sought to establish whether the earliest Christian groups were pro- or anti-marriage. One strand of theologically oriented scholarship on early

---

[50] Nathan, *The Family in Late Antiquity*, 214, on fictive kin groups.

Christianity, developed in dialogue with Michel Foucault's *History of Sexuality*, has seen asceticism as a core impulse of the early Christian movement. According to this view, the eroticized bonds of friendship in early ascetic communities represented the core contribution of Christian ethics to the ancient Mediterranean.[51] This strand of scholarship sees the ethics of the emerging Christian household as a repressive force, and seeks to establish that this householder Christianity is a secondary development, a reaction to an early tradition of Christianity as a movement of 'liberation'.[52] The present study takes a different approach, one rooted in the questions and methods of social history rather than theological engagement. Our interest here is in reconstructing the social dynamics governing participation in Christian institutions.

While we consider the literary evidence produced by bishops and visionaries, our interest is less in these exceptional figures than in the hidden landscape inhabited by a 'silent majority' of religious 'minimalists', sane and practical people who simply wanted to find a way to live as painlessly as possible within the framework of existing ideas and institutions. That these minimalists also, on occasion, lent the weight of their participation to one idea or institution rather than another, means that they were not without a voice in the historical process, but it is a voice which has all too often been neglected by historians, in part because the medieval librarians who preserved the evidence from our period perceived the texts by and for these 'minimalists' as unimportant.

From the mid-fourth century onward, the 'silent majority' begins to be more visible in the sources. This is essentially because it is only after the conversion of Constantine that we see the conversion of large numbers of men and women rich enough to appear in the documentary record even if they were not famous. What this means for the historian is that many questions about lay participation in Christian institutions can only really be asked after a certain watershed moment in the evidence; for the West, this is roughly the reign of Pope Damasus (366–84).

Our best evidence for the earlier centuries suggests that Christian writers were ambivalent about marriage and the biological family.[53] The first Christian writer, the apostle Paul, had expected the *eschaton* (the end of

---

[51] Virginia Burrus, *The Sex Lives of Saints: An Erotics of Ancient Hagiography* (Philadelphia, 2004).
[52] Mark Jordan, *The Ethics of Sex: New Dimensions to Religious Ethics* (Oxford, 2002), 71, with discussion in Burrus, *Sex Lives of Saints*, 2–3.
[53] Carolyn Osiek, 'The Family in Early Christianity: "Family Values" Revisited', *Catholic Biblical Quarterly* 58 (1996), 1–24. See also Elizabeth A. Clark, 'Antifamilial Tendencies in Ancient Christianity', *Journal of the History of Sexuality* 5 (1995), 356–80.

the world) to take place within his own life-time, and he had therefore discouraged his followers from making long-term plans for their private lives. In 1 Corinthians he says, 'I think that, in view of the impending crisis, it is well for you to remain as you are. Are you bound to a wife? Do not seek to be free. Are you free from a wife? Do not seek a wife' (1 Corinthians 7:26–7). For Paul, to be 'bound to a wife' is to embrace, along with the hoped-for pleasures of conjugal life, anxieties and responsibilities that may be crushing in the context of the coming *eschaton*. Paul did not see much value in procreation, given his firm expectation that the end of the world was approaching, but he did see fornication – sex outside the marriage bed – as an important stumbling-block for Christians, who needed to cultivate ritual and spiritual purity as they faced the coming end of time.[54] Paul's plan of action in the battle against fornication was to fight fire with fire. He saw what Kathy Gaca has called 'the pure blue flame of marital sex'[55] as his most powerful weapon in the war against fornication. Paul allows that those who wish to marry may do so, not so that they can have children, but so that their sexual cravings can be satisfied without harm to the community.

Later generations, however, fought what Dennis MacDonald has called 'the battle for Paul', attempting to establish whether the apostle should be remembered as the founder of the Christian family or its most trenchant critic.[56] Some remembered Paul as the founder of a radical view of virginity. The reason can be found if one looks ahead a few lines in the same letter to the Corinthians:

Yet those who marry will experience distress in this life, and I would spare you that. I mean, brothers and sisters, the appointed time has grown short; from now on, let even those who have wives be as though they had none, and those who mourn as though they were not mourning . . . For the present form of this world is passing away. I want you to be free from anxieties. The unmarried man is anxious about the affairs of the Lord, how to please the Lord, but the married man is anxious about the affairs of the world, how to please his wife, and his interests are divided (1 Corinthians 7:28–30, 32–4).

Paul's ideas here draw on a standard debate among pagan philosophers about whether a man committed to philosophy could afford to involve himself in the emotionally unbalancing business of raising children. We

---

[54] Michael Newton, *The Concept of Purity at Qumran and in the Letters of Paul* (Cambridge, 1985).
[55] Gaca, *The Making of Fornication*, 240.
[56] Dennis MacDonald, *The Legend and the Apostle: The Battle for Paul in Story and Canon* (Philadelphia, 1983).

will be in a better position to grasp what was at stake in this debate if we remember that first-century social and medical conditions forced even the very rich to expect to lose a majority of their offspring to infant and child mortality.[57]

Clearly these words meant one thing in the context of an imminent end to the world, and another if those who embraced Paul's message had to wait, generation after generation, for an end that never seemed to come. A generation after Paul, the author of the Gospel of John remembered Jesus as having challenged the claims of biological kinship by offering, through the medium of the Christian *ecclesia*, a form of elective kinship. His version of the passion narrative records Jesus speaking from the Cross to his mother, who stood vigil with her sister and Mary Magdalene. Calling out to her and pointing to the Beloved Disciple, 'he said to his mother, "Woman, behold your son!" Then he said to the disciple, "Behold your mother!" And from that hour the disciple took her to his own home' (John 19:26–7). A second-century tradition in the *Apocryphal Acts of the Apostles* celebrated the dedication of Christian wives who refused to sleep with their husbands, despite the apostle Paul's having made it clear that the point of Christian marriage was no more nor less than to offer an acceptable vehicle for sexual recreation.[58] By the middle of the second century, however, the re-reading of Paul as a 'teacher of virginity' was in turn challenged.

Having noticed that the end of the world had failed to arrive, one or more anonymous second-century authors decided that Christian norms for the family should be put into place.[59] The resulting texts, the first and second Letters to Timothy and Letter to Titus of the New Testament, are known as deutero-Pauline epistles because they were written in Paul's name, and accepted by later generations as his authentic writings. Ironically, it was the pro-marriage writers of the second century who abandoned Paul's idea of marriage. They saw marriage as the cornerstone of a new, Christian social order to be established in this world so long as it lasted, and as the source of a new community of saints to be raised as children within the faith.

The pagan philosophical tradition was more suspicious of the bonds of biological kinship as a force that could undermine the solidarity of a community. Both Plato and the early Stoics had seen some form of

---

[57] Bruce W. Frier, 'Natural Fertility and Family Limitation in Roman Marriage', *Classical Philology* 89 (1994), 318–33.

[58] For discussion, see Cooper, *The Virgin and the Bride*, Ch. 3, 'The Bride that is no Bride'.

[59] MacDonald, *The Legend and the Apostle*, and Margaret Y. MacDonald, *Early Christian Woman and Pagan Opinion: The Power of the Hysterical Woman* (Cambridge, 1996).

communism as a crucial measure for shielding the common good from the ill effects of unrestrained desire. Greed, they argued, not desire (lust) *per se*, was the most important social danger. Greed was ultimately the fruit of the procreative impulse, evident in the fact that parents tend to hoard whenever they can for the sake of their offspring. A truly rational society, they argued, would break the hold of biological reproduction as the point of gravity for cohabitation and social allegiance.[60]

Under the influence of the Septuagint, Christian 'procreationists' began to develop an idea of 'fornication' – *porneia* – as a betrayal of the bond between God and Israel. While *porneia* in pagan texts refers in a comparatively neutral descriptive sense to prostitution, in the Septuagint it refers to sexual transgressions against the authority of God. As Gaca puts it, 'sexual defilement and dishonor are incorporated into a new order of wrongdoing – disobeying a deity who requires unconditional obedience and devotion.'[61] As imagined by both Jews and Christians, God is a jealous lover, whose people must humble themselves on the model of an adulterous wife hovering in fear of punishment. Here a specific demographic threat to the growth of Israelite religion – that of intermarriage with women who will raise the couple's children in a gentile faith – takes on a metaphorical life of its own.

We will see below that among the later patristic writers Augustine of Hippo and John Chrysostom were rather more interested in Plato's sense of the tension between the household and the common good than in a procreationist repudiation of sexual pleasure *per se*. We saw above that Augustine was acutely conscious of the narrowing scope of the wife in Christian marriage. His view of marriage, we will see, was deeply paradoxical. On the one hand, he stood against Jerome as a passionate defender of what Robert Markus has called 'Christian mediocrity';[62] while Jerome encouraged ascetics to cultivate a 'holy arrogance' with regard to those whose religious aspirations were not as exalted as their own, Augustine made every effort to offer the married a place within the Christian polity which, if not exalted, was at least a place of honour. But later in his career, Augustine found himself in controversy with Julian, the young bishop of Eclanum in southern Italy, who believed that Augustine's views on human nature were perilously close to the views of the Manichaeans. Thus by the early fifth century, the Pelagian controversy had developed into a debate

---

[60] Gaca, *The Making of Fornication*, 28–55.   [61] Gaca, *The Making of Fornication*, 126.
[62] Markus' ch. 4, 'Augustine: A Defence of Christian Mediocrity', in his *The End of Ancient Christianity* (Cambridge, 1990), 45–62, remains an immensely useful exposition of this theme.

over Christian marriage, a debate in which Augustine found himself trying to defend himself against the argument that his views of grace and free will led irretrievably to undermine the foundation of the married estate.

AUGUSTINE, PELAGIUS, AND THE LATIN READERS OF JOHN CHRYSOSTOM

It is useful to begin our consideration of the late fourth-century debate with a discussion of John Chrysostom, whose authority would become a central point of contention in the controversies over marriage of the 420s. It is easy to see why Chrysostom was chosen as an iconic figure in the debate over Christian marriage. His exegetical sermons on Paul, for example, repeatedly sound the theme of the importance of marriage, both as a tonic to the passions and as a school for harmony whose results will ramify beyond the walls of the Christian home and into the Christian city. In his twelfth homily on Colossians, John suggests that a chaste wedding will attract Christ as a guest: 'Christ himself will come to your wedding, and where Christ goes, the choir of the angels follows. If you so desire, He will work for you an even greater miracle than he worked in Cana: that is, he will transform the water of your unstable passions into the wine of spiritual unity.'[63]

In his twentieth homily on Ephesians he specifies that desire itself is not an obstacle to the chaste marriage but can in fact serve as a crucial agent to further the marriage's social purpose: 'Nothing welds society together so much as the desire (*eros*) of husband and wife ... when harmony (*homonoia*) prevails, the children are raised well, the household is kept in order, and neighbours, relatives, and friends enjoy the fragrance. Great benefits, both for families and for states, are thus produced.'[64] This may be related to a passage in the *Baptismal Instructions*, where sexual intercourse is understood precisely as a means granted by God to unify man and woman after the Fall has sundered them.[65]

A classically trained Christian preacher such as Chrysostom could easily adapt his praise of virtue in terms which remembered the tension between the individual and the common good. Chrysostom was known for passionate preaching on the dangers of avarice and cupidity, and his sense

[63] John Chrysostom, *Hom. XII in Col.* (*PG* 62, 389).
[64] John Chrysostom, *Hom. XX in Eph.* (*PG* 62, 136).
[65] John Chrysostom, *Baptismal Instructions*, 2.7 (*SC* 50, 2nd edn, 137).

of the possible obstacles to a well-made marriage dwelt less on lust than on money. His instinct was that parents cared less for moral probity than financial prospects as they arranged the marriages of their children, and thus the family's standing for the next generation.[66] Against this tendency, John posed the formidable wherewithal of his irony.

What, then, is the reason for marriage, and on what account has God established it? Listen to Paul, saying, 'on account of fornication, let each man have his own wife' (1 Cor. 7:2). He did not say, for the sake of deliverance from poverty, or on account of the acquisition of means, but why? So that we might shun fornication; so that we might check lust, so that we might be yoked together in temperance (*sōphrosynēi*), so that we might please God . . .[67]

Seen in this light, lust was a lesser evil, posing a straightforward danger whose remedy was well known. Greed, on the other hand, was insidious, and it could lurk behind the seemingly honorable concern for the welfare of one's family.

Sexual desire would only constitute sin in cases where immoderate use deformed it to the likeness of greed, for the root of sin was not in the body but in the heart: 'Desire is not sin, but whenever it slips into immoderation, not wishing to remain within the law of marriage but attaching itself to other men's wives, then the business becomes adultery, but not through desire: rather through excessive grasping where desire is concerned.'[68] John saw sexual desire as an accompanying factor – rather than the cause – of the soul's internal conflict with the vices of intemperance and cupidity. However, that it was a factor which held a particular rhetorical interest was not lost on him. Thus the wedding night itself became an occasion for the confrontation of philosophy not with sexual pleasure but with greed: 'From that very night on which he first receives her into the bridal chamber, let him teach her temperance, gentleness, and the holy life, casting away all love of money at the beginning and from the very threshold.'[69] Note that it is love of money, not lust, that must be banished from the marriage as a matter of first importance. It was by the cultivation of temperance and open-heartedness, and not by anti-sexual calisthenics, that marriage could become a veritable school for virtue, a school second only to

---

[66] Blake Leyerle, 'Too Close for Comfort: John Chrysostom, Authority Issues, and Ascetical Couples', North American Patristics Society Annual Meeting, Chicago, 1990, reminds us that these rhetorical exhortations to poverty were directed to an audience of substantial means: they can only be understood as exhortations to poverty in relative terms.

[67] John Chrysostom, *Quales ducendae sint uxores* (*PG* 51, 232).

[68] John Chrysostom, *Hom. in Ep. ad Romanos* 7.14 (*PG* 60, 508–9).

[69] John Chrysostom, *Hom. in Eph.* 5.22 (*PG* 62, 145).

the desert. After lovingly describing a husband and wife in earnest debate over the spiritual meaning to be drawn from the sermons they have heard in church together, Chrysostom concludes: 'if anyone marries in this way and on these terms, he or she will not be inferior by far to the monks, nor the married be inferior to the unmarried.'[70]

It is somewhat ironic that Augustine was suspected of enmity to marriage, because he approached the theme of the virtuous householder in a way very similar to Chrysostom's. In book 5 of his *City of God*, he dwelt with particular emphasis on vigilance for the city's well-being as he reviewed the traditional Roman ideal of immaculate conduct. This concern of the earthly city was especially vivid to a mind which saw as the defining force of human sin its tendency to draw the individual away from life-giving communion with other human beings, and into a sterile privacy of intent.[71] That Augustine came to shun the hope of an earthly city made whole by the reciprocity of its inhabitants should not lead us to underestimate his sympathy for the civic aspirations of Graeco-Roman ethics. In his catalogue of the vices which the worthy conduct of the *maiores* had scorned, pride of place was given to the most explicitly anti-civic of these:

They took no account of their own material interest compared with the common good, that is the commonwealth and the public purse; they resisted the temptations of avarice; they acted for their country's well-being with disinterested concern; they were guilty of no offence against the law; they succumbed to no sensual indulgence.[72]

Sensual indulgence fell behind avarice and the questionable use of public funds because of their perniciousness as vices which furthered the individual's private (or familial) good at the expense of the wider community. Traditionally, avarice was understood as the refusal of prosperous citizens to contribute their share of the benefactions on which cities depended – a vice whose result was explicitly civic. Christian writers would attempt to define it increasingly in terms of a refusal to contribute to the work of the Church rather than the city, but it remained the paradigmatic betrayal of community.

For a writer such as Augustine, the sins of the flesh were not in themselves as troubling as the immoderation of men or families who would betray the common good for the sake of financial gain. The insubordination of the

---

[70] John Chrysostom, *Hom. in Eph.* 5.22, (*PG* 62, 147).

[71] Robert Markus has taken care to underline the coincidence of privacy and spiritual deprivation in Augustine's thought. On the result of this insight for Augustine's view of human community, especially in defining the particular calling of monastic communities, see now Markus, *The End of Ancient Christianity*, 78ff.

[72] *Civ. Dei* 5.15 (*CSEL* 40, 242).

sexual urge was a revealing symbol for the danger which this self-interest posed to the common good,[73] but it was not the cause of the problem.[74] During the years around 400, Augustine had famously taken up against Jerome, whose *Adversus Jovianianum* argued that marriage could not offer a path to virtue equal to that offered by asceticism.[75] Jovinian, himself a monk, had argued that Christian marriage and asceticism were equally valid. It was Augustine who brokered the terms of compromise in his *De sancta virginitate* and *De bono coniugali*, both written around 400. Marriage should be honoured as a virtuous path, even if widowhood and virginity were incrementally better.[76] Here the metaphor of the thirtyfold, sixtyfold, and hundredfold fruit from the Gospel of Matthew (Matthew 13:23) was put to work, with virginity representing the hundredfold. At the same time, Augustine reminded his readers, there was no cause for praise in ascetic achievement if it came at the expense of charity and humility.

We turn now to the passionate debate in the 420s between Augustine of Hippo and Julian of Eclanum, a young married bishop whose senatorial mentors in southern Italy included Paulinus of Nola. In his *Contra Iulianum Pelagianum* (c. 421), Augustine defended himself against Julian's accusation that, in addition to calling into question God's justice and his status as the benevolent creator of humanity, Augustine's view of original sin would deny the remission of sins in baptism and would thus condemn marriage. During the course of his debate with Augustine, Julian effectively branded Augustine's views as neo-Manichaean, and set them in opposition to Chrysostom's. Whether he did so maliciously or in ignorance of the many similarities between the two writers' views need not

[73] For a ramifying explication of Augustine's use of the sexual urge as a symbol of the dislocation of the will, see Peter Brown, 'Sexuality and Society in the Fifth Century AD: Augustine and Julian of Eclanum', in E. Gabba, ed., *Tria Corda: scritti in onore di Arnaldo Momigliano* (Como, 1983) 1, 49–70. The intent of the present study is to modify the polarity posed by Brown between 'Julian's essentially physiological view of sexuality ... hand in hand with an ancient faith that sexuality, like any other instinctual drive, was amenable to the will', and Augustine's 'novel manner of interpreting the physiology and psychology of sex ... at variance with all current medical opinion', by suggesting that if viewed in light of ethics rather than medicine, the two authors would be seen to differ not in their understanding of sexuality (primarily in terms of a semiotics of male self-control), but rather in their prescriptions for the tension between *caritas* and immoderation.
[74] See Kate Cooper and Conrad Leyser, 'The Gender of Grace: Impotence, Servitude and Manliness in the Fifth-Century West', *Gender and History* 12.3 (2000), 536–51.
[75] On this controversy, see now David G. Hunter, *Marriage, Celibacy, and Heresy in Ancient Christianity: The Jovinianist Controversy* (Oxford, 2007).
[76] For more extensive discussion, see Markus, *End of Ancient Christianity*, Ch. 5, 'A Defence of Christian Mediocrity', and Cooper, *The Virgin and The Bride*, Ch. 5, 'The Whispering Critics at Blaesilla's Funeral'.

concern us here, although we will see below that a minor scholarly industry emerged in the fifth century to emphasize divergences between Augustine and Chrysostom.

Although Julian's critique of Augustine developed from concerns about grace and free will, sexual ethics and the role of married householders took centre stage in the 420s. This may explain why an obviously Latin letter like *Ad Gregoriam in palatio* was copied under the name of Chrysostom from as early as the sixth or early seventh century.[77] Indeed, Dom Morin argued nearly a century ago that it was in the context of the debate between Julian and Augustine that our few surviving conduct manuals for the married laity were produced, but there is little real evidence to support this hypothesis.

It may be misleading to see the debate over sexual ethics as an aspect of the Pelagian controversy, despite Augustine's efforts to frame Julian as a Pelagian, since it is impossible to identify a coherent 'Pelagian' position in this area. Gerald Bonner suggested over thirty years ago that the affiliates of Pelagius were not 'a party with a rigidly defined doctrinal system; they were a mixed group, united by certain theological principles which nevertheless left the individual free to develop his own opinions on particular topics,'[78] and this is nowhere truer than in the context of sexual ethics. A case has recently been made by Jean-Marie Salamito for the coherence of a Pelagian 'party' in the first quarter of the fifth century,[79] but it is a view that is very difficult to defend.

Pelagius himself, for example, was long believed by scholars to have been a proponent of radical asceticism, but this view must now be abandoned. It relied on the inclusion among Pelagius' writings of *De castitate*, a radical ascetic work which De Plinval attributed to Pelagius,[80] but which is now understood as an exaggeration of Pelagius' teaching in the direction of radical asceticism.[81]

---

[77] Isidore of Seville records it as a letter of Chrysostom: *De viris illustribus* 19 (s.v. Johannes Chrysostomus): 'Ad personam quoque cuiusdam nobilissimae matronae Gregoriae reperitur opus eius insigne de conversatione vitae et institutione morum, sive de compugnantia virtutum et vitiorum' (*PL* 83, 1095–6).

[78] Gerald Bonner, *Augustine and Modern Research on Pelagianism* (The Saint Augustine Lecture, 1970) (Villanova, 1972), 31.

[79] Jean-Marie Salamito, *Les Virtuoses et la multitude: aspects sociaux de la controverse entre Augustin et les pélagiens* (Grenoble, 2005).

[80] Georges De Plinval, *Pélage: ses écrits, sa vie et sa réforme* (Lausanne, 1943), 44–5.

[81] On the authorship of the *De castitate*, see S. Prete, 'Lo scritto pelagiano "De castitate" è di Pelagio?', *Aevum* 35 (1961), 315–22, and Robert F. Evans, *Four Letters of Pelagius* (New York, 1968), 24ff. On Pelagian views of marriage, Carlo Tibiletti, 'Teologia pelagiana su celibato/matrimonio', *Augustinianum* 27 (1987), 487–507.

Across our period, the primary meaning of *castitas* was as the virtue of sexual modesty associated with a fertile and honourable Roman wife, the virtue of exemplary conjugal fidelity within a reproductively active marriage.[82] *De castitate*, however, offered a new and tendentious definition of *castitas* as sexual renunciation. The treatise stood at the radical end of what was in fact a wide spectrum of views on sexual ethics among the followers of Pelagius; at the conservative end, Julian of Eclanum saw the logical outcome of Pelagius' views as leading in precisely the opposite direction, toward a reaffirmation of marriage.

The view of *De castitate* should probably be understood as a 'fringe' view in its fifth-century context, and certainly not as characterisic of 'Pelagian' sexual ethics, if there was such a thing. As Robert F. Evans put it, Pelagius

[did not] share the view of the author of *De castitate* that *castitas* [defined, idiosyncratically for the period, as continence] is the '*fundamentum* ... *sanctitatis atque iustitiae*', a view which sets the latter author's treatment of the subject quite apart from the opinion of Pelagius that the fulfilment of *iustitia* is the common vocation of all Christians and that the continent accomplish something over and above this, the '*consilium perfectionis*'.[83]

It has also been suggested that Pelagius' own writings were tampered with in transmission. For example, it has now been argued that a much-quoted passage on marriage as appropriate only for the spiritually ill in Souter's text of Pelagius' *Expositions on Thirteen Epistles of Saint Paul* was in fact a later interpolation,[84] a distortion of his meaning by a later ascetically minded writer.

In 1967 a remarkable study by François-Joseph Thonnard[85] approached the question of how John Chrysostom's authority figured in the polemic between Augustine and Julian of Eclanum. Julian had called Chrysostom among others to witness against Augustine; Augustine's response was to assert systematically, through a recapitulation of John's works known to him, that John showed no sign of differing from his own exegesis on this point. He was able to do this largely because Chrysostom did not address

---

[82] Kate Cooper, 'Chastity', *Encyclopedia of Religion* (2nd edn, Framington Hills, Michigan, 2004) 3, 1557–60, at 1558; Helen North, *Sophrosune: Self-Knowledge and Restraint in Classical Antiquity* (Ithaca, 1966).

[83] Evans, *Four Letters of Pelagius*, 25.

[84] See Evans, *Four Letters of Pelagius*, 25 n. 67; the passage under discussion is the commentary on 1 Cor. 7:3–5. Celestin Charlier, 'Cassiodore, Pélage, et les origines de la Vulgate paulinienne', *Studiorum Paulinorum Congressus Internationalis* (Rome, 1963), 2, 461–70, calls into question Souter's choices in editing the *Expositions* in light of his own inquiry into the idiosyncratic transmission process.

[85] François-Joseph Thonnard, 'Saint Jean Chrysostome et Saint Augustin dans la controverse Pélagienne', *Revue des études byzantines* 25 (1967) (Mélanges Venance Grumel 2), 189–218.

the question of original sin; but this does not invalidate his point. Thonnard characterized Augustine's approach as essentially disingenuous: 'cette "charité doctrinale" qui préfère, en lisant un auteur aussi attaché à la foi catholique que saint Jean, prolonger sa pensée dans le sens de la vérité.'[86] The fact was that Augustine himself had written in defence of marriage on terms not dissimilar to John's. Julian, however, had found what he believed was an inconsistency in Augustine's thinking, and he drove the point home with relish.

An important study by Pier Franco Beatrice in the 1980s explored the Pelagian sympathy with the Eastern tradition of the Church, suggesting that Julian's interpretation of John Chrysostom was not only made in good faith but substantially correct.[87] Further, Beatrice explained the Eastern theological context which informed Julian's anxiety that Augustine's views would lead to a condemnation of marriage and to the ever-present danger of Manichaeism.[88] The men who rallied to the defence of Pelagius against what they perceived as a threat of Manichaeism were motivated both by their study of Eastern handbooks against the early heresies condemning marriage, and by the provocation closer to home of a lively Western Manichaean faction, whose place in Augustine's own past was well advertised.[89] The concern in the late fourth century to protect marriage against a threat posed by Manichaeism has also been stressed by David Hunter, who has made it clear how urgent a figure like Jovinian felt it was to defend marriage against the learned and numerous Manichaean contingent at Rome, who found it despicable.[90]

The career of a little-known figure among the Pelagians, Anianus of Celeda, shows that the translation of Chrysostom's writings into Latin was an important commitment of Julian's circle. What is known about Anianus with certainty is that he translated at least two works of John Chrysostom from Greek into Latin, providing what seem to have been the

---

[86] Thonnard, 'Saint Jean Chrysostome', 218.

[87] Pier Franco Beatrice, *Tradux peccati: alle fonti della dottrina agostiniana del peccato originale*, Studia patristica mediolanensia 8 (Milan, 1978), 191–202. Similarly, Panayiotis Papageorgiou, 'Chrysostom and Augustine on the Sin of Adam and Its Consequences', *St Vladimir's Theological Quarterly* 39 (1995), 361–78, suggests that Augustine misunderstood his Greek colleague.

[88] Beatrice, *Tradux peccati*, 243–78. It is beyond the scope of the present study to judge the question of whether or how Pelagian writers misunderstood Augustine even as he misunderstood Chrysostom, or indeed whether Augustine entirely understood them. Augustine clearly felt that the accusation that his position could lead to Manichaeism was not made in good faith, e.g. *Contra Iulianum*, 1.1.3.

[89] See R. A. Markus, 'Manichaeism revisited: Augustine's *Confessions* and the controversy with Julian', *Collectanea Augustiniana: Mélanges T. J. Van Bavel* (Louvain, 1990), 913–25.

[90] David G. Hunter, 'Resistance to the Virginal Ideal in Late-Fourth-Century Rome: the Case of Jovinian', *Theological Studies* 48 (1987), 45–64.

earliest versions of Chrysostom's work for a Latin audience. There are preserved two prefatory letters to these translations, that to Evangelius prefaced to Chrysostom's seven homilies in praise of Saint Paul[91] and one to Orontius, prefaced to Anianus' translation of at least 25 of Chrysostom's 91 *Homilies on the Gospel of Matthew.*[92] Anianus' own known compositions, the two letters prefacing his translations, coincide precisely with Julian in accusing Augustine of Manichaeism. It is also possible that Anianus was the author of one or more of the anonymous Latin pseudo-Chrysostom texts which have survived.[93] At the same time, the deep hostility to marriage of another surviving fifth-century Latin pseudo-Chrysostom text, the *Opus imperfectum in Matthaeum*, suggests that in the fifth century the Gospel of Matthew, and perhaps more specifically Chrysostom's view of the Gospel of Matthew,[94] was an important point of contention in what might be called the 'culture wars' of the debate begun by Augustine and Julian.[95]

We know from Anianus' prefaces that he saw himself as calling Chrysostom to witness against a perceived insinuation on Augustine's part that the human will was bound by a determinism (*necessitas*) springing from original sin.[96] Chrysostom's homilies on Paul were important because they specifically countered a Manichaean denial of human

---

[91] Anianus of Celeda, *Epistula ad Evangelium* (*PG* 50, 472–3).

[92] Anianus of Celeda, *Epistula ad Orontium* (*PG* 58, 975–6). These have been dated by Dom Chrysostomus Baur to the periods 415–19 and 419–21 respectively: Chrysostomus Baur, 'L'Entrée littéraire de saint Chrysostome dans le monde latin', *RHE* 8 (1907), 249–65; the dates are suggested at 254 and 257 respectively.

[93] A hypothesis originally proposed by Garnier and reopened by Baur, 'L'Entrée littéraire', 254–5. It has continued to attract inquiry: B. Altaner, 'Altlateinische Übersetzungen von Chrysostomusschriften', *Kleine Patristische Schriften* (Berlin, 1967), 418–19, warned against attributions of the Latin versions of Chrysostom while philological data are incomplete; nonetheless, approaches to the problem have been made by Anne-Marie Malingrey, 'La Traduction latine d'un texte de Jean Chrysostome: *Quod nemo laeditur*', *Studia Patristica* 7 (Berlin, 1966), and Jean Dumortier, *Jean Chrysostome: A Théodore* (*SC* 117).

[94] It is not certain whether the *Opus imperfectum* was intended to masquerade as a genuine work of John Chrysostom in translation, or whether the attribution to Chrysostom entered the manuscript tradition at a later date.

[95] While Frederick Schlatter, 'The Author of the *Opus imperfectum in Matthaeum*', *Vigiliae Christianae* 42 (1988) 364–75, believes that the text could have come from the pen of Anianus, I have argued that the conflicting views of marriage in the two texts make shared authorship extremely unlikely: Kate Cooper, 'An(n)ianus of Celeda and the Latin Readers of John Chrysostom', *Studia Patristica* 27 (1993), 249–55. The affinites of the *Opus imperfectum*, traditionally studied as an Arian text, with Pelagian thought are brought forward by Joseph H. Crehan, 'Sinful Marriage and the Pseudo-Chrysostom', in *Kyriakon: Festschrift Johannes Quasten* (Münster, 1970) 490–8. (For history of scholarship on the *Opus imperfectum*, see Hermann Josef Sieben, s. v. 'Jean Chrysostome (Pseudo-)', *Dictionnaire de spiritualité* 8 (1974), 362–9.)

[96] '... clarissimi sideris vice, noctem Manichaei erroris exagitat. Quantum vero nobis consolationis exoritur, cum cernimus, tam eruditio tamque illustri orientis magistro, eam, quam in nobis

perfectibility, adducing the example of Paul the Apostle's own perfection; the homilies on Matthew were similarly understood as summarizing the correct position on grace and free will. Adolf Primmer's manuscript discovery of the original version of the *Epistula ad Orontium*, the preface to Anianus' translation of the homilies on Matthew, makes it clear that this translation was intended to furnish ammunition against a threat of Manichaeism.[97] What has circulated since antiquity is a form expurgated by readers who were offended by its harsh words against Augustine and against the condemnation of Pelagius; the original version (which Primmer identified in the twelfth-century Latin MS Bibliothèque Nationale 14468) dwells insistently on the 'Manichaei rabiem'[98] which had arisen against Pelagius. This fits neatly with the charge of Manichaeism made by Anianus in his preface to Chrysostom's homilies in praise of Saint Paul, and finds support in Augustine's defence of his own views on the *concupiscentia nuptiarum* in *Letter 6** to Atticus, Bishop of Constantinople, a text which may also derive from the period c. 420–1.[99] There may have been more common ground, however, between Augustine and Pelagius himself.

CELANTHIA AND OPTATUS: THE PERMANENCE OF THE MARRIAGE BOND

Curiously, Augustine's own exploration of how to balance the claims of the marriage vow with a vocation to asceticism may have been the spur for Pelagius to write his only known treatise to a married woman, the *Epistula ad Celanthiam*.[100] It is interesting to note that rather than taking issue with Augustine's approach to Christian marriage, Pelagius – if the author of the

---

Traducianus [Augustine] oppugnat, astrui veritatem, quam certe beatus Joannes, ita his quoque ab omni munitam latere custodit, armat, accendit, ut videatur non tam praesentes informasse discipulos, quam nobis contra verae fidei oppugnationem auxilia praeparasse. Quantus enim ille adversus necessitatem, quantus pro libero surgit arbitrio, quam nostrorum libris ubique concinens, voluntatis jure servato divinae gratiae praesidia commendat, quam contra omnium vitiorum tenebras, quam pro cunctarum speculo virtutum splendidissimum vas electionis opponit!' (*Epistula ad Evangelium* (PG 50, 471–2)).

[97] Adolf Primmer, 'Die Originalfassung von Anianus' epistula ad Orontium', in Rudolf Hanslik, ed., *Antidosis: Festschrift für Walther Kraus* (Vienna, 1972), 278–89. I am grateful to Professor Primmer for generous discussion of the problems related to Anianus.

[98] Primmer, 'Die Originalfassung', 280, line 29. Similarly, ll. 21ff.: 'Certe beatus Iohannes cum in aliis operibus tum in hoc quoque tantus fere ubique tamque infestus assurgit, ut non tam evangelistae dicta interpretari quam nobiscum deproeliari Manichaeorum decreta videatur.'

[99] For this letter's context and possible date, see M.-F. Berrouard, 'Les Lettres 6* et 9* de saint Augustin', *Revue des études augustiniennes* 27 (1981), 264–77, and Brown, 'Sexuality and Society', 50 n. 5.

[100] On authorship of the letter, see Evans, *Four Letters of Pelagius*, 22.

letter is indeed Pelagius – simply echoes Augustine's reasoning. Whether this is because the two letters were written before the Pelagian controversy had gained momentum, or because the authors in fact agreed where the pastoral repercussions of the debate on marriage and asceticism were concerned, is unclear. Both authors take care to qualify their encouragement of the pursuit of ascetic virtue if it is brought into direct conflict with marriage.

Augustine's Letter 262 to Ecdicia is an object lesson in how asceticism could become a mere travesty of the Christian perfection to which its practitioners aspired.[101] From Augustine's letter we can reconstruct the conflict in Ecdica's household as follows. Having pronounced a unilateral vow of continence without consulting her husband, Ecdicia then began to dress as an ascetic when she left the house in order publicly to document her own abstinence. Up to this point, the husband had acceded to her inclination out of respect for her pious intentions, however humiliating to him her awkward way of realizing them. However, there was worse to come. Ecdicia's scorn for marital concord led her to compromise even the parental duties which she and her husband shared. (Here, Augustine relied for his information not on the letter which Ecdicia sent him, but on what he was able to extract from the letter's bearer.[102]) We are told that in a gesture of pious liberality Ecdicia signed over a substantial portion of her wealth to passing monks at a time when her husband was not present to object.[103] Augustine could not hide a certain sympathy with the husband, who at this point lost his temper with Ecdicia and, despising her vow of continence, turned to adultery.[104] Augustine noted that the husband certainly *would* have objected, since he was counting on Ecdicia's riches to provide for their son and heir, who had himself (we are astutely reminded) shown no sign of being called to a life of renunciation. Augustine wryly reminded her that an ascetic must preserve against his or her own inclinations the inheritance of children left under his or her care.

---

[101] On this text, see now Rebecca Krawiec, '"From the Womb of the Church": Monastic Families', *Journal of Early Christian Studies* 11 (2003), 283–307; E. Ann Matter, 'Christ, God, and Woman in the Thought of St. Augustine', in Robert Dodardo and George Lawless, eds., *Augustine and his Critics: Essays in Honour of Gerald Bonner* (London, 2000), 172–3; Claudia Koch, 'Augustine's Letter to Ecdicia: A New Reading', *Augustinian Studies* 13 (2000), 173–80. My own views are discussed more fully in Cooper, 'Insinuations of Womanly Influence', 159–60, and Cooper, *The Virgin and the Bride*, 106–8.

[102] Augustine, *Ep.* 262.5 (*CSEL* 57, 624).   [103] Augustine, *Ep.* 262.5 (*CSEL* 57, 625).

[104] Augustine, *Ep.* 262.5 (*CSEL* 57, 625): 'Tunc ille detestans eos tecum et non dei servos sed domus alienae penetratores et tuos captivatores et depraedatores putans tam sanctam sarcinam, quam tecum subierat, indignatus abiecit. Infirmus enim erat et ideo tibi, quae in communi proposito fortior videbaris, non erat praesumptione turbandus sed dilectione portandus . . .'

Had she curried her husband's favor by cultivating the virtues of patience and humility herself (maintained Augustine), Ecdicia would certainly have been able to sway his will to her purpose by the enticements of wifely charm, a woman's most expedient medium for her husband's edification. 'Then God would have been praised in your works, because they would have been accomplished in such trustful partnership, that not only the height of chastity but even the glory of poverty would have been yours.'[105] The terms in which Augustine described this idealized partnership were those of his monastic writing: however limited his hopes for the *saeculum*, in practical terms Augustine meant the Christian family to strive for a communion no less deeply rooted in charity than that of his own monks.

It was in the context of advice on domestic quandaries such as that of Ecdicia that the Christian writers of the fifth and sixth century would begin to give shape to the idea of the marriage bond as a permanent and lasting union of persons which 'neither infidelity nor even valid divorce can remove'.[106] Modern historians have confusingly begun to use the terms 'chaste marriage' and 'spiritual marriage' to refer to marriages like Ecdicia's, in which one or both partners took a vow of continence.[107] Both terms are warmly to be resisted. The first, because it reflects ignorance of the meaning of the latin word *castitas*, a term which carries a connotation of sexual fertility. The second, because it implies that there was no spirituality of the marriage institution *per se*, at the same time as it misleadingly suggests that the practice of continent marriage bore a privileged relationship to theological allegories such as the marriage of Christ to the Church or the Soul to Christ, even though what the allegories meant to invoke about marriage was in fact its fecundity.[108] Ascetic writers from the fifth century onward began to propose that continence could be accepted as a form of *castitas* despite its infertility, and while traditionalists would not have been pleased, the usage eventually gained wide currency. But this

---

[105] Augustine, *Ep.* 262.5 (*CSEL* 57, 625): 'et laudaretur deus in operibus vestris, quorum esset *tam fida societas*, ut a vobis *communiter* teneretur non solum summa castitas verum etiam gloriosa paupertas' (italics my own).

[106] On the marriage bond, see Reynolds, *Marriage in the Western Church*, 210–11.

[107] See, e.g., Dyan Elliot, *Spiritual Marriage: Sexual Abstinence in Early Medieval Wedlock* (Princeton, 1993).

[108] Reynolds, *Marriage in the Western Church*, 226 notes that the twelfth-century writer Rupert of Deutz refers to a husband and wife who part company in order to dedicate themselves to prayer as *casti coniuges*; what this demonstrates, however, is that continence is a category within *castitas*, not that it *replaces* the older definition, as Rupert himself clarifies in his *Commentary on John*: 'Hoc manifeste legitimi atque casti sed tamen carnalis coniugii fidem atque unanimitatem commendat' (Rupert of Deutz, *Commentaria in evangelium sancti Iohannis* 2 (*CCCM* 9, 112)).

meaning never displaced the older meaning of modesty and loyalty to the marriage bed.

The letter addressed to Celanthia, another woman who has taken a vow of continence without first having consulted her husband, is clearly more ambitious as a letter of spiritual advice: the narrative occasion for writing seems almost to be a literary conceit. Indeed, it is possible that the theme of the unilateral vow was itself a conceit: we will see that Fulgentius of Ruspe takes it up as well. If it was a conceit, it was a useful one, in that it made it possible to look deeply into the nature of marital *consensus*.[109] It was in large part through these letters that the Christian ideal of marriage as a permanently binding vow began to take shape, although it was not until the Carolingian period that a concentrated attempt was made to enforce the ideal.[110]

The letter to Celanthia opens with a *captatio benevolentiae* less perfunctory than many: the writer is at pains to stress the repeated and urgent quality of Celanthia's entreaties that he write. It is possible that the writer in this particular case did struggle with a genuine reluctance to write: any spiritual adviser would be cautious about seeming to countenance a vow such as Celanthia's, and would certainly not wish, by offering her advice after the fact, to be laid open to the charge of having encouraged her to take such a vow without consulting her husband. Nonetheless, she has asked that he prescribe a fixed rule for directing the course of her life according to the teachings of scripture, and he has come to believe that to refuse would be false modesty. His task, then, is to demonstrate how, 'you may be able, by holding firmly to your place in marriage, not only to please your husband but also Him who allowed marriage Himself'.[111]

This leads to a long discussion of the desirability of keeping the commandments, both those which prohibit sin and those which enjoin good works. The writer goes on to clarify that to warn against even the smallest of sins should not be equated with the position of the Stoics, who do not make a distinction between the various levels of transgression and error. Celanthia should hope to be as blameless as Job, laying her spiritual house not on shallow sand but on solid rock. She must seek to draw a line not

[109] See Riccardo Orestano, *La struttura giuridica del matrimonio romano dal diritto classico al diritto giustinianeo* (Milan, 1951) 1, 261ff., on the concern of patristic writers to emphasize that a cessation of sexual union did not absolve the duty of spouses to preserve the *consensus* which bound them in marriage. In the case of Ecdicia, Augustine is quite explicit: 'non enim, quia pariter temperabatis a conmixtione carnali, ideo tuus maritus esse destiterat', Augustine, *Ep.* 262.4 (*CSEL* 57, 624).

[110] Pierre Toubert, 'La Théorie du mariage chez les moralistes carolingiens', in *Il matrimonio nella società altomedievale*, Settimane di Studio del Centro Italiano di Studi sull'Alto Medievo 24, 2 vols. (Spoleto, 1977) 1, 233–85.

[111] Pelagius, *Ad Celanthiam* 2 (*CSEL* 29, 437; tr. Rees, 128).

only between herself and the pagans, but also between herself and those who profess to live a Christian life, but whose conduct reveals them to be 'living a pagan life under the Christian name'.[112]

Here begins an excursus on the ubiquitous theme of the Two Paths. She should remember that every step she takes commits her to one direction or the other; with this in mind, seemingly inconsequential decisions – such as whether or not to listen to a flatterer, whether or not to harbour resentment against an enemy – are listed. The path to life, our writer argues, is a lonely path, because even those who intend to follow it may by a wrong turning return to the way of the crowd – even one to whom she looks as a guide may turn out to be her companion in error. But despite the uncertain spiritual fate of those whom she encounters in this life, she can hardly claim that she is bereft of a sure example on whom to pattern herself. The words of the apostles and evangelists are invoked in order to encourage her to look to Jesus himself as the example in whose footsteps she must follow. The study of scripture, then, is a matter of seeking to see the examples of Jesus and of the saints 'as if they were present now, and to learn from its advice what is to be done and what has to be avoided'.[113] Not only should she meditate God's commandments as she encounters them in the scriptures; she must turn them over continually in her mind, seeking constantly to embody them in her actions.

She should hold the Golden Rule of the Gospel of Matthew (Matt. 7:12) like a mirror always to hand; it will help her to examine her conduct and determine whether she is on the path of righteousness, simply by asking herself whether she has done by another as she would wish to be done by. It is implausible, he argues, that anyone should claim that the commandments of God are too difficult to carry out, or too difficult to understand, when the whole meaning of the Law and the Prophets is simply to bind the People of God together by mutual acts of consideration and kindness.

He returns to the list of specific actions which she must avoid, this time in greater detail and with an emphasis on how they undermine the bonds of charity. Refusing not only to disparage others, but to listen to those who do so, will protect her not only from spiritual confusion but also from finding that her relationships with others have been damaged more seriously than she intended. Similarly, she should avoid flatterers, and respect the honesty of those who speak the truth bluntly, rather than despising them as jealous or proud. She should cultivate a careful modesty in her speech, avoiding

[112] Pelagius, *Ad Celanthiam* 8 (*CSEL* 29, 442; tr. Rees, 131).
[113] Pelagius, *Ad Celanthiam* 13 (*CSEL* 29, 445; tr. Rees, 134).

both oaths and untruth, and think of her heart as a temple of God, her soul as an altar adorned with the jewels of virtues.

In a passage echoing Pelagius' *Letter to Demetrias*, a text to which we will return in the following chapter, the writer encourages Celanthia to cultivate the virtue of humility. But this exhortation develops into a passage which by no means shares Pelagius' concern to strike a balance between praise for earthly nobility and the need to contain its claims. Here, we see an unambiguous rejection of accidents of birth as a criterion of spiritual standing. 'What can be nobler before God and men than Peter, who was a fisherman and poor? What more illustrious among women than the blessed Mary, who is described as a carpenter's bride? . . . nor does it matter what are the circumstances of anyone's birth, when all of us without exception are reborn in Christ.'[114]

Similarly, Celanthia is warned against the arrogance which might arise from her thinking herself morally superior to others on the basis of fasting and abstinence, or of failing to follow the more mundane commandments on account of her great feats of asceticism. This treatment of a standard theme differs slightly from the others in that it stresses specifically the spiritual dangers of pride. 'But what does it profit a man that his body be reduced by abstinence, if his spirit be swollen with pride?'[115] Abstinence of the body only has moral value where the spirit is starved of vices. Although she should avoid pride, she should not fail to be conscious of reputation, so that she may shine as a lamp unto the world, attracting others to the faith by the seemliness of her conduct.

The writer turns finally to Celanthia's home life. Amid the cares of the household, he encourages her to set aside a part of each day for reading and prayer, so that she may return to her duties refreshed and able to set an example for the rest of the household. She should seek to be loved by all as a mother rather than a mistress, for obedience stemming from fear is less reliable than obedience stemming from love. She should see that her husband's authority is upheld, setting for the rest of the household an example of how to honour him. Her gentle and quiet spirit should be her only adornment, although by this he does not mean that her clothing should be extravagantly ragged – merely that it should be of a becoming modesty. This last statement is a veiled reference to our writer's final topic, for the figure of the wealthy *matrona* dressed in rags, who by altering her manner of dress intended to signal to the world that she was no longer

---

[114] Pelagius, *Ad Celanthiam* 21 (*CSEL* 29, 452; tr. Rees, 138).
[115] Pelagius, *Ad Celanthiam* 22 (*CSEL* 29, 452; tr. Rees, 139).

sleeping with her husband, was on its way to becoming a literary topos, as we saw above in Augustine's letter to Ecdicia. It is to the question of Celanthia's sexual relationship with her husband that our writer means to turn.

Here the tone of the letter – and its level of specificity to Celanthia's own stituation – alter dramatically. The writer has discovered that several years ago she had taken a vow of continence, and he praises her for her virtue in renouncing the pleasure of the marriage bed, a sacrifice all the greater than that of a virgin, since a pleasure already experienced is far more difficult to renounce than one which one can only imagine. But he was disturbed to discover that Celanthia had taken this step without the consent of her husband, since the apostolic writings make clear that the wife has an obligation to protect the husband from fornication by granting him con-jugal rights, an obligation which the husband in turn owes the wife.[116] He wishes her to understand the seriousness of this action. Both of them, he reminds her, have heard of cases where such contempt for the spouse has led to the dissolution of the marriage, as well as, equally distressingly, cases in which the abandoned partner has consoled himself with adultery.[117] Celanthia should not flatter herself that the Lord is pleased by her vow, since what she has offered was not hers to give.

Imagining that Celanthia could only have taken so perilous a step in ignorance, the writer proposes to set out the apostolic teaching on this subject from the ground upwards. He reminds her that Paul's teaching is essentially moderate on the subject of legitimate sex within marriage, neither claiming with Jovinian that continence is no greater than marriage, nor arguing with the Manichaeans that marriage is to be condemned. Rather, the idea of marriage as a remedy for lust is one which accords it spiritual value, even while the continent are able to strive for yet greater heights. Of course there is value in continence, but the apostle is clear that it is a decision which couples must make jointly, and that they should practise continence for fixed intervals of time, rather than plunging into permanent continence without building up long collaborative experience. Only continence achieved through a shared commitment has any real chance of lasting. If one of the two partners presumes to make a decision on behalf of both, this is not virtue but egotism. Celanthia's position now is not enviable. Continued contempt for her husband is not admissible, but to betray a vow which she has already made to God is a matter of fear and trembling. Her only real hope is to behave so endearingly to her husband

---

[116] Citing 1 Cor. 7:4.
[117] Possibly a reference to Ecidica, although there is no reason to think her case was unique.

that he is moved of his own will to come to her assistance, choosing of his own accord to share in her vow of continence. The writer closes by attempting to strike a more generic tone. He turns to the broader theme of the praise of chastity, and ends with a meditation on the blessedness of those who watch and wait for the final Day of Judgement, and who live their lives in vigilance to meet it with a pure heart.

Both Augustine and the author of the letter to Celanthia did their best to bury the fact that Ecdicia and Celanthia could have found support for their challenge to the husband's conjugal rights in earlier Christian literature such as the *Apocryphal Acts*. The strategy in addressing these women is to place emphasis on the impossibility of the situation they have put themselves in, and to dissuade other women from following in their footsteps.

If the letters to Ecdicia and Celanthia find no solution to the quandary of the unilateral vow of continence, an early sixth-century letter on the same theme, this time addressed to a husband, finds a solution. This letter, written by Fulgentius of Ruspe during his second exile in Sardinia, c. 515–23, takes up the same question of a wife's unilateral vow of continence, with a corresponding exploration of the permanence of marriage, from a more sympathetic point of view. Something of the context can be reconstructed from the letter itself, although in the majority of manuscripts the name of the addressee is lacking, perhaps on account of the sensitive nature of the subject matter. (A few manuscripts give an otherwise unknown Optatus as the addressee.)[118] It is a delicate pastoral situation: the writer's beloved wife seems to have taken a vow of continence while on her deathbed, though whether in anticipation of meeting her maker or as a bargain for a return to health is not entirely clear. Whatever the precise nature of the vow, the bishop's brief summary of the situation as he understands it makes clear that her health has been restored, and that her husband has written to the bishop to inquire whether it would be permissible to resume marital relations.

Fulgentius' letter is clearly meant at some level as an *hommage* to Augustine, a writer for whom he had great affection. But it carries a more reassuring message than Augustine's letter. This may be in part because he believes that the husband and wife are not fundamentally in disagreement; rather they are uncertain about what is required in order to be scrupulous in their Christian observance. Fulgentius takes the

---

[118] A point made by Robert B. Eno in the introduction to his translation of the text, *Fulgentius: Selected Works* (Washington, D.C., 1997), 279.

opportunity to offer a discourse on the nature of conjugal sexuality before coming to his judgement, which is essentially that the marriage vow is binding, and takes precedence over any other vow, unless the later vow is made with the the spouse's consent. If the husband did not knowingly concur in a vow of continence, then the wife did not have it in her power to make a vow, and can therefore be excused for returning to sexual relations within marriage. On the other hand, if the husband admits that he knowingly concurred in a vow of continence, it is incumbent on both to fulfil the vow. The importance of the letter to the majority of its readers, who did not share the couple's predicament, was in the bishop's reasoning.

Fulgentius clearly wishes to take the opportunity to set the record straight on what Paul intended. He begins by explaining that there are two issues at stake: the nature of Christian marriage and the nature of Christian vows. Lest the reader be confused by the misleading claims of some proponents of some ascetic writers, he states categorically that for the married, chastity and not continence is the required virtue. Chaste conjugal intercourse should not be understood as a failing in the eyes of God – only 'immoderate lust' can make it so. 'In spouses, therefore, excess is censured by the law, but nuptial dignity is not deprived of the gift of honour conferred on it by God.'[119] He moves on to an explication of Paul's First Letter to the Corinthians, chapter 7, in which the idea of the conjugal debt is elaborated.

> The thrust of the reading from the Apostle shows that the wife should have intercourse with her husband and the husband with the wife by reason of a certain mutuality of what is owed. Without a doubt, the Apostle would not have called this a debt unless he knew that it had legitimately to be paid; nor would he command that it be paid by the duty of mutual consent, if it were an evil demand on the part of the one asking.[120]

It follows that conjugal intercourse is an honourable duty, and a sharp distinction is made between conjugal intercourse and illicit sexuality.

> If a married man fornicates, he sins mortally. But if he does not desert the faith of his bed, but intemperately exceeds a little bit with his wife, in the natural usage only, not only seeking to beget but sometimes obeying the lust of the flesh, he does not do this without fault; such a fault, however, is quickly forgiven to the one who does good and prays because marital love preserves the fidelity for the spouse . . .[121]

---

[119] Fulgentius, *Ad Optatum* 4 (*CC* 91, 190; tr. Eno, 281).
[120] Fulgentius, *Ad Optatum* 5 (*CC* 91, 190; tr. Eno, 281–2).
[121] Fulgentius, *Ad Optatum* 8 (*CC* 91, 191; tr. Eno, 283).

This passage in fact reflects a point made in Augustine's *De bono coniugali*, and in fact the letter up to this point is noticeably steeped in a valorization of marriage which was almost certainly self-consciously based on the writings of Augustine.[122]

But in fact, Fulgentius' defence of marriage goes further than that of Augustine. By placing emphasis on the conjugal debt, Fulgentius clears the way for approaching conjugal intercourse as the fulfilment of a vow rather than the result of moral weakness. This in turn lays the groundwork for his circumspect attitude to the vow of continence. While Augustine and the author of *Ad Celanthiam* had seen the vow of continence as binding, even if it were unfortunate that it had been taken without the consent of the partner, Fulgentius places stress on the prior vow, the vow of marriage itself.

The full ability to vow bodily continence is not available to the married man or woman, whose body is not in his or her own power but in that of the spouse ... When someone wishes to make profession of the continence of his body which is under the power of his spouse, it is like someone trying to give alms or offer a sacrifice from what belongs to someone else.[123]

If marriage is a Christian institution, Fulgentius argues, then the vow of marriage must take precedence over any later vow – unless the later vow was taken under the aegis of marital consent it is not in fact valid.

If anyone up to this point is more worried about his own weakness than secure in the power of the Lord, if he has not known the continence of the flesh, let him keep himself from iniquity and use his wife as is fitting. Let him flee evil and greed and he will not be condemned if he pays the debt to his spouse. Let him not be drunk, nor envious, not contentious, nor a hypocrite, nor a quarreller, not proud, nor rapacious, nor greedy.[124]

The text continues with a lengthy exhortation to cultivate the virtues of the Christian *paterfamilias*, turning to the problem of the just exercise of power with respect to slaves, children, and other subordinates which we have seen in texts such as the acephalous Bobbio letter and *Ad Gregoriam*. In concluding, the bishop strives to connect the problem of sexual ethics to the wider ethical commitments of the Christian householder: 'Above all, let faithful spouses always remember that they must stand firm in prayers and almsgiving; let them not always wish to wallow in the

---

[122] Augustine's defence of marriage is well explicated by Markus, *End of Ancient Christianity*, ch. 4, 'A defence of Christian mediocrity', 45–62.

[123] Fulgentius, *Ad Optatum* 14 (*CC* 91, 194; tr. Eno, 286).

[124] Fulgentius, *Ad Optatum* 20 (*CC* 91, 196; tr. Eno, 289).

weakness of the flesh, but let them hasten to rise to the level of a more controlled life.'[125]

Writing to the young widow Galla, the daughter of Quintus Aurelius Memmius Symmachus (consul. 485) and sister-in-law of the philosopher Boethius (consul. 510), Fulgentius again defends Christian marriage, although in this case he is writing in order to encourage her to remain a widow rather than remarrying.

The marriages of Christians are holy because in them chastity is kept in the body and purity of faith is preserved in the heart ... and because the spouses pay each other the debt of the flesh, insofar as they do it in modesty, they keep the commandments of Christ because they depart in no way from conjugal charity and chastity.[126]

The bishop turns, however, to console her by recourse to the old hierarchy of marriage, widowhood, and virginity as ascending virtues. Her husband's death should be understood as offering an added blessing:

For he who showed you the way to be followed for a better life has not deserted you. The lord wanted you to climb to better things by degrees, so that first you might live faithfully married to one husband, and afterwards you might remain apart from a husband without difficulty.[127]

The matter-of-fact approach to the husband's death should not deceive us: the bishop's intent here is to place value on the marriage between Galla and her dead husband. The conjugal bond is so strong, Fulgentius argues, that it can not be replaced by a second marriage, and Galla and her husband will be reunited in the afterlife.

AD GREGORIAM IN PALATIO AND AUGUSTINIAN MEDIOCRITAS

The Augustinian theme of the wife who draws her husband toward virtue is garnished with idiosyncratic detail in *Ad Gregoriam*, but the text nonetheless reflects John's deep loyalty to an Augustinian understanding of Christian marriage and indeed of the Christian laity. Augustine of Hippo had made his radical re-evaluation of the marriage bond years earlier, probably long before John and Gregoria were born. There is little reason to believe that his views on this subject were immediately influential, or even known to the majority of fifth- and sixth-century Christian writers,

---

[125] Fulgentius, *Ad Optatum* 22 (*CC* 91, 197; tr. Eno, 290).
[126] Fulgentius, *Ad Gallam* 9 (*CC* 91, 201; tr. Eno, 296).
[127] Fulgentius, *Ad Gallam* 10 (*CC* 91, 201; tr. Eno, 297).

but in the now largely unknown John Augustine found a very attentive reader indeed, and one who would represent his views in the vividly metaphorical language so beloved by the élite lay readership whom the ideas most needed to reach.

What strikes us when we turn to *Ad Gregoriam* is how strongly the text is marked by military and juridical language, already from the very first lines. Gregoria's imagined request to John is a case in point: 'I ask, may you deign to give a ruling (*responsum*)[128] on what place a wife will be able to find before God, or to clarify to what extent she will have paid compensation for the licence of the marital state (*maritalis licentiam potestatis*).'[129] Surely, John has in mind the Day of Judgement, but it is no accident that his text is posed as a *responsum*, in the formal language of Roman law. The military theme, too, crops up immediately.

For already at the very beginning of marriage (*conubii*), because the Enemy saw you handed over after the training of your parents to the embraces of a most Christian man, in whom no disgrace of concubines, no immodest conceit of female friends, was able to prevail, in whose heart as in his whole estate purity of morals (*castitas*) holds sway; then, I say, the author of all crime presaged that you would be his assassin, nor from any other motive did he attempt either at first to incite quarrelling between you, or afterwards to plant the seed of various instances of discord except in order that he – the Devil – might separate those joining together against him and wishing to live in the love of Christ.[130]

The cultivation of wifely piety finds its glamour here, and even the very fact of restraint and modesty – of *castitas* in its primary sense of faithfulness to her husband – is recast as an act of military aggression. Her troubles are the result of her own cultivation of virtue; they are caused by 'the Adversary whom you yourself bestirred to enmity by loving morality (*castimonia*) and embracing the footsteps (*vestigia*) of the Lord Jesus Christ'.[131] Toward the end of the letter, John casts his recommendation for further reading equally in military lanaguage: 'I have above shown you the units of fighters, so that you might learn that you yourself could not arrive at eternal life except by the passage-way of this battle. Go to Paul, the *magister militum*, so that he may place the breastplate of faith on you, and the helmet of hope and salvation.'[132]

Certainly, Gregoria's is not a continent marriage; the repeated references to sex and procreation, while discreet, make this clear. In chapter 7

---

[128] *responsa* were the authoritative opinions through which authorized Roman jurists (initally, pontifices) contributed to the development of the law.
[129] *Ad Gregoriam praef.* (*CC* 25A, 191).   [130] *Ad Gregoriam* 1 (*CC* 25A, 192–3).
[131] *Ad Gregoriam* 1 (*CC* 25A, 193).   [132] *Ad Gregoriam* 17 (*CC* 25A, 224) (cf. 1 Thess. 5:8).

Gregoria is reminded of her obligation to pay the 'conjugal debt' to her husband (1 Cor. 7:4), and of his reciprocal obligation to do the same. John imagines that Gregoria might see this fact as a reason for discouragement, or, still worse, an excuse not to pursue the life of virtue. Toward the end of the treatise, he summarizes her possible objections: ' "But", you say, "that searching and observance (*inquirere et servare*) are the duty of those, who are not held by the bond of marital union (*copulationis vinculo*)."¹³³ And how does Christ make you as a married person conform to His grace, if He perceived that His charity could not find a place in you through the charity of marriage (*per caritatem coniugii*)? "¹³⁴ Missing is any statement that the couple have vowed continence, an omission that would be difficult to explain if it were the case. Emphatically, *caritas coniugii* – not bodily asceticism – is the vehicle through which she must conform to God's grace.

This means that we must be careful in reading the opening passage of the treatise, in which John represents her as having approached him with fear about the coming judgement: ' "I ask, may you deign to give a ruling on what place a wife will be able to find before God, or to clarify to what extent she will pay compensation for the licence of the marital state (*maritalis licentiam potestatis*)." "¹³⁵ At the same time, John states that Gregoria has 'freed her heart bound fast by a lawful bond' and 'left behind' her 'fleshly cares'.

John is essentially flattering his reader here by implying that it is from a sense of duty, rather than carnal desire, that she fulfils her office as a married person. Perhaps he sees an Ecdicia in the making and wants to redirect her enthusiasm, but he may simply think it is more flattering to picture a Roman *materfamilias* as being 'above' sex.

Where the letters of Ecdicia and Celanthia mean to define the requirements for a vow of continence within marriage, in *Ad Gregoriam* it is chaste – which is to say monogamous but sexually active – marriage that is defended as a spiritual calling. This is a point driven home by persistent incidental reference to the sexual aspect of the bond. We see this in chapter 1, 'The Enemy saw you handed over after training by your parents to the embrace of a most Christian man (*christianissimi viri amplexibus*)', and in the same passage praise for the husband's character in that he is known to keep no concubines and 'in [his] heart as in his whole estate *castitas* holds sway (*in suo praedio castitas dominatur*)'.¹³⁶ Gregoria herself is

¹³³ On *copulatio* see *CTh* 9.42.2. ¹³⁴ *Ad Gregoriam* 24 (*CC* 25A, 241).
¹³⁵ *Ad Gregoriam praef.* (*CC* 25A, 191). ¹³⁶ *Ad Gregoriam* 1 (*CC* 25A, 192).

certainly faithful, if the speech which John imagines for her can be trusted: '"I have given myself over to the embraces of purity (*castitas*), in such a way that I may not suffer to be severed from her even if I could both learn which day would be my last, and clearly know the hour at which I will be called to return [to God]."'[137] John's view of Gregoria in the embraces of chastity echoes the language of a thousand funerary inscriptions for Christian wives during the early centuries, in which *castitas* was celebrated as a sign of the beloved's loyalty to her husband and to the marriage bed.[138]

It is difficult to assess the tone of the relationship between Gregoria and her husband. What signposts we can find seem to suggest that the *domina* of the text was intended as a generic figure, rather than a direct description of the lady to whom the text was addressed. This is especially true where John strays onto topics which would have been seen as an affront to the lady's honour if they were understood as referring specifcally to her own circumstances.

There is a hint of misbehaviour on the husband's part in the text, but very little is detail is given: 'And although you assert that you are able to endure a great martyrdom in order to protect Christ's commandments, would you disdain the same commandments on account of a slight affront of marital loyalty (*levem maritalis fiduciae iniuriam*)?'[139] What this *iniuria* involves is unclear, but it clearly refers to the 'seed of discord' planted by the Devil.[140] In chapter 2, we come as close as we are likely to to an outright accusation against the husband:

'But it is wrong (*nefas est*)', you will say, 'for a free-born and noble woman, weak with the fragility of a pampered body, to undergo unremitting conjugal raving (*adsiduum furorem maritalem*), and to be reduced to the dishonour of outrages (*iniuriarum opprobrium*) within domestic walls, where I am valued (*existimer*) as if a mere slave.'[141]

The *furor maritalis* here could refer to outrageous behaviour by the husband, but it could also be an ascetic's somewhat catty way of referring to the marriage act itself. The *inuriarum opprobrium*, however, is not so easy to explain away. It could be a an echo of the *cubilis iniurias* suffered by

---

[137] *Ad Gregoriam* 15 (*CC* 25A, 217–18).

[138] Jos Janssens, S. J., *Vita e morte del cristiano negli epitaffi di Roma anteriori al sec. VII* (Rome, 1981), 117–27.

[139] *Ad Gregoriam* 6 (*CC* 25A, 201); possibly a reference here to the *cubilis iniurias* tolerated by Monnica in *Confessions* 9.9 (*CC* 27, 145), although in that case the affront seems to be Patricius' direct affront to the marriage bed by chasing after other women.

[140] *Ad Gregoriam* 1 (*CC* 25A, 193).

[141] *Ad Gregoriam* 2 (*CC* 25A, 193).

Monnica in *Confessions* 9,[142] but since the *iniurias* in that case referred to Patricius' infidelity, and John elsewhere affirms that Gregoria's husband is faithful to her, the intertextual reference would still leave an unsolved problem. It may also be a reference to the martyr romance known as the *Passio Anastasiae*, in which the saint is imprisoned by her husband, an episode alluded to in *Ad Gregoriam* with the phrase *maritalem iniuriam.*[143]

We have to be aware that if Gregoria's husband were known for conduct unbecoming to a man of his standing, John would be far more careful in speaking about it than is the case in *Ad Gregoriam in palatio.*[144] It would have been an affront to Gregoria's honour for someone who was probably her social inferior to speak of it directly, especially in a text that was intended for circulation, as this one seems to have been. The surviving letters from bishops to ladies of exalted standing are uniformly bland in their descriptions of a noble husband's behaviour, even when the husband's behaviour was very bad indeed. (We have seen this above in the case of Ecdicia.) Bishops who were called on to mediate in the case of marital abuse seem to have done so willingly, but they seem to have done so as discreetly as possible.[145]

This said, no Christian letters of advice to a wife experiencing domestic violence are known to survive from antiquity, even though there is good evidence that domestic abuse took place. The surviving documentary papyri do include a number of petitions and affadavits *from* women in this situation, who mention having sought the assistance of priests or bishops.[146] Yet a contemporary example of the 'correct' mode of address in such a case can be extracted from the martyr romance known as the *Passio Anastasiae*. When Anastasia's husband imprisons her the saint makes a passionate plea for help to the holy Chrysogonus. In a highly euphemistic reply without prefatory protests of his compassion or condemnation of the husband, the holy man passes over the details of her situation and dwells on instead on Anastasia's own temptation to sin. 'Take care that you not be

[142] *Confessions* 9.9.19 (*CC* 27, 145).
[143] *CC* 25A, 198.
[144] On the disapproval of moral writers, both pagan and Christian, toward spousal violence, see Joy A. Schroeder, 'John Chrysostom's Critique of Spousal Violence', *Journal of Early Christian Studies* 12 (2004), 413–32, at 414–17. Robert A. Kaster explains the issue of 'face' when criticizing the conduct of an associate: 'The revelation that a friend was ethically deficient implied that you had misplaced your friendship ... this impulse toward self-protection applied *a fortiori* to members of your own household, whose exposure to *pudor* implicated you in still more intimate ways.' Robert A. Kaster, 'The Shame of the Romans', *Transactions of the American Philological Association* 127 (1997) 1–19, at 16.
[145] See Cooper, 'Closely Watched Households'.
[146] Bagnall, 'Church, State, and Divorce', 58–9; P. Arnaoutoglu, 'Marital Disputes in Greco-Roman Egypt', *Journal of Juristic Papyrology* 25 (1995), 11–28.

deceived by trials in the midst of an otherwise holy life. It is not that God
has tricked you; rather, God is testing your faith."[147] (We can only assume
that the sin against which she is warned is that of despair, but this is
the closest he comes to alluding to her desperate circumstances.) There is
every reason to believe that John knew this text, since he offers extended
praise for the virtues of Anastasia in chapter 5 of *Ad Gregoriam*. It is just
possible that John means obliquely to approach what could be a desperate
situation; on this reading, the choice of Anastasia for praise might well be a
pointed one.

However, the decorous language of the passage implies that the *iniuriae*
referred to in the text were, if not hypothetical, at least well within the
bounds of comportment sanctioned by Roman law and custom.[148] We saw
in Chapter Four above that, at least for the sake of argument, John raises
the possibility that Gregoria herself could abuse the power she holds over
dependents such as slaves. That accusation, too, would be out of place in a
prestige text like *Ad Gregoriam* if she were actually known to be doing so.
There is reason to imagine that where the *domina* feared violence from the
dominus, her own dependents could also expect to feel its brunt, not only
directly but through the *domina*'s resulting agitation and frustrated anger,
but again, this is not a subject John intends to explore.[149]

We must consider in greater depth the likelihood that 'Gregoria' as John
constructs her is herself a literary fiction, the late Roman precursor to the
distressed lady in a tower who would figure as a heroine in medieval
romance. This would explain what is otherwise a disturbing mismatch
between the literary aspirations of *Ad Gregoriam* and the rather alarming
pastoral situation at which it hints. In a situation of genuine crisis, the
pastor involved would hardly divert his effort to composing a stunningly
pretentious literary pastiche making light of the situation. If we are not to
judge John a monster, we must imagine a more humane *Sitz im Leben* for
his act of literary composition.

It is more likely that in writing his treatise for Gregoria John discovered a
literary synergy between the legend of Anastasia, a saint dear to his patroness, and the painful commentary of Augustine on the estate of woman in
marriage. On this hypothesis, he would have meant to address the trials of
'woman' in the abstract rather than the details of Gregoria's individual

---

[147] *Passio Anastasiae* 5 (Delehaye, 224). For fuller discussion of the exchange of letters between Anastasia
and Chrysogonus, see Cooper, *The Virgin and the Bride*, 119–26.

[148] Nathan, *The Family in Late Antiquity*, 104: Theodosius II (in 449) allowed unilateral divorce in the
case of wife-beating, but Justinian revoked the penalty, substituting a fairly slight fine.

[149] Clark, 'Women, Slaves, and the Hierarchies of Domestic Violence'.

situation. This is far more compatible with what we know of the relationship in the fourth and fifth centuries between literary men and the aristocratic ladies to whom they addressed letters of spiritual instruction: on the whole, the letters find an opportunity for flattery wherever possible.[150] They rarely go into unpleasant matters, and in the rare instances in which they do, such as Augustine's *Letter* 262 to Ecdicia, one can see that the writer knows full well how his reader's dignity will be wounded by his opening discussion of such a humiliating topic, and is using the 'shock-value' to make a pastoral point worthy of such extraordinary emphasis.

There would be no comparable pastoral excuse for humiliation in the case of *Ad Gregoriam*, by contrast, since unlike Ecdicia, the *matrona* whom John imagines is not at fault, but rather is pictured as suffering unjust wrongs at the hands of another. According to the logic of our period, there would be no pastoral value whatsoever in humiliating a woman in desperate circumstances by referring openly to the indignities to which she was being subjected. This is all the more the case since the text is clearly aimed at a wider readership, one comprising the highly educated men and women at court, who would have been Gregoria's peers. By addressing what he must imagine to be a literary tour de force to a well-placed *domina*, John clearly hopes to gain a wide audience for his ideas, and humiliating his patroness at court would be the last thing that he would want to do. So it is very likely that the 'you' of John's letter should not be understood as a precise description of his historical addressee Gregoria, but rather as a generic *domina christiana*, a figure through whom he believes he can explore the pastoral issues affecting the senatorial women of his day. His cajoling tone, seeking constantly to explain away the difficulties of what was in fact, of course, a comparatively fortunate social position, reflects a situation in which he is playing with abstract questions rather than facing painful pastoral realities. There is every reason to think that *Ad Gregoriam*'s evocation of the plight of the married *domina* was designed to evoke a literary *pathos* not dissimilar to Venantius Fortunatus' *Elegy on the Death of Galswintha*, written some decades later.[151]

This said, in his conversations with women of Gregoria's rank John has clearly been listening. He understands, for example, that noble women are

[150] Anne N. Kurdock, '*Demetrias ancilla dei*: The Problem of the Missing Patron', in Kate Cooper and Julia Hillner, eds., *Religion, Dynasty, and Patronage in Early Christian Rome, 300–900* (Cambridge, 2007), 190–224; Andrew Jacobs, 'Writing Demetrias: Ascetic Logic in Ancient Christianity', *Church History* 69 (2000), 719–48.

[151] See Michael Roberts, 'Fortunatus' Elegy on the Death of Galswintha (*Carm.* 6.5)', in Ralph W. Mathisen and Danuta Shanzer, eds., *Society and Culture in Late Antique Gaul: Revisiting the Sources* (Aldershot, 2001), 298–312.

not happy with the Christian approach of allowing the husband 'to value [the wife] as if [she] were a slave'. He admits that it is not Roman law but Christian history that has led to current situation in which 'each woman has been committed . . . to a single Lord' whose will she must not oppose:

> For before it was prohibited that male authority be despised (Gen. 3:16), the female had it in her power (*habuit in potestate*) to will what [that authority] deplored, but thereafter each and every woman has been committed by divine and human authority to a single lord, with the result that she knows that by no means may she oppose his will; by what shame would she pose as an impediment her free status or her original authority (*potestatis*), when at the time when she had it in her power to will (*velle*) what she would, it is agreed that she herself cut herself off from all of this right to rule?'[152]

In addition to the introduction of a biblical justification for male authority, we see the disturbing change in the perception of the marriage contract which we discussed at the beginning of the present chapter: 'nor to be sure did you enter your husband's home as a bride (*ingressa es ad maritum*) unless also with the result that you would not be able to have authority (*potestas*) over your body itself, given that even the apostolic authority [1 Cor. 7:4] witnesses, that where her husband is concerned a wife should not have power over her body.'[153] The context is a discussion of the reciprocal obligation to pay the conjugal debt, and he does go on to acknowledge that the husband is also bound, but the language is strikingly asymmetrical. The theme of the quasi-servile role the Christian wife is asked to assume comes up repeatedly in *Ad Gregoriam*.

John clearly grasps that a woman of Gregoria's standing would balk at the role she is being asked to assume. But his response is essentially palliative. What he offers is not a challenge to the new ideal of wifely submission, but rather an interpretative strategy to help her cope with what is being asked of her.

> Naturally, I will take care to defend nobility (*nobilitatem*) by every effort. I am delighted to join with you in protesting on account of your noble birth (*generositate*). But at any rate you will not be able to deny that there are two nobilities of your origin: the one by which you are called a daughter of God, the other by which you are called the daughter of a mortal. Of which one, then – the human or the divine – will you have us take up our defence first of all? If the human, you are overcome; if the divine, you have won.[154]

---

[152] *Ad Gregoriam* 7 (CC 25A, 202).   [153] *Ad Gregoriam* 7 (CC 25A, 202).
[154] *Ad Gregoriam* 2 (CC 25A, 193).

What we see here is perhaps the first, pragmatic step of trying to smooth the problem away, or to prevent its arising in the first place.

Central to the strategy proposed is what will be an extended motif of *imitatio*, calling on Gregoria to meditate on both Christ and the martyrs.

Do you suffer outrages (*iniurias*) justly, or unjustly? If justly, consider it due, if unjustly, turn to Christ, and you will not be able to make a pretext of outrages. In the face of outrages and affliction by mortals, reflect on the Son of God who suffered flagellation; against the reproaches and derision of mortals, [consider] His face touched with spittle and His defiled countenance; instead of the horror of death itself, look on Him Crucified. And so, in every dispute, in every punishment (*laceratio*), in every blast of insults, and, too, in every trial (*supplicio*), not to abandon endurance is to imitate Christ.[155]

As a precaution, John follows the invitation to *imitatio Christi* with the subtler strategy of praise mixed with shame:

'But', you will say, 'as a guardian of my own nobility, firm in discipline, a follower (*pedisequa*) of all good morals (*morum*), in chasteness (*castitate*) a teacher, in dignity outstanding, in honour most careful, in speech true, in prayer capacious, in matters of fair dealing most just, sparkling in the stewardship of the life of the household, swift and successful in the most useful work – I ought not to let anything in family life sadden me; no conjugal affront (*maritalis indignatio*) should stir up my emotions (*meos motus*), if I am to persevere in this just path.' O argument of injustice, battling against justice! It is right and true, a true gem and a true coin are not to be tested, but it is unjust if they are afraid to be tested.[156]

First, a sympathetic hearing is given to the point of view of an aristocratic *domina*, but the argument is swiftly rejected, in language drawn from the same lexicon of Roman honour.

John is sure that the Christian tradition bears affirmation of the wifely role, even if it is not obvious to the untrained eye. He answers Gregoria's concerns by recourse to the theme of *imitatio martyrum*:

How will she endure the unpredictablilty of the barbarians (*varietas barbarorum*), who was horrified by a single citizen's raising his voice? But let me admit that you might be able to find a place among those wives whose *Passiones* and *Gesta* are witnessed by reliable documents (*evidentia scripta*). In sum, why would you not be willing to bear the small trials [of the married state], you who are sure you can bear great ones?[157]

The price of access to the imaginative landscape of saints and martyrs is to reimagine her own situation on the same terms.

[155] *Ad Gregoriam* 4 (*CC* 25A, 197).   [156] *Ad Gregoriam* 4 (*CC* 25A, 197–8).
[157] *Ad Gregoriam* 5 (*CC* 25A, 198).

And if this is so – nay, because it is so – I ask what foolish line of thinking persuades you to judge that Christ, for whose will you stand prepared to die at the hands of a tyrant, may be defied where a husband is concerned? For in the case of a husband, will you scorn His precepts (*praecepta*) even though you say you would observe them with regard to a tyrant?'[158]

If she fails to reinvent herself on these terms, John warns, it is a betrayal not only of the Christian tradition, but of Christ himself. We will return to discuss this theme at greater length in Chapter Five.

Gregoria is encouraged to think not only of the martyrs but of a host of married women as her forebears, and the Bible is the place to look for them.

The whole company of matrons will be with you: with you most enduring Sarah, with you gentlest Rebecca, with you holiest Rachel, with you Aseneth, wife of the most chaste (*castissimi*) patriarch [Joseph], with you Zipporah, wife of the man who spoke with God, with you Deborah, vanquisher of arrogance, with you Jael, piercing through the head of the Devil, with you Judith, killing the enemy of chastity (*castitatis*), with you marches (*pergit*) Hannah, the mother of the one seeing God, with you the Shunamite, about to perceive the glory of sojourning in a foreign country, with you Anna, the daughter of Phanuel, who first recognized the Saviour, with you Magdalene, with you Martha – with you the host who, because they have recognized you as one of their number, will be with you even here in this world, and will fight down the enemy battle-lines for you; they throw the very father of crimes to the ground under your feet. Behold what sisters celestial nobility has given you: behold by what kind of women matronly glory is attended; behold by what kind of force the nobility that is eternal is defended.'[159]

The *domina* is encouraged to ask them how they were able to progress from the married estate while on earth to the 'peak of angelic dignity' which is now theirs. 'Take care to question them with these words, "I ask you, O most blessed of all women, by what art or by what approach did your step (*gradus*) enter into the sanctuary of such majesty? Show how you delighted in the softness of marriage when placed on earth, and yet now in heaven possess the peak of angelic dignity." '[160] We should presumably understand this as a reference to meditative Bible study, though their response is represented as live dialogue:

You will hear that with one voice they all respond to your question thus, 'We loved endurance with our whole hearts, and it was endurance that led us to this [lofty] seat. For it is she who gives birth to the other virtues and nurses them with the milk of her own breasts, nor is there any other virtue at all which can be conceived or be created without endurance. For truly we have preserved the *castitas* of our

---

[158] *Ad Gregoriam* 6 (*CC* 25A, 200–1).   [159] *Ad Gregoriam* 2 (*CC* 25A, 194–5).
[160] *Ad Gregoriam* 3 (*CC* 25A, 195–6).

husbands through endurance; through endurance we believed in the rewards of Heaven; through endurance we held to the signs of hope; through endurance we scorned the world, and for the love of chastity (*castitas*) we scorned the threat of disgrace.'

The great task of these women, we are told, is that they were able to preserve the *castitas* of their husbands – by *castitas* we understand that the husbands were faithful to the marriage bed, not that they abstained from legitimate married intercourse. The ability of chaste women to 'bring their husbands into line', sexually and otherwise, had been highly prized since the time of Augustus.[161] At the same time, they are able to reconcile the requirements of Roman honour with the ethics of Paul's first letter to the Corinthians:

'Through endurance we have desired nothing which is accompanied by fear of the laws or shame before others (*hominum pudor*). Through endurance we have scorned every pleasure which could be held in common with beasts, and we have loved only that virtue, which we are known to hold in common with the angels. Through endurance we have longed for nothing regrettable; and through endurance we have laughed at many things which we have suffered against our moral sense. Through endurance we have believed in God, and through endurance we have kept His commandments (*iussa servavimus*); through endurance we have nourished faith, hope, and charity; nor has there been any leader at all other than endurance (*patientia*), to lead us to that pinnacle of worthiness.'[162]

John returns repeatedly to the theme of wifely persuasion, and again he draws on 1 Corinthians as a point of reference. Above, we discussed a passage in which John imagined Gregoria's objection that Paul saw the power over the spouse's body as applying equally to wife and husband. John seems to accept her point, but in fact turns to a sustained meditation on how a wife should use her sexual attractiveness (Paul's discussion of the conjugal debt is the topic from which he leaps off) and 'sweetness' (*dulcedo*) to ensure that her husband does not object to being guided by her will in all things.

I cede readily to this worthy saying, and I maintain that nothing else is meant in the letter [to the Corinthians], than that you should bind your husband by so much charity, and hold him fast by so great a compliance of manner (*morum obtemperantia*), that with you guiding all [his affairs] he should now altogether be

---

[161] Cooper, 'Insinuations of Womanly Influence', 153–5. An interesting fifth-century example can be found in *Letter* 9.6 of Sidonius Apollinaris to his colleague the bishop Ambrosius, in which an unnamed young man is praised for leaving a slave concubine in order to marry a girl of noble family and character, who has steered him toward *bonos mores* (*PL* 58, 620–1); for discussion, see Evans Grubbs, *Law and Family*, 315–16.

[162] *Ad Gregoriam* 3 (*CC* 25A, 195–6).

reluctant to assume the burden of authority (*potestatis curam*). For why should he reserve anything for his dominion, with you taking care of the matter better [than he could himself] because he had willed it? And might he not rejoice, that not only having never encountered contradiction in any matter, but even having encountered unanimity (*consensus*), to such a point that what he wished might better be fulfilled? For sweetness (*dulcedo*), not authority (*potestas*), has handed you over to his dominion, from which, accordingly, you have determined that nothing else should occupy your thoughts exclusively, unless to see to it that you alone among all women manage to be beautiful for him. Therefore, just as you take care lest you show yourself unsightly to his eyes by any blemish of face, so cultivate a beauty of manner, lest therein some unsightliness be able to show forth.[163]

Physical beauty is clearly an asset here, though it should always be accompanied by its ethical counterpart:

Show rather how beautiful of soul you are, how beautiful in intention (*voto*), and how fine (*elegans*) you are in the service of charity, how charming (*decora*) in compliance to a command (*iussionis*), so that – bound by consideration of this – [your husband] may cease to keep his own counsel, and will receive your whole will as a divine pattern (*regulam*), and shiver at your displeasure as at sacrilege.[164]

John obviously delights in the idea of seeming obedience as a strategy of power. Her 'compliance to a command' shows the emptiness of the husband's authority at one level, but at the price of not seeking to dislodge it.

The wifely trickery here reaches back to Augustine's advice to Ecdicia, and almost certainly to his praise of Monnica for her ability to manage the intemperate Patricius.[165] In Gregoria's case, the reader is invited to take pleasure in the *frisson* of proposed duplicity. This, too, was an idea with venerable patristic authority; we will see in the following chapter that Tertullian's treatise *On Patience*, a treatise John clearly knew since he cites it, offers a similar proposal to take one's pleasure in the small ironies of accommodating to the power of others. This said, the advice is given in earnest, for there is a great deal at stake, both for Gregoria and her husband.

A hard story from the desert, about a husband and wife who could not stop fighting and were eventually struck dead in punishment, drives home the point. John imputes a remorseful speech from beyond the grave to the hapless pair:

'Do not', they say, 'do such things as we have done, lest you should suffer what we are suffering.' You see that both could have been saved by one: you see how much

[163] *Ad Gregoriam* 7 (*CC* 25A, 202–3). [164] *Ad Gregoriam* 7 (*CC* 25A, 203).
[165] Augustine, *Confessions* 9.9.19 (*CC* 27, 145).

happiness she could have introduced on the spot, had she soothed (*delinisset*) [the will of] her enraged husband with due endurance (*patientia debita*), and freed by that embrace of legitimate flatteries, the man whom the Enemy had bound tightly by the fetters of ire (*iracundiae nodo*).[166]

What John means here, and he means it honestly, is that abuse from her husband will be the least of Gregoria's worries if she fails to sooth his nerves when he is being impossible. Not only his soul but her own hangs in the balance. When they come to the Last Judgement she will be called to account, and John is confident that she will be able to give a fair case for herself.

You will be blessed if, standing in front of the tribunal of Christ on that day [of Judgement], you are able to say: 'Here, Lord, is the man whom You ordained should be my husband: I guided him by so great a compliance of manner (*morum obtemperantia*),[167] that he never held out against my will. When by great endurance I achieved this very thing, I urged him at once to worshipping and blessing You, so that just as I complied with him when he was ordering, so he would hearken to You, the gracious Lord ordering him, and just as I shunned all those things which he prohibited, so would he abstain from everything which Your holy law prohibits.'[168]

If Gregoria is the indirect beneficiary of the strategy of spoiling her husband, so, too, is God himself.

We can see that in trying to persuade Gregoria to take up her post within the institution of Christian marriage as he understood it, John made every effort to reconcile conflicting strands of tradition, and a somewhat jumbled and over-rich metaphorical wherewithal is the result. John seems to be aware that a figure such as Gregoria might have good reason to balk at the role offered her, and though he tends to cast her possible objections in as unflattering a light as possible, he is aware that he needs to be persuasive. Of course we have no way of knowing whether Gregoria was convinced, since no record of her reaction survives. We should also consider an equally interesting – and equally difficult – question: what, really, was the point of persuading a woman like Gregoria to play along?

There is a self-serving inconsistency to Gregoria's position as John constructs it. On the one hand, she is worried that her task as a married Christian is not worth much in the eyes of God; on the other hand, she

---

[166] *Ad Gregoriam* 8 (*CC* 25A, 205).
[167] Compare Augustine, *Ep.* 262.5 (*CSEL* 57, 625) to Ecdicia, on managing a husband: 'infirmus enim erat et ideo tibi, quae in communi proposito fortior videbaris, non erat praesumptione turbandus sed dilectione portandus ...'
[168] *Ad Gregoriam* 8 (*CC* 25A, 203–4).

chafes at what is asked of her even in this comparatively modest role. (Naturally, our author does not openly consider the possibility that married women are asked to accept rather less praise for a role that is in fact rather more difficult than the better-rated vocations.)

If the degradation of the wifely role is what disturbs Gregoria, John's anxieties are clearly elsewhere. What troubles him is not so much the possibility that the wifely role is too difficult, but rather that a married layperson – male or female – might see the demands of Christian ethics as largely irrelevant to his or her estate. A recent article by Alan Kreider has suggested that post-Constantinian bishops despaired at the prevalence of 'non-participation' by the laity.

> Augustine thought of the early days of the church, recorded in Acts 2, when people were 'thoroughly and perfectly' converted. Even in his day, he knew some people who sought to follow Christ, to pray for their enemies, and to distribute their goods to the needy. To their behaviour . . . the response of many baptized people was incredulous: 'Why are you acting crazy? You're going to extremes; aren't other people Christians?'[169]

John is clearly worried that Gregoria has every reason to join this faction.

> 'But these', you say, 'are not commands (*mandata*) for married people.' Listen to the voice of the Lord responding to this: *Every tree*, he says, *which does not produce a worthy fruit, is destroyed, and is put to fire* (Matt. 7:19). This saying does not exempt any station (*dignitas*) or assign any exception whatsoever to spouses.[170] For marriage (*nuptiae*) would be bad, if it could not exist without prevarication regarding the precepts (*praecepta*) of God. For when God blessed marriages (*coniugia*), and ordered that from the womb of mothers should come forth [both] males and females for the sake of procreation, He took counsel well enough indeed, and allowed that men should be able with their own wives to serve Him.'[171]

The perfectly reasonable position taken here is that the deity would hardly be likely to create a society in which reproduction of the species was considered dishonorable; this was probably a majority view in late

---

[169] Alan Kreider, 'Changing Patterns of Conversion in the West', in idem, *The Origins of Christendom*, 3–46 (here, 34), citing *Sermons* 88.12–13 and 14.4 respectively, in the translation of Edmund Hill (New York, 1990–). For further discussion, see Kate Cooper, 'Ventriloquism and the Miraculous: Conversion, Preaching, and the Martyr Exemplum in Late Antiquity', in Kate Cooper and Jeremy Gregory, eds., *Signs, Wonders, and Miracles*, Studies in Church History 41, (Woodbridge, 2005), 22–45.

[170] Chrysostom frequently stresses similar ideas. E.g.: *Adv. oppug.* 3 (*PG* 47, 319–86): 'The difference between [a monk and a regular Christian] is that one is married and the other is not; in all other respects they will have to render the same account.'

[171] *Ad Gregoriam* 23 (*CC* 25A, 239).

antiquity, but it could only remain so if the married laity involved themselves enough in the Christian community to make their views heard.

It is a point which he returns to repeatedly.

No matronly necessity excuses you: *If you would attain life, keep the commandments (serva mandata)* (Matt. 19:17). This is the voice of Christ, not of just anyone, who might be capable of telling an untruth. Tell me, sweet daughter, do you not wish to attain life, because you have been placed (*posita*) under [the care of] a husband? Without doubt you do. Accordingly, if you wish to attain life, keep the commandments.[172]

The justice of John's position is that the requirements of husband and deity must coincide in order for the system to be just, which of course it must be.

For it is quite unjust if the divine law makes you be adorned by a manner [pleasing] to your husband, but leaves you unadorned [by a manner pleasing] to God, if it orders you to do the will of your husband, and not to do that of your creator – that you fulfil your husband's commands for the sake of a brief life, and do not see to the will of God for the sake of eternal life.[173]

John may or may not have known Augustine's letter to Ecdicia – there is every reason to suspect that he did – but he has clearly absorbed its spirit with regard to the tactics of wifely persuasion.

If John has a particular contribution to make to the ethics of Christian marriage, it is not so much in the novelty of his position as his effort to reach a new audience. *Ad Gregoriam* is pitched at a higher cultural register than the comparable letters of Augustine or Fulgentius, and while this strategy may have narrowed its potential readership across the centuries, it is possible that it succeeded in gaining the attention of a literate readership in John's own day.

It is not entirely clear, however, whether *Ad Gregoriam* was intended to steer the spiritual ambitions of a specifically female readership, or whether the point was to conjure a heroine in distress for the edification of men and women equally. We can consider both possibilities in turn, since they may not be mutually exclusive.

To the degree that John was addressing a female readership, the first danger which he would want to obviate was that a woman of Gregoria's standing and kind might see the Church as irrelevant to her role as a great lady in the traditional Roman manner. If she believed the Church to be a rallying-point for hostility to the old Roman values, she might hold herself apart from accepting a role as patron or friend to the clergy. All parties

---

[172] *Ad Gregoriam* 17 (*CC* 25A, 221).   [173] *Ad Gregoriam* 17 (*CC* 25A, 222).

knew that if she could be persuaded to use her own wherewithal – and ideally her influence with her husband – in support of the good causes sponsored by the Church, a well-placed, pious *domina* was an indispensable ally.

A second, very different kind of danger would involve her electing the route taken by Ecdicia and, later, Radegund: embracing the Church but holding herself apart from her husband, on the grounds that married life was not a role of honour. Hagiographers tended to praise such women fulsomely after the fact, but the truth was that a bishop would do better to talk her out of it if he got there in time. Not only did such women cause trouble between the Church and their powerful husbands; they also created a ripple of discontent throughout the community of the faithful.

To the degree that *Ad Gregoriam* was addressed to a readership of both men and women, we should remember that its literary motif of *teichoskopia*, the viewing of a battle from the high city walls, was as old as Homer. Even if its antiquity was instantly recognizeable, the motif would have seemed uncomfortably contemporary to a reader in the late fifth or early sixth century. Yet if Gregoria is a new Helen and the battle being waged on the plain below the city is a battle over who will win her, in this instance it is the soul, not the body, that is contested. The battle, of course, is being fought not only over Gregoria but over every reader.

We should remember, finally, that the historical Gregoria may have been perfectly happy as she was, and that *Ad Gregoriam* tells us a great deal about John's imagination and rather less about the lady whom he imagined. The literary register of the text suggests that it was probably intended as a bravura display of John's wide reading rather than as a specific pastoral intervention. Nothing is known, of course, about how John's literary effort was judged by his contemporaries. The lady to whom it was addressed – and her husband – may or may not have been delighted by its literary originality. Whether their sensibilities were offended by the writer's evocative treatment of sensitive areas is not recorded. In all likelihood, they found at least part of the text at least mildly alarming. If their unease led to soul-searching John would certainly have been well pleased.

CHAPTER 5

The invisible enemy

> The afflictions which we suffer must soften the hardness of our hearts,
> for, as was foretold by the prophet: 'The sword reacheth unto the
> soul' [Jeremiah 4:10]. Indeed, I see my entire flock being struck down
> by the wrath of God, as one after another they are visited by sudden
> destruction . . . Every one of us, I say, must bewail his sins and repent,
> while there is still time for lamentation. We must pass in review all
> those things we have done which we ought not to have done, and we
> must weep as we think of our trespasses . . .[1]

As his last act before going into hiding to avoid being enthroned as Pope,
the Christian deacon and former urban prefect Gregory made a famous
speech to the Roman people, a speech known to posterity in the *Histories* of
his contemporary Gregory, bishop of Tours. The occasion was the out-
break in Rome during the winter of 589–90 of a plague, which had caused
the death of Pope Pelagius II and was caused in turn by a prodigious
flooding of the Tiber. The deacon Gregory's first recorded address to the
People of Rome was a call to arms against the plague.

Since earthly medicine could do nothing to stop the disease's fierce
progress, Gregory proposed that his people look to their own hearts, whose
hardness might be the cause. The plague had been sent by God to warn his
people of their failings. A collective imprecation could bring down God's
mercy, 'For God is full of mercy and compassion, and it is His will that we
should win his pardon through our prayers.' By a concrete act of penitence,
the Roman people could send a message to the deity. Gregory's advice was
reassuringly practical:

Therefore, dearly beloved brethren, with contrite hearts and with all our affairs in
order let us come together, to concentrate our minds upon our troubles, in the
order which I will explain in a minute, as day dawns on the Wednesday of this
week, to celebrate the sevenfold litanies. When He sees how we ourselves condemn

---

[1] Gregory of Tours, *Decem libri historiarum* 10.1 (*MGH SRM* 1, 479; tr. Thorpe, 544–5).

our own sins, the stern Judge may acquit us of this sentence of damnation which He has prepared for us.[2]

Each of the seven deacons of the Roman Church would assemble a phalanx of the faithful at one of the Roman shrines of the martyrs: the clergy at Cosmas and Damian, the abbots and monks at Protasius and Gervasius, the abbesses and their assembled nuns at Marcellinus and Peter, the children at John and Paul, the laymen at Stephen Protomartyr, the widows at Euphemia, and the married women at Pope Clement. 'Let us all process with prayers and lamentations from each of the churches thus appointed', exhorted Gregory,

to meet together at the basilica of the blessed Virgin Mary, Mother of our Lord Jesus Christ, so that there we may at great length make our supplication to the Lord with tears and groans, and be held worthy to win pardon for our sins.[3]

Gregory's strategy of empowerment, in the face of an overwhelming threat, may seem beside the point to a modern sensibility, but we too have seen how the invocation of sweat and tears can serve a wartime leader.

Three years later, according to his earliest biographer, Gregory demonstrated that the same kind of bravura display had the power to save his city from the Lombards. A century after his death, his first hagiographer records:

[The King] marched his army against Rome intending to devastate it. Saint Gregory went to meet him and spoke to him before them all and thus, by his unique eloquence and holy instruction, so mollified the King's frenzied spirit that he promised so long as Gregory was Pope in that city and he was King, his nation would never lead an army against them.[4]

The story is doubtless an elaboration of the famous account of Pope Leo's face-off with Attila the Hun outside the gates of Rome in 451, an account preserved by Prosper of Aquitaine. Although we need to be wary of the myth-making, the story is nonetheless firm evidence for the cluster of expectations that attached to a person such as Gregory. Even the Lombards, it was believed, could not overcome his indomitable faith in the power of the Almighty. Gregory's imperturbability, and its basis in his confident insight as a reader of Scripture and of hearts and minds, would become legendary.

The second book of his *Homilies on Ezekiel*, preached in the summer of 593 to a small circle of intimates eager to understand the prophet's vision of

[2] Gregory of Tours, *Decem libri historiarum* 10.1 (*MGH SRM* 1, 480, tr. Thorpe, 545–6).
[3] Gregory of Tours, *Decem libri historiarum* 10.1 (*MGH SRM* 1, 481, tr. Thorpe, 546).
[4] *Vita Gregorii* 23, ed. and trans. B. Colgrave, *The Earliest Life of Gregory the Great by an Anonymous Monk of Whitby* (Cambridge, 1968), 115.

the Temple, shows that Gregory himself saw a link between scriptural exegesis and the Lombard problem. Indeed, it may be the grain of sand around which the above-mentioned episode developed.

> There are two things that concern me. One is that this vision [of the Temple] is shrouded in such thick obscurity that it seems difficult to throw any light on it. The other is that I have learnt that the Lombard King Agilulf has crossed the Po and is moving at top speed to besiege us.[5]

What is important about these narratives for our purposes is the light they shed on the discourse of sin and self-examination at the end of antiquity. Far from demeaning its practitioners, the strategy of self-examination offered a means of facing larger-than-life obstacles with indomitable conviction. We know, for example, that when the Lombards besieged Naples in 587, the bishop ordered at least one monk to proceed with the normal work of the scriptorium, in this case, correction of a manuscript of Eugippius' *Excerpta Augustini*. (Our source is the monk's subscription on the sixth-century manuscript itself, Paris Lat. 11642, which has survived.)[6] It bears emphasis that this way of drawing a connection between external crises and inner spiritual conflict had deep roots in Roman Stoicism, but it had acquired a thick patina of Christian associations over the early centuries. Both the fascination of miraculous power and a more introspective tradition of Christian spirituality played their part.

At the same time, the peculiar effectiveness of Christian structures of belonging offered a material advantage, in times of difficulty, to members of the Christian network of mutual support. It has been suggested, for example, that one of the key factors in Christianity's rapid expansion was a distinctive ethos which encouraged Christians to act on behalf of the community's best interest even where this meant courting unnecessary danger individually. In the face of such an ethos, even a scourge such as the plague could bring with it hidden opportunities. Rodney Stark has argued that during the great plagues of the second and third centuries Christian communities gained dramatically in membership, in part because their members were far more likely than non-members to receive adequate nursing care. In addition, sociology worked in their favour: a group with such a strong ethos of close interdependence and mutual care would be well positioned to attract new members from among those

---

[5] Gregory the Great, *Hom. in Ez.* 2 praef. (*CC* 142, 205).
[6] Discussion in T. S. Brown, *Gentlemen and Officers: Imperial Administration and Aristocratic Power in Byzantine Italy AD 554–800* (Rome, 1984), 19.

survivors who had lost family members or access to other structures of belonging.[7]

The logic of Christian stoicism was to cut every obstacle down to size. Though not reductionist in the theological sense, this strategy of thought is profoundly reductionist psychologically. To the degree that the enemy is powerful, the faithful believe, he is not real; rather, each adversity is an illusion, a puppet on strings held by the Devil. Further, the Devil, too, has no real power: he only has a hold on the Christian to the degree that the Christian allows him to. Ergo: the enemy is not real. To put it another way: to the degree that the enemy is real, the enemy is one's own doubt.

This logic would form the core of what became the warrior Christianity of the early Middle Ages. The predilection of early medieval Christians for elements of magic and the miraculous has sometimes been misunderstood as a rejection of the ethical strands of earlier Christianity, but this is incorrect. To the contrary, the Christianity of spiritual warfare that cristallizes at the end of antiquity is in fact a deeply perceptive reflection of strands of thought that reach back to the New Testament and to Hellenistic Judaism. The miraculous sensibility of late Roman Christianity should not be understood as the result of a decline in literacy, at least where the motif of spitirual warfare is concerned. In fact, the use of the motif may have served as a badge of literacy.[8]

An episode in the early sixth-century *Vita* of bishop Epiphanius of Pavia, shows the interpenetration between this imaginative landscape of spiritual warfare, and the harsh realities of an Italy repeatedly exposed to civil war. Written by his successor Ennodius, the *Vita* records a speech made by the holy man Epiphanius in 471, when he had been brought to Rome to try to broker a peace between the emperor Anthemius and his barbarian son-in-law the patrician Ricimer, who had been the king-maker in Italy since the early 460s. Ricimer's marriage to Anthemius' daughter Alypia in 467 seems to have been part of the deal which had brought Anthemius to power. The splendid festivities of the marriage had been seen by contemporaries as offering new hope for the safety of the Roman state, a view confirmed by the panegyric addressed in January 468 to the new emperor Anthemius by Sidonius Apollinaris, who had travelled from Gaul to bring a petition.[9] But by 470 it was clear that the allegiance would not hold. In 471 the

---

[7] Rodney Stark, *The Rise of Christianity: A Sociologist Reconsiders History* (Princeton, 1996), 73–94.

[8] Kate Cooper, 'Ventriloquism and the Miraculous: Conversion, Preaching, and the Martyr Exemplum in Late Antiquity', in Kate Cooper and Jeremy Gregory, eds., *Signs, Wonders, and Miracles*, Studies in Church History 41 (Woodbridge, 2005), 22–45.

[9] See Penny MacGeorge, *Late Roman Warlords* (Oxford, 2002), 235.

situation escalated toward civil war. It was at this juncture that the holy bishop of Pavia was brought in to try to restore order, a mission which ultimately failed.

It should come as no surprise that the bishop's attempt to bring peace draws on a moral language closely related to what we have encountered in the conduct manuals for the powerful laity. Here is Epiphanius addressing the emperor:

> The patrician Ricimer has requested my humble oratory, believing without doubt, that a Roman will confer, as a gift to God, the peace which is requested by a barbarian[10] . . . I know of no kind of warfare which requires greater courage than to struggle against rage . . ."[11]

Anthemius' reply, as reported by Ennodius, sustains the theme of interior examination:

> Shall we now grant this man peace? Shall we sustain an internal enemy under the cloak of friendship, when neither the bonds of friendship nor of marriage have been able to hold him to his agreements? It is a great advantage to have known the mind of an enemy, for then he at once feels he has been beaten.[12]

The enemy hidden by the cloak of friendship inverts a metaphor in the *Passio* of Sebastian, where the *miles Christi* hid his true identity under the cloak of a Roman soldier.[13] A 'feedback loop' of sorts is probably in play as Ennodius tells the story of Epiphanius and the emperor. He wants to give value to this strand of Christian rhetoric by suggesting that it was on such resources that great men drew when the future of the Roman state hung in the balance. At the same time, the more value accorded to the language, the more likely that it could be put into use.[14]

---

[10] Ricimer was probably descended from the Visigothic royal family through his mother, although his father was a Sueve (MacGeorge, *Late Roman Warlords*, 178).

[11] Ennodius, *Vita Epifani* 64–5 (*MGH AA* 7, 92): 'Ricemer patricius parvitatem meam oratu direxit, indubitanter coniciens, quod pacem Romanus deo munus tribuat, quam precatur et barbarus . . .. Simul nescio quae species fortior possit esse bellorum quam dimicare contra iracundiam,' (trans. MacGeorge, *Late Roman Warlords*, 249). Note that MacGeorge's text is slightly different to that of the *MGH*.

[12] *Vita Epifanii* 69–70 (*MGH AA* 7, 92–3): 'Huic nos pacem dabimus? Hunc intestinum sub indumento amicitiarum inimicum sustinebimus, quem ad foedus concordiae nec adfinitatis uincula tenuerunt? Grandis cautio est adversarii animum cognovisse: etenim hostem protinus sensisse superasse est.'

[13] *Passio Sebastiani*, 2.

[14] Peter Brown, *Power and Persuasion: Towards a Christian Empire* (Madison, 1992), offers an exploration of the moral languages developed in the late Roman East, while Leyser, *Authority and Asceticism, from Augustine to Gregory the Great* (Oxford, 2000), charts the attempt to create a legacy of episcopal authority in the West that reconciled ascetic and civic moral languages.

In the early sixth century, we see writers across the Latin West borrowing the metaphor to explore the problems of Christian public authority. Thus, as we saw in Chapter One, Ferrandus of Carthage, writing to Reginus in the early 530s, used the visibile–invisible opposition – 'those fight against visibile enemies, these against invisible ones' – to distinguish between the *miles Christi* and the *miles saeculi*. But it was Cassiodorus who voiced a more threatening reading of the metaphor of the internal enemy, one which must always have hovered just below the surface in a society troubled by rival political and ethnic groupings. At around the same time as Ferrandus' treatise, the *Edictum Athalarici* composed by Cassiodorus (c. 533–4) on behalf of the young king Athalaric, takes up the theme of internal and external threats to the kingdom: 'For long an ominous whisper has reached our ears that certain persons, despising *civilitas*, affect a life of beastly barbarism, returning to the wild beginnings of society, and looking with fierce hatred on all human laws . . . The internal enemy is even more dangerous than the external.'[15] Like the plague, the prospect of war sharpened the urgency and the rhetorical point of the habit of self-examination.

A poem from early fifth-century Gaul, the *Carmen de providentia Dei*, captures the intermittent mood of self-examination that arrived with the barbarian invasions, and never really left.

You, who weep over overgrown fields, deserted courtyards and the crumbling terraces of your burnt-out villa, shouldn't you rather shed tears for your own losses, when you look at the desolate recesses of your heart, the beauty covered over with layers of grime, and the enemy rioting in the citadel of your imprisoned mind? If that citadel hadn't been surrendered . . . these beauties created by the hand would still remain to bear witness to the virtue of a holy people . . . If any mental energy remains, let us shake off the servile yoke of sin, break the chains, and return to freedom and the glory of our native land . . . Let us not fear, because we have collapsed in a flight in the first contest, to take a stand and embark on a second battle.[16]

To offer the hope of a hidden spiritual dimension, in such circumstances, was an invaluable tool, making it possible to find scope for agency and self-belief. But these ideas, if timely, were by no means opportunistic; they

---

[15] *Edictum Athalarici*, *Variae* 9.18 (*MGH AA* 12, 282): 'diu est, quod diversorum querellae nostris auribus crebris sussurationibus insonarunt quosdam civilitate despecta affectare vivere beluina saevitia, dum regressi ad agreste principium ius humanum sibi aestimant feraliter odiosum . . . sed tanto gravius grassantur vitia quanto probantur interna.'

[16] *Carmen de providentia dei* (translation, cited here, and commentary in Roberts, M., 'Barbarians in Gaul: The Response of the Poets', in J. Drinkwater and H. Elton, *Fifth-Century Gaul: A Crisis of Identity?* (Cambridge, 1992), 97–106).

had roots in a patrimony going back to the days of the early Church. Latin writers at the end of antiquity were steeped in the patristic tradition that preceded them, and could thus draw on deep currents of spiritual reflection, reaching back beyond the beginning of Christianity to the anguished questioning of the Psalms, to find the hidden meaning in whatever their God might have in store for them.

THE PARADOX OF INVISIBLE POWERS IN EARLY PATRISTIC TRADITION: TERTULLIAN AND CYPRIAN

Two streams of patristic reflection converged into a powerful current. One stream explored the spiritual power that the individual Christian might gain by cultivating forbearance in the face of difficulty, while another developed an analysis of the parallel inner conflict between the vices and the virtues in the Christian's soul, on the understanding that self-examination was the first step to empowerment. The result was a vivid image, applicable to women and children as easily as to men, of the individual Christian as both a martyr and a soldier, engaged in a life-or-death conflict with those who would persecute the faith, and at the same time with the armies of Satan.

The late Roman spirituality of allegorical battle is best known through its distinctive expression in the monastic writings of Evagrius and John Cassian – a prologue to the medieval tradition of the Seven Deadly Sins.[17] But the instinct that the troubled soul could better be understood through the metaphor of a battle between the vices and the virtues was both more widespread and more ancient than the lore of the Christian desert. The construction of the conflict between good and evil within the human soul as an allegorical battle between the vices and virtues[18] derives through Alexandrian Neoplatonism from Hellenistic astrology. This manner of thinking reached the Latin West by way of Ambrose of Milan,[19]

---

[17] Columba Stewart, *Cassian the Monk* (New York, 1998). See also Adolf Katzenellenbogen, *Allegories of the Virtues and Vices in Mediaeval Art from Early Christian Times to the Thirteenth Century*, tr. A. J. P. Crick (London, 1939), and Richard Newhauser, ed., *In the Garden of Evil: The Vices and Culture in the Middle Ages*, Papers in Mediaeval Studies 18 (Toronto, 2005).

[18] Given its importance in late antiquity, the subject of personification allegory has received astonishingly little attention. For the West, see Morton W. Bloomfield, *The Seven Deadly Sins: An Introduction to the History of a Religious Concept, with Special Reference to Medieval English Literature* (Michigan State College Press, 1952).

[19] On Ambrose as allegorist, see the sensitive article of Hervé Savon, 'Maniérisme et allégorie dans l'oeuvre d'ambroise de Milan', *Revue des études latines* 55 (1977), 203–21.

whose thought was steeped in the writings of Origen of Alexandria, and subsequently through Rufinus of Aquileia's translations of Origen's own works.[20]

Yet the theme had already been taken up, centuries earlier, by Tertullian and Cyprian, the writers whose vigorous prose brought 'Christian Latin' into being. Both played a crucial role, along with the early Latin translations of the Bible, in establishing the terms of discussion for most topics of what has been called 'Christian Latin'. Unsurprisingly, both writers made an important contribution to the Christian spirituality of endurance, and to the imaginative construct of spiritual warfare.

The themes which they established – such as the importance of the virtue of endurance, the necessity of keeping the commandments of God, or the struggle within the soul between the virtues and the vices – have frequently been understood by a scholarship insufficiently grounded in the earlier patristic period as either, on the one hand, superficial borrowings from a more developed monastic literature, or, on the other, as heretical or insufficiently Christianized borrowings from the pagan philosophical literature. We will see, however, that the tradition of concern for the spirituality of the literate laity is as old as our evidence for Latin Christianity itself.

Written around the turn of the second to third century, the first extended exploration of the spirituality of endurance, Tertullian of Carthage's brief treatise *De patientia* ('On Endurance'), was written in unknown circumstances.[21] Tertullian addressed another treatise, *Ad martyras*, to the problem of martyrdom, but *De patientia* is designed specifically to address the distresses of daily life, from serious matters such as the death of a family member, to the petty grievances among friends and family.

It is Tertullian who develops the kernel of what will become the idea that the soul's besiegement by vice is the work of the Devil.

Therefore I detect the birth of impatience in the Devil himself, at that very time when he impatiently bore that the Lord God subjected the universal works which He had made to His own image, that is, to man. [Ps. 8: 4–6]. For if he had

---

[20] Bloomfield, *Seven Deadly Sins*, 51ff. Perhaps not incidentally, Rufinus was also responsible for the translation into Latin of Evagrius of Pontus, the great student of Origen's works, and author of the *Praktikos*, the first mannual for ascetics specifically to outline a battle-plan for the soul's conflict, seriatim, with the vices. On the intellectual milieu of Rufinus and the Western students of Origen, see Caroline P. Hammond, 'The Last Ten Years of Rufinus' Life and the Date of his Move South from Aquileia', *Journal of Theological Studies*, n.s. 28 (1977), 372–429, and Elizabeth A. Clark, *The Origenist Controversy: The Cultural Construction of an Early Christian Debate* (Princeton, 1992).

[21] A concise and judicious survey of the scant evidence on Tertullian is given in James B. Rives, *Religion and Authority in Roman Carthage from Augustus to Constantine* (Oxford, 1995), 273–85.

endured (that), he would not have grieved; nor would he have envied man if he had not grieved.[22]

Tertullian hints as well at what will become a standard topos of Christian devotional literature, the battle within the Christian soul between the vices and the virtues.[23]

Drawing on commonplaces of Hellenistic moral philosophy, he emphasizes the social dangers of hypocrisy and the 'affectation of virtue'[24] and of striving after great spiritual accomplishments while neglecting the seemingly minor occasions through which the texture of a person's moral life is established,[25] or the relevance of the virtue of endurance to the wrongs of daily life.[26] The propertied milieu to which Tertullian is addressing himself is revealed when he exhorts the reader to take his or her expectations of slaves as an index of what God expects of each Christian.[27]

Tertullian suggests that endurance is not only required of the Christian, who should learn from the example of God's own willingness to endure suffering and death for the sake of humanity, but it is a useful tool of self-protection. Endurance offers, he suggests, a strategy by which the Christian can insulate him or herself from forces beyond his or her control. This is especially true of life with other human beings. Tertullian is not above giving sly advice on the social psychology of human aggression:

I will add (somewhat) touching the *pleasure* of endurance. For every injury, whether inflicted by tongue or hand, when it has lighted upon endurance, will be dismissed with the same fate as some weapon launched against and blunted on a rock of most steadfast hardness. For it will wholly fall then and there with bootless and fruitless labour; and sometimes will recoil and spend its rage on him who sent it out, with retorted impetus. No doubt the reason why any one hurts you is that you may be pained; because the hurter's enjoyment consists in the pain of the hurt. When, then, you have upset his enjoyment by not being pained, *he* must needs he

[22] Tertullian, *De patientia* 5 (*CSEL* 47, 6–7; tr. *ANF* 3, 709).
[23] E.g. Tertullian, *De patientia* 14 (*CSEL* 47, 21): 'patientia ... adversus onmem subvertendae fidei vel puniendae paraturam, ut verbera, ut ignem, ut crucem bestias gladium constantissime toleret, quae prophetae, quae apostoli sustinendo vicerunt.'
[24] Tertullian, *De patientia* 1 (*CSEL* 47, 2) on philosophers: 'in illam adfectatione virtutis unanimiter student.'
[25] Tertullian, *De patientia* 8 (*CSEL* 47, 13), 'absit a servo Christi tale inquinamentum, ut patientia maioribus temptationibus preparata in frivolis excidat!'
[26] Tertullian, *De patientia* 9 (*CSEL* 47, 14): 'nam omnis iniuria, seu lingua seu manu incussa, cum patientiam offenderit, eodem exitu dispungetur, quo telum aliquod in petra constantissimae duritiae libratum et obtusum.'
[27] Tertullian, *De patientia* 10 (*CSEL* 47, 15–16): 'servulis nostris adsumentibus sibi de conservis ultionem graviter offendimur eosque, qui nobis patientiam obtulerint suam, ut memores humilitatis servitutis suae, dominici honoris diligentes non probamus modo, sed ampliorem, quam ipsi sibi praesumpsissent, satisfactionem facimus.'

pained by the loss of his enjoyment. Then you not only go unhurt away, which even alone is enough for you; but gratified, into the bargain, by your adversary's disappointment, and revenged by his pain. This is the *utility* and the *pleasure* of endurance.[28]

His sense for the pettiness of human interaction here is truly impressive, and perhaps reflects the circumstances of mutual surveillance that characterized Roman domestic arrangements.

As it happens, we have direct evidence that three centuries later Tertullian's *De patientia* was being read very carefully, since the author of *Ad Gregoriam in palatio* used it at length.[29] The most striking point of contact between the two texts is a somewhat altered, but extensive, direct borrowing in *Ad Gregoriam* of a characterization of the virtue of endurance from Tertullian's text.[30] Here is Tertullian's version of the passage:

What a great thing is allowed to endurance, that she should have God as her debtor! Not unjustly: for she watches over all His prescriptions, and interposes herself in His mandates: she defends peace, rules faith, assists love, teaches humility, awaits penitence, confers confession, rules the flesh, serves the spirit, bridles the tongue, stays the hand, treads down temptations, drives away scandals, consummates martyrdoms, consoles the poor, moderates the rich, does not destroy the weak, does not over-extend the strong, delights faith. She invites the foreigner, commits the slave to the care of the master and the master to that of God, beautifies the woman and establishes the man; she is loved by the boy, praised by the youth, admired by the old man; she is beautiful in either sex and every age.[31]

Ad Gregoriam recasts Tertullian's passage to reflect its own theme of inclusion of the various estates in the pursuit of Christian perfection. The passage appears in *Ad Gregoriam* as follows:

What a great thing is allowed to endurance, that she should have God as her champion! Not unjustly: to be sure, He watches over all her actions, and is present in all her good deeds. She defends peace, sustains faith, drives away scandals,

---

[28] Tertullian, *De patientia* 8 (*CSEL* 47, 14; tr. *ANF* 3, 712–13), altered.

[29] This said, *Ad Gregoriam* bears no discernible relation to Tertullian's *Ad uxorem*, one of the very few other texts to have been addressed to a married woman in antiquity.

[30] *De patientia* 15 (*CSEL* 47, 1–24).

[31] Tertullian, *De patientia* 15 (*CSEL* 47, 22): 'quantum patientiae licet, ut deum habeat debitorem! nec inmerito [enim]. Omnia enim placita eius tuetur, omnibus mandatis eius intervenit: fidem munit, pacem gubernat, dilectionem adiuvat, humilitatem instruit, paenitentiam expectat, exhomologesin adsignat, carnem regit, spiritum servat, linguam frenat, manum continet, temptationes inculcat, scandala pellit, martyria consummat, pauperem consolatur, divitem temperat, infirmum non consumit, valentem non extendit, fidelem delectat, gentilem invitat, servum domino, dominum deo commendat, feminam exornat, virum adprobat; amatur in puero, laudatur in iuvene, suspicitur in sene; in omni sexu, in omni aetate formosa est.'

confers charity, preserves marriages in purity, refreshes virginity dedicated to God, sustains widowhood, assists those serving God, quickens married couples living in continence, bestows honour upon the priests of God, and strengthens the martyrs of Christ: she confers faith, encourages the friend, consoles the sad, comforts the sick, and sustains the needy. She is loved in children, praised in men, revered in the old, and extolled in women. She is beautiful in those of every dignity, either sex, or any age: she makes the wealthy moderate, raises up the poor, and sustains the needy.[32]

The author of *Ad Gregoriam* probably knew Tertullian's text directly, rather than from a citation in another author or a florilegium, since he develops a number of themes from *De Patientia*, such as the dangers of hypocrisy and the 'affectation of virtue'[33] or of striving after great spiritual accomplishments while neglecting the more important minor ones,[34] the exhortation to imagine one's expectations of one's own slaves as an index of what is expected of one by God.[35] Numerous verbal echoes rebound between the two works, especially where the battle between the vices and the virtues is concerned,[36] or the relevance of the virtue of endurance to the wrongs of daily life.[37] Occasionally, in addition, the descriptions of serenity of spirit in *Ad Gregoriam* echo Tertullian's description of endurance herself.[38] There is much confluence of subject matter but it would be misleading to suggest that *Ad Gregoriam's* overall structure was related to that of *De patientia*. Although Tertullian established many of the motifs on which later spiritual writers would draw, it was another Carthaginian, the third-century bishop Cyprian, bishop of Carthage from 248/9 to 258, who found a way to join the motif of endurance with other motifs to form a distinctive ethos of spiritual warfare.

---

[32] One can see *Ad Gregoriam's* systematic innovation on Tertullian's language: not only are new elements added, but frequently a synonym is substituted where Tertullian's meaning is retained. See *Ad Gregoriam* 16 (*CC* 25A, 219): 'O quantum patientiae licet, ut deum habeat defensorem! Nec inmerito: omnia enim opera eius tuetur, omnibusque eius virtutibus interest: pacem munit, fidem regit, pellit scandala, caritatem adsignat, servat in castitate coniugia, virginitatem deo dicatam exhilarat, viduitatem sustentat, deo servientes adiuvat, coniuges vegetat continentes, sacerdotes dei ornat, martyras quoque Christi conroborat: adsignat fidem, amicum confirmat, tristem consolatur, infirmum confortat, egentem sustentat. Haec amatur in pueris, laudatur in viris, veneratur in senibus, magnificatur in feminis: in omni honore, in omni sexu, in omni aetate formosa est: divitem communicat, pauperem sublevat, cadentem sustentat.'

[33] See n. 24 above.

[34] Tertullian, *De patientia* 8 (*CSEL* 47, 13): 'absit a servo Christi tale inquinamentum, ut patientia maioribus temptationibus preparata in frivolis excidat!'

[35] See n. 27 above.   [36] See n. 23 above.   [37] See n. 26 above.

[38] Tertullian, *De patientia* 15 (*CSEL* 47, 23): 'vultus illi tranquillus et placidus, frons pura, nulla maeroris aut irae rugositate contracta; remissa aeque in latum modum supercilia, oculis humilitate, non infelicitate deiectis; os taciturnitatis honore signatum . . .'

Cyprian's *De bono patientiae*[39] shares much in general terms of theme and vocabulary with Tertullian's *De patientia*, but it is his *De mortalitate*,[40] an exhortation to fortitude delivered to the faithful of Carthage during the pestilence of 252, which takes up a systematic treatment of the problem of discouragement among Christians and provides the pattern for the later treatments of the theme. We can see in Cyprian how powerfully the ancient moral strategy of self-introspection in the face of difficulty could flourish on the new sustenance of biblical imagery. It is a creativity forged in the heat of real hardship, and there was every reason for it to become an enduring moral language. The stimulus of hardship was never hard to come by in the Roman period, but it was felt ever more sharply as the Roman social order began to unravel. A moral language proposing hardship as a spur to spiritual prowess would come to seem ever more valuable.

De mortalitate begins by trying to understand why so many of the faithful are unable to face the agonies of the plague with an untroubled spirit. Some are unsteady, the bishop suggests, 'either through weakness of mind, or through paucity of faith, or through the sweetness of secular life, or through the weakness of their sex,[41] or – what is worse – through straying from the Truth'.[42] Cyprian goes on to explain that the true Christian is not one who reposes in an easy faith, but rather is one who battles for God, 'posted in the heavenly camp'.[43] The trials of the present – his own historical moment – should not be a cause of distress, since they are a sign of the arrival of the end time.

Cyprian develops the inherited idea of the Christian as a *miles Christi*, a soldier fighting in God's army, in a new and vivid way.[44] Spiritual adversity is figured graphically in military terms, the 'darts and weapons' of the Devil being the soul's own vices.[45] The *pugna adversus diabolum*[46] establishes a new kind of personification allegory, in which the vices and virtues

---

[39] Cyprian, *De bono patientiae* (*CC* 3A, 118–33).   [40] Cyprian, *De mortalitate* (*CC* 3A, 17–32).

[41] *Ad Gregoriam* 10.18 (*CC* 25A, 307, 224).   [42] Cyprian, *De mortalitate* 1 (*CC* 3A, 17).

[43] Cyprian, *De mortalitate* 2 (*CC* 3A, 17): the Christian defined as 'qui Deo militat, qui positus in caelestibus castris divina iam spirat'.

[44] Adolf von Harnack, *Militia Christi: the Christian Religion and the Military in the First Three Centuries*, trans. David McInnes Gracie (Philadelphia, 1981), is still valuable on the early period.

[45] Cyprian, *De mortalitate* 4 (*CC* 3A, 18–19): 'Ceterum quid aliud in mundo quam pugna adversus diabolum cotidie geritur, quam adversus iacula eius et tela conflictationibus adsiduis dimicatur? cum avaritia nobis, cum impudicitia, cum ira, cum ambitione congressio est, cum carnalibus vitiis, cum inlecebris saecularibus adsidua et molesta luctatio est. Obsessa mens hominis et undique diaboli infestatione vallata vix occurrit singulis, vix resistit: si avaritia prostrata est, exsurgit libido: si libido compressa est, succedit ambitio: si ambitio contempta est, ira exasperat, inflat superbia, vinolentia invitat, invidia concordiam rumpit, amicitiam zelus abscidit.'

[46] Cyprian, *De mortalitate* 4.57 (*CC* 3A, 18–19).

themselves are endowed with the attributes of human soldiers on the field of battle, so that the Christian's inner struggle becomes a *psychomachia* (lit. 'soul-battle'). This is a theme which we have already seen in the literature of classically orientated Christians such as Prudentius; it will become equally important to monastic literature – we will encounter it in Evagrius and Cassian – and it will thrive as a motif across medieval literature.

Another point developed by Cyprian is the exhortation to imitate Christ in his forbearance faced with suffering. The theme of 'following Christ' had been associated primarily with the martyrs through the first two centuries to the time of Tertullian.[47] The notion of the Christian life as *imitatio* is one whose roots lie deep in the period of the persecutions. The historical martyr her- or himself was expected to engage in *imitatio* – to re-enact by his or her own endurance the passion of Christ – a topos which reaches back to the letters of Paul himself.[48]

Another influential text from the New Testament had explicitly linked forbearance when faced with domestic mistreatment to the suffering of Christ:

Servants, be submissive to your masters with all respect, not only to the kind and gentle but also to the overbearing. For one is approved if, mindful of God, he endures pain while suffering unjustly. For what credit is it, if when you do wrong and are beaten for it you take it patiently? But if when you do right and suffer for it you take it patiently, you have God's approval. For to this you have been called, because Christ also suffered for you, leaving you an example, that you should follow in his steps. He committed no sin; no guile was found on his lips. When he was reviled, he did not revile in return; when he suffered, he did not threaten; but he trusted to him who judges justly. He himself bore our sins in his body on the tree, that we might die to sin and live to righteousness. By his wounds you have been healed. (1 Peter 2:18–24)

Drawing on this strand of biblical tradition, Cyprian was able to make vivid the problem of the member of the community who is discouraged, in the face of the martyrs' heroism, by the seeming inconsequence of the daily pursuit of simple virtues. As a remedy, he offers the sufferings of biblical figures as *exempla* whose virtues may be imitated. In *De mortalitate* the list is headed by Job;[49] we will see that in *Ad Gregoriam* and other texts of the fifth and sixth centuries, the *exempla* are male or female depending on the gender of the addressee.

---

[47] Simone Deleani, *Christum Sequi: étude d'un thème dans l'oeuvre de saint Cyprien* (Paris, 1979).

[48] See the exhortation in 1 Cor. 11:1 ('Be imitators of me, as I imitate Christ'), a text which will be picked up as a starting-point by later writers such as the author of *Ad Celanthiam*.

[49] Cyprian, *De mortalitate*, 10ff (*CC* 3A, 21ff.).

Finally, *De mortalitate* ends with an invitation to consider the soul's return to paradise, its true home.[50] The themes of hastening to one's own country, of the Christian as a pilgrim on earth, of the crowd of apostles, prophets, martyrs, virgins, and loved ones waiting to welcome the Christian to heaven, are brought together for an epic finale[51] which served as the model for numerous imitations in the fourth, fifth, and sixth centuries, from Jerome's letter 22 to Eustochium to *Ad Gregoriam*. Cyprian's strategy of chiding the Christian who claims to be eager to face martyrdom, but shows himself demoralized by a less heroic fate would find numerous imitators, as we shall see below.[52] While Cyprian's task was to console those who fear the genuine threat of death from the plague, *Ad Gregoriam* takes up the motif as a way of pointing out the spiritual value of the minor trials of daily married life – but the spirit, and indeed the wording, of the two passages is very close.

Cyprian's fear that the faithful might be swayed from their spiritual purpose through discouragement drew, of course, on a vigorous tradition of philosophical writing, ubiquitous enough to serve as a standard school exercise.[53] We have seen that the most eminent of Christian *consolationes*, the sixth-century *De consolatione philosophiae* of Boethius, develops similar themes, although it draws not on Cyprian but directly on the pagan philosophers whom Cyprian, too, had read. We will see that Cyprian's theme of the battle between the vices and the virtues became ever more influential in the fourth and fifth centuries. By the fifth century, Christian use of allegory had a widespread audience both as the province of Christians of no mean intellectual pretence, and equally as the province of those for whom uncomfortable aspects of the biblical tradition could best be reconciled through an intellectualist approach.

ORIGEN AND AMBROSE

The ground-rules of Christian allegory would come to rest on the prodigious contribution of one of Cyprian's Greek contemporaries, Origen of

---

[50] See also Cyprian, *De mortalitate* 18 (*CC* 3 A, 27): 'quid ergo oramus et petimus ut adveniat regnum caelorum, si captivitas terrena delectat?'

[51] Cyprian, *De mortalitate*, 26 (*CC* 3A, 31–2). 'Magnus illic nos carorum numerus expectat, parentum . . . et copiosa turba.'

[52] Cyprian, *De mortalitate*, 17 (*CC* 3A, 25–6): 'Sed fortasse aliquis opponat et dicat: "hoc me ergo in praesenti mortalitate contristat quod qui paratus ad confessionem fueram et ad tolerantiam passionis toto me corde et plena virtute devoveram martyrio meo privor, dum morte praevenior."' On Cyprian's fifth-century influence, see Hervé Savon, 'Une Consolation imitée de Sénèque et de Saint Cyprien (Pseudo-Jérôme, *epistula 5, ad amicum aegrotum*)', *Recherches Augustiniennes* 14 (1979), 153–90.

[53] See Savon, 'Consolation imitée', 154–9, and literature cited there.

Alexandria, although his influence would not be felt in the West until a century after his death. In his fifteenth *Homily on Joshua*, Origen had explained his view of the matter in terms drawn from his reading of Paul. The apostle had spoken of putting on 'the whole armour of God', (Eph. 6:11): his meaning was obviously not a literal one, 'For we know that the law is spiritual' (Rom. 7:14). In his bounty, the Lord had provided in the Hebrew Bible a glittering array of battle narratives in order to fortify followers of the new dispensation for a moral and a spiritual battle to rank with the great wars of the ancient Israelites.[54]

Origen's development of a Christian allegorical vocabulary was designed to bring Christian literature into alignment with the Alexandrian intellectual milieu. Yet it served another equally important function, that of defending aspects of the Judaeo-Christian inheritance which might otherwise come under attack.[55] (We will encounter a similar use of allegory as a strategy for defending difficult-to-explain aspects of tradition in the cult of the martyrs.) Thus, for example, Origen used allegorical claims to silence critics of the Hebrew Bible who found its chronicles of Israelite military history incompatible with the New Testament message of peace. What the ancient wars of Joshua and the modern struggles of Christians had in common was their adversary: all fought alike against the serried ranks of the Devil and the other angels who had followed him into apostasy.[56] The book of Joshua and the epistles of Paul, correctly read, spoke with one

---

[54] Origen, *Homilia in Iesum filium Navis* 15 (*SC* 71, 330): 'Unde denique sciens Apostolus nulla nobis iam ultra bella esse carnaliter peragenda, sed animae certamina contra spiritales adversarios desudanda, velut magister militiae praeceptum dat militibus Christi dicens: "induite vos arma Dei, ut possitis stare adversus astutias diaboli" [Eph. 6:11]. Et ut horum spiritalium bellorum ex veterum gestis habere possimus exempla, istas nobis rerum gestarum narrationes in ecclesia voluit recitari, ut nos, si spiritales sumus, audientes quia "lex spiritalis est" [Rom. 7:14], in his quae audimus "spiritalibus spiritalia comparemus" [1 Cor. 2:13] et contemplemur ex his gentibus, quae carnalem Istrahel visibiliter oppugnarunt, quantae sint gentes contrariarum virtutum ex his spiritalibus, qui dicuntur "spiritales nequitiae in coelestibus" [Eph. 6:12] quae adversus ecclesiam Domini, quae est verus Istrahel, suscitent bella.'

[55] On 'un principe d'exégèse bien établi depuis Philon: l'absurdité ou l'indécence d'un épisode raconté par les livres saints est signe qu'il faut aller au-delà du sens obvie', see Savon, 'Maniérisme', 211, and J. Pépin, 'Théorie de l'exégèse allégorique', in *Philon d'Alexandrie, Lyon 11–15 septembre 1966*, Colloques nationaux du CNRS (Paris: 1967), 161–7.

[56] Origen, *Homilia in Iesum filium Navis*, 12.1 (*SC* 71, 294): '... bella, quae per Iesum geruntur, et regum atque hostium strages coelestium "rerum umbra et typus" [Heb. 8:5] esse dicenda sunt, eorum dumtaxat bellorum, quae noster Dominus Iesus cum suo exercitu et magistratibus, id est credentium populis atque eorum ducibus, contra diabolum et eius angelos proeliatur. Ipse est enim, qui in Paulo et in Ephesiis pugnat "adversus principatus et potestates et rectores tenebrarum, adversus spiritalia nequitiae in coelestibus" [cf. Eph. 6:12].' See also *Homily* 15.1: 'Nisi bella ista carnalia figuram bellorum spiritalium gererent, numquam, opinor, Iudaicarum historiarum libri discipulis Christi, qui venit pacem docere, legendi in ecclesiis fuissent ap Apostolis traditi. Quo enim iis bellorum

voice. In the West, a similar defensive use of spiritual allegory came to
prevail, although the context in which it was deployed evolved over time. It
was not until the heady years of the end of the fourth century that a
conjunction of intellectual confidence and cultural conflict arose which
would make full use of the instability and multiplicity of meaning which
allegory made available.

It was Ambrose, Bishop of Milan from 374 to 397, who made Origen's
thought widely available in the West. In Ambrose's hands, the allegorical
approach to the experience of the individual which we have seen in Cyprian
proved capable of absorbing the allegorical method of scriptural exegesis
which he received from Origen. Similar developments were taking place in
the Egyptian desert at around the same time – see, for example, the writings
of Evagrius Ponticus – but it was Ambrose who engineered the confluence
of diverse traditions of spiritual guidance, and developed the approach to
the struggle of the Christian martyrs as an *exemplum* to guide 'average'
Christians as they faced the struggle within the soul. His contribution was
all the more distinctive and lasting, in that he drew a connection which
would take centre stage in the Latin spirituality of the early Middle Ages.
This was the metaphorical link between the interior battle of the Christian
represented by the martyr's fight, and the powerful language of the Psalms,
with their meditation on the soul's need for divine sustenance in the face of
tribulation.

Early in his *Expositio in Psalmum 118*, Ambrose establishes the lines of
orientation for the biblical discussion of the spititual tests to be undergone
by the righteous: 'many will persecute me . . . but I will not turn away from
witnessing to you [Psalm 118:157].'[57] Job is brought forward to begin with,
as the example of the man who understands that he must continue to bless
God even in the face of disaster, then the Book of Acts, to remind the

proficeret ista descriptio, quibus dicitur ab Iesu; "Pacem meam do vobis, pacem meam relinquo
vobis" [John 14:27] et quibus per apostolum iubetur et dicitur: "Non vosmet ipso vindicantes"
[Rom. 12:19] et "magis iniuriam percipite" et "magis fraudem patimini" [1 Cor. 6:7]?'
[57] Ambrose, *Expositio psalmi CXVIII* 20.43 (*CSEL* 62, 466): 'Sequitur versus quintus: "multi perse-
quentes me et tribulantes me; a testimoniis tuis non declinaui" [Ps. 118:157]. Non est magnum, si
tunc a dei testimoniis non declines, cum te nullus adfligit, nullus persequitur. Quis enim inoffense
sibi prosperorum eventuum secundante successu fieret ingratus? Quis divitiis adfluens, iugi salute
robustus non ad dei gratiam referat quod sibi illa concessa sint? Denique cum sanctum Iob dominus
praedicaret, ait adversarius: "numquid gratis colit Iob dominum? Nonne tu omnia dedisti ei? Mitte
manum tuam in omnia quae habet, si non in faciem te benedicet" (Job 1:9–11). Tunc igitur plus
probatus est, quando amissis opibus et filiis a domini cultu et gratia non recessit. Sed non unus
persecutor est, multos ministros habet. Sed non te terreat. "Per multas" enim "tribulationes oportet
nos introire in regnum dei" [Acts 14:21]. Si multae persecutiones, multae probationes; ubi multae
coronae, multa certamina. Tibi ergo proficit quod multi persecutores sunt, ut inter multas persecutiones facilius invenias quemadmodum coroneris.'

Christian that 'it is through many tribulations that we shall reach the kingdom of God [Acts 14:21]'. Next the Roman martyr Sebastian – on whose feast day the *Expositio* was delivered[58] – is brought forward. Ambrose then asks the congregation to consider their own interior struggle:

But what is worse, not only the visible but also the invisible are persecutors, and there are more of these by far . . . For who can be exempted, when the lord himself suffered the temptations of persecution? Avarice, ambition, extravagance, pride, and fornication all attack the soul.[59]

The bishop clarifies that the struggle against these interior obstacles is far more daunting to the Christian than any externally imposed trial.[60] Each Christian will continuously be called to witness for Christ, so he or she must take special care to show allegiance to Him in every action, even the most trivial.[61]

For how many are hidden martyrs of Christ every day, and confess Jesus as Lord! The Apostle recognized this martyrdom and faithful witness to Christ when he said, 'This is our glory and the testimony of our conscience' [2 Cor 1:12]. How many have confessed externally while internally they denied the faith!

The silent suffering of these is contrasted to the sham piety of others, for whom the faith is merely an instrument for some worldy craving:

For indeed many are brought forward who for a time, for the sake of marrying a wife whose Christian parents refused to let her marry a pagan husband, have externally confessed, with a feigned faith, what they internally denied.[62]

---

[58] Ambrose, *Expositio psalmi CXVIII*, 20.44 (*CSEL* 62, 466): 'Utamur exemplo Sebastiani martyris, cuius hodie natalis est.'

[59] Ambrose, *Expositio psalmi CXVIII*, 20.45 (*CSEL* 62, 466–7): 'Sed quod peius, non hi solum persecutores sunt qui videntur, sed etiam qui non videntur, et multo plures persecutores . . . Quis enim exceptus potest esse, cum ipse dominus persecutionum temptamenta toleraverit? Persequitur avaritia, persequitur ambitio, persequitur luxuria, persequitur superbia, persequitur fornicatio.'

[60] Ambrose, *Expositio psalmi CXVIII*, 20.46 (*CSEL* 62, 467): 'Isti sunt persecutores graves, qui sine gladii terrore mentem hominis frequenter elidunt, qui inlecebris magis quam terroribus animos expugnant fidelium. Hi tibi hostes cavendi, hi graviores tyranni, per quos Adam captus est. Multi in persecutione publica coronati occulta hac persecutione ceciderunt. "Foris", inquit, "pugnae, intus timores" [2 Cor. 7:5]. Advertis quam grave certamen sit quod est intra hominem, ut se cum ipse confligat, cum suis cupiditatibus proelietur? Ipse apostolus fluctuat haeret adstringitur, captivari se adserit in lege peccati et mortis corpore debellari nec potuisse evadere, nisi esset domini Iesu gratia liberatus.'

[61] See, e.g., Ambrose, *Expositio psalmi CXVIII*, 20.47 (*CSEL* 62, 468): 'Quod est amplius, non sermonis tantummodo, sed etiam operis testimonium praebuisti. Quis enim locupletior testis est quam qui confitetur dominum Iesum in carne venisse, cum evangelii praecepta custodit? Nam qui audit et non facit, negat Christum; etsi verbo fatetur, operibus negat.'

[62] Ambrose, *Expositio psalmi CXVIII*, 20.48 (*CSEL* 62, 468): 'Quanti ergo cotidie in occulto martyres Christi sunt et Iesum dominum confitentur! Novit hoc martyrium apostolus et testimonium Christi fidele, qui dixit: "haec est enim gloriatio nostra et testimonium conscientiae nostrae" (2 Cor. 1:12). Quanti foris confessi sunt et intus negaverunt! Namque uxoris ducendae gratia, quae gentili viro a

Ambrose here reminds his listeners how easy it is to lay claim to the Christian faith, and how difficult to act on its ethical teaching.

Inspired by Ambrose, Latin writers and preachers of the fifth century took care to draw a connection between the prowess of the historical martyr and the experience of ordinary Christians wherever possible. The martyrs themselves were figured as taking part in the spiritual wrestling match with the vices with which the faithful were presumed daily to struggle.[63] Equally, Christian audiences were encouraged to identify their own struggle with the vices with the more patently heroic struggle of the martyrs against an earthly persecutor:

Beloved, if you wish we should have a share in the heavenly seat, as God promised to the victors, let us in the first instance imitate the faith of the holy martyr confessing, and let us follow his path in virtue, nor should we be afraid in the love of God to set our hearts against the bloody hands of the persecutor ... for it is not beyond you to be a victor daily in any respect, if you will only reject the desires of the flesh.[64]

Such exhortations served to strengthen the sense of Christian identity among the faithful. They accord precisely, as it happens, with the shift noted by Charles F. Altman in a 1975 article from 'diametrical' to 'grada-tional' models in hagiographical writing from the fourth century onwards.[65] Altman suggested that the shift can be accounted for by the changing social function of hagiographical narrative as the Church itself was transformed progressively from an embattled group of 'outsiders' to a normative cultural institution. For the present discussion, it will suffice to acknowledge the wider problem of the social function of *imitatio*.

---

christianis parentibus negabatur, simulata ad tempus fide plerique produntur quod foris confessi sunt intus negasse. An fornicationis causa tantummodo putamus dominum deum nostrum in populum Iudaeorum tam severe esse commotum, ut viginti tria milia de populo necarentur, propterea quod Madianitae gentis feminis concubitu miscerentur ac non eo, quod per illos concubitus alienigenarum discedere a fide, negare dominum cogerentur?'

[63] Victricius, *De laude sanctorum* 6 (*CC* 64, 76–9) characterizes the martyr as imitator of Christ, tamer of passion, crusher of ambition, despiser of wealth, suppressor of lewdness, persecutor of arrogance.

[64] Valerianus of Cimiez, *Homilia XV de bono martyrii* 5 (*PL* 52, 740): 'Si vultis ergo, dilectissimi, ut sit nobis in coelesti sede portio, quam victoribus Dominus repromisit, imitemur primo loco sancti martyris fidem in confessione, et sequamur viam eius in virtute, nec dubitemus in amore Domini cruentis lictoris manibus pectus opponere ... non deest autem in quo possis quotidie vincere, si volueris carnis desideriis repugnare.'

[65] Charles F. Altman, 'Two Types of Opposition and the Structure of Latin Saints' Lives', *Medievalia et Humanistica* 6 (1975), 1–11. On the whole, according to Altman, the *passiones* of the pre-Constantinian period served to pose a diametrical opposition between the forces of good and evil, while the *vitae* of the post-Constantinian period place stress on development and transformation within an individual, and the possibility that others may be transformed by contact with the individual in question.

IMITATIO

With this in mind, we turn to another important purpose of the claim that the faithful must imitate the martyrs: to legitimate martyr piety against its critics. In his *Contra Faustum* Augustine defended the orthodoxy of martyr piety against accusations of idolatry:

We revere the martyrs with the same reverence based in love and fellowship which we also offer to holy men of god in this life … But we neither offer nor teach others to offer the reverence called *latria* in Greek to anyone except the one God, because it is a kind of subjection owed properly to a divinity.[66]

To defend martyr piety against those who saw it as merely a Christianized form of idolatry, it was helpful to underline its edificatory nature. Augustine stressed that martyrs 'should be honoured with an intention of imitating them; they should not be revered with an intention of actual worship.'[67] If it was to find a place within the pale of orthodoxy, the literature of martyrdom would have to maximize its claim to a unique role in the moral training of the faithful.[68]

Such an approach may equally have parried the accusations of those who saw in the feasts of the martyrs merely an occasion for drunkenness, but it would by no means have been taken for granted. A common view of the martyrs was that their holiness consisted precisely in their *difference* from the mortals who venerated them. Augustine's account in the *Confessions* of his mother's sober intentions in bringing her libation to the memorial shrines of the saints belies an assumption that the intent of the majority was rather toward revelry; there is no reason to doubt, however, that the intoxication was intended to produce an uplifting sense of communion and awe.[69]

Indeed, André Vauchez has suggested that the prevailing stand-point of hagiography before the twelfth century was to stress the supernatural power of the saint to the exclusion of the possibility of *imitatio* – and that only in the aftermath of the Gregorian reforms do we see the invention of the saint's life as a *règle de conduite* for the laity.[70] While Vauchez's proposal might

---

[66] Augustine, *Contra Faustum* 20.21 (*CSEL* 25, 562): 'Colimus martyres eo cultu dilectionis et societatis quo in hac vita coluntur homines Dei … atillo cultu qui graece "latria" dicitur, cum sit quaedam proprie divinitati debita servitus, nec colimus, nec colendum docemus nisi unum Deum.'

[67] Augustine, *De vera religione* 55.297 (*CSEL* 77.2, 77): 'Honorandi sunt propter imitationem, non adorandi propter religionem.'

[68] Peter Brown, 'Enjoying the Saints in Late Antiquity', *Early Medieval Europe* 9 (2000), 1–24, discusses the development of Augustine's thought on this point.

[69] Augustine, *Confessions*, 6.2.2 (*CSEL* 33, 114–16).

[70] André Vauchez, 'Saints admirables et saints imitables: les fonctions de l'hagiographie ont-elles changé aux derniers siècles du moyen-âge?', in *Les Fonctions des saints dans le monde occidental*

superficially seem to be confirmed by twelfth-century citations of patristic *auctoritates*,[71] the presence of such citations is misleading. Put simply, almost any position on *imitatio* could be defended by recourse to the fathers. It is more appropriate to speak of a spectrum of possibilities whose use was not governed by chronology.[72]

Let us consider, for example, the frequently cited opinion of Gregory the Great, explaining to his interlocutor in the *Dialogues* that not all qualities of the spiritually great are to be imitated:

> The freedom of their life must not be taken as an example by the weak, lest, while someone presumes that he is similarly filled with the Holy Spirit, he should disdain to be a disciple of a man and become the master of error ... Thus Moses was taught his mission in the desert by an angel, not instructed by a man. But these things, as I have already said, must be venerated – not imitated – by the weak.[73]

What becomes apparent, if we compare the citation from Gregory with its converse ('an intention of imitating them, not ... of actual worship') which we encountered above in Augustine, is that the approach to *imitatio* varied according to context.

This was not mere sophistry. What made the difference was an assessment of the consequences for the well-being of the faithful, with pastoral strategies governed by awareness of social factors in the congregation that are now very difficult to recover. The tendency of fifth- and sixth-century writers, where *imitatio* was concerned, was to emphasize its ethical benefit. Reforming a Church which they feared was prone to complacency or idolatry was the point, although there was some uncertainty about how far the reform agenda might be pushed before it led to equal and opposite complications.

The exhortation to *imitatio* might solve the theological problem of idolatry, but it also gave rise to a thorny pastoral problem. Not only must the *exemplum* attract interest and sympathy: empathy was equally important if the *exemplum* was to bestow a sense of participation in virtue

---

(*IIIe–XIIIe siècle*): *Actes du Colloque organisé par l'École Française de Rome avec le concours de l'Université de Rome 'La Sapienza', Rome, 27–29 octobre 1988*, Collection de L'École Française de Rome 149 (Rome, 1991), 161–72, here 164.

[71] Discussed by Bruce C. Brasington, 'Non imitanda sed veneranda: The Dilemma of Sacred Precedent in Twelfth-Century Canon Law', *Viator* 23 (1992), 135–52.

[72] Brown, 'Enjoying the Saints', cites Brigitte Cazelles, *Le Corps de sainteté d'après Jean Bouche d'Or, Jehan Paulus et quelques vies XIIe et XIIIe siècles* (Geneva, 1982), to make a complementary point at the other end of the chronological spectrum, showing that later medieval texts did not necessarily engage with *imitatio*.

[73] Gregory the Great, *Dialogues* 1.1.7 (*SC* 251, 22). Brasington, 'Non imitanda sed veneranda', 143, discusses the importance of the citation for medieval debate over legal precedent.

on the faithful. The devotee had to be able to find some 'hook' of similarity with the *exemplum*, some point of identification, lest *imitatio* seem an aspiration beyond reach.[74]

These are concerns which surface repeatedly in the devotional literature for women. We saw in Chapter Three that the anonymous author of the *Letter to Claudia* warned that there was no excuse for moral failure in a layperson who had been exposed to the full range of *exempla* from the Hebrew patriarchs forward to the *Lives* of the saints, and that this warning was picked up by other writers such as the author of the *Ad Gregoriam*.

The acephalous Bobbio letter discussed in Chapter Three explores the problem of *imitatio* from alternative perspectives. Early in the text, an excursus on exemplars emphasizes the importance of the women of the Hebrew Bible, such as Anna and Judith (Duval 219). Turning to the New Testament and citing 1 Peter 2:21–4, the anonymous author reveals that *imitatio* is not governed by gender, since Jesus himself came to earth to offer an *exemplum*, so that we may follow in his footsteps.[75] For the married woman, he reminds his reader, it is also important to remember that as a mother she will herself be called upon to act as an *exemplum* for her child.[76]

At the same time, the idea of the invisibility of the Christian's struggle with the vices captured the imagination of monastic writers. The manual of advice for handling each of a series of vices seems to have had great popularity as a phenomenon of the desert: we meet it, for example, in *De diversis malignis cogitationibus*[77] and *De octo vitiosis cogitationibus*,[78] both of Evagrius Ponticus. Monks were not the only recipients of this kind of instruction, as *Ad Gregoriam* attests, but they were certainly its stereotypical readers.[79]

In his second *Conference*, John Cassian explains, following Evagrius,[80] that the invisibility of his struggle places the ascetic in danger of perdition unless he find a reliable guide to these secret matters:

[74] Discussion in Cooper, *The Virgin and the Bride*, 117–27.   [75] *Acephalous Bobbio Letter* (Duval, 231).
[76] *Acephalous Bobbio Letter* (Duval, 227).
[77] Evagrius Ponticus, *De diversis malignis cogitationibus* (*PG* 79, 1200–33).
[78] Evagrius Ponticus, *De octo vitiosis cogitationibus* (*PG* 40, 1272–8).
[79] On the struggle with the vices in fourth- and fifth-century Egyptian monastic literature, see now David Brakke, *Demons and the Making of the Monk: Spiritual Combat in Early Christianity* (Cambridge, Mass., 2006).
[80] Evagrius, *Praktikos* 48 (*SC* 171, 608).

For [the ascetic's] enemies are not visible but invisible and merciless; the daily and nightly encounter is a spiritual battle not against one or two, but against innumerable companies, whose destructive power is all the more dangerous, insofar as the enemy is the more hostile, and the contest the more hidden.[81]

It was an idea which laid the groundwork for the Psychomachy, one of the most popular genres of medieval literature.

ARNOBIUS THE YOUNGER

The fifth-century Roman Church would develop a literature steeped in this imagery of the conflict in the human soul, and the interest in these themes reached across genres and across the divide between ascetic and lay readers. To understand the imaginary landscape of the Roman Church in this period, one can do no better than to turn to the *Commentary on the Psalms* written by the monk Arnobius, possibly a native of North Africa, who lived in Rome during the turbulent years between the death of Valentinian in 455 and Ricimer's siege of the city in 471.[82] Very little is known about Arnobius. The *Commentary* is dedicated to the bishops Leontius (or Laurentius) and Rusticus, but their identities are disputed. Von Schubert argued a century ago that Arnobius was a Roman monk,[83] and he may be the protagonist of the anonymous *Conflictus Arnobii cum Serapione*, a dialogue on Christ's two natures recorded (or imagined) between two learned Roman monks, one from Africa and one from Egypt,[84] probably dated to the late 440s, in the run-up to the Council of Chalcedon. During the twentieth century efforts were made to assign a number of works to Arnobius' authorship on the basis of often very slim points of overlap between other anonymous texts and his commentaries on the psalms, but none of these attempts has been entirely successful. Nonetheless, he is a crucial figure for understanding the Roman Church in the time of Leo the Great and Attila the Hun.

---

[81] Cassian, *Coll.* 2.11 (CSEL 13, 52): 'Habet enim non adversus visibiles, sed invisibiles atque inmites hostes diurnum nocturnumque conflictum nec contra unum seu duos, sed contra innumerabiles catervas spiritale certamen, cuius casus tanto perniciosior cunctis, quanto et infestior inimicus et congressus occultior.'

[82] MacGeorge, *Late Roman Warlords*, 247ff.

[83] Hans Von Schubert, *Der sogennante Praedestinatus: ein Beitrag zur Geschichte des Pelagianismus* (Leipzig, 1903).

[84] H.-M. Diepen, 'La Pensée christologique d'Arnobe le Jeune: théologie de l'Assumptus Homo ou de l'Emmanuel?' *Revue Thomiste* 59 (1959), 535–64; at 538 Diepen suggests that this was the formal *procès-verbal* of an actual debate, similar to the debates held between Arians and Catholics under Thrasamund.

Arnobius saw the great metaphor of the psalms, of God's help to the soul beset by enemies, as one peculiarly suited to an age of military uncertainty. Meditation on the psalms stood at the core of fourth- and fifth-century Latin Christian spirituality, and Arnobius teased out the pastoral implications of this practice for his own generation. Although it is distinctively his own, his advice on how to read the psalms reflects the mood of the age: 'Let cities perish, let provinces perish, because the teachings are perishing. Moreover, let Phineas stand so that he may pray for us, that is to say, let the people of the martyrs stand, who like Phineas were not afraid to shed blood.'[85] It is not too far-fetched to see this language as reflecting the sense of uncertainty as the mid-fifth-century Roman Church attempted to find a secure footing in a politically volatile climate.

Another passage, in his commentary on Psalm 140, sees this awareness of the perilous military situation compounded by a sharp concern for the problem of heresy: 'Our bones have been scattered in hell . . . they are in hell, when they are with those who bring us the tinder for doing evil . . . when we are joined to heretics and feign friendship although we see them undertake a battle, and do not fight them openly, as the Romans do the barbarians.'[86]

In a number of passages, Arnobius develops the insight that there is a connection to be made between the metaphor of the soul's besiegement and the other great tradition of embattled Christian spirituality, the passion narratives of the Christian martyrs. Nearly a century ago the Italian scholar Maria Monachesi suggested that Arnobius could have been the author of the enigmatic *gesta martyrum*, the anonymous hagiographical romances constructed around the memories of the early Roman martyrs.[87] The suggestion derives from Arnobius' reference to the passage in Psalm 19 in which the psalmist promises the Eternal One to record for future generations his merciful intervention on behalf of Sion. In his commentary on Psalm 101, having proclaimed his veneration for the remains of the earthly martyrs, Arnobius tells his readers that 'we wrote their *passiones* for another generation, and the people who will be created

---

[85] Arnobius, *Commentarii in psalmos* (PL 53, 485).
[86] Arnobius, *Commentarii in psalmos* (PL 53, 552): 'Dissipata sunt ossa nostra secus infernum . . . juxta infernum sunt, quando iuxta illos sumus, qui nobis fomitem tribuunt delinquendi . . . quando iungimur haereticis et quasi sub specie amicitiae cum his videmur inire conflictum, et non aperta fronte, ut Romani contra barbaros, repugnamus'; cf. Diepen, 'La Pensée christologique', 538.
[87] Maria Monachesi, 'Arnobio il Giovane ed una sua possibile attività agiografica', *Bolletino di studi storico-religiosi* 1 (1921), 96–109.

praise God in His saints until the end of time.'[88] There is more than a whiff
of escatological expectation here, and it is unclear whether Arnobius' first-
person plural – *scripsimus* – means that he himself wrote hagiography, or
whether he speaks for his entire generation.

In his discussion of eleven out of the 150 psalms, Arnobius finds an
opportunity to explore in depth how the heroic suffering of the martyrs
could be adopted as a model for Christians in his own day. Arnobius develops
the metaphor of the internal and external battle that had been made famous by
Evagrius and John Cassian. For Arnobius, 'invisible enemies' await the
Christian: 'Just as the holy ones despised punishments and visible enemies,
so we, too, fight off invisible enemies.'[89] But for Arnobius the martyrs are now
the champions of orthodoxy, and *imitatio martyrum* is the strategy of those
who wish to cleave to a threatened doctrinal purity. The 'invisible enemies'
Arnobius speaks of seem to be insidious people who want to lead the Catholic
faithful into heresy. The following extended passage sums up his approach:

All the torments inflicted by the faithless on the martyrs during the persecutions
are inflicted on us by the invisible enemies, if we profess ourselves to be slaves of
Christ. Therefore, when you read about their battles meditate on your own, which
are internal and invisible, and you, in the secret places of your soul, resist the
malicious spirit, as did those who were able to stand up against those who wanted
them to sacrifice to the gods. Let your victory have the same origin as theirs, but
while it was a cause of death for them, for you let it be life; even if where you are
concerned it isn't the case to speak of violence, since you only have to do battle
with persuasion, let us imagine that you have to cope with both, and that your
battle is both with violence and with the persuasion of demons, but aid will come
to those who are prepared . . . insist with prayers, vigils, pray for the favour of God;
with all this, you will profess yourself a follower of the martyrs.[90]

The martyrs here are both *exempla* whom the Christian should imitate, and
heavenly strong-men into whose retinue the soul should seek to insinuate
itself.

[88] Arnobius, *Commentarii in psalmos* (PL 53, 471): 'Scripsimus passiones eorum in progenies alteras, et
populus qui creabitur usque in sempiternum laudat Dominum in sanctis suis.'
[89] Arnobius, *Commentarii in psalmos* (PL 53, 569): '. . . sicut sancti contempserunt poenas, hostes
visibiles, ita nos invisibilis hostis delectationes ingestas abjicimus.'
[90] Arnobius, *Commentarii in psalmos* (PL 53, 525–26): 'Quidquid martyribus in persecutionibus
fecerunt homines increduli, hoc nobis, si tamen exhibemus Deo servitium, in tentationibus
invisibiles faciunt inimici. Cum ergo illorum visibiles legeris, pugnas tuas invisibiles cogita. Et ita
tu animo contradicito spiritui quod injustum est suggerenti, sicut illi homini sacrificium persua-
denti. Unde illi vicerunt, inde vince. Illorum victoria mors fuit, tua victoria vita sit; et persuasio ibi et
vis operata est, pone quod et tecum sic agatur, et persuasio tecum et violentia praeliantur, quanquam
sola persuasio tecum agat . . . ora, vigila, clama, tene propositum, martyrum pedissequum
profiteris.'

Ad Gregoriam in palatio, whose author seems to have known Arnobius' *Commentary on the Psalms*, takes a similar approach, encouraging the senatorial *domina* to see her own struggle as an attempt to gain the protection of the most powerful. When she is faced with the temptation to bewail her estate, she should turn against temptation and 'protest vigorously and unsparingly: use the privilege (*officium*) of your nobility, claim for yourself the prerogative of power to rule (*imperium*); bring in as counsel the Apostles, interpose the white-clad army of martyrs ... urge your kinsfolk (*parentes*), the most holy angels. Press the point (*insiste*), follow [the matter] through, and constantly demand deliverance.'[91] The themes of kinship, patronage, and military prowess, so critical in the troubled atmosphere of late fifth-century Italy, lie close to the surface even as they are overlaid with a spiritual meaning.

In chapter 5 of the treatise, introducing an extended meditation on *patientia*, the virtue of endurance, John returns to the old Cyprianic theme of the Christian who wishes for martyrdom even as he or she fails to contend with superficial hardship:

For the voice of inexperienced impatience is often heard to say, 'I long to show forth my steadfastness before an unbelieving persecutor. As a matter of fact, I know that if I do this, I'll be able to join the company of the saints.' Oh, new boxer in the glorious battle! Oh, outstanding athlete and master of wrestling-matches! The one who asserts that she is able to bear the force of punches and kicks without flinching in the sight of a whole crowd, of kings and judges, turns out to be the one who fell over in private, shaken by one touch of the wrestler's wax. The one who claims she will fight bravely in battle against the enemy actually is the one who quaked at the [sight of men] training for battle, before ever leaving the camp. And how will the one who was unnerved by a whinnying horse be fearless before the lion's roar? How will she who was horrified by a single citizen's raising his voice endure the surprises the barbarians have in store?[92]

In the face of this kind of witless self-importance, John brings the tonic of the martyr *exemplum*.

But let me admit that you might be able to find a place among those wives whose *Passiones* and *Gesta* are witnessed by reliable documents. In sum, why would you not be willing to bear the small trials, you who are sure you can bear great ones? There are many whom you believe to have fought victoriously against the battle-lines of tyrants and to have laughed at all manner of tortures, whom you believe to have entered the abode of the heavens crowned by the flowery gore of their own blood.

---

[91] *Ad Gregoriam* 2 (CC 25A, 194). [92] *Ad Gregoriam* 5 (CC 25A, 198).

It is worth noting that it is specifically the wives among the martyrs whom John singles out as appropriate objects of *imitatio*.

It should come as no surprise that *Ad Gregoriam* shows more than a passing interest specifically in the martyrs of Rome, the protagonists of the *gesta martyrum* discussed above. We have seen the importance of *exempla* from the Bible – including the Bride of the Song of Songs. Equally important, however, are the mother of the Maccabees and the three married women martyrs venerated in Latium, Felicitas, Symphorosa, and Anastasia.[93]

Why should I remember you, glorious mothers, who with seven sons each[94] subdued the diverse powers of tyrants, although in different times and by different trials (*suppliciis*)? The province Palestine remembers (*tenet*) you, Maccabea; the Tiburtine city [Tivoli] venerates and accepts you too, Symphorosa, with seven brothers put forth from your womb. The city of Rome heaps you, true Felicitas, with due praise and due honours, O true Felicity and teacher of all faithful matrons... None of your [pl.] torments, none of those of your children disturbed you. You showed your countenances joyous to your children – although they were being tortured – lest, when they saw you weeping, they should bow their souls to affliction. For when the will alone (*sola voluntas*) was importuned by an unjust torturer, it was in [its] power (*arbitrio*) to be unwilling to be twisted by torture.[95]

The *passiones* of Symphorosa and Felicitas, as they have come down to us, are clearly literary embroideries on the story of the Maccabees, in that each mother has seven sons whom she encourages in martyrdom before being martyred herself, and there is almost no detail about the individual women beyond their similarity to the biblical heroine. But this does not mean they were not prized as Roman heroines of the faith in the fifth and sixth centuries. At the end of the sixth century, Gregory the Great will remember Felicitas as one of the *rectores*, the emblematic figures of Christian authority, in his *Homilies on the Gospels*.[96]

The third married martyr, Anastasia, serves as an especially important model for two reasons. First, she is the only one of the three whose *passio* discusses the trials of marriage in any detail. Indeed, they are rendered in vivid colour, since her husband Publius was believed to have flown into a rage upon hearing of her conversion to Christianity, placing her under

[93] On the genesis of the *passio Symphorosae*, see Kate Cooper, 'The Widow as Impresario: Gender, Authority, and Legendary Afterlives in Eugippius' *Vita Severini*', in Walter Pohl and Maximilian Diesenberger, eds., *Eugippius und Severinus: Der Autor, der Text, und der Heilige* (Vienna, 2000), 53–64, and literature cited there.
[94] Symphorosa and Felicitas were each recorded as having suffered with seven children; their *passiones* presumably intended an imitation of the mother of the seven Maccabees martyred in 4 Macc. 8–12.
[95] *Ad Gregoriam* 5 (*CC* 25A, 200).   [96] Gregory, *Homiliae in Evangelia* 1.3 (*CC* 141, 20–5).

house arrest in order to keep her from maintaining contact with her companions in the faith.

With how great forbearance (*tolerantia*) did you manage the affront suffered in marriage (*maritalem iniuriam*), who endured with tranquil soul the cruelty of a tyrant, just as after the blows of the executioners and after all manner of tortures you rejoiced in allowing yourself even to be burned alive (*assari*)? . . . Think in this respect how many wives sprung from a lowly condition scoffed at physical threats and in the face of a raging tyrant, not pale with fear but eager in the Lord, when they saw that you, who are noble and dainty, had constantly scorned all kinds of torments for the defence of honour and faith?[97]

If Anastasia is significant because of her personal history, she is also significant because of her place in the liturgical calendar. Since her feast day falls on 25 December, it coincides with the liturgical celebration of the Incarnation.[98] John makes it clear that her cult is specifically relevant to married women in their capacity as mothers:

Justly Christ took you up into the heavens on the same day on which he himself descended to earth, and he permitted the anniversary of your martyrdom to occur on the same day as the nativity of his assumption [of the flesh], because you, by suffering martyrdom, offered to many what he offered to all by being born. And just as, having despised majesty, he took on the form of a servant,[99] so that he might assist us all, so you yourself, having despised the glory of nobility, took on an ignominy of person, so that you might be imitated by others, and so that you might provide a model of Christian endurance for all. You will receive everlasting glory as much because you set an example for the edification of all matrons (*pro aedificatione omnium matronarum*) as because of your own martyrdom.[100]

Through her privileged connection to the Incarnation, Anastasia offers not only a martyr *exemplum* tailored to *imitatio* by a married woman, but even a bridge to a privileged relationship with Christ.

It is significant that the prologue of the *Passio Anastasiae* adapts the metaphor of the invisible battle to a polemical use, to furnish a succinct

---

[97] *Ad Gregoriam* 5 (*CC* 25A, 198–9). Anastasia's imprisonment is discussed at length in Cooper, *The Virgin and the Bride*, ch. 5, 'The Imprisoned Heroine'.

[98] See Kate Cooper, 'Contesting the Nativity: Wives, Virgins, and Pulcheria's *imitatio Mariae*', *Scottish Journal of Religious Studies* 19 (1998), 31–43, for discussion of evidence in both East and West in the fifth century, that there was competition between wives and virgins over their spiritual 'ownership' of the Nativity.

[99] This phrase echoes another passage of the *Passio Sebastiani* (*BHL* 7543), *Passio Sebastiani* 44 (*AASS Jan.*, 2, 3rd edn, 636): 'Numquid servi tui, qui te negaverunt dominum suum, dum te in habitu servili respicerent, non potuerunt ut rebelles occidi? Ita et qui negant Christum Dominum suum pro hoc quod semetipsum a maiestate exinanivit, et formam servi suscepit, nullatenus poterunt aeterni ignis poenas evadere.'

[100] *Ad Gregoriam* 5 (*CC* 25A, 199).

apologia for martyr piety. The text defends the public reading of the martyr
acta by insisting that the faithful must study the struggles of the martyrs
because they themselves will be expected to duplicate the struggles of their
spiritual forebears: 'we furnish an *exemplum* for those to come . . . for we
know that every day we will be called out invisibly to the battles which they
endured visibly . . .'[101] The Decretals of Gelasius, written in the early sixth
century, record that the Roman Church was unusual in not permitting the
public reading of the *gesta martyrum* as part of the liturgy, because versions
were believed to be circulating in which heretical views were slipped in
among the martyrs' confessions of faith.[102] However, the *Passio Anastasiae*
prologue subsequently gained a wide circulation at the head of a handful of
hagiographical texts.[103]

  Less direct but equally significant is *Ad Gregoriam*'s invocation of the
passio of Sebastian, a martyr whose importance we have already seen above.
We see this in the passage cited at the beginning of the encomium to *patientia* –
'O, new boxer in the glorious battle! O, outstanding athlete and master of
wrestling-matches!'[104] – echoing a string of exclamations addressed by
Sebastian to the Christian *viri illustri* Marcus and Marcellianus.[105]
Ironically, given that *Ad Gregoriam* is a treatise on wifely piety, Sebastian's
speech is delivered to the two young men at the point when the youths are
allowed a visit with their wives, whose job it is to persuade them that if they
renounce the faith they can return to their homes. These wives try to persuade
their husbands away from virtue rather than towards it, but since in the *Passio
Sebastiani* we are in the realm of hagiography, it is of course the Christian
husbands who persuade their pagan wives – and indeed the rest of their
families – to join them in martyrdom.[106] A second parallel can be found in a

---

[101] *Passio sanctae Anastasiae* 1 (Delehaye, 222).
[102] The connection between the two documents, which has yet satisfactorily to be clarified, was first
    suggested by Baldouin de Gaiffier, 'Un prologue hostile au Décret de Gélase?' *Analecta Bollandiana*
    82 (1964), 341–53.
[103] On its diffusion, see de Gaiffier, 'Un prologue', 341–3.
[104] *Ad Gregoriam* 5 (*CC* 25A, 117).
[105] *Passio Sebastiani* (*BHL* 7543), 9 (*AASS Jan.*, 2, 3rd edn, 630): 'At ubi vidit athletas Dei immenso
    certaminis pondere fatigari, in medio eorum se obiiciens, dixit: "O fortissimi milites Christi,
    O instructissimi divini prælii bellatores, per nimiam virtutem animi fortiter pervenistis ad palmam,
    et nunc per misera blandimenta coronam deponitis sempiternam? Discat nunc per vos Christi
    militum fortitudo, fide potius armari quam ferro. Nolite victoriarum vestrarum insignia per
    mulierum blandimenta abiicere, et subiectas pedibus vestris hostis devicti cervices ad victricia
    et rediviva iterum bella laxare, cuius quamvis sæva contra vos extiterit et periniqua a instantia,
    saevior tamen efficitur ira repetita."'
[106] On the family orientated model of conversion in the *Passio Sebastiani*, see Cooper, 'Ventriloquism
    and the Miraculous'.

passage where John dissuades his wifely reader from the vice of avarice. She is told to address the vice besieging her with the following speech:

For in this world everything that I experience is uncertain to me, and – as in a dream – I perceive what passes as a sort of shadow. And so I must not miss a good offer. I will indeed give up small things in order to receive the large ones; I will let go of what is temporal, so that I may discover the eternal. For why should I be afraid to give of my own accord what an idle heir (*otiosus heres*) makes off with against my will (*mihi invito*)? For that reason I make over the things that are mine to Him, because I am not able to take them away with me. I will make altogether my own that which in truth is not my own, and I will show my true love for my riches, when I have sent them ahead of me instead of letting them perish. I must press on to reach the most sacred retinue, from which I will no more be allowed to absent myself; there I will build myself a house; in that place I will build storehouses.[107]

Here again, we find a verbal echo of a speech of Sebastian to the wives of Marcus and Marcellianus.[108] In all likelihood it is no accident that here John has taken up a martyr text which places extended emphasis on the potential of the conjugal relationship to be a force for Christian conversion.

The *Passio Sebastiani* itself offers a compelling summary of the themes we have seen so far, in a speech in which the *Miles Christi* makes the connection between the invisible battle and the need to place one's riches in the one storehouse invulnerable to the barbarians.

Say you were to cross through the centre of a barbarian battle-line, and you were to find the strong man who always cleaved to you, who had even given you a bag full of money. He would say to you: 'Give me the money I gave to you for safekeeping, because those barbarians are plotting to take it from you, and when they have robbed you, they will put you to the sword.' Surely you would not hesitate to throw yourself at his feet, and to ask him to take the money back – he whom you know you can trust to give back more even than he had received, and to free you from the enemy? The bottom line, then, is that you may have Christ as the protector of your wealth.[109]

---

[107] *Ad Gregoriam* 12 (*CC* 25A, 210–11).

[108] Similarly *Ad Gregoriam* 12 (*CC* 25A, 210): 'Pergendum mihi est ad sacratissimum comitatum ...' echoes *Passio Sebastiani* 12 (*AASS Jan.*, 2, 3rd edn, 631): 'Haec vos instigat, O parentes sanctissimi, ut filios vestros proficiscentes ad Comitatum caeli, ad honorem incorruptibilem, ad amicitias Imperatoris aeterni, stultissimis lamentationibus revocetis. Ista est quae vos, o castissimae coniuges Beatorum, per pietatis colorem impietatem martyrum mentibus fecit tradere, et necem pro liberatione afferre. Si enim consensissent revocationi vestrae, pauco quidem tempore vobiscum esse poterant; postea vero separari, et ita habuerant separari a vobis, ut numquam vos nisi inter tormenta perpetua videretis; ubi edax flamma incredulorum animas devorat, ubi dracones blasphemantium labia comedunt, ubi serpentes morsibus suis incredulorum pectora depascuntur.'

[109] *Passio Sebastiani* 16 (*AASS Jan.*, 2, 3rd edn, 631–2): 'Numquid si transires per medias acies barbarorum, et invenires fortem virum qui te semper dilexit, qui tibi etiam sacculum pecuniis

Toward the end of the *Passio*, the *vir illustris* Marcus himself takes up the task of explaining what the war against the Devil involves for every Christian.

Marcus said: 'Learn, dearest kin, and your spouses, let your bonds of affect be taught to use the shield of virtues against the assault of the Devil, and against all the arrows of the feelings of carnal desire. And learn not to yield to the enemy when in the midst of the tyrants' ranks, to fight harder, to hold your ground, and so bravely to reach the King. Let the Devil's minions rise up as often as they want, do their savage worst, wreak whatever punishments they please upon our bodies; they can kill the body, but the soul, fighting for the faith in truth, they cannot overcome. Wounds received for the emperor make his soldiers the more glorious. On this account, the Devil now rages with the madness of a tyrant, because he foresees that he can fall victim to the standard of your capacity to endure. And as he brings on his tortures, let his hope perish. He threatens death, to terrify you: he promises life, so as to rip it away; he promises safety, only to remove it. This is his stratagem of war, this his counsel of deceit: to relieve the body of its tortures, and so to subjugate the soul to vice. It is for us, in confronting him, to strive not to yield to the foe, to show contempt for the body, and to come to the aid of the soul. Why should the strongest of generals turn their backs to become the most wretched of foot soldiers, and fail in that fight when victory is in their grasp? Why should they be afraid to die, when they know that to die is the nature, not the punishment of man?'[110]

With its discussion of 'the arrows of carnal desire', the text proposes that ascetic renunciation is the truest way to fight the good fight. In *Ad Gregoriam*, by contrast, the same image of the soldier in the King's service has been domesticated.

I will not forsake endurance, until I reach my most victorious King. It is endurance herself who will offer me the safety of the city: let her bring me forward in the

donaverat plenum, dicentem tibi: "Da mihi custodiendas pecunias quas dedi tibi; quia isti barbari insidiantur ut eas tibi auferant, quas dum tibi abstulerint suis te gladiis laniabunt"; numquid non pedibus eius advolutus rogares eum, ut eas ipse susciperet, de quo certus esses quod et ampliora quam acceperat redderet, et te ipsum ab hostibus liberaret? Restat nunc ut divitiis vestris tutorem possitis habere Christum.'

[110] *Passio Sebastiniani* 27 (*AASS Jan.*, 2, 3rd edn, 633): 'Marcus ait: "Discite parentes carissimi, et vester, o coniuges, discat iugalis affectus, aduersus pugnam diaboli, et contra omnes sagittas affectuum carnalis desiderii clipeum virtutum opponere, atque inter acies tyrannici exercitus hosti non cedere, dimicare acrius, a gradum tenere, et ad Regem fortiter pervenire. Insurgant quantum volunt, et saeviant satellites daemonum, et quibus volunt poenis corpora dilanient nostra; corpus occidere possunt, sed animam vincere non possunt pro fidei pugnantem veritate. Gloriosiores faciunt milites vulnera pro Imperatore suscepta: in hoc enim diabolus tyrannidis suae furore nunc saevit, in quo praevidet perseuerantiae vestrae tropaeo se posse torqueri: et ideo tormenta infert, ne spes eius pereat: mortem minatur, ut terreat: vitam promittit, ut eripiat: securitatem pollicetur, ut tollat. Haec tota belli calliditas, hoc fraudis consilium, a suppliciis eripere corpus, et vitiis animam subiugare. Nos e contra contendamus hosti non cedere, corpus contemnere, animae subvenire. Cur enim fortissimi duces militibus miserrimis terga convertant, et in eo bello deficiant, in quo possunt esse victores? Vel qua ratione mori timeant, qui sciunt hanc hominis naturam esse, non poenam?"'

presence of the King whom I long for. When I entrust an affront (*iniuriam*) to his care, he is a protector; when I make harm known to him, he is a restorer; if I tell him of trials, he is a consoler.[111]

The last lines of *Ad Gregoriam* offer an image of the reader as having finally reached the heavenly *comitatus*. Having fought honourably, she stands with the company of the Virtues, looking back down over the battlefield from the safety of the heavenly city.

Let Truth call you her darling, let Purity (*castitas*) call you her sister, let Seriousness be a mother to you, let Wisdom count you as her own sister, let Reverence (*pietas*) be a kinswoman to you, let Mercy recognize you as a friend, let Faith hold sway in you, let Hope and Charity always attend you. Stand up straight among these ranks, noblewoman, and, exhibiting something like a holy arrogance,[112] pride yourself that you are a member of their company . . . United to the companions of Christ and the angels, you despise the whole world, which will perish quickly with those who love it.[113]

In closing, John offers his blessing, both to Gregoria and to the husband of whom we have heard so little in the course of his letter. 'Already you embrace Him whom you love more than your husband – that is, the Lord Jesus Christ – along with that very husband. May He strengthen you and him by an ample felicity in His love, so that here in the present you may rejoice . . . and there [in the future world] you may be glad at having found perpetual glory.'[114]

THE RAIMENT OF MORTAL FLESH

The themes discussed in this chapter formed an important strand of the legacy of late Roman Christianity to the medieval church. This can be seen especially clearly in one of the crucial manuscripts of the Italian ascetic legacy, MS Lat. 12634 of the Bibliothèque Nationale. This manuscript, which Lowe believed was produced around the end of the sixth century in one of the cities north of Naples, possibly Capua, is best known because it preserves the so-called 'Rule of Eugippius', a short monastic rule very similar in structure to the mid-sixth-century *Rule of Saint Benedict* and, like its more celebrated counterpart, quoting extensively from the earlier *Regula Magistri*. Besides the 'Rule of Eugippius', the other texts copied into

---

[111] *Ad Gregoriam* 16 (*CC* 25A, 219).
[112] Compare Jerome to Eustochium, *Ep.* 22.16 (*PL* 22, 403): 'ad hominis coniugem dei sponsa quid properas? disce in hac parte superbiam sanctam, scito te illis esse meliorem'; see also Paulinus of Nola, *Ep.* 12.7 (*CSEL*, 79–80).
[113] *Ad Gregoriam* 25 (*CC* 25A, 243).   [114] *Ad Gregoriam* 25 (*CC* 25A, 243–44).

Paris 12634 are mostly monastic in orientation, but three texts bear witness to the sixth-century laity. One, the *passio* of the Roman saints John and Paul, will not concern us here, although it is one of the Roman *gesta martyrum* and bears important connections to the *Passiones* discussed above.[115] More important for the present discussion are two sermons on the Resurrection preserved, like so much other early medieval literature, under the name 'Iohannes episcopus'. Whether these sermons were produced by one of the Roman or Neapolitan bishops bearing that name in the sixth century is not known; equally, they may possibly be from the hand of the enigmatic figure known to scholars as 'Johannes mediocris', 'John the mediocre', a preacher working out of Naples in the fifth or early sixth century, whose works were transmitted under the name of John Chrysostom, and whose interest in the imitation of the martyrs is well attested.[116]

Early in the second of his two sermons, this *Johannes episcopus* develops the theme of the transience of human life. The *saeculum*, he argues, is merely a place of pilgrimage, and can not be understood as our true home; its tribulations, therefore, should not be the cause of despair.

Truly, truly, everything that we experience is a pilgrimage. For in the here-and-now we are like pilgrims, we have no fixed abode, we strive, we mop our brows, taking difficult paths, full of dangers. From all sides, there are traps laid by spiritual and physical foes, and everywhere we go our we can find we have taken a wrong turning. And because our ways are beset with so much danger, not only do we wish to be freed from these dangers: even when we are free, we grieve and we make plaint as though we were lost.[117]

This allegiance to another country is not only a consolation; it is also a command. The Lord of the heavenly country does not sit easily with the negligence of those whose minds are too deeply enmeshed in the affairs of

---

[115] On the *passio* of John and Paul, see now Conrad Leyser, ' "A Church in the House of the Saints": Property and Power in the *Passion* of John and Paul', in Kate Cooper and Julia Hillner, eds., *Religion, Dynasty, and Patronage in Early Christian Rome, 300–900 CE* (Cambridge, 2007), 140–62. On the relationship of the *Regula Magistri* to the Roman *gesta martyrum*, see Kate Cooper, 'Family, Dynasty, and Conversion in the Roman Gesta Martyrum', in *Hagiographische Überlieferung im Frühmittelalter – zwischen Niederschrift und Wiederschrift*, ed. M. Diesenberger, (Vienna, forthcoming).

[116] On Johannes Mediocris, see A. Wilmart, 'Les 38 sermons attribués à Saint Jean Chrysostome', *JThS* 19 (1917), 305–27.

[117] Iohannes, *De consolatione mortuorum sermo* 2 (*PL* 40, 1162): 'Vere, vere peregrinatio est omne quod vivimus: nam sicut peregrini in saeculo, sedes habemus incertas, laboramus, desudamus, vias ambulantes difficiles, periculis plenas: indique insidiae, a spiritalibus, a corporalibus inimicis, undique errorem calliculi sunt preparati. Et cum tantis periculis urgeamur, non solum ipsi non cupimus liberari, sed etiam liberatos tanquam perditos lugemus et plangimus.'

the *saeculum*. Even as the reader is told that the *saeculum* is not the soul's true home, we encounter yet again the strategy of casting spiritual matters into language reflecting the this-worldly social anxieties of the reader's historical reality:

If an earthly king summons a man to his palace or into his company, does not the man hasten with gratitude in his step? How much the more should we hasten to the King of Heaven, who not only receives us there into his company, but also makes us his attendants, as it is written: 'If we be dead with him, we shall also live with him. If we suffer, we shall also reign with him [2 Tim. 2: 11–12].'[118]

The Christian reader is exhorted to see that human fragility – more tangible now than it ever has been – is merely an illusion. The truth of the matter is that just as the soul is eternal, so the body will be restored to wholeness in the Resurrection. Here bishop John draws on imagery from the prophet Jeremiah, God's presence with the unborn child in the womb, as a guarantee of God's ability to restore the body at the last.

He who formed you from a drop of formless fluid in your mother's womb, who commanded you to grow in sinew, blood, and bone – he can, believe me, bring forth again from the womb of earth. Perhaps you are afraid that he does not have the power to clothe your dry bones in flesh as before? Do not, do not reckon the majesty of God by the scale of your own powerlessness. He is God, the creator of all things, who clothes the trees in leaves, and the fields in flowers. And in that springtime of the Resurrection, he will be able to clothe your bones.[119]

Now the martyrs are brought to witness. The martyrs, of course, are the paramount example of faith in the Resurrection. After discussing the contribution of the apostles as preachers of the Resurrection, he turns to the martyrs:

What, then, of the holy martyrs? Did they have certain hope of the Resurrection, or not? If they had not, they would not have borne so many ordeals, and the punishment of death for the greatest of prizes. It was not their ordeals in the here

---

[118] Iohannes, *De consolatione mortuorum sermo* 2 (*PL* 40, 1162): 'Si rex terrestris ad suum palatium vel convivium aliquem vocet, non cum gratiarum actione properabit? Quanto magis ad coelestem currendum est regem, qui quos receperit, non solum convivas, sed etiam conregnatores efficiet, sicut scriptum est: "Si commortui sumus, et convivemus; si sustinebimus, et conregnabimus"' (2 Tim. 2:11 and 12).

[119] Iohannes, *De consolatione mortuorum sermo* 2 (*PL* 40, 1163): 'Qui te ex gutta informis liquoris in tuae matris utero, in nervas, venas et ossa iussit excrescere, poterit, mihi crede, de utero terrae iterum generare. Sed times ne forte ossa tua arida vestiri pristina carne non possit? Noli, noli secundum tuam impotentiam Dei estimare maiestatem. Deus ille rerum omnium procreator, qui vestit arbores foliis, et prata floribus: poterit et tua ossa illico veris tempore in resurrectione vestire.'

and now that spurred them forward, but rather the rewards that were to come. For they know it is written: 'For the things which are temporal are seen, while the things which are not seen are eternal' [2 Cor. 4: 18].[120]

Bishop John next reaches beyond the Christian martyrs to invoke the mother of the biblical Maccabees, whom we have seen above as an *exemplum* beloved of the Roman martyrs themselves, as they were known to the Roman faithful in their *gesta*.

Listen, brethren, to this example in virtue. The mother was urging on her seven sons, and she was not grieving, but rather rejoicing: she saw her sons being torn with hooks, cut with blades, roasted in a frying-pan, and yet she herself was not washed with tears, she raised no howls of grief, but she devoted herself to urging her sons to bear the pain. It was not cruelty on her part, but rather loyalty: she loved her sons, not tenderly, but fiercely. She encouraged her sons to suffer the ordeal that she herself gladly also undertook. For she was sure of the resurrection of her sons and of herself [2 Macc. 7]. What shall I say of such men, such women, what of such boys, and such girls? How they ordered death itself for themselves, the way they went at full tilt for heavenly service? They could have lived on earth, had they wanted; that was the choice they had, to live while denying Christ, or to die confessing him. But they chose rather to discard a life in time, and to choose instead an eternal life; to be cut off from earth, and to dwell in heaven. What place is there here, brethren, for any doubt?'[121]

We have changed gears now; we are no longer engaged in anything like an abstract discussion of the problem of the Resurrection. The clockwork of Christian *consolatio* is now gathering momentum, and we are with the fearful and the bereaved: with the parents who have lost children, with those who fear for children yet living. To grieve inconsolably over these, we are told, is to betray the martyrs who have sacrificed all for their hope in the Resurrection.

---

[120] Iohannes, *De consolatione mortuorum sermo 2* (*PL* 40, 1164–5): 'Quid autem sancti martyres? Habuerunt certam spem resurrectionis, an non? Si non habuissent, non utique per tantos cruciatus et poenas mortem pro lucro maximo suscepissent: non cogitabant supplicia praesentia, sed praemia secutura. Sciebant dictu. Quae videntur, ad tempus sunt; quae autem non videntur, aeterna sunt.'

[121] Iohannes, *De consolatione mortuorum sermo 2* (*PL* 40, 1164): 'Audite, fratres, virtutis exemplum. Mater septem filios hortabatur, et non lugebat, sed potius laetabatur: videbat filios suos ungulis radi, ferro concidi, sartagine assari; et non lacrymas fundebat, non ululatus tollebat, sed sollicite ad tolerantiam filios hortabatur. Non enim erat illa crudelis utique, sed fidelis: amabat filios, non delicate, sed fortiter. Hortabatur filios ad passionem, quam gaudens ipsa quoque suscepit. Erat enim de sua et suorum filiorum resurrectione secura [2 Macc. 7]. Quid loquar viros, quid feminas, quid pueros, quid puellas? Quomodo sibi de ista morte iusserunt, quomodo summa celeritate ad coelestem militiam transierunt! Poterant utique ad praesens vivere, si voluissent; quia in ipsis erat positum, Christum negando viverent, aut confitendo morerentur: sed magis elegerunt vitam proiicere temporaneam, et vitam assumere sempiternam; excludi de terra, et incolere coelum. Inter haec, fratres, quis dubitationis est locus?'

Where is our residual fear of death? If we are the children of the martyrs, if we wish to be found among their companions, let us not grieve for the dear ones who go before us to the Lord. For if we wish to grieve, the blessed martyrs themselves will heap insult upon us, saying: 'O ye faithful, O ye who seek the kingdom of God, you who grieve and shed tears for those dear to you dying in comfort, on feather beds – if you had seen them tortured and killed among the infidels for the name of God, what would you have done then? Would that not have been an example for you to follow?'[122]

Even Abraham was ready to kill his son with a sword, at God's request – a sacrifice repaid by God's own sacrifice when He gave His son for the salvation of His people. 'For he who sheds impatient tears for one he has lost, when can he come to the martyr's arena? But the man who is loyal and great-hearted here, he is already stepping up to greater things.'[123] Bishop John reminds the faithful, too, that their pagan forbears had shown exemplary forbearance when required to sacrifice their children.

Now, there is an example from pagan history. There was once a pagan emperor, who had a son, his only child, much loved. When the prince was on the Capitol, sacrificing to his heathen idols in error, the news came to him that his son had died. He did not set aside the sacred task which he had in hand, he shed no tears, nor did he let out a sigh. Listen, rather, to what he replied. 'Let him be buried', he said, ' as a reminder to me that he was born mortal.' Look on this reply, look on the virtue of this pagan man, that he did not command that they should wait for him, but that his son should be buried straight away.[124]

It is a strategy calculated to shame. Instead of showing the great fortitude in the face of bodily danger for which they had once been known, the Christians of his own time – Bishop John insinuates – have fallen away from the stoic virtue of their pagan forebears. There is something oddly

[122] Iohannes, *De consolatione mortuorum sermo 2* (PL 40, 1164–5): 'Ubi potest adhuc mortis residere formido? Si martyrum sumus filii, si eorum socii volumus inveniri, non contristemur morte, non lugeamus charos, qui nos praecedunt ad Dominum. Nam si plangere voluerimus, ipsi nobis insultabant beati martyres, et dicent, "O fideles, o regnum Dei cupientes, vos qui charos vestros delicate morientes, in lectis utique et plumis cum maerore plangitis et lugetis; si eos a Gentilibus propter nomen Domini cruciari et interfici videretis, quid facturi essetis? Aut non vobis praecessit exemplum?"'
[123] Iohannes, *De consolatione mortuorum sermo 2* (PL 40, 1165): 'Sic qui plangit impatienter ammissum, quando poterit ad martyrii pervenire certamen? Nam qui in his constans et magnanimus existit, iam sibi gradum ad potiora substernit.'
[124] Iohannes, *De consolatione mortuorum sermo 2* (PL 40, 1166): 'Exemplum autem de paganorum historia est. Fuit quidam princeps paganus, qui habebat filium unicum, satisque dilectum. Hic cum in Capitolio idolis suis gentili errore sacrificaret, nuntiatur ei filius ille unicus defuisset. Non reliquit sacra quae gerebat in manibus, non lacrimavit, nec omnino suspiravit: sed quid respondit, audite. "Sepeliatur", inquit: "memini enim me illum genuisse mortalem." Vide responsum, wide hominis pagani virtutem: ut nec expectari se iusserit, vel ut praesente se sepulturae filius traderetur.'

reassuring about the way the stoicism of the Roman father is invoked to shame his descendants: at a time when the certainty of Roman self-definition in Italy is ebbing away, undermined by decades of civil war, tactical ethnic identification, religious confusion, and – perhaps most damagingly – ambivalence about the contemporary Roman emperors as 'Greeks' rather than really being Romans at all, it is still possible to resort to Livy to find an anecdote to shame one's neighbour into doing the right thing.

At the same time, of course, something has changed. When Roman fathers and mothers were asked to sacrifice their children, it was to appease the gods, to uphold a principle, to avenge the family honour. Violence and disease, of course, had always laid claim to the most vulnerable, even during the centuries when it had been possible to keep the arena of military conflict far from the children of Roman citizens. But when Christian fathers and mothers considered the loss of their children, they were asked to imagine their way into an alternative history, with their example a woman who stood against everything that was Roman, the mother of guerrilla rebels in a fallen kingdom that would one day become a Roman province.

A new concept of family unity is offered here, one in which it is the hope of the Resurrection that holds the biological family together in the here and now. This is a different way of offering solace for the painful realities of child mortality, which remained distressingly high in Europe for centuries up to the late nineteenth and early twentieth century. Death is domesticated in these texts, becoming a passage which, however irreversible, poses no obstacle to the bonds of affection uniting parents and children. At the same time, the theme of the beloved child's death in the *Passio Sebastiani* and other hagiographical texts reflects a changed institutional culture, in which parents are asked to offer their children in a new kind of pact with death. The forbearance of parents when required to sacrifice a beloved child is one of the central themes of the Roman *gesta martyrum*,[125] and it is not too difficult to find support for the idea that the emphasis on this theme reflected the pastoral needs of the monasteries which almost certainly sponsored their production.[126] The earliest known Italian monastic rule, the *Regula Magistri*, written south-east of Rome in the first quarter of

---

[125] For discussion, see Kate Cooper, 'The Virgin as Social Icon: Perspectives from Late Antiquity', in Mathilde Van Dijk and Renée Nip, eds., *Saints, Scholars, and Politicians: Gender as a Tool in Medieval Studies*, Medieval Church Studies 15 (Leiden, 2005), 9–24, at 22–3.

[126] Kate Cooper, 'Family, Dynasty, and Conversion'.

the sixth century, draws on the *Passio Sebastiani* and a number of the other *gesta*; it forms the basis, in turn, for the extracts collected in the so-called 'Rule of Eugippius' preserved alongside the sermons of Bishop John in the late sixth-century Paris manuscript mentioned above.[127]

Citing another martyr narrative, the *Passio Juliani et Basilissae*, the *Regula Magistri* gives detailed advice to the abbot who is called upon to accept a *filius nobilis*, the son of a noble family, into the monastery. The anonymous writer warns that a struggle can be expected between the family and the youth. But the son's cause will prevail, because it draws its vigour from God's own power: 'For if there was opposition, even forcible, to his being brought to God, then the claims of the monastic cloister will be upheld, "because the Lord is powerful to defend his own, and his right hand is stronger in the protection that it offers than is the hand of the Devil in causing harm".'[128] We are back in the territory, here, of fathers giving way to their sons.

But the *militia* to which the sons are conscripted is no longer that of the emperor. It is the *militia Christi*, indeed, a very specific earthly version of the *militia Christi*, that of the post-Chalcedonian monasteries, with their increasing autonomy from direct lay ownership, and their evolving place in an episcopally administered ecclesiastical hierarchy.[129] Yet there is a further twist to the story. We saw in Chapter One that young men and women could elect the life of continence and that this often – though not always – represented an act of defiance against the judgement of parents who wished, more than anything, for legitimate grandchildren. From the time of Melania the Younger, ascetic parents had dedicated their children to virginity – a practice commended by Saint Jerome, with characteristic irony, as justifying marriage 'in order to produce new virgins'.[130] But as we saw in the case of the celebrated virgin Demetrias, as often as not,

[127] On the *Regula Magistri* in general, and its appearance in Paris Lat. 12634 in particular, see Conrad Leyser, *Authority and Asceticism from Augustine to Gregory the Great* (Oxford, 2000), at 103–6 and 112–15 respectively.

[128] *Regula Magistri* 91.3–4 (*SC* 106, 398): 'Quod si contrarii extiterint interim usque ad vim pro eo Domino inferendam, claustro monasterii vindicentur, "quem potens est Dominus defendere propter se, quia fortior est dextera eius ad protegendum, quam diaboli iniquitas ad ledendum",' citing the *Passio Juliani et Basilissae*. (For further discussion of this passage, and other borrowings from hagiographical sources in the *Regula Magistri*, see Cooper, 'Family, Dynasty, and Conversion'.)

[129] A brief overview of this process can be found in Kate Cooper, 'Poverty, Obligation, and Inheritance: Roman Heiresses and the Varieties of Senatorial Christianity in Fifth-Century Rome', in Kate Cooper and Julia Hillner, eds., *Dynasty, Patronage, and Authority in Early Christian Rome, 300–900* (Cambridge, 2007), 165–89.

[130] Jerome, *Ep.* 22 (*PL* 22, 406).

ascetics lived into old age in the context of the *domus* into which they were born.[131]

After the Council of Chalcedon, however, monasteries began to exist as institutions juridically independent of lay ownership, accountable to the local bishop by preference over the *dominus* who owned the land. In this context, we begin to catch sight of a new phenomenon, in which parents contracted for their children to join free-standing, institutionally established monasteries. This practice, known as 'child oblation', would become a standard feature of the business transacted between lay and monastic establishments. How this took place, and the new opportunities and tensions it introduced into the bonds of biological kinship, falls beyond the scope of this study.[132] To understand how these ideas about parental sacrifice and otherworldly belonging would crystallize into a legacy to be handed down in the post-Roman West, we may return once more to Gregory of Tours, this time to his *Life of the Fathers*. Among the stories collected there is the life of Monegund, who died a recluse in Tours although she had begun her adult life as a married householder in Chartres. One hears in the opening of the narrative how Gregory's ear is steeped in the traditions we have encountered.

From the beginning of this rude age, the Saviour of the world showed himself for patriarchs to see, and prophets to foretell. At last he deigned to be received into the womb of the ever-virgin and intact Mary. The all-powerful and immortal Creator suffered himself to be garbed in the raiment of mortal flesh. He died to make reparation for mankind who had died through sin and He rose again victorious. We were wounded by the arrows of criminal deeds and hurt by the blows of robbers who had ambushed us, but he cleansed us with a mixture of oil and wine and led us to the store of heavenly medicine, which is the teaching of the Church. He exhorts us with the gift of His incessant teaching to live by the saints' example. And as examples, He provides not only men but members of the inferior sex who are not sluggish in fighting the good fight but full of manly vigour.[133]

After a skeletal description of Monegund's early life as a wife and mother, Gregory comes swiftly to spring the trap of his narrative. 'Struck by fever, the girls paid their final debt to nature. Mourning for them, bewailing her bereavement, the sorrowful mother never ceased to weep by day and by night. Neither her husband nor her friends nor any other intimate could

---

[131] See also Kate Cooper, 'The Household and the Desert: Monastic and Biological Communities in the *Lives* of Melania the Younger', in Anneke Mulder-Bakker and Jocelyn Wogan-Browne, eds., *Household, Women, and Christianities in Late Antiquity and the Middle Ages* (Leiden, 2005), 11–35.

[132] Mayke de Jong, *In Samuel's Image: Child Oblation in the Early Medieval West* (Leiden, 1996).

[133] *Vita Monegundis* pref. (*MGH, SRM* 1.2, 286).

console her.' Eventually, however, Monegund passed to a second stage in her grief.

... At last she came to herself and said: 'If I can find no consolation for my daughters' deaths, I fear I shall give offence to my lord, Jesus Christ. Now I will give up this lamentation and be consoled. Like the blessed Job, I shall repeat, "The Lord giveth and the Lord taketh away; as it pleaseth the Lord, so shall it be done; blessed be the name of the Lord" [Job 1:21].' So saying, she put off her mourning garb. She ordered a little cell prepared for herself, fitted out with a small window through which she might see a little light. Turning with contempt from the world and spurning the company of her husband, she devoted all her time to God alone, placing her faith in Him, pouring out prayers for her own sins and those of the people.[134]

Eventually, Monegund left Chartres, fearing that she was attracting too much praise for her piety, and went on pilgrimage to visit the shrine of Saint Martin. When she reached the Touraine, however, she established a new cell and found her vocation as a miracle-worker. At first, her husband importuned her to return to her native city, but after she offered to do as he asked, he relented and 'asked nothing further from her'.[135] Monegund returned to the Touraine and to her cell, where she resumed working miracles, and continued to do so even after her death.

With Monegund, we are far, both geographically and culturally, from the world of a Proba, a Celanthia, or a Gregoria. It is more or less taken for granted by the ecclesiastical literature that a truly Christian husband will support the pious aspirations of a Monegund (whether this proved true in historical reality is another matter altogether, and one which the sources do not allow us to judge). The old civic ideals, to the degree that they survived, came to do so through the institutions of the Church, while new ideas emerged which accorded more squarely with biblical and hagiographical tradition as a frame of reference.

Marriage, too, took on a new colour under the Church's aegis. It was now the thirtyfold fruit, an institution less exalted than that of avowed virginity or continence. Yet the Roman institution of marriage, as a mechanism for protecting the legitimacy of a man's offspring by his chosen reproductive partner, had been reinvented on terms which would secure its efficacy in a post-Roman future. At the same time, a change took place whose repercussions none of those who contributed to the transformation of marriage would have been able fully to appreciate. A new ideal of permanence of marriage as a bond not only on earth but also for eternity

---

[134] *Vita Monegundis* 1 (MGH, SRM 1.2, 286).   [135] *Vita Monegundis* 2 (MGH, SRM 1.2, 288).

had taken root in the imaginations of Christian writers and churchmen. The invention of this ideal represented nothing less than a revolutionary shift in the landscape of Roman (and post-Roman) family life. Through a permanently binding vow of marriage, men and women could now aspire to establish a durable, irreversible bond. If the ideal of marriage as a union for eternity was revolutionary, however, it must also be remembered that it is an ideal which every generation of Christians since the end of the Roman empire has found its own way to undermine.

Appendix. Ad Gregoriam in palatio

English translation by Kate Cooper[1]

Most admirable daughter, I marvel that, after turning your back on fleshly cares and freeing your heart from the lawful bond which fixed it, you have turned your countenance to the Holy Spirit, saying[2]: 'What I ask, is that you give a ruling[3] on what place a wife will be able to find in the sight of God, or clarify how far she may have compensated for the licence of the marital state (*maritalis licentiam potestatis*). Long afflicted by trials and adversities, I have taken refuge in this sole point of comfort, that I might discover whether somehow there is anything which in the future life may bring assistance to a woman placed under the authority of a husband, lest I should also dread the pain of future punishments, being deprived of the joys of security in the present.'

CHAPTER I. THAT THE HUMAN RACE IS TO BE ALLOWED
TO BE TESTED FOR A TIME, SO THAT IT MAY REJOICE
FOREVER IN THE FUTURE[4]

O height of the riches of the wisdom and knowledge of God; how unfathomable are His judgements! [Rom. 11:33]. For the world is allowed to rage, and sadness is let loose to take control of minds, so that those whom a deceitful enjoyment had unyoked from Christ may come back and conquer themselves to rise above the pleasures. Dear girl, I would not have you fear a fleeting sadness, through

---

[1] I am grateful to Carole Hill, Nicholas Horsfall, Peter Brown, and Janet Martin for assistance with this translation, though none bears responsibility for its shortcomings. I have used Daur's edition (*CC* 25A) as the basis for this translation.

[2] Tore Janson, *Latin Prose Prefaces: Studies in Literary Conventions*, Acta Universitatis Stockholmiensis: Studia Latina Stockholmiensia 13 (Stockholm, 1964), 21ff. and *passim*, on the allusion to a letter of request as a strategy for suggesting the importance of what follows. Here, however, it should be understood in light of a wider dialogic program at work in the treatise.

[3] *responsa*: the authoritative opinions through which authorized Roman jurists (initally, *pontifices*) contributed to the development of the law.

[4] The chapter headings here and below are integral to the ancient text.

which you will have been able to come upon the sweet promises of your Lord, at least if you believe the truth of what you sing: *those who sow in tears shall reap in joy* [Ps. 125:5]. This is why the apostle James exclaims: *count it all joy, my brethren, when you meet various trials, for you know that testing (probatio) produces endurance,⁵ moreover, let endurance work to its full effect, that you may be perfect and guileless in the sight of God* [James 1:2–4]. And the vessel of election, the apostle Paul, also repeats the same things, saying, *because suffering produces endurance, endurance produces experience (probatio), experience produces hope, and hope does not confound, because God's love has been spread through our hearts by the Holy Spirit which has been given us* [Rom. 5:3–5]. And the voice of our Lord Jesus Christ, foretelling the future, also deigns to forewarn his own servants in these words: *The world*, he says, *will rejoice, but you will be sad; yet your sadness will be turned to rejoicing, and to your rejoicing there will be no end* [John 16:20–2]. And so, I do not want you to conclude that your trouble is fruitless, if you meet it [sadness] as one well-established in charity;⁶ rather, you should know that, through whichever person it has come upon you, it is inflicted by the Devil. Were there no reason why the Enemy of the human race should be jealous on your account, and for which he might reveal the green flame of his envy, he would never have beset you with his battery of woes. And not without cause is the Devil tormented by the pain of his envy, since he is lamenting that you – a rare thing among respectable married women (*matronae*) – have taken up arms against him. The King of Vices grieves that you are fighting boldly against his soldiers, battling to be sure against the whole regiment of the sins, and he is terrified that the drawn sword of your faith is threatening the necks of his generals, the crimes and sacrileges which hold sway in this world. That is, you traverse the course of this life, cutting off the heads of all those transgressions which are the beginning of sin, when with resisting soul you lop off the first shoots of sin, so that the branches which would have sprung from them are stunted.

For already at the very beginning of marriage (*conubii*), because the Enemy saw you handed over after training by your parents to the embraces of a most Christian man, in whom not the disgrace of concubines, not the shameless pride of keeping mistresses, had been able to gain a hold, in whose heart as in its own estate purity of morals plays the lord (*castitas dominatur*);⁷ then, I say, the author of all crime had the presentiment that

⁵ *Patientia*, the virtue of Stoics and martyrs: I have translated *patientia* as 'endurance' throughout.
⁶ MS A has *castitate* where MS C has *caritate*; I have accepted C's reading.
⁷ *Castitas* in this treatise is used in its classical sense, 'purity of morals', and is (precisely) not understood as incompatible with the lawful sexual activity of the married.

you would be his assassin, and it was not for any other reason, save to separate people who had joined against him and who wished to live in the love of Christ, that he – the Devil – tried first of all to sow dissension between you, or later, to plant the seed of angry outbursts. So do not shut your eyes and try to ignore the Adversary whom you yourself bestirred to enmity by holding morality (*castimonia*) dear and following in the foot-steps (*vestigia*) of the Lord Jesus Christ, whose followers the Enemy knows can enter there, where Christ has entered.

For that reason he places himself as an obstacle in their path, so that even if he is unable to draw [any believer] away [from Heaven], he can at least impede the one hastening. Since therefore you understand that what holds you back is of the Devil, despise the one holding you back and give heed to the one who is calling you forward; hasten on (*curre*) in the service of charity and take trouble (*satage*) [on its account]; run (*curre*) hard to outstrip your husband. No arrow of impatience will strike you, if you protect yourself with a shield of forbearance (*tolerantia*). You who follow Christ the King, and who desire to evade the hostile tyrant pursuing you, flee him whom you flee and follow Him whom you follow; do not hesitate at any cost: let no instances of material loss or verbal injury hold you back. For if by some struggle with himself he should arrest you, the one whom you were fleeing will draw nearer, and the one whom you were following will draw further away.

CHAPTER 2. THE NOBILITY OF THE SOUL IS TO BE DEFENDED

'But it is utterly unacceptable (*nefas est*)', you will say, 'for a free-born and noble woman, weak with the fragility of a pampered body, to meet with a husband's unremitting frenzy (*adsiduum furorem maritalem*),[8] and to be reduced to the dishonour of affronts (*iniuriarum opprobrium*) within domestic walls, as a result of which I am accorded the standing of a mere slave (*mancipium*).'

Naturally, I will take care to defend nobility (*nobilitatem*) by every effort. I am delighted to join with you in protesting on behalf of your noble birth (*generositate*). But you won't be altogether able to deny that there are two noble lines in your birth: the one by which you are called a

---

[8] The addressee's complaint here is difficult to understand, and may best be understood by reference to the *Passio Anastasiae*, in which Anastasia's initial test of endurance was mistreatment by her husband. It is also possible, however, to take *furor maritalis* as a reference to the sex act itself. On this reading, the addressee could be threatening to take a unilateral vow of continence.

daughter of God, the other by which you are called the daughter of a mortal. Of which one, then – the human or the divine – will you have us take up our defence first of all? If the human, you will be refuted; if the divine, you have won. So defend the nobility of your lineage, and when the daughter of the Devil – that is, without doubt all pleasure in any sin whatsoever, or a provocation (*occasio*) to any kind of misdeed – attempts to hinder you, then protest that you, the daughter of the high King, have been unlawfully dishonoured by the daughter of a captive barbarian.

Then indeed, I say, cry aloud and spare not [cf. Isaiah 58:1]: use the privilege (*officium*) of your nobility, claim for yourself the prerogative of sovereign status (*imperium*); bring in as counsel the apostles, interpose the white-clad army of martyrs; and also, O soul, press forward your kinsfolk (*parentes*), the most holy angels. Press your case (*insiste*), pursue it through the proper channels, and exact a formal confirmation of your freedom. And first of all, strive to make your case against shamelessness from the distinguished lineage (*natalibus*) of moral purity (*castitas*), against injustice from the nobility of justice, against impatience from the glory of endurance (*patientia*), against faithlessness from the splendour (*claritas*) of faith, against arrogance from the heights of humility, against avarice from the riches of almsgiving, against harshness from the origins of mercy; and against dissension – come! – see that you do not hold your tongue about the illustrious glory of charity and of all the heavenly virtues, of whose nature by God's action your soul has taken part, either when it was created, or when it was restored again to life. O soul, show forth the distinguished lineage of these virtues, I say, of which heavenly nobility has made you the near relation, and – mindful of this shining nobility – be angered against ignoble vices in defence of noble virtues. Let endurance (*patientia*) as conqueror place her yoke on the neck of impatience, let modesty put a bridle on lust (*libidini*), let generosity fetter avarice, and let the charity of Christ hold in chains the impulses [toward] all crimes, until the day on which He will hail them before the Judge to answer for themselves. The whole company of matrons will be with you: with you most enduring Sarah,[9] with you gentlest Rebecca,[10] with you holiest Rachel,[11] with you Aseneth, wife of the most chaste (*castissimi*) patriarch,[12] with you Zipporah, wife of the man who spoke with God,[13] with you Deborah, vanquisher of

[9] Wife of Abraham: Genesis 11ff.   [10] Wife of Isaac, Gen. 22ff.   [11] Wife of Jacob, Gen. 29ff.
[12] i.e. Joseph: Gen. 41:45–50, 46:20; and the Hellenistic romance of *Joseph and Aseneth*.
[13] i.e., Moses: Exodus 2:21ff., Exodus 4:18.

arrogance,[14] with you Jael, piercing through the head of the Devil,[15] with you Judith, killing the enemy of chastity (*castitatis*),[16] with you marches (*pergit*) Hannah, the mother of the one seeing God,[17] with you the Shunamite, about to perceive the glory of sojourning in a foreign country,[18] with you Anna, the daughter of Phanuel, who first recognized the Saviour,[19] with you Magdalene,[20] with you Martha – with you the host who, because they have recognized you as one of their number, will be with you even here in this world, and will fight down the enemy battle-lines for you; they throw the very father of crimes to the ground under your feet. Behold what sisters celestial nobility has given you: behold by what kind of women matronly glory is attended; behold by what kind of force the nobility that is eternal is defended.

CHAPTER 3. IT IS THROUGH ENDURANCE (*PATIENTIAM*)
THAT ALL VIRTUES ARE ABLE TO EXIST

Cast your mind's eye back and forth across them all, and – afire with yearning to be associated with them – take care to question them with these words, 'I ask you, O most blessed of all women, by what art or by what approach did you set foot in the sanctuary of such majesty? Explain how it is that while on earth you enjoyed in the pleasures of marriage, and yet now in heaven possess the peak of angelic dignity.'

You will hear that with one voice they all respond to your question thus, 'we loved endurance with our whole hearts, and it was endurance that led us to this lofty seat. For it is she who gives birth to the other virtues and nurses them with the milk of her own breasts, nor is there any other virtue at all which can be conceived or be created without endurance. For it is through endurance that we have preserved the self-control (*castitas*) of our husbands;[21] through endurance we believed in the rewards of Heaven;

---

[14] It was the courage of Deborah which made possible the unified action of the tribes of Israel against the Canaanites: Judges 4:5.

[15] Jael (Judges 4:4–22, 5:2–31) murdered Sisera by taking a hammer (or possibly a tent peg) to his skull when he took refuge in her tent.

[16] Judith's murder of the lascivious Holfernes, this time by decapitation, is recounted in the Book of Judith.

[17] i.e., Samuel; 1 Samuel 1ff.   [18] 2 Kings 4:8–37, 8:1–6.   [19] Luke 2:36–8.

[20] The reference to the Magdalene as a matron is unusual; compare the Pseudo-Jerome *Commentary on Mark* (PL 30, 640B), discussed in Germain Morin, *Études, textes, découvertes* (Paris, 1913), 328 n. 1, and idem, 'Un commentaire romain sur saint Marc de la première moitié du Ve siècle', *RB* 27 (1910), 352–62.

[21] The reference here is to husbands who are persuaded by their wives to hold to the straight and narrow path of monogamy; cf. the praise in ch. 1 of Gregoria's husband for having no sexual partner other than his wife.

through endurance we held to the signs of hope; through endurance we scorned the world, and for the love of chastity (*castitas*) scoffed at the threat of disgrace. For in this way the world betrays the reputation of modesty, so that it may undo her works, and it takes care to represent as holy those whom it has caused to wallow in the filth of sin. Through endurance Susanna was not afraid to be called an adulteress, lest, fearing to be called so, she might have been so;[22] for she wished reputation to serve virtue, not to govern it. Through endurance we have desired nothing which calls forth shame before others (*hominum pudor*). Through endurance we have scorned every pleasure which could be held in common with the beasts, and we have loved only that virtue, which we are known to hold in common with the angels. Through endurance we have longed for nothing regrettable; and through endurance we have laughed at many things which we have suffered against our moral sense. Through endurance we have believed in God, and through endurance we have kept His commandments (*iussa servavimus*); through endurance we have nourished faith, hope, and charity; nor has any other leader (*dux*) than endurance, led us to the very pinnacle of honour.'

CHAPTER 4. WHAT KIND OF THING IN PARTICULAR
IS ENDURANCE

Here, you have heard the ruling you demanded.[23] We have heard you asking and them answering. I imagine they left nothing for you to ask, except carefully to inquire what is endurance itself, which you learned is your sole necessity when you received a reply from the holy matrons. Hear then what is endurance, which you have just learned is the mother of all virtues, and their guardian. Endurance is the daughter of innocence, whom the Enemy of humankind disposes the reckless to call the daughter of wickedness (*nocentiae*). For thus is the name of vice is attached to every kind of virtue: the faithful one is called false, and the faithless, clever (*urbanus*).[24] By this means the vices take the place of the virtues in

---

[22] The story of Susanna, whose unsuccessful seducers put her to trial as an adulteress, appears in Daniel 13.
[23] Janson, *Latin Prose Prefaces*, 118ff., on the escalation of verbs of demanding used to characterize the addressee's initial request in the later Latin prose prefaces; this process accords with the development of a Christian rhetoric of simplicity and particular reluctance. See also Averil Cameron, *Christianity and the Rhetoric of Empire: the Development of Christian Discourse*, Sather Classical Lectures 55 (Berkeley, 1991), 84ff.
[24] On the ambivalence of *urbanus* in Christian Latin, and its shift in meaning from connoting the classical ideal of civic humanism to a slur indicating 'a perverse attitude to things Christian', Edwin S. Ramage, *Urbanitas: Ancient Sophistication and Refinement* (Norman, Oklahoma, 1973), 151–2.

human minds, so that the simple and less educated person takes what is approved by mortals as a model to follow. This is why the crowds of the immodest accuse the pure (*castos*) of being impure (*incestos*) and discolour with the stain[25] of bad conscience cheeks hued only with the rosy glow of modesty. It then follows that cunning is ranked above the innocent, and the crafty one is judged more acceptable than the pure in heart. Thence it is that disreputable talk (*infame conloquium*) is prized in public, and the speech which witnesses purity (*puritatis index loquella*) is spurned; that prattling chit-chat (*garrula conversatio*) jeers at those living in quiet, and the slyness of fawning wins the prized position. The test is now that endurance should come forward and show herself to be a truly precious gem, and not as a glass fake that is exposed when tested. For in vain does she boast of the decorations of victory who is afraid to be tested yet wishes to be adorned.

What are you weeping for? I ask you, Christian soul, answer: why has the pallor of an indignant spirit taken hold of you? Why does the frown on your forehead rout the holy Cross from its place? Why is the clear gaze of your eyes clouded over, and all the tranquility of your soul cast down? Do you suffer affronts (*iniurias*) justly, or unjustly? If justly, consider it due, if unjustly, turn to Christ, and you will lose your taste for making a case on account of outrages. As you face outrages and affliction by mortals, reflect on the Son of God who suffered flagellation; against the reproaches and derision of mortals, [consider] His face touched with spittle and His defiled countenance; against the horror of death itself, look on Him Crucified. And so, in every dispute, in every attack, in every blast of insults, and, too, in every torment (*supplicio*), not to abandon endurance is to imitate Christ. 'But', you will say,[26] 'as a guardian of my own nobility, a woman firm in discipline, a follower (*pedisequa*) of all good morals (*morum*), in chaste conduct (*castitate*) a teacher, in dignity outstanding, in honour most careful, in speech true, in prayer capable, in matters of fair dealing most just, sparkling in the stewardship of the life of the household, swift and successful in the most useful work – in the course of family life I ought not to be disturbed in any way, no conjugal affront (*maritalis indignatio*) should stir up my emotions (*meos motus*), if I am to persevere in this path of righteousness.'

---

[25] *fuco*: i.e., cosmetic paint.
[26] The language of this passage parallels that of the honorary inscription dedicated by Anicius Hermogenianus Olybrius and his wife, Anicia Juliana, to his mother, Anicia Faltonia Proba, *CIL* 6.1755, discussed in Anne N. Kurdock, The Anician Women: Patronage and Dynastic Strategy in a Late Roman Domus, 350 CE–600 CE (PhD thesis, University of Manchester, 2003), 52.

O argument of injustice, battling against justice! It is right and true, a true gem and a true coin are not to be tested, but it is unjust if they are afraid to be tested. If you recognize that in this life it is time not for rewarding but for testing, take on in a spirit of endurance the temporary testing, so that you may be able to accept the eternal remuneration.

CHAPTER 5. THAT THE KIND OF PERSON WHO DISDAINED THE VIRTUE OF PATIENCE IN TIME OF PEACE IS NOT LIKELY TO BEAR THE PERSECUTIONS OF MARTYRDOM SUCCESSFULLY

It is clear what love of contention is contributing here; it is certainly not absent. For untried impatience has the habit of saying, 'I long to show forth my steadfastness before an unbelieving persecutor. As a matter of fact, I know that if I do this, I will be able to join the company of the saints.'

Such a new boxer in the glorious match! Such an outstanding athlete and master of wrestling-matches! The one who claims that, under the gaze of the entire populace and of the kings and judges, she will be able to withstand the force of punches and kicks without flinching, turns out to be the one who fell over backstage at the wrestling-ground, shaken by one touch of the wrestler's wax.[27] The one who claims she will fight bravely in battle against the enemy is actually the one who quaked at the training for battle, before ever leaving the camp. And how will the one who was unnerved by a whinnying horse be fearless before the lion's roar? How will she endure the unpredictablilty of the barbarians, who was horrified by a single citizen's raising his voice? But let me concede that you might be able to find a place among those wives whose *Passiones* and *Gesta* are witnessed by reliable documents. Why, then, should you not bear with small trials, you who are sure you can bear great ones? These are the women whom you believe to have fought victoriously against the battle-lines of tyrants and to have laughed at all manner of tortures, whom you believe to have entered the abode of the heavens crowned by the bright gore of their own blood.

And to make mention of a few out of the many, or out of the countless at least three or four, I must recall, though briefly, an example particularly dear to God, yours, O holy Anastasia. Illustrious (*illustris*) in this world, you took care to be even more distinguished before God, since you obtained even more precious treasures in your character than you scorned among your possessions. Rather, we believe, you obtained the true value of

---

[27] *ceroma*: the embrocating wax applied by massage before a wrestling match; the massage itself was strenuous.

your moral worth, and did not lose wealth and property but made an exchange of it with the Lord to receive it back in the future a hundredfold and to regain eternal life along with it. With how much capacity to forbear, do you think, did you manage the affronts of married life (*maritalem iniuriam*), you who endured the cruelty of a tyrant with so tranquil a soul that after the blows of the executioner and after all manner of tortures you happily allowed yourself to be burned alive (*assari*)? This ornament of all Christian matrons, how was it, do you think, that for love of chastity she boldly scorned what was allowed, who so willingly desired for the sake of Christ to bear what caused pain? How many wives sprung from a lowly condition scoffed at physical threats and in the face of a raging tyrant, do you think, not pale with fear but eager in the Lord, when they saw that you, who are noble and dainty, had constantly scorned all kinds of torments for the defence of honour and faith? Justly Christ took you up into the heavens on the same day on which he himself descended to Earth, and He permitted the feast of your martyrdom to occur on the same day as the nativity of His Incarnation,[28] because you, by suffering martyrdom, offered to many what He offered to all by being born. Just as He set aside his majesty and took on the form of a slave (*servi*), so that He might assist us all: so you yourself set aside the glory of nobility and took on an ignominy of person, so that you might be able to be imitated by others, and so that you might provide a model of endurance for all Christians, as one who will receive everlasting glory as much because you set an example for other matrons as because of your martyrdom.

Why should I not bring up the memory of you, glorious mothers, who with seven sons each[29] subdued the diverse powers of tyrants, although at different times and through different tortures (*suppliciis*)? The province Palestine possesses (*tenet*) you, Maccabea[30]; you too, Symphorosa, with seven brothers born from your womb, the Tiburtine city[31] venerates and accepts. On you, her true Felicity, the city of Rome heaps due praise and due honours, O true Felicity and teacher of all married women of the faith. What women do you [sing.] think should be afraid of losing their one life for love of Christ, when they have contemplated your glorious examples,

---

[28] *adsumptionis*: a word whose theological implications in the early-to-mid fifth century bear discussion, especially given the connection in this text between Anastasia and Christ's *adsumptio*.

[29] Symphorosa and Felicitas were each recorded as having suffered with seven children; their *passiones* presumably intended an imitation of the mother of the seven Maccabees in 4 Maccabees.

[30] The mother of the Maccabees; the relics of the Maccabees (parents and children) were at Antioch until 551, when they were translated to Constantinople; a portion was then translated to S. Pietro in Vincoli in Rome under Pope Pelagius I (556–61).

[31] Or, City of Tibur (Tivoli); the shrine of Symphorosa was on the Via Tiburtina.

and seen perceived that you fought for the defence of justice all the way to death, through many trials and without any hesitation, despite your love for your children? None of your [pl.] torments, none of those of your children disturbed you. While they were being tortured, you showed them your joyous faces lest they should bow their souls to affliction if they saw you weeping. For it was in their power (*arbitrio*) not to yield to torture, when their witness was set upon by an unjust torturer.

And so, most blessed wives of Christian husbands, Christian wives, whichever of you have heard and believe these things: how glittering an ornament from the jewels of their martyrdoms do these women carry around you to sanctify you, since you have seen that your own peers – wives, that is to say – have entered the starry regions with their children, without doubt to prepare a place for all women in the station of marriage. As their followers, you [pl.] will be able to enter there, where you believe them to have entered.

CHAPTER 6. EXCEPTING BY THE WILL OF GOD, THE WIFE
SHOULD NOT DESPISE THE WILL OF THE HUSBAND
IN ANY MATTER

For in fact, all you women who believe know yourselves to be debtors of Christ, so that not only are you to behave humbly towards your husbands out of the duty of forbearance, but you are also to offer your necks to savage tyrants in such a way as to bear every kind of torment should it be necessary. And if this is so – rather, because it is so – I ask what foolish line of thinking persuades you to judge that Christ, for whose will you stand prepared to die at the hands of a tyrant, may be defied where a husband is concerned? For in the case of a husband, will you scorn His precepts (*praecepta*) even though you say you would observe them with regard to a tyrant? And although you assert that you are able to endure a great martyrdom in order to protect Christ's commandments, would you disdain the same commandments on account of a slight affront of marital loyalty (*levem maritalis fiduciae iniuriam*)? For the same One who commanded that you should not fear those who kill the body,[32] but rather, having scorned the temporary afflictions of the body, fear only Him, and who can banish both the body and the soul to Gehenna, Himself teaches (*praecipit*) that a wife should love her husband in the same way that the Church loves Christ,[33] and accordingly that she should not oppose him in

---

[32] Cf. Matt. 10:28.   [33] Cf. Eph. 5:25.

any matter of the will, just as the Church does not oppose the Saviour, so that, just as Christ is not contradicted by the Church, a husband never should suffer the contradiction of his will, setting aside only the authority of a command of his that renders her who obeys it an apostate and imposes the penalty of eternal fire: so that both scorn and obedience in a wife should be linked to obedience to the divine command. I can find no way to contemplate, wife, how you have the nerve to think you can despise your husband when he gives orders, or out of scorn bewail him when he is angry, if his will has only been cast out – I repeat – where it goes against the will of God.

CHAPTER 7. WITH RESPECT TO WHAT DUTIES AND BY WHAT
JUDGEMENTS A TRUE WIFE IS TO BE JUDGED

And so the whole crowd of married women (*matronarum turba*) stands firm either through fear or through love, and does not attain the dignity of privileged status for any other reason except to show either a ready love to good husbands or due fear to the bad-tempered. For before it was prohibited that male authority be despised, the female[34] had it in her power (*habuit in potestate*) to will what [that authority] deplored. But since the time when every single woman has been committed by divine and human power to one lord in such a way that she may not by any means oppose his will, [only] with the greatest shame may she put forward her free status or her original authority (*potestatis*) as an impediment, since at the time when she had it in her power to will (*velle*) what she would, it is agreed that she herself cut herself off from all of this right to rule. You have been bought, O *matrona*, and purchased by the contracts of your dowry agreement (*instrumentis dotalibus*), bound by as many fetters as [you have] limbs, nor to be sure have you known your husband carnally (*ingressa es ad maritum*)[35] for any other reason than that you cease to have authority (*potestas*) over even your very body, since the apostolic authority (1 Cor. 7:4) witnesses, that a wife should not have power over her body. You may perhaps respond that the apostle ruled as well, that a husband also does not have authority (*potestas*) over his own body before his spouse. I cede readily to this worthy saying, and I maintain that nothing else is meant in the letter [to the Corinthians], than that you should bind your husband by so much charity, and hold him fast by so great a compliance of manner (*morum obtemperantia*), that with you

---

[34] The reference here is to the Garden of Eden (Gen. 3:16).
[35] J. N. Adams, *The Latin Sexual Vocabulary* (London: Duckworth, 1982), 176, cites Vulgate Genesis 6:4, 'ingressi sunt filii . . . ad filias', with this meaning.

guiding all [his affairs[36]] he should now altogether be reluctant to assume the burden of authority (*potestatis curam*).[37]

For why should he reserve anything for his own power, with you taking care of the matter better [than he could himself] because he had willed it? And might he not be glad, that not only has he never encountered contradiction in any matter, but that there has been such unanimity (*consensus*), that what he wished might better be carried out? For sweetness (*dulcedo*), not authority (*potestas*), has handed you over to his dominion, from which, accordingly, you have determined that nothing else should occupy your thoughts exclusively, unless to see to it that you alone among all women manage to be beautiful for him. Just as you take care not to present yourself to his eyes looking ugly because of some blemish on your face, therefore, cultivate beauty of manner in the same way so that no ugliness may appear. For just as one face is compared to another, so manner to manner. Indeed, a face – however unsightly – is agreeable, if it is beautified by the soul's demeanour, and however beautiful the face is, it is rendered unsightly if it be sullied by unsightliness of soul. Thus, this is your real need to please: just as you take care to please nuptial eyes, take care to please the ears, and do not allow any bitterness (*amaritudinem*) at all to come out of your mouth which, having entered marital ears, might declare that you possess an unsightly soul. Show rather how beautiful of soul you are, how beautiful in intention (*voto*), and how fine (*elegans*) you are in the service of charity, how charming (*decora*) in compliance to a command (*iussionis*), so that – bound by consideration of this – [your husband] may cease to keep his own counsel, and will receive your whole will as a divine pattern (*regulam*)[38], and shudder at your displeasure as at sacrilege.

CHAPTER 8. BY COMPLIANCE HUSBANDS CAN BE WON OVER BY WIVES, AND CAN BE CALLED OUT TO THE GRACE OF THE HOLY SPIRIT FROM THE TRAFFIC OF THE FLESH

How blessed you will be when you have attained this result, that a wealthy citizen[39] should have been called to the service of holiness through you. How blessed you will be if, standing on that day [of Judgement] before the

---

[36] Following MS A, *sua*.

[37] This reading is based on Morin's emendation of '*curam*' for '*coram*' (MS A) and '*te iam*' (MS C).

[38] On the semantic range of 'regula' in this period, understood as, e.g., 'norme di vita apostolica', Salvatore Pricoco, *L'isola dei santi: il cenobio di Lerino e le origini del monachesimo gallico* (Rome, 1978), 82ff.

[39] MSS M and C substitute 'maritus tuus' for A's 'adsiduus' (A represents the *lectio difficilior*). This meaning is known in late antiquity: 'Assiduus dicebatur apud antiquos, qui assibus ad aerarii expensam conferendis erat', Isid. *Orig* 10, 17.

tribunal of Christ, you are able to say, 'see, Lord, this man whom you ordered me to take as my husband, I have guided him by such great compliance of manner (*obtemperantia morum*),[40] that he proved never to be opposed to my will. When once through great forbearance I achieved this, I immediately urged on him the need for him to worship and give thanks to You, so that exactly as I obeyed him when giving orders, so he should listen to You, gracious Lord, when you instructed him ; and exactly as I shunned all those things which he prohibited, so would he abstain from everything which Your holy law prohibits.'

For how wicked it would be, how very bitter if, God forbid, being bound in the knots of any sins, he should cry out before the Judge: 'The woman whom you gave to me, it was she herself who caused a spirit of fury and anger to overmaster me and caused me to sin by her constant contempt, I fell into this crime because of her, because of her I ran headlong into that charge, her sloth has caused this sin, her haughtiness has caused that one.'

What trembling there will be then, what darkness, what wailing when, after being summoned so many times, warned by the prophets so many times, urged on by the apostles so many times, encouraged by the Gospels so many times, the day of death finds us still incorrigible. Indeed, let this be the punishment for those people whom no fear of hell at present perturbs and no love of the kingdom of Heaven draws on. Your female slave certainly takes on a husband on this condition, that both of them should be subject to you in their servitude, and if the man she takes on as husband happens to be sprung from a free-born line, union with her nevertheless brings him under your rule. And is it not impermissible that, through your handmaid, you yourself should obtain as slave a man who owes you nothing, and that through yourself as His handmaid God should lose His servant, a man he bought with his own precious blood?

We have read that certain people in Palestine[41] once perished in the following way. A married couple used to use the same, too-often repeated words of abuse between themselves and when, at a banquet and inflamed by mutual insults, they were pelting one another with bread, in which God

---

[40] Compare Augustine, *Ep.* 262.5 to Ecdicia, on managing a husband: 'infirmus enim erat et ideo tibi, quae in communi proposito fortior videbaris, non erat praesumptione turbandus sed dilectione portandus . . .'

[41] Morin, 'Un traité inédit d'Arnobe le Jeune', *RBen* 27 (1910), 156, specifies that the 'Bishop of Seleucia' who appears below must be the bishop of Seleucia Pieria, presumably because of Syria's proximity to Palestine. However, we know from the travels of Egeria that Seleucia of Isauria was on the pilgrimage route to Palestine. Neither Seleucia, however, fell *within* Palestine at any point, but *in Palestinam* is occasionally used in late Roman sources as a general term for the Near East. The source of the anecdote is unknown.

established the height of his mystery, a figure appeared to them, the story goes, bearing a flaming sword and, before striking them, he addressed them in the following way. 'Do not any further provoke God,' he said, 'whom you ask for daily bread only in order to fatten your devilish ire. The divine retribution attends you, that you may perish by this [*isto*] sword.' The ears and the sight of all were blocked; the only ones able to see and hear were the two themselves, who were struck down by the fiery sword. The blow was hidden from all, but the punishment was plain to all. They were allowed to survive for one month in their suffering. Judging the crime to be one to which the mercy of penitence should be denied, the bishop of the city of Seleucia when asked would scarcely have bestowed a penitence on them [at all], had he not been much influenced by many in a line of reasoning in which the brief extension of life to the wretches was said to be for the purpose that they should not be punished to the full. Hear how wrong-doing associates itself with anger, hear how much godlessness crime lets in: both hear and beware, you people in whom that evil dwells not as an occasional fault but as a habit. These people have been cut down before the Day of Judgement and are receiving the punishment for their deed before the time of retribution. Somehow those already dead cry out, and call upon us as witnesses. 'Do not', they say, 'do such things as we have done, lest you should suffer what we are suffering.' You see that both could have been saved by one: you see how much happiness she could have introduced on the spot, had she soothed her bad-tempered husband with due endurance (*patientia debita*), and by the embrace of legitimate sweet-talk, freed the man whom the Enemy had bound tightly by the fetters of ire (*iracundiae nodo*).

CHAPTER 9. IT IS BETTER TO TEACH THE THINGS TO BE AVOIDED RATHER THAN THOSE TO BE SET ARIGHT [AFTER THE WRONG IS DONE]

My lady, I am setting out this matter of the behaviour of others for you to learn what you should guard against rather than trying to root out problems after they have arisen; I am pointing out the pitfalls set up in the dark places of the world, and into which the careless rush and the heedless charge. I insist that I am not applying ointment to healthy eyes, but am pointing out the blind to the seeing, so that they should know what to steer clear of, if they are not to be afflicted by a similar blindness. For it is better to give warnings to the healthy than to the sick, and both divine and human laws are recited with pleasure by those at peace with themselves, but are heard by the guilty with anguish and lamentation. What good is it to a

murderess to learn the law only then, when she is being punished, to grasp
what she ought to have shunned only then, when she cannot call back the
crime into which she has stumbled? So let us shy away from evil actions,
eagerly chasing after good ones; and, on fire with ardour for virtue, let us
not congratulate ourselves because we have avoided sin, but fear[42] lest we
lose the rewards made ready for us. For standing opposite us is a hostile
adversary, fully armed in order to strike at once at the exposed target of the
Faith. And so the shield is not to be thrown away, in case one's flank is
exposed; nor is the sword to abate in case the Enemy should begin not to be
afraid. What is more, once he has seen his opponent is fully armed, he will
lose his daring.

CHAPTER 10. A VIEWING-TOWER IS SET UP IN
CONTEMPLATION, ASCENDING WHICH THE SOUL TURNS ITS
ATTENTION EITHER TO THOSE WINNING OR TO THOSE LOSING,
IN ORDER TO IMITATE THEM

Now climb this tower, which is set in this life, and look from it to the
battle-lines of those who are fighting. Look from the right-hand side of
the tower, so that you see not the losers, whom you mean to flee, but
the winners, whom you should imitate. Both because you have raised the
standards of the Church of Christ the king within the palace (*intra
palatium*)[43] and have taken up arms against the Foe; and because, posted
(*posita*) on campaign in the passage through this life, for you it is there
[that] you must fight against the army of vices and for the defence of the
virtues, until you arrive at the higher court (*comitatum*) in which perpetual
peace reigns. Turning away, then, from the sight of the left side, look from
the right-hand side of the tower, and see on this field of battle the army of
souls fighting for each of the virtues. For it is the soul which is both victor
and vanquished, which both takes and is taken prisoner. And on that
account we make mention of the soul in this context, lest the more fragile
sex believe the necessity of [fighting] this battle not incumbent on itself,
since the soul, moulded into a form without shape and constructed from
invisible materials, is not allocated by gender, but being invisible, allies
herself in an invisible act of consent either to good or to evil, either to our
lord Jesus Christ or to His Enemy, the patron of all crimes and the enemy
of holiness. So, then, I have placed you at the top of a high tower and laid

---

[42] From 'but fear' to the end of the chapter, the text closely parallels *Ad Clavdiam* 2, *CSEL* 1, 220.
[43] The reference is to Gregoria's location *in palatio*.

out for your eyes the view on the right side; and next, with the pointing finger of the following little speech, I will indicate to you the battle of every single one of them. The battle with these adversaries is a real one; they cannot be bought off at any price; and there is no other route, except through the middle of this battle-line, by which one may journey to the city of Jerusalem, in which the true King reigns with his victors. And so, everything whatsoever that presents itself as an obstacle to those wishing to pass through [the line] is a battle-engine of the Enemy: happy or harsh, sweet or bitter, favourable or adverse, such things as may try to hold back a man moving forward are well known to be devices of the Enemy. In true combat, one must have a true opponent, and especially the person who knows he or she is pushing on to that place, where only the victors can enter. So, look with interior eyes from the height of this tower, to which the wisdom of Christ has led you, and see the soldiers of Christ fighting mightily for each of the virtues in turn, and see that not a single one of those attacking or defending slows his pace, however far he has come. Look at the swords, the spears, the pikes, the bows, the arrows and quivers: see that the adversaries do not let up, and see the soldiers fighting back relentlessly. Pay particular attention to the King of the Vices himself, and how in answer to the downfall of any one of the sins he calls forward the [most] effective soldiers: for when he sees one of his army wounded, for example when he sees mendacity grievously wounded by a soldier of Christ, the Enemy himself, in the place of his general, opposes with the barbs of the following arguments that soldier as he fights back, and he harasses him with these taunts.

CHAPTER 11.[44] THE BATTLE OF TRUTH AGAINST FALSEHOOD[45]

'Why, madman, do you turn the enmity of humankind against yourself? Truth gives birth to hate, separates friends, sharpens up enmities, stokes up wrath, and inflicts loss on its followers in proportion to how well they have guarded it.'

You have seen arrows striking the soldier of God in a dense flight: look now at what kind of sound his cuirass gives off when battered. 'My truth is Christ, who alone is enough for me against the enmity of all the world, and

---

[44] Generally, the pattern in the next few chapters is that the vice speaks first, accusing the addressee and misunderstanding her Christian intentions, then the narrator introduces her defence by the relevant virtue.

[45] *mendacium*: Salvian, Cassian, Chrysostom, and the *Passio Sebastiani* permit *mendacium* in certain kinds of situations; Augustine does not (*De mendacio* and *Contra mendacium*).

who provides abundant compensation for any loss. And if riches are to be sought, what is richer than Christ? Or if enmity is to be feared, what is worse than his hatred? And if friendships are to be cherished, what better than His love? Or if anger is to be feared, what more ruinous than His indignation? And if wealth is to be embraced and losses fled, the more so those which know no end. But why should I be concerned with riches? Let wealth pass away and let riches vanish: Christ alone suffices for me, he alone is everything to me, everything is Him alone, who is the truth and the fountain of truth, whence everything flows that is true, so that everything that is false may be refuted.'

Look again to where my finger is pointing (*ad digitum meum*), for I will show you another division contending against that of avarice. For hear then how many times its sides are struck by the blows of weapons, though protected by shields.

CHAPTER 12. THE FIGHT OF LIBERALITY (*BENIGNITAS*)
AGAINST AVARICE

'Why are you proving, in a fruitless struggle, to be the enemy of your own wealth and wish by excessive liberality to be the ally of your own losses? All men, the mighty and the low, even the bishops of God, will look up to you and honour you only to the extent that you have money, and not to the extent that you have had the capacity to be holy. Why do you weaken your power (*potestate*) and grant away the profit from your own riches? For what else was the hand of the Enemy about to do to you, than that which your own hand inflicts? Better to let the coins remain in [your] purse; to let the seeds from the crops remain sound in the storehouse, for them not to be wasted on the lowliest of people but planted out in the most fertile fields; and to let wines marked on the exterior [with the stamp of] consuls of old remain untouched on the barges, so that their wholesaler is prompted by their bouquet into pouring out his money to you. Is it not ridiculous to weigh out your harvest on the little tables of the poor, and to pour forth your surplus oil for the little lamps of beggars? One has to consider those adverse conditions which habitually overturn good fortune in a sudden, swift reversal; they usually give guidance to any fortune wishing to transfer [itself] to someone else.'

We have heard the clang of blows rained down by the demons, let us now listen to the buckler of the good soldier bouncing them back: 'If the consuls of this world do not shy away from the profitless throwing away of their wealth, in order to enrich chariot-drivers and actors, and make brothel-keepers and mimes rich men, but rather glory in these excesses, so long as by this loss of possessions they purchase the favour of the contemptible crowd, why, with the approval of the angels, should I myself be afraid to offer a coin for the relief of the servants of god, a coin which I trust is to be given back to me a hundredfold by the right hand of my King (*regis mei dextera*)? And if the earth returns a seed more fruitful than when she received it, why should I not believe that it will be returned to me by the Lord Jesus Christ, especially when I have His signed contract (*chirografum*) of promise and warning: *Amen, Amen, I say unto you, whatever he has done to the least of those who believe in me, he has done to me?*[46] I am saying that I possess the pledge of Him whose word alone one could trust without that signed contract; he promises that he himself will return a hundredfold together with eternal life, and will make restoration in that place in which there is no end to a life of delight. For in this world everything that I experience is uncertain to me, and – as in a dream – I perceive what passes as a sort of shadow. And so I must not miss a good deal. I will indeed give up small things in order to receive the large ones; I will let go of what is temporal, so that I may discover the eternal. For why should I be afraid to give of my own accord what an idle heir (*otiosus heres*) makes off with against my will (*mihi invito*)? For that reason I make over the things that are mine to Him, because I am not able to take them away with me. I will make altogether my own that which in truth is not my own, and I will show my true love for my riches, when I have sent them ahead of me instead of letting them perish. I must press on to reach the most sacred retinue, from which I will no more be allowed to absent myself; in that far place I will build myself a house; there I will build storehouses.

And because no conveyance, no beast of burden, on which I might convey my riches to the other side, will have been able to enter there, I will set all of my belongings on the shoulders (*cervicibus*) of the servants of God. With these porters nothing of mine is allowed to perish; it is necessary that those of whom Christ is the teacher, and the holy angels the protectors, be the ones to carry my riches to the heavens. Let the stomachs of the poor, in which Christ witnesses that he both hungers and is filled, be the storehouses for my crops. Why should an heir mock me with a false blessing, and with lying lips wish [me] life while he grumbles in his heart that [my] death comes slowly? I have been taught by Christ, how my riches may go on my path before me, so that they cannot be without me.

Avarice, it is through him that I have taken up arms against you in this wonderful manner: I have been seized by a greater avidity than you yourself

---

[46] Cf. Matt. 18:5–6, Mark 9:42, Luke. 17:2.

were able to urge. To this end, money-lenders, convert (*convertite*) both your rapacity and your souls: for I have found a most reliable and fitting debtor, to whom we may lend for a hundredfold return. He has never cheated anyone; He has caused absolutely no one to lose what He took into His possession, for he does not request what he has borrowed in order to make use of it, but in order that he may return a hundredfold what he has received. He is in need, in order that he may enrich; he hungers, in order that he may refresh; he asks, in order that he may grant; he begs, in order that he may bestow. Of course, emperors kept back gold and precious stones, and refused to lend them to Him, imagining they might lose them, while fishermen eagerly brought forth whatever they might possess – as it were, the earnings of a single hour.[47] For you see what glory the fishermen were worthy to receive, what ignominy the rulers to meet with. What glory do you think is shown in heaven by the angels to the living souls of those to whose dead bodies so much honour attaches itself on earth, when the knees of an emperor are bent to the memory of a fisherman? What have you ever bought, O miser, that is so great that you are unwilling to share the lot of those fishermen, by expending a coin which you may recover on favourable terms, and by showing mercy to those who serve Christ, and indeed to your own self?'

In response to this, I see Avarice, buffeted by a deadly blow, but supported by Faithlessness. It remains, then, that the soldier of Christ should strike at Faithlessness as well, so that when he has shattered the weapons of both, he may bring both captives under his own sway.

CHAPTER 13. THE BATTLE OF FAITHLESSNESS IN SUPPORT
OF AVARICE AGAINST THE DESPISER OF THE WORLD
(*CONTEMPTOREM MUNDI*)

These, then, are the arrows with which Faithlessness enters the fight to defend Avarice: 'Has specious beggary devised for itself a new way of lending, by which it may bestow fortune on those who are like itself? "Give", it says, "what you may receive a hundredfold in the Kingdom of Heaven." O insupportable argument (*articulum*) of beggary! What would indigence (*calamitas egestuosa*) not claim, she who will return what was given her after death, and this a hundredfold, with eternal life in addition? I, too, might undertake to offer such a bargain, that is if I should find

---

[47] Here the reference is possibly to Acts 4:32–5, the community of goods, coloured by Matt. 4:18–20/ Mark 1:16–18, the calling of Andrew and Simon Peter, who immediately cast aside their nets to follow Jesus.

anyone so daft that I could induce him to lend me a thousand *solidi* without hesitation which he is to get back in the underworld after he is dead. Where do you think this senseless person is lurking, who might think that as a dead man he will get back what he lent out as a living person?'

Finally, Faithlessness has brought out a sword for the defence of Avarice, up to now kept hidden in a sheath, and – not knowing that the soldier of God is clothed beneath his/her linen by a breastplate – she thinks that [the soldier] can be pierced by this point (*mucrone*). Look out from the height of the tower, and lend your ear for a little while, and hear the One bringing his armed and triumphing right hand to bear upon the neck of Faithlessness. 'Come here, O wretched Faithlessness, come here, I say, and converse with me, the One making this promise. Point out anyone who has at any time regretted that he or she had placed trust in Him: I on the other hand will hold forth a countless populace, who rejoice in having done so. You, show someone who has lost that which he or she had lent; I will show that he or she has received more than a hundred times a hundred thousand. What, I ask, did John, what Peter, what Andrew, what did James scorn? On account of His name, they scorned the poor man's small fishing net; what do you think they gained? Reckon it up, if in fact that which is immeasurable can be reckoned.

Examine thoroughly, then, if you please, the question whether [the gain] can either harm or help someone after death: both so that you confirm by impossible and irrational signs that very promise [that is], according to you, impossible and irrational. For the leper cannot be healed by touch, and yet he is certainly healed; demons cannot be put to flight by a command, and yet by a command they were to flight;[48] a flow of blood cannot be dried up by the touch of garments, and suddenly it dried up on brushing against them.[49] At a single word of command, a paralysed man cannot possibly get up and then be ordered to carry away the bed on which he was lying as proof of his fully recovered health[50] – both of which were accomplished by the One ordering. How is it that five thousand banqueters got their fill from five loaves of bread,[51] seas were traversed by dry feet,[52] and the dead – already in their tombs – were raised up as though merely asleep,[53] He gave commands to the blowing of the winds,[54] and by an

---

[48] Cures of demoniacs: the Gerasene demoniac: Matt. 8:28ff.; the daughter of the Syro-Phoenician woman: Matt. 15:21ff.; healing of the epileptic: Matt. 17:14ff.; demoniac of Capernaum, Mark. 1:28.
[49] The woman with the issue of blood: Matt. 9:20.   [50] The healing of the paralytic: Matt. 9:2ff.
[51] The feeding of the five thousand: Matt. 14:19ff.   [52] The walking on the sea: Matt. 14:25ff.
[53] The raising of Lazarus: John 11:38ff. The words 'mortui . . . excitati sunt', are difficult, and perhaps best interpreted as an unsuccessful chiasmus.
[54] The stilling of the storm: Matt. 8:24ff.

invisible power broke the stones that were set to restrain bodies, from which the dead, rising, could bear testimony for His truth?

O Incredulity, what is left for you, from which you might live? You have been destroyed by the standard (*vexillo*) of faith, for all these wonders have been performed by Christ and His disciples to this end, that no one might justifiably be made by you to doubt whether he or she can receive a hundredfold, and eternal life besides. He confirmed impossible things therefore and things lacking in reason by signs both impossible and unreasonable, so that He could take away from you, O Incredulity, any power by which you could be given life. For after the Resurrection He was seen not only by Peter, but by all the Twelve, and not only by the apostles but even by more than five hundred brethren at the same time.[55] And because He promised that he would return riches in heaven, He ascended to heaven with all the apostles watching, and we are strengthened – so that we may be fearless – by the testimony of not two or three witnesses (which would be enough), but by the witness of a greater number than is necesssary for belief, namely of those who in His name raised the dead, and were performing the wonders which might confirm their claims (*asseverantia*).'

Behold, you have seen the soldier of Christ at the victory memorial of Faith, a victor over Avarice and Faithlessness; now see which arguments he will use as weapons to fight against Gluttony and Voraciousness.

CHAPTER 14. THE BATTLE OF ABSTINENCE AGAINST GLUTTONY

'Why do you [masc.] vex yourself with idle and worthless pains? Why do you give yourself over before death to deadly torments, why do you deny bread to your stomach which is the victim of hunger, and despise (*abuteris*) like an ingrate the grand banquets given by God?'

I do not want you to reckon that my speech is contrary to the divine word, since you will be well aware that the Lord Himself said, *Not the things which enter into the mouth, but the things which come out of it, pollute a person* [Matt. 15:11]. Now pay attention to the soldier of Christ steadily striking the adversary with his missiles. 'I know this saying of my King is an objection to the Judaic superstitions, by which the meat of cattle is declared pure, the meat of pigs impure, and all the practice (*observantia*) of holiness is dedicated to discrimination among foods; the cuttle-fish is avoided, the eel fled, and the blood of the just is unhesitatingly poured out, although it is feared to spill that of the pig. With this saying (which you are using

[55] Cf. 1 Cor. 15:5–6.

against me) Christ accuses the hypocritical teachers of these superstitions; He teaches His soldiers, then, so that they may vanquish you by prayers and fasts and that just as in the beginning you gained the upper hand by a man eating, and just as you rejoiced that the ones eating were cast out of Paradise, so now you may mourn that the fasting have entered the Kingdom of Heaven, with the Lord himself offering guidance to His soldiers, and distinguishing between the two paths in this saying: *enter by the narrow gate, for the path that leads to death is wide and spacious, and they are many who enter on it* [Matt. 7:13]. You yourself also, most artful inventor of persuasions, when you had challenged him to make loaves from stones so that with them he could relieve the hunger of the [flesh of] man He had taken on, did he not cast you down with the utterance of this refutation, in which He said, that *a person does not live by bread alone, but by every word of God* [Luke 4:4]? Whence he even saw fit to order us, saying, *take pains for the food which does not perish* [John 6:27]. Moreover, let the body be in need, so that the soul may feast, for I hear Christ exclaiming in the Gospels: *Woe to you, who feast in this world, because in the next you will be hungry* [cf. Luke 6:25]. And so you strive to call me back from fasting, as if I did not know that Jacob, become fat, gross, and swollen, abandoned the God who made him and departed from the God of his salvation. Surely I will eat, I will eat of the banquets of the divine precepts, I will eat and drink without end. I will suffer no sluggishness from the food, no drunkenness from the wine, nor will I suffer any discomfort from satiety.'

Behold, you have seen a most diligent soldier wresting the standards from the enemies of his king and bringing them back to the camp; now in his place see with what kind of weapon the enemy strives to kill another fighting against the desire of his own flesh.

CHAPTER 15. AGAINST DESIRE OF THE FLESH [*CONCUPISCENTIA*]

'Are you the only solider who is to be rejected by the mercy of God? Look at that one, inflamed by the heat of youth, that one swollen up with desires, that one dedicated to licentiousness, and that one having feasted on every pleasure, who have suddenly attained a remission of the charges against them. For just as immaculate youth loses the reward for its purity of morals (*castitas*) if it has sinned in old age, so the immodest flame of youthful licentiousness (*luxuriae*) will not be able to pose an obstacle, once it has been extinguished by the chill of old age. For only then indeed will you present to God the fruit of purity (*castitas*) in a blameless manner, when you disdain the beautiful [fem.], esteem lightly the desirable [fem.], and shudder at the very things [neut.] which are agreeable in the present [world].'

You have heard with how forceful a blow the enemy struck the soldier of Christ: now hear by what kind of loud whirring of spear the soldier drives back his opponent. 'That comeliness which you have brought to me as a pretext for licentiousness, I will honour for the praise of its Maker, so that glory may be to the Creator, when his creature is praised. Certainly, if beauty is something to be loved, what can be found that is more beautiful than purity (*castitas*), or more refined than modesty, since we ourselves become beautiful as we willingly strive for it? Accordingly, modesty surrenders our gaze [pl.] freely to heaven, having in itself far greater delights than the embrace of the flesh. In sum, from its mouth, a serene manner of speech (*oratio secura*) is brought forth, gaiety is enjoyed, and wholesomeness is attained. For how is it that the pleasures of shamelessness are so sweet, since lust itself, being deceptive and poisonous, is as sweet to behold as it is deadly to the touch? Why do you tinge the rim of this poisonous cup for me with the honey of duty towards God (*divinae pietatis*) so that the sweetness which is tasted first at least superficially cloaks the subsequent venom? Why do you believe that as a young man (*iuvenem*) I am unable to shoulder that burden which as a tiny child (*infantulus*) I bore without shirking, and which as you [masc.] yourself maintain, I will be able as an old man to carry?

'It is wrong for me to bow to justice less while I am capable of more, and only to wish to serve modesty at that time when shamelessness has scorned to have me as her servant. For the saints do not accept something which has been rejected, nor is the offer of that gift which the usurper (*tyrannus*) has cast off accepted by the king, nor does the rich man accept what the beggar has disdained as not worth having. Finally, why should I risk things which are certain for the sake of uncertain ones, and having lost what I now possess, take up at this point what I am uncertain whether or not I can find? For what kind of thing is it, then, if, like a madman, I exchange the friendship of the king which I have for his displeasure, to beg tearfully for the forgiveness of the one whose service I had borne? It must be added, that there is no state of human life and no certain measure by which I can be sure that I may obtain forgiveness through a final supplication. Accordingly I must look to death, and guide my mind's whole attention toward it, because although the fact of it is certain, its time and circumstance are unpredictable. Considering this, then, I have given myself over to the embraces of purity (*castitas*), so completely that I would not allow myself to be severed from her even if I could both learn which day would be my last, and clearly know the hour at which I will be called to return [to God].'

Behold, you have seen a man contending on behalf of love of purity of morals (*castitas*); now see the lover of endurance counting all adversities as nothing for the sake of her love.

CHAPTER 16. OF ENDURANCE

Endurance is brought forth through injury to property, through times of want and exile, and [the soldier] follows her with a light heart: through the defiance of a slave, through the betrayal of a friend, through the loss of riches, through the scorn of mortals, through the ruin of slander, through the dissension of loved ones, through the reproaches of kinsfolk, through other people's disparagement, through need, through hunger and thirst; and too, through the very variety of torments endurance hastens and takes care, and the one who loves her never forsakes her at all. I beg you, listen carefully to the sort of enemy darts, sent flying after her, by which Endurance is attacked.

'Where are you rushing to, you mad thing, where are you hurrying and bustling off to? Why do you open yourself to the reproaches of mortals and to the despising of the mob? See, everyone who looks at you is despising you, to such an extent that you have been made the censure of your neighbours. Was this the only way you found for pleasing God, that you should unflinchingly put up with maddening disasters, and should not quake at the animosity of mortals? Why, indeed, when you are accused despite your own knowledge of your innocence, do you refrain from speaking, so that you seem to confirm an accusation which you do not refute? Do rouse yourself, and speak: let the proud be met with a retribution measured to their cunning. Leave off being silent, now, with your head bowed; have a ready tongue for revenge in the defence of justice. For in you, virtue suffers an outrage, and modesty is tormented by the shameless. Others will have cause to fear, when you take vengeance on these: let each person (whom it may concern) meditate on what he or she will have to reckon with, and let him or her learn from other Christians what to fear, if he or she should be delivered by you to just punishment.'

Listen to the lover [masc.] of endurance [responding] to this. 'Oh, most ingenuous (*inperitissime*), nay, most deceitful (*dolosissime*) persuader to this madness! I flee impatience with her father, that is, the Devil, and I follow endurance, the daughter of the highest God: I flee the impious barbarian and you direct me to linger; as I follow the pious King, you prevail upon me to stop, so that the one whom I am following may distance him/herself, and the one whom I am fleeing may draw nearer. The person who is fleeing from a battle-line of swords in hot pursuit has no leisure for tarrying, and pondering over verbal affronts (*iniurias verborum*); the one who hears the roar of the pursuer behind him or her does not have time to linger and calculate the harm done by his or her attackers. While I am busying myself, making haste, and taking care, I could be taking refuge within the city. After all, let all [my concerns] perish, provided that I am able to escape the enemy, even stripped of my clothing. For clearly I can restore them, but they cannot restore me; I am more important than they, not they than I, since they were created on account of me and not I on account of them. But if punishment is to be demanded, it is not in a field where the sword rages that records can be drawn up and formal actions brought. In the field of battle, let conversation cease.[56]

I will not forsake Endurance, until I reach my most victorious King. It is Endurance herself who will offer me the safety of the city: let her bring me forward to the presence of the King whom I long for. When I entrust an affront (*iniuriam*) to His [masc.] care, He is a protector; when I make harm known to Him, He is a restorer; if I display my wounds, He is a healer. Oh, how much is granted to Endurance, that she should have God as her champion! Not unjustly: to be sure, He watches over all her actions, and is present in all her good deeds. She defends peace, sustains faith, drives away scandals, confers charity, preserves marriages in purity (*castitas*), refreshes virginity dedicated to God, sustains widowhood, assists those serving God, fosters (*vegetat*) married couples living in continence, bestows honour upon the priests of God, and strengthens the martyrs of Christ: she confirms the faithful one, encourages the friend, consoles the sad, comforts the sick, and sustains the needy. She is loved in children, praised in men, revered in the old, and extolled in women: She is beautiful in those of every dignity, either sex, or any age: she brings the wealthy into balance, raises up the poor, and sustains the needy.'

CHAPTER 17. THAT A WOMAN PLACED IN MARRIAGE SHOULD
SEARCH THE WILL OF GOD THROUGH HIS LAW, AND KEEP THE
COMMANDMENTS OF HER HUSBAND FOR THIS LIFE JUST AS
[SHE KEEPS] THOSE OF CHRIST FOR THE LIFE TO COME

See, I have set you atop the tower of wisdom, and I have shown you both those struggling (*dimicantes*) and those who are winning (*vincentes*). On this field of battle all the victors have become saints; there every day the glorious mother Church obtains passage with her sons and daughters, not one of her children will be able to reach the unconquered (*invictam*) city, who has not

---

[56] *Sileant inter arma sermones*: the reference here is to Cicero, 'silent enim leges inter arma' (*Pro Mil.* 11 and *Att.* 7.3.5)

crossed these lines by fighting. Whence the apostle, the trainer (*domitor*) for this engagement, warns his recruits with this saying: *Take up*, he says, *the arms of God, that you may be able to fight on the day of doom. For ours is not a battle against flesh and blood, but against the leaders of this world and the masters of the darkness* [Eph. 6:12–13]. So, dearest one [fem.], take up the weapons of God; they are not very heavy – nor should you fear feminine weakness; they are possessed of an easy yoke and a light burden. Indeed, you will be taking up arms, if you take pains to learn what you absolutely should and should not do. The writings of your King well known open to you, which you are by no means allowed to ignore, if indeed you do not deny that you are a daughter of the Church, who – when she conceived you and bore you and began to nurse you from the most pure milk of her own breasts – taught you this directly before all other things, that she might show you your Father in Heaven, to whom you might say, *Let Thy will be done on earth as in heaven* [Matt. 6:10]. Therefore see where you can look for the will of God: for unless you know it, you will not at all be able to do it.

Indeed, it is greater to do the will of God than to know it, but one must first know it in order to do it: the first precedes the second in merit, the second [precedes] the first in order. For it can come about that you stumble in your commitment to obedience, if you do not first learn how you ought to obey. No wifely necessity excuses you: *If you would attain life, keep the commandments* (*serva mandata*) [Matt. 19:17]. This is the voice of Christ, not of just anyone, who might be capable of telling an untruth. Tell me, sweet daughter, do you not wish to attain life, because you have been placed (*posita*) under [the care of] a husband? Without doubt you do. Accordingly, if you wish to attain life, keep the commandments. Perhaps you may say, I want to know what [kind of] mandates they are. Let no one seduce you with vain words: it is this you should hear as sufficiently truthful, which is veiled by no cloud of fawning or eloquence. So, then, you wish to attain life, and therefore, you wish to keep the commandments. I will show you the friends of life: let them instil their advice, let them instil His will into you; let them themselves acquaint you openly with the unadulterated (*mera*) commandments, just as they came out of the mouth of Christ. No man better than Matthew understands them, none more outstandingly than John; Luke has followed them step for step, and Mark did not break them in any way. These are the four witnesses of life: here you will find the commandments which you must keep. Let the pomp of human speech fall silent:[57] where the divine voice does not speak we make the ears ring by puffing out air; here the path that leads to Life (*vitae ratione*) is to

---

[57] *Sileat humani pompa sermonis*: now, a play on 'sileant inter arma sermones'.

be discussed. Listen to Life herself pronouncing her commandments. Do not
seek either the order or the number of the commandments in this little work
(*opusculum*): we hasten (*currimus*) to this end, that Truth be known in her
own works (*opusculis*), not in human words. And so read the God and Lord
Jesus Christ himself in His own works (*opusculis*) [the Gospels]. Don't let
anyone seduce you by vain proofs. If you wish to attain Life, read the writings
of the four witnesses: everything they say is Christ's; they have added nothing
their own. To be sure, we have assessed the order of the commandments for
you in this work, in order to explain them clearly, if briefly. And, if only you
have begun for the sake of your life to examine the Lord's commandments so
closely that you may keep them with your whole heart (because He ordered
that His commandments be kept with exceeding care), you will have to
discover that these great commandments are of two kinds, so that one kind
is of ordering and one of prohibiting: and just as it falls to you not to do what
is prohibited, so it falls to you to do what is ordered. I appeal to you, do not
examine too much or too little, that when you have read, you not open your
eyes to some commandments and close them to others, as if you had not read
them at all. For it is quite unjust if the divine law makes you fitted for the
requirement of your husband, but leaves you ill-suited for those of God, if it
orders you to do the will of your husband, and not to do that of your creator –
that you fulfil your husband's commands (*iussa*) for the sake of a brief life, and
do not see to the will of God for the sake of eternal life.

Take care you do not add yourself as well to the number of those women
who, faint from the poison of their carelessness, set their dainty dispositions
(*pectus*) against the divine banquets. For indeed, in order to excuse themselves by the appearance of being straightforward, such women deceive many
women in agreement with themselves by this stratagem: Nothing, they say, is
better than for each and every one to declare him/herself a Christian
straightforwardly (*simpliciter*). Tell me, commentator [fem.] on this saying,
what is so straightforward, as that you become acquainted with the writings
which your Lord addressed you, just as you have addressed directions to your
slaves? What so artless, what so true, what so harmless, as that you cultivate
the precepts of your redeemer with regard to yourself, by the same law as that
by which you desire that your slaves know and fulfil your will? And
conversely, what is so full of guile, so not-artless but rather cunning and
artful, as that you wish not to know [your duty] lest you do [it]?

Friends do not put up with it if their written instructions are neglected
even by friends, much less masters by their young slaves, or superiors by their
inferiors. But indeed if the laws (*scripta*) of the princes of [this] world be
overlooked, on one side you may see a sword threatening, on the other the

imperial treasury (*fiscum*) gaping open for your fortune. But those laws which punish here in the present [world] are not scorned, and those are scorned which punish in the future. It is not allowed to anyone to be unaware of these [earthly] laws, but not only is it profitable to be unaware of divine [laws], but even to know them is believed to be a sin. For that saying borrowed by the ignorant resounds throughout nearly the whole world: *Be not proud* (*noli altum sapere*), *but stand in awe* [Rom. 11:20]. O most ignorant, or rather most cunning crowd of sinners! You have read this saying only in Paul's book (*in codice Pauli*) but surely the following, too, is written there: *I entreat you, by the mercy of our Lord Jesus Christ, that you seek to know what is the will of God, what is just and good, and what perfect* (Rom. 12:1–2). But whether you like it or not, he himself says, *be not proud, but stand in awe*. What, then, did he set for himself sayings struggling against one another, so that one would be destroyed by the other? No. What, therefore, does *be not proud, but stand in awe* mean? Look carefully at the lesser meaning of the saying, that you may understand the greater. So by saying *but stand in awe* after he has said *be not proud*, he has held you in check, who neglect the commands of your redeemer with a haughty neck, for he knows that arrogance is proud when it does not take care to know the will of its Lord, being untouched by awe.

As a result the divine wisdom gives testimony, saying: *who fears the Lord will seek to know what things are pleasing to Him, and his or her meditation will be on the precepts of the Most High* [Eccl. 2:19; 9:23]. For the Saviour Himself, too, proclaims in the Gospels: *come to me, and learn that I am gentle and lowly in heart* [Matt. 11:28–9]. And God proclaims by the Prophet: *Learn my will and learn to do good* [cf. Isaiah 1:17]. And the Holy Spirit: *Unless someone has learned righteousness on earth*, it says, *he or she will not serve the truth* [cf. Isaiah 26:10]. And, too, in the very beginning of the psalms a blessing is offered him/her alone, *who meditates on the law of the Lord day and night* [Ps. 1:2]. And he or she is called blessed and untainted who carefully examines the witnesses of the law, and with whole heart seeks to know them thoroughly [Ps. 118:1–2]. But why should I offer light as if to blind eyes, and call out as if to deaf ears, believing that I am calling forth to knowledge those who do not want to know the will of God? And if they do not care to know the writings of the Lord himself, when will they read my writings? You, then, outstanding ornament (*decus*) of all Christian matrons, if you recognize that you are a daughter of the Church, nourish yourself at her breasts and suck at her paps flowing with inviolable milk: for insofar as you approach there as one capable of faith, to that degree will you draw grace and piety there. I have above shown you the units of fighters, so that you might learn that you yourself could not arrive at eternal life except by the passage-way of this battle. Go to

Paul, the *magister militum*, so that he may place the breastplate of faith on you, and the helmet of hope and salvation [cf. 1 Thess. 5:8]. Run under the wings of the Church, where you will get an understanding of the divine teachings: for she herself protecting you under her wings teaches you how you may fight and win, so that protected by the shield of God's right hand you shall not fear a terror in the night, or a flying arrow in the day, or a problem prowling about in darkness, or ruin or the mid-day demon (*nec ruinam aut daemonium meridianum*)[cf. Ps. 90, 5–6]. Through these things you will be immortalized in that number, to whom it is said, *be still, and the Lord will expel the Egyptians on your behalf* [Exodus 14:14].

CHAPTER 18. A RESPECTABLE CHRISTIAN MARRIED WOMAN MUST BE SO HEEDFUL IN ALL HER WORKS AND IN THE CARE OF THE HOME, THAT ON NO ACCOUNT DOES SHE SCORN THE COMMANDS OF HER LORD, AND THAT TO THOSE WHO ARE UNDER HER POWER AND TO HER SLAVES SHE IS A GENEROUS MISTRESS (*LIBERALIS DOMINA*)

Consequently, if you wish the invincible mother to take you in under her wings, so that you may be worthy to enter there, where those enter who conquer the vices and hold to the virtues, although on account of the weakness of your sex you will have been left out of even the most trifling battle, and the giants[58] will have been taken away, and the enemies will be banished from the field, and the barbarians will be far from you to be sure, beware, please, lest you be shaken by a trifling blow, when (through one of your handmaids) wool or weaving has begun to unsettle you. For that age-old snake is artful in undermining the mercy by which God sees fit to protect us from the great temptations, and he goads you with exceedingly slight provocations, by which, God forbid, you may be induced to violate God's laws.

And directly, if you open well the ears of your discretion, you will hear him thus stirring up against you a dispute before God: 'Why do you take this woman away from my dominion, and add her to the number of holy women? You attach to the company of your attendants her whom you see slighting your teachings on account of a single thread, whom the cares of the mortal more than of the divine life concern, whose hands the crafting of human attire occupies more than the study of the holy writings (*lectio divina*)[59] sent from Heaven to earth, that your will be known to all. Surely

---

[58] The sons of Earth and Tartarus; cf. Claudian's *Gigantomachia*.
[59] See Jacques Rousse, 'Lectio divina et lecture spirituelle', *DSp* 9 (1976), 470–510.

she herself should be both her own witness and her judge. Now if she herself were to address writings to her slaves, in which she prohibited some things and ordered others, would she not lament if they were despised, and by some sort of severe punishment crush this scorning of herself? How can you suffer her with impunity to disregard what is sacred to you, and with impunity not to know, and, not knowing, not at all to do [your commandments]? Or is it from some other cause that one of her handmaids, weighed down by a burden, importunes you, and tearfully appeals to your favour? Or is it not on this account that one [of her household] is hungry, that one is naked, that one goes about ragged, because she entirely neglected the doing of those things which your justice (*aequitas*) wished to be known and fulfilled? What slave of her household did she ever bring up for you out of her own means? Which of her little maids (*ancillulis*) has she dedicated to your service? When has she enforced a rule of your discipline which had been neglected by her slaves (although to be sure she never passed over an instance of herself having been taken lightly)? Which day brought her afresh into your presence? Which night made her remain awake, having been snatched from sleep on account of your love? – especially since she should have made you the equal of human love, to the point of desiring you (her redeemer) as much as she has desired her husband, whose salvation she has obtained by the generosity of your favour.'

Blessed are you [fem. sing.], if you bear in mind these menaces of the Enemy, and examine all you are about to do or say beforehand by a careful consideration within yourself! There is no means by which things said or done can revoked. Let no handmaid groan under a heavy burden, nor let any mistake of weaving agitate you. Let a garment of reverence (*pietas*) be woven for you by your handmaidens, which no moth may eat away, nor old age weaken, so that in like manner they may wish life to a mother and not death to a taskmistress. Let the widows weave [tunics] for you woven with gold, the virgins of Christ [weave tunics] of silk, when they present themselves (*se repraesentant*) before your Lord, decked in your gifts. Then you will have these clothes prepared for putting on when your Creator orders you to lay aside the garment of this body; then, I say, you will put on exceedingly splendid clothes, when you will have cast off the garment of the body. Take care, I beseech you, Lady, that no one should see filthy limbs (*squalentia*) among the rags of any one of your home-born slaves (*vernaculorum*), lest any one of yours should freeze in the cold of winter on account of poverty; let none suffer hunger, none be wearied by starvation, none by beatings, for there is not one of your slaves – male or female – for whom you may believe that you will not have to give account before God. For to this end mortals were made masters over other mortals, that they might receive the care of the image of God during its sojourn in this world, and should keep safe the riches destined for souls, which the plunderer of all that is good bestirs himself each day to snatch away.

So then be a model (*forma*) for all your servants: let them see you boldly standing guard over the riches of truth in your mouth, and of the riches of purity (*castitas*) with respect to your body, of reverence (*pietas*) in your breast, of innocence in your hands, of integrity in your expression. Let them see your eyes continually lifted to the heavens, let them see that the jewels of your ears can in no way be snatched away by the verbal piracy (*piraticis sermonibus*) of your detractors, nor the boundaries of your charity be violated by a deceitful garrulity (*loquacitate*). By this model (*exemplum*) you will secure your own salvation and that of those [women] over whom you have been worthy to rule. For what they have seen you love, they do; what they see delight you, they imitate. They will call on God continually, and they will bend their knees to Him, by whom they [fem.] were made. When you were present, not one of them should ever have dared to speak impudently, or – what is shameful to mention – to gossip in base, vain, and empty chatter; for your ears reveal your character. You are believed willingly to do what you have been seen willing to hear. Be adorned by the society of friends [fem.] by whose example (*exemplo*) you may live: by whose endurance you may be made mild, by whose conversation (*alloquio*) you may grow in beauty. Do not be led by the feigned praises of fawning women of ill-repute; nor let the fluttering of hearsay make you either happy or sad: for you may see many women abandoning the witness of their breast, rejoicing in being what they are vaunted as being, and lamenting what they are believed to be. Believe me, a harmlessness (*innocentia*) which wants to live by the esteem of the harmful (*nocentum*) is not secure enough, for, after abandoning God – for whose sake one practises righteousness (*iustitia*) – it will be prey to the fickleness of humanity, and may cease to be what it wished to be said to be. For when public opinion (*fama*) is more important than the virtues, and the vices of others hold sway, [innocence] is set afire by the varied kindling of misdeeds. For one person delights in one vice, another in another, and both of them must be pleased, lest what we love be taken from us – a reputation, that is, that rises and falls in the world, and, just like the world, is bound to pass away. But you, my Lady, while you pass through these dregs of corruption (*feculentas clades*), sing out the verse of the 52nd psalm, saying, *God has scattered the bones of those who please human beings: they are bewildered, because God has rejected them* [Ps. 52:6]. And say also with Paul the Apostle: *if I wished to please mortals to such a degree, then I would not be a handmaid (ancilla) of Christ* [cf. Gal. 1:10]. And hear the voice of the Lord Jesus Christ in response to this, saying, *woe when mortals will have praised you and blessed you* [Luke 6:26]. Whence he encourages his apostles with this word: *By this*, he says, *know that you are my disciples: if the world have hated you* [cf. John 15:18ff.]. But I cannot see at all how I should mention this without a sigh, for the divine authority has been led right up to the point that it is warning, that *he or she is made the enemy of God whom the world cherishes* [James 4:4]. O, I am a wretch! What will we do, that the world should not love us, lest in our wretchedness we should fear that God hold us in enmity? Let us hold to righteousness with our whole heart, and we will have all the unjust as our enemies; among the unchaste let us hold to modesty (*pudicitiam*), and we will be accused as shameless (*impudici*). Thus Joseph, having endured his mistress,[60] thus Susanna the elders: lest they be unchaste, were reviled as being so; lest they be base, they were brought into disrepute, for if they had wished to serve not God but their own reputation, they would have made God their enemy. Behold, both we men are taught and women are taught as well by the example (*exemplo*) of these two: and we apply our minds to what needs to be done and what needs to be held to [during our sojourn] in the world. For we have come into the world on this account, that we may do battle. He or she is wrong, and greatly wrong, who prepares her/himself to dwell in the peace of this world or reckons the time of persecution to be [only] then, when martyrs are confirmed as sacrifices to God. Do not feign that you do not see what you are looking at – we do not wish to speak the truth, lest we displease others. For the battle through which we may justly attain the crown of the martyrs as victors, if we struggle with an unspoiled valour (*sincera virtute*) of spirit, is for all time.

CHAPTER 19. HOW MASTERS (*DOMINI*) SHOULD BEHAVE
TOWARD SLAVES

Conscientiously inspect and examine your own justice (*aequitas*) concerning your younger slaves (*servulos*).[61] As one who does not doubt that you will have to give account to God, analyse yourself in a conscientious examination, and ask yourself what you may have praised in that one, what in that one you may have punished, what you may have loved in this one, what you may have shrunk from in that one. For if, on the Day of Judgement, you pin your faith on Christ himself standing as witness, what explanation will you give for words spoken in vain? Why do you suppose yourself to be set apart (*te praeteriri*) from

---

[60] For the story of Joseph and Potiphar's wife, who accused him publicly of having made sexual overtures to her after he refused hers to him, Genesis 39:6ff.

[61] The force of the diminutive here is ambiguous: *servulus* can mean 'young slave', and this passage introduces a section on the education of younger slaves. Still, the diminutive here is also part of a larger pattern, with *oratiuncula* and *muliercula*.

the soul of humanity, for whom Christ poured forth his blood? Or rather do you not see that He cherishes nothing more in you than your character, nor – deferring to your noble birth – does He allow that you come to Him in one way and someone else in another way. You will enter the audience chamber of the mother Church in the same way as he or she does: father Christ speaks to you and to him or her with the same voice. He or she was conceived by the same heat of the divine seed as you were, and was born by the same birth of the mother Church: together with you he or she enters as guest to the King's presence, together with you, he or she is called forward as a friend. And do you think all these things can be passed over as really of the smallest importance, when an explanation about the matter is going to be demanded of you? O unbelief (*incredulitas*), begotten of the Devil! O mother of all worst things, and enemy of perpetual life, you who pass with closed eyes by Him who shared in human nature! Power that will fall swiftly, why do you trouble yourself? This one, whom the human condition has made your slave, the second birth has made to be your brother or sister. Or if because you believe too little, you do not look after him or her because he or she has been reborn, look after him or her because he or she has been born, since you do not feel too little.

Why do you exact [of others] what you are not strong enough yourself to bear, and impose a burden which you yourself cannot bear? You look down on the one weeping, in addition, you are more furious than you need to be with the one sighing, you laugh at the one who hungers, you set the worn out one back to work again (*reapplicas*), you set at nought the grey hairs of the old, and in all of these things you go beyond the legitimate contract of slavery (*ius servitutis*). I know you claim that these [your slaves] deserve all this. In that case, teach righteousness (*justitiam*), to prevent their deserving it. Admonish your slave as you are admonished by the Lord, and with encouragement offer them this saying, the saying which our Lord sees fit to offer us, saying, *Come, children, hear me; I will teach you the fear of the Lord* [Ps. 33:12]. Since in your household the childishness of the younger slaves (*servulorum*) spills over into unruly behaviour, and in the older ones you require what you neglected to cultivate in the younger, teach those of tender years what will make you happy in the future; and may it both find you a crown with the Lord, and in the present allow you to live in peace. With difficulty will you exact righteousness (*justitiam*) from them, who do not have it within themselves at all; and yet, they would have it, if they had received it when they were small. Is it other than if you unexpectedly compel a Hebrew to speak forth in Greek, or if you force a Greek suddenly to deal in Latin?

Hear the almighty God rebuking His badly behaved people: *If the Ethiopian*, He says, *changes his skin, and the panther (pardus) his dappling* (*varietas*), you too will be able to do good, although you have the habit of evil [Jer. 13:23]. Do you see, pray, that the fault is ours, if in the time for learning we do not teach good to those, whose faults entrenched by long habit we punish? Believe me, there is no other remedy left, except that we should conquer the bad with goodness, and prevail over the impious with piety. For it is impetuousness (*animositas*), rather than justice (*aequitas*), which has the habit of exacting revenge, allowing each individual to suffer what he or she has earned. And where is the passage, in which we call to God, *O Lord, if you mark iniquities, Lord, who will stand* [Ps. 129:3]? Or perhaps God loves mercy (*pietas*) where you are concerned, yet embraces justice (*aequitas*) with respect to your slave? And if you wish adequately to teach that God loves justice (*aequitas*), why do you teach and at the same time refuse to be taught? For anger (*animus*) arises veiled in the blasphemous darkness of wrath and proclaims itself the champion of righteousness (*iustitiae*), at the very moment it has expelled that very righteousness from its mind. And if God so loves righteousness that he does not spare sinners at all, how is it we are still allowed to enjoy the brightness of the day, and have not all descended into the avenging darkness of Gehenna, but rather we pray daily that our debts be cancelled?[62]

'But God loves discipline (*disciplina*)', you will say. I think you should be careful more on your own account than on that of your slave: for to the degree that your stomach is filled with better food, your body dressed in more expensive clothes, so much more does your soul demand to be adorned by better works of discipline, and to be furnished abundantly with rich and magnificent gifts. Most often, then, show your slaves your compassion (*indulgentiam*), and most often grant forgiveness of their offences (*peccatorum*). Because your Lord Himself took care that you know by His own witness: that just as you yourself have judged, so you will be judged, and just as you yourself have measured, so it will be measured to you. O mortal, if you followed this saying of the Lord with a whole faith, you would never belabour your badly behaved young slaves (*servulos*) with all sorts of blows. So it is that one is wearied with blows, another cast down, another driven out, another expelled, that one banished entirely from your presence, another handed over to a heavier yoke of servitude, and after this – cursing yourself – you yourself ask your Lord to forgive your debts by the same terms as [those by which] you have forgiven [the debts] of your slave? Behold, the day is approaching, in which you may be ordered to leave this body, and to be brought to your Lord's presence (*repraesentari aspectibus*): do you want,

---

[62] The allusion here to the Lord's Prayer develops a recurring theme, calling attention to the spiritual meaning of perhaps over-familiar liturgical practice.

then, for Him to demand this sort of reckoning for your misdeeds in order to impress Himself on you as one who is just (*iustum*) and a lover of discipline? To be sure, I believe firmly that unless He has shown us His mercy (*pietatem*) in every possible regard, we will be found guilty even on those things in which we [think ourselves] worthy of praise.

Therefore let us hasten (*festinemus*) to be the friends of mercy (*misericordiae*), yet let us not pull so hard on the reins of justice (*justitiae*) that we never allow her to run at all, but let us allow her to run in such a way that mercy (*pietas*) may overtake her. And let the former take care justly (*juste*) to reward the good, and the latter mercifully (*pie*) to raise up the evil, the former to punish offences, and the latter to absolve the dying of their guilt (*a reatu pereuntes*), the former to punish the guilty one together with the crime, the latter to rescue the criminal after the crime has been punished. And so let each be allowed to fulfil her own office, so that for the sake of salvation there may be as much the indignation of justice (*iustitiae*) as the gentle soothing of mercy (*misericordiae*); while one is angry at the wrong-doer, the other sustains the petitioner. In the end, your pattern of behaviour will be the teacher of everyone, from which fair dealing (*aequitas*) and mercy (*misericordia*) demand this, that without violation of kindness (*salva humanitate*), it should put away from itself those whose reform must be despaired of, with God Himself ordering, *Cast out from the council,* He says, *the contagious one and iniquity will depart together with him/her* [Prov. 22:10]. And indeed, a holy way of life does not endure what is inimical to tranquillity, even if that very thing seems to be indispensable to many other useful things, with the Saviour Himself ordering that if your right hand offends you, that is, if that one is the one whom you can use as a right hand in your dealings (*conversatione*), and this person offends you, that is, he or she makes an obstacle for the one wishing to live in a holy way, cut him/her off and cast him/her away from you, for it is expedient to live without this one person, [rather] than to be punished with him/her. This is why the holy Church condemns heretics as ones who will perish, and casts out of her assembly, because of a single fault (*pro uno incommodo*), those from whom she has attained great profit: the benefit is that once the evil person has been cast out, the rest may be able to continue steadfastly in good, so that the work of cultivation on behalf of the character of your slaves may not be made vain by his/her contagion. Rightly, take care most intently, lest you cling to the privilege of bodily nobility to the degree that you resolve to follow the examples set by your ancestors in a misguided way: but – having set aside all the good [precedents] – cut off the evil, which they now regret, and put them at a distance from yourself; nor should you press things that have been done badly even to the point of an increase of their punishment. For our forebears are weighed down, when we ourselves persist in deeds contrary to the divine precepts; so let us call upon God to have mercy on them while we put their misdeeds right. Why then do you slight your own soul, so that although according to the spirit it is the daughter of God, you make it emulate mortal forebears? Behold, the crackling of eternal fire and the strength of flames increase: reckon for me the nobility of your family (*prosapiae*), and you will begin to follow after the customs (*mores*) of your ancestors.

CHAPTER 20. IT IS BETTER TO PROTECT THE NOBILITY
OF THE SOUL THAN THAT OF THE BODY

I have said already, and now I repeat: believe me, the soul is much nobler than the body. For she is begotten from a heavenly lineage (*caelesti stirpe*), to whom God speaks, saying, *hear, daughter, and see* [Ps. 44:10]. Nor does He gratuitously call the soul his daughter, which He created as a sharer in His eternity, and which in a certain sense He made to be the body's God, whose seed is from Heaven, whose image resembles God, and the whole structure of whose members is angelic. By contrast, the nobility of the body is empty, its seed arises from depravity, its progeny from pollution, its very essence from dirt. Born from the filth of fleeting pleasure, it is dragged out from the birth pangs of a woman in pain,[63] drowned in the groans of a nursing woman. It arrives with its own weeping and with another's pain; it departs with its own pain and with another's weeping. In the meantime between its birth and death, surrounded by unpredictable circumstances, it causes and experiences pain; it is laughed at and laughs; it strikes others and is itself beaten; it is embellished and it spoils. Now in childhood, it tastes the bitterness of schooling; next, to youth, the ruin of sin is sweet; it glories in being robbed of holiness, it is delighted when it is seduced, and it hurries on to attain to the chains of sin. It buys life of a little time in exchange for the loss [entailed by] perpetual death, and it craves an exchange of the bitterness of eternal time for the sweetness of one hour.

Such are the stinking dealings of this body, such are the bargains made and accepted, so that the delight of a single hour may be given and a sadness which can never end at all may be endured. And, O sorrow! Believing we were made by God for this one thing, to persist night and day in the desires of the flesh (*carnis desideriis*), and – led by greed for those pleasures – we sense no harm to the soul. We prepare warm clothes for the body lest it feel the cold of winter,

---

[63] The curse of Eve: Genesis 3:16.

and cool ones for the summer, lest it be hot; for the body, lest it be hungry, we hoard food, and lest it be thirsty, drink; for the body, lest it be sad, we prepare enjoyments, and lest it be anxious, relaxations; for the body, houses are constructed shining with gilded panelled ceilings, decorated with precious marbles, and frescoed with unending wonders, for the body, elaborate furnishings, silver vessels are made; for the body, an abundance of sheep and fish and fowl is prepared; for the body, fragrant wines mixed with floral extracts are poured out; for the body, [we cultivate] apple orchards, vineyards; for the body, we purvey to the eyes whatever is beautiful, the ears, whatever is tuneful, the throat, whatever sweet; whatever is fragrant we covetously appropriate (*adferimus*) for our sense of smell, and – pity me! – subjecting even our very soul, which was made to govern the body, to the whims of the body, we do not allow it to meditate on anything, except what the habit of the body has ordered. What do you think we are counting on being able to say in God's presence, or what delay of this fleeting existence [are we counting on], that we are not ashamed of being willing still to be unprepared [for death]?

I believe we are expecting to say,[64] 'Lord, we did not know that You existed, You did not send prophets, You did not give the Law to the world, we saw no patriarchs, we read no examples of the saints' [lives] (*sanctorum exempla*), your Son was never on Earth, Peter remained silent, Paul refused to preach, the evangelist did not teach, there were no martyrs, whose example we might follow, no one foretold your coming judgement, no one commanded that the poor be clothed, no one urged that passion (*libidinem*) be checked. We fell by lack of information (*inscientia*) and we sinned by lack of knowledge (*ignoratione*); for those sins which we committed knowing no better, we deserve mercy (*veniam*).'

But perhaps it is the sheer number of our years that has prompted this calamity, so that we resist the temptations of the flesh rather feebly, while we contemplate life's great length. What do you think, will the years be so long that they do not pass quickly? What wealth (*census*) is so worthwhile, that for its sake we rightly may not fear a perpetual death? What do you think so delights, that it may never cause revulsion? What is so craved for, that it can create no aversion by over-satiety? Yesterday, crowned with roses and encircled in flowers, flashing with gold and resplendent with jewels, the king – as he was considered – marched in glory, accompanied by the praise of all the world. But today he is dead, and see, it will seem that he never existed at all. For now all is taken at naught which either does not exist at present or has ceased to exist, so that no wealth or money can restore it. But grant that

---

[64] From 'Lord' to the end of the paragraph, the text closely parallels *Ad Claudiam* 3, CSEL 1, 200–1.

we were able to subsist through the space of three hundred years and yet still on the last day, by ending life were to cut off what we have lived, I ask you, what sort of long duration is it, which is destroyed by an ending?

But we are fettered by the fragility of human nature – the very saying of this should be an offence to the Creator – if by this you mean that he originally made you so frail that you were not strong enough to defy His will, and now you cannot fulfil what He ordered. Let me allow for the time being, that, because, as you see it, the body, having been overcome [masc.] by the weakness of the flesh, you believe that all things should be furnished for it, lest the body be wearied by the discomfort of life itself sinking away. On what account do you charge your soul with having injured you? In what, I will say, do you establish that your soul is an enemy to you? In what is it hostile or arrogant, so that you prefer the pride (*gloriam*) of the flesh to it and place the enjoyment of bodily pleasure before it? Or, if you do not do this, show what kind of houses you have caused to be prepared for your soul in Heaven, when we see what kind your body has on Earth. Teach what estates (*possessiones*) you have made ready there for the soul, so that when you have been ordered to depart from these you will be accepted there by the inhabitants, that is, by the angels, and with Him introducing you, whose contract you kept here, by which He guaranteed that He would return a hundredfold all that you had paid out for His servants.

How heated will be the repentance then – God forbid – if the Lord should say to him or her: 'You have not provided for the needs of my servants, in whom I have given witness that I am both poor and rich, am condemned and lifted up, am refreshed and hunger, according to the contract (*chirografum*) which I offered you. O miser [*avare* – masc.], I wrote that with a ready will I would repay you a hundredfold; the provisions (*cauta*) speak, the writings witness, and lest there should remain anything whence the soul might doubt, I gave you the Holy Spirit as a pledge, who would not leave you until that day, on which you would receive all things a hundredfold. Where are those things now, which on earth you enjoyed possessing? For they all have passed away like a shadow, and leaving you behind, they have moved on to another person. Now someone else is gladdened by the things for which you are suffering punishment; another grows rich and profits, from whom you departed, needy and a beggar. What if he or she should profit to this end, that, believing my words, by the contract (*chirografum*) which you yourself [masc.] have despised, he or she lends at interest to my servants? Will you not be tormented endlessly by a redoubled mourning, both because he or she has spent the fruit of your cares on Earth, and because he or she has made himself or herself an eternally rich person in Heaven, by lending what had been yours?'

But why am I bringing up the reproach of the righteousness (*iustitiae*) of God, to your grief; it is either so you should lament because you have once and for all lost your riches, or that you groan because you [masc.] have suddenly been given over to eternal beggary? And would that these punishments, inflicted for scorning the Lord, were sufficient: for not even the binding flame of everlasting burning may make you amid the torments a companion of the one who called to Abraham, asking that the poor man Lazarus be sent to him, in order to dip the end of his finger in his mouth to refresh it.[65] O how blessed we would be, if we cherished our riches so much, that we never allowed them to be taken away from us, and sent them ahead to our own city, and took them away from this place, from the land in which we have become settlers, and, because we had proved that they could not in any way follow us when we die, we freely permitted them to precede us! But perhaps you think the saying of the apostle Paul is in vain, by which we are taught that, having here been stripped of the tunic of the body, there we will not be found naked and wretched [cf. 2 Cor. 5:3]? And if we do not believe that the righteous (*iustos*) are rewarded there with eternal riches, nor sinners punished by perpetual torments, how do we claim for ourselves the authority (*dignitas*) of the Christian name, which a whole faith engenders, and the work (*factura*) of all virtues fosters?

CHAPTER 22. THAT A CHRISTIAN IS [A] TRUE [CHRISTIAN] THROUGH THE TESTING (*EXERCITATIONEM*) OF THE CHRISTIAN LIFE; IF THE OBSERVANCE OF THE COMMANDMENTS (*MANDATA*) OF CHRIST CEASES, HE OR SHE CANNOT BE A TRUE CHRISTIAN

'Far be it from me', you say, 'that I should suffer myself to be added to the number of the unbelieving: I believe in Christ wholly, and I confess Him with the Father and the Holy Spirit in one Trinity.'

You will hear the apostle responding to this: *You*, he says, *believe that there is one God. You do well: even the demons believe, and they tremble* [James 2:19]. And listen as well to the same Lord Jesus Christ calling out: *why do you say to me, Lord, Lord, but do not do the things which I will?* [Luke 6:46] And again: *Amen, I say to you, that the person who hears my words and*

---

[65] The story of the rich man and Lazarus (Luke, 16:19ff.) is ubiquitous in late Roman sermons.

does them is the one who loves me [cf. Matt. 7:24; John. 14:21]. And again: *If you love me, keep my precepts (praecepta mea servate)* [John. 14:15]. And also nearing [the time of] his ascension the Lord Jesus Christ is said at the last to have handed down this [teaching] to his saints: *Go*, he says, *baptize all nations in the name of the Father and the Son and the Holy Spirit* [Matt. 28:19]. And having said these words, he was not silent, but added clearly what it is that can keep (*custodire*) baptism whole, saying: *teaching them to keep (custodire) everything which I have bidden (mandavi) you. And behold, I am with you, in all the days until the end of time* [Matt. 28:20]. Oh, most devout shepherd! Oh, unutterable protector (*custos*) of redeemed souls! I am with you, he says, during all the days until the end of time; moreover, keep whatever commandments I have left you. You see, therefore, that when we despise his precepts (*praecepta*), it is not He who abandons us, but we who shun Him. And we are making excuses, if we are heard somewhat later seeking mercy, we who pass with deaf ears over that saying, with which through [the Prophet] Zachariah the Lord warns those who despise him, saying: *Just as I called out*, he says, *and you did not listen, so will you call out, and I will give no heed, says the all-powerful Lord* [Zach. 7:13]. And indeed, is it not a thing of great arrogance (*superbiae*), that you should plead that you [masc.] have been despised by Him, Whom you yourself have already despised? Let him or her hearken before God, who hopes to be heard by God.

CHAPTER 23. THAT THE SAFEKEEPING (*CUSTODIA*) OF THE
DIVINE PRECEPTS (*PRAECEPTORUM*) IS INCUMBENT ON ALL
THOSE WHO CONFESS CHRISTIANITY, NOR MAY ANY CHRISTIAN
WITH IMPUNITY DESPISE THEM

'But these', you say, 'are not commandments (*mandata*) for married people.'

Listen to the voice of the Lord responding to this: *Every tree*, he says, *which does not produce a worthy fruit, is destroyed, and is put to fire* [Matt. 7:13]. This saying does not exempt any station (*dignitas*) or assign any exception whatsoever to spouses.[66] For marriage (*nuptiae*) would be bad, if it could not exist without deviation from the precepts (*praecepta*) of God. For when God blessed marriages (*coniugia*), and ordered that for the sake of a fruitful progeny both males and females should be born from the womb of mothers, He took counsel well enough indeed, and will have

---

[66] Chrysostom frequently stresses similar ideas, e.g. *Adv. oppug.* 3, 'The difference between [a monk and a regular Christian] is that one is married and the other is not; in all other respects they will have to render the same account.'

foreseen that men should be able to serve Him with their wives. For if the nature of marriage (*coniugii*) were such, that it might hamper those who wished to serve the Lord, never would the prince of the faithful Abraham with Sarah have been found acceptable (*placuisset*); nor would Isaac with Rebecca, nor Jacob with Rachel, nor Joseph with Aseneth, nor Moses with Zipporah, nor Joachim with Susanna, nor any at all of those have reached such a height of perfect worthiness (*dignitas*) before God, if the tethers of marriage (*coniugii retinacula*) had hampered them from so great an achievement. Finally now in our own time, according to what plan would Christ sanctify the yoking of marriage (*nuptiarum*) through His priests, if He knew it to be inimical to his precepts (*praeceptis*) to so great a degree, that it would debar those wishing to fulfil His laws (*iussa sua conplere*)? Or on what account would God by the mystery of the second regeneration[67] adopt as His children those placed (*positos*) in marriage, if He saw that being hampered by this bond (*hoc praepeditos vinculo*) they could not hasten toward His kingdom?

'But', you say, 'this is a great and a holy thing, allowed perhaps to those who hold to the good of the unmarried state (*singularitatis*) without pause; but these hidden and holy things cannot exist among the cares of the married (*coniugum*).'

Let us see, then, which is greater, the granting of a reward (*munus praemii*), or the observance of the commandments (*mandatorum custodia*). I believe that the observance (*custodia*) is lesser, and the reward (*praemium*) is greater: because the reward (*praemium*) is given for the observance; the observance is not offered for the reward. For the observance is in our own power (*in opere nostro*), but the reward is in the hand of God, which is paid out for the observance. And how can you [fem.], placed in marriage (*in coniugio posita*), demand to receive the reward (*praemium*) of life in the mystery of the body of Christ, if you assert that you are not able to keep (*servare*) the observance (*custodia*) for which it is given? For if you absolutely refuse to hand over your bronze coin to someone who has turned up to collect it in return for the completion of some job, unless he has absolutely finished what he came to be paid for, and not only do you not offer [payment], but you even become angry, on account of the outrage itself, that he has fallen short of the agreement (*a placito*), then why ever would God have given eternal life, adoption of [ourselves as His] children, the remission of sins, victory over enemies, participation in his kingdom and in his heavenly banquet, and the

---

[67] That is, the sacrament of baptism (Prosper of Aquitaine, *Chronicon* I.1252: 'sacramentum adoptionis' (*PL* 27, 709).

communion of his very eternity to married people together with all believers, if he perceived that they could not at all keep (*servare*) those [commandments] for which all these [benefits] are given?

God asks the impossible of no one: what he exacts of all, all could fulfil, if with their whole hearts they were to fly to His aid. The irresolute (*dubii*) perish, not because God despises them, but by their own vice. For He offers all things when He is asked, and, to put the matter more fully, He himself requires of us that He be asked: for no benefit is granted, excepting by Himself. And the devout donor: *Ask*, He says, *and it shall be given you: seek, and you shall find: knock, and it will be opened to you: for each who asks, receives, and who seeks, finds, and to the one knocking, the door is opened* [Matt. 7:7–8]. Consequently, by saying 'each who asks, receives', He has refused the petition of none, but He, who wishes to give to all, has wished that all should ask. It is we who cheat ourselves, then, by our own self-deception, and we who do not wish to change our own lives change the will of the Lord, saying in a sort of blasphemous explanation, that He does not trouble himself (*curet*) that we be worthy, who it is certain poured forth his blood for the salvation (*salute*) of all people, who it is certain can not in any way be an acceptor of persons. But you say that the fragile structure of human nature is not capable of carrying out the will of God.

CHAPTER 24. OF THE QUALITY OF HUMAN NATURE

Come now, consider the nature of your situation.[68] Do you think that your Creator made you with the intent of making it possible that through you a human being should carry out the will of a human being, and not of making it possible for His will to be fulfilled? Was His intent not to make it possible for human beings to be free from crimes, but rather for human beings to be sinners? Was His intent to make it possible for Him Himself to be despised, and not for what He has ordered (*iussit*) to be heard? Was His intent to make it possible for the will of the Devil to be enacted, and not to make it possible for the will of God to be enacted?

'But', you say, 'that searching and observance (*inquirere et servare*) are the duty of those, who are not held by the bond of marital union (*copulationis vinculo*).'

---

[68] *condicio*: situation, rank, circumstances. The meaning here can be construed in two ways: first, 'the married estate': cf. *TLL* s.v. *condicio* I.B, 'speciatim de -e uxoria, de sponsalibus vel nuptiis contrahendis, sive agitur de re uxoria sive de concubinatu', e.g. *Laud. Turiae* 2.35 (*CIL* 6, 1527), 'tu ipsa dignam condicionem quaereres p(ara)resque.' Or: 'your created condition (as a human being)'.

And how does Christ make you as a married person conform to His grace, if He perceived that His charity could not find a place in you through the charity of marriage (*per caritatem coniugii*)? How, then, does the Divine judgement (*sententia*) commend once-married [men as] bishops?[69] How does legal authority give preference to (*eligit*) once-married women (*univiras*)?[70] How is the Church open to all married people? How do wives together with their husbands as well, receive holy mysteries (*sacrosancta mysteria*) which they will not be able at all to obtain from the hand of Christ, if they have wished not to fulfil his orders (*iussa facere*), or if they have wished to effect what is forbidden? In truth, they seem to partake of the heavenly table, but they are only partakers of an earthly table; they seem to bear themselves about in the heights of the Church, but they are lingering in the lowest depths of Hell (*inferioribus inferis*); and no strength against the assaults of the Devil is gained from the divine banquets, by those who, made weak by vices and passions, despise the precepts of their Lord.

CHAPTER 25. THAT ALL SCRIPTURE AND ALL SOUND DOCTRINE POINT TO THIS, THAT HUMAN BEINGS SHOULD DO THE WILL OF GOD, AND THAT THIS IS THE ESSENCE OF JUSTICE

And so, ascending from the earth gradually, we reach the highest step (*gradum*), which is next to the heavens. Here everything is awe-inspiring, if we open the eyes of our souls. For we have attained the very gates of heaven: our eyes are already fixed on what we should long for. Accordingly, let us lift up our hearts (*sursum itaque corda*), as we have responded that we have done,[71] and, as we progress, let us avert our eyes entirely from below, lest, shaken when we look down by fear of the dizzying height and cast headlong by the whirling, we should tumble down into the lower depths from the very heights of heaven. Let the eyes be so fixed on heaven, that our feet mount this one step (*gradum*) with an unhindered gait; having done so, we will rejoice that we are within, where the everlasting joy of eternal life

---

[69] 1 Timothy 3:2.

[70] Morin emends '*universas*' to '*univiras*' on the basis of a presumed reference to 1 Tim 5:9 ('Let a widow be enrolled if she is not less than sixty years of age, having been the wife of one husband . . .'). See Michel Humbert, *Le Remariage à Rome: étude d'histoire juridique et sociale*, Università di Roma, Pubblicazioni dell'Istituto di diritto romano e dei diritti dell'oriente mediterraneo 44 (Milan, 1972) 360ff., on Christian-inspired reversal of the Augustan legislation preferring remarriage and compromising the legal status of the *univira*.

[71] A marginal note in MS A makes explicit the liturgical reference to the 'sursum corda'; in the Roman liturgy, the response to 'sursum corda' is 'habemus ad Dominum.'

abides. For this step is that one, which we promise the heavenly Father that we will climb. For as we beg for our daily dole of bread (*annonam*) we say, 'thy will be done on earth as in heaven.' Therefore, as we have said, this one last step is understood to remain, that we should most devotedly search the will of God, for in this door heaven is either closed or lies open to us. At this point all distinction of sex, age, station (*condicio*) ceases, for none crosses the threshold of eternal life, except him or her who has so ascended the steps of the will of God, that he or she steers entirely clear of what is prohibited, and adheres completely to what is commanded. Thus far the thread of this little homily has drawn you along to this, that you may learn that it is absolutely incumbent on you, that no aspect of the gospel teachings be unknown to you.

Search unceasingly, therefore, after that which it is utterly forbidden you not to know, and either on account of love for eternal life learn what you should do, or on account of terror of perpetual death learn what you should avoid. The sayings of Peter the Apostle and the recorded rulings (*responsa*) of Paul the legal expert will give you advice in this respect; the evangelists will show you the ways of your Lord, and they will devotedly suggest what he loves or dreads. Climb this one step which remains to you with a steady foot, so that the ascent of so great a mountain may help you onward, near to the starry heights. Press forward daily, and from day to day grow in the holy honours: let Truth call you her darling, let Purity (*castitas*) call you her sister, let Seriousness be a mother to you, let Wisdom count you as her own sister, let Reverence (*pietas*) be a kinswoman to you, let Mercy recognize you as a friend, let Faith hold sway in you, let Hope and Charity always attend you. Stand up straight among these ranks, noblewoman, and, exhibiting something like a holy arrogance,[72] pride yourself that you are a member of their company. Rejoice that among the blind you see, among the ill you have health, among the dead you live. Because of this your name is written in the Book of Life.

For the Lord has poured the light of his many blessings on you. And as that light spreads through your members He separates you from the shadows of this world, and makes you show forth varying capacities (*virtutes*) to all. Finally – before all else – Christ has in you a handmaid,[73]

---

[72] Jerome to Eustochium, *Ep.* 22.16: 'ad hominis coniugem dei sponsa quid properas? disce in hac parte superbiam sanctam, scito te illis esse meliorem'; see also Paulinus of Nola, *Ep.* 12.7.

[73] There are interesting epigraphic parallels in which a woman's importance to those whom she encountered is underlined, e.g. *ILS* 1259 '... munus deorum, qui maritalem torum/nectunt amicis et pudicis nexibus,/pietate matris, coniugali gratia,/ aetatis usu, consecrandi foedere,/ iugi fideli simplici concordia/ iuvans maritum, diligans, ornans, colens.'

the Church a worshipper, [your] husband a sweetheart, [your] children a teacher, [your] relatives one most dear, [your] friends a most extraordinary [friend], maidservants a mistress, orphans a mother, the sorrowful a bringer of joy, the anxious a consoler, the wretched a merciful one, the poor a protector, the oppressed a bulwark (*repugnaculum*), the weary a relief, the falling a staff, the labouring a help, and you are raised up by the intercession of all to whom you are bound by generosity in every way. United to the fellowship of Christ and the angels, at the same time you reject the whole of a world about to pass swiftly away with those who love it; already you embrace Him whom you love more than your husband – that is, the Lord Jesus Christ – along with that very husband. May He strengthen you and him by an ample felicity in His love, so that here in the present [world] you may rejoice in having escaped indictment on account of all your failings, and there [in the future world] you may be glad at having found perpetual glory.

Here ends – happily – the book of the blessed John, bishop of Constantinople, to the matron Gregoria. Lady, read my saving warnings. And rejoice in the Lord. You have carried out all these things before you read them. Live happily in God with your holy husband. And may the Lord from Zion bless you so that you may encounter good in all the days of your life, and the children of your children. Peace to your house forever. Amen.[74]

---

[74] The subscription of the Reichenau MS (recorded but not preferred by Morin) is 'Exp[licit] libellum iohannis episcopi constantinopolitani scriptum ad Gregoria[m] de officiis matronalibus vel quid uxor deo om[ni]p[otenti]. debeat quid marito.'

Bibliography

PRIMARY SOURCES

Anon., *Acephalous Bobbio Letter*, ed. Yves-Marie Duval, 'La Lettre de direction (acéphale) à une mère de famille du MS 954 de Vienne (CPL) 755: Édition des divers fragments dans leur ordre original', in Michel Soetard, ed., *Valeurs dans le stoïcisme: du Portique à nos jours* (Lille, 1993), 203–43

Anon., *Ad amicum aegrotum* (*PL* 30, 61–104)

Anon., *Ad Claudiam* 1 (*CSEL* 1, 219–23)

Anon., *Ad Demetriadem*, ed. Sister M. Kathryn Clare Krabbe, *Epistula ad Demetriadem de vera humilitate: A Critical Text and Translation with Introduction and Commentary*, CUA Patristic Studies 97 (Washington, DC, 1965)

Anon., *Ad Gregoriam in palatio constitutam* (*CC* 25A), also ed. Germain Morin, *Études, textes découvertes* (Paris, 1913), 383–438, repr. in *PLS* 3.

Ambrose, *Expositio in psalmum CXVIII* (*CSEL* 62)

Arator, *De actibus apostolorum* (*CSEL* 72)

Arnobius Iunior, *Commentarii in psalmos* (*PL* 53, 327–568)

Arnobius Iunior, *Conflictus cum Serapione* (*PL* 53, 239–322)

Athanasius, *Vita Antonii*, tr. Evagrius of Antioch (*PL* 73, 126–70)

Augustine, *De sancta virginitate* (*CSEL* 41, 235–302)

    Confessiones (*CC* 27)

    Contra Faustum Manichaeum (*CSEL* 25)

    De civitate Dei (*CSEL* 40)

    Contra Iulianum (*CSEL* 85 and 86)

    De bono coniugali (*CSEL* 41, 187–231)

    De doctrina christiana (*CSEL* 89)

    De vera religione (*CSEL* 77.2)

    Epistulae (*CSEL* 34, 44, 57, 58, 88)

    Epistulae ex duobus codicibus nuper in lucem prolatae (*CSEL* 88); this edition was subsequently revised by its editor (J. Divjak) as: *Lettres 1*–29*: nouvelle édition du texte critique et introduction*, Bibliothèque Augustinienne 46B (Paris, 1987); tr. R. Eno, *Saint Augustine, Letters VI (1*–29*)*, *FC* 81 (1989)

    Sermones (*PL* 38, 39); ed. F. Dolbeau, *Augustin d'Hippone, vingt-six sermons au peuple d'Afrique* (Paris, 1996); tr. Edmund Hill, *The Works of St Augustine*, part 3, *Sermons*, 11 vols. (Brooklyn, 1990–7)

Avitus of Vienne, *Epistulae* (*MGH AA* 6/2); tr. D. Shanzer and I. Wood, *Avitus of Vienne: Selected Letters and Prose* (Liverpool, 2002)

Boethius, *De consolatione philosophiae* (*CC* 94)

Cassian, *Collationes* (*CSEL* 13)

Cassiodorus, *Variae* (*MGH AA* 12); tr. S. J. B. Barnish, *The Variae of Magnus Aurelius Cassiodorus Senator* (Liverpool, 1992)

Cassiodorus, *Instititutiones divinarum et saecularium litterarum*, ed. R. A. B. Mynors (Oxford, 1937); tr. James W. Halporn with an Introduction by Mark Vessey, *Cassiodorus, Institutions of Divine and Secular Learning: On the Soul* (Liverpool, 2004)

Cassiodorus, *Ordo generis Cassiodori* (*Anecdoton Holderii, MGH AA* 12, v–vi); see in addition the edition and translation of A. Galonnier, *Antiquité tardive* 4 (1996), 299–312

Cicero, *De Officiis*, ed. C. Atzert (Leipzig, 1941)

Codex Justinianus, ed. P. Krueger, *Corpus iuris civilis*, II (Berlin, 1929)

Codex Theodosianus, ed. T. Mommsen and P. Meyer, *Theodosiani libri XVI cum constitutionibus Sirmondias* 1 (Berlin, 1905); tr. Clyde Pharr, *The Theodosian Code and Novels and The Sirmondian Constitutions* (Princeton, 1952)

Commodianus, *Instructiones adversum gentium deos* (*PL* 5, 201–62)

Croke, Brian, and Jill Harries, *Religious Conflict in Fourth-Century Rome: A Documentary Study* (Sydney, 1982)

Cyprian of Carthage, *De bono patientiae* (*CC* 3A)
    De mortalitate (*CC* 3A)

Ennodius, *Epistulae* (*MGH AA* 7); Stéphane Gioanni, *Ennode de Pavie, Livres 1. et 2., texte établi, traduit et commenté* (Paris, 2006)
    Paraneisis didascalia (*MGH AA* 7, 310–15)
    Vita Epifani (*MGH AA* 7, 84–109)

Eugippius of Lucullanum, *Excerpta ex operibus S. Augustini* (*CSEL* 9.1)
    Commemoratorium vitae sancti Severini (*SC* 374)
    Regula (*CSEL* 87)

Evagrius, *Praktikos* (*SC* 170–1)
    De diversis malignis cogitationibus (*PG* 79, 1200–33)
    De octo vitiosis cogitationibus (*PG* 40, 1272–8)

Ferrandus, *Ad Reginum Comitem Paraneticum* (*PL* 67, 928–50)

Pseudo-Ferrandus, *Vita Fulgentii*, ed. G. Lapeyre (Paris, 1929); tr. Antonio Isola, *Pseudo Ferrando di Cartagine: Vita di San Fulgenzio* (Roma, 1987)

Fulgentius, *Opera* (*CC* 91); tr. Robert B. Eno, *Fulgentius: Selected Works* (Washington, DC, 1997)

Gaius, *Institutiones*, ed. T. De Zulueta, *The Institutes of Gaius* 1, *Text with Critical Notes and Translation* (Oxford, 1946)

Pseudo-Gelasius, *De libris recipiendis et non recipiendis* (*TU* 38)

Gennadius of Marseilles, *De viris illustribus* (*TU* 14, 57–97)

Gerontius, *Vita Melaniae Iunioris (SC* 90); tr. Elizabeth A. Clark, *The Life of Melania the Younger: Introduction, Translation, and Commentary* (Lewiston, 1984); also:

La Vie latine de Sainte Mélanie: édition critique, traduction et commentaire, ed. and tr. Patrick Laurence (Jerusalem, 2002)

Gregory, *Dialogi* (*SC* 251, 260, 265)
  Homiliae in Hiezecihelem Prophetam (*CC* 142)
  Homiliae in Evangelia (*CC* 141)
  Moralia in Iob (CC 143, 143A, 143B)
  Registrum epistularum (*MGH Epp.* 1 and 2, also *CC* 140, 140A)
  Regula pastoralis (*SC* 381, 382)

Gregory of Tours, *Decem libri historiarum* (*MGH SRM* 1); tr. Lewis Thorpe, *Gregory of Tours: History of the Franks* (Halmondsworth, 1974)
  Vita patrum (*MGH SRM* 1)

Hilary of Arles, *Sermo de vita sancti Honorati* (*SC* 235)

Jerome, *Epistulae* (*PL* 22)
  De viris illustribus (*TU* 14, 1–56).

John Chrysostom, *Adversus oppugnatores vitae monasticae* (PG 47, 319–86)
  Homilia [XIII] in Ep. ad Romanos 7:14 (PG 60, 507–24)
  Homilia [XX] in Eph. 5:22 (PG 62, 135–50)
  Homilia [IV] in Matthaeum 1:17 (PG 57, 13–794)
  Paranaeses ad Theodorum (*SC* 117)
  Quales ducendae sint uxores (PG 51, 225–42)
  De subintroductis, ed. Jean Dumortier, *Les Cohabitations suspectes: comment observer la virginité* (Paris, 1955)

Pseudo-John Chrysostom, *De legislatione 3* (*PG* 56)

John the Deacon, *Epistula ad Senarium* (*PL* 59, 399–408)

John the Deacon, *Vita Gregorii* (*PL* 75, 63–242)

Iohannes, *De consolatione mortuorum sermones II* (*PL* 40, 1162–68)

Joseph and Aseneth, ed. Christoph Burchard, Pseudepigrapha Veteris Testamenti Graeca 5 (Leiden, 2003)

Leo I, *Epistulae* (*PL* 54, 1204–5)

Liber Pontificalis, ed. Louis Duchesne, 3 vols. (Paris, 1955); tr. Ray Davis, *The Book of Pontiffs (Liber Pontificalis to AD 715)* (2nd edn, Liverpool, 2000)

Martianus Capella, *De nuptiis Philologiae et Mercurii*, ed. James Willis (Leipzig, 1983)

Mathisen, Ralph, *Ruricius of Limoges and Friends: A Collection of Letters from Visigothic Gaul* (Liverpool, 1999)

Maximus of Turin, *Sermones* (*CC* 23)

Methodius of Olympus, *Symposium*, ed. G. N. Bonwetsch, *Die griechischen christlichen Schriftsteller* 27 (Leipzig, 1917)

Novellae Valentiniani, see *Codex Theodosianus*

Origen, *Homilia in Iesum filium Navis* (*SC* 71)

Passio Anastasiae (*BHL* 401); ed. Hippolyte Delehaye, *Étude sur le legendier Romain: les saints de novembre et de décembre*, Subsidia Hagiographica 23 (Brussels, 1936), 221–49
  Passio Felicitatis (*AASS Iul.* 3, 12–13)
  Passio Sebastiani (*BHL* 7543) (*AASS Ian.* 2, 265–78, 3rd edn, 628–42)

Passio Symphorosae (*AASS Iul.* 4, 358–9)

Paulinus of Nola, *Carmina* (*CSEL* 30)

   Epistulae (*CSEL* 29)

Pelagius, *Ad Demetriadem* (*PL* 30, 13–45); tr. B. R. Rees, *The Letters of Pelagius and his Followers* (Woodbridge, 1991)

   Epistula ad Celantiam (*CSEL* 29, 436–59); tr. Rees, as above

Pomerius, *De vita contemplativa* (*PL* 59, 415–520); tr. M. J. Suelzer, *Julianus Pomerius: The Contemplative Life*, Ancient Christian Writers 4 (Westminster, Md., 1947)

Proba, *Cento* (*CSEL* 16, 511–609); tr. Elizabeth A. Clark and Diane F. Hatch, *The Golden Bough, The Oaken Cross: The Virgilian Cento of Faltonia Betitia Proba*, American Academy of Religion Texts and Translations Series 5 (Chico, Ca., 1981)

Procopius, *Wars*, ed. and tr. H. B. Dewing, Loeb Classical Library 81 (Cambridge, Mass., 1914–40)

Prudentius, *Psychomachia*, ed. H. J. Thomson, *Prudentius* (Cambridge, Mass., 1969)

Salvian, *Adversus avaritiam* (*CSEL* 8, 224–316)

Seneca, *De ira*, ed. E. Hermes, *Dialogorum libri XII* (Leipzig, 1907)

Sidonius, *Epistolae* (*MGH AA* 8); tr. W. B. Anderson, *Poems and Letters*, Loeb Classical Library, 2 vols. (Cambridge, Mass., 1936–1965)

Symmachus, *Epistulae* (*MGH AA* 6.1, 1–278)

Tertullian, *De patientia* (*CSEL* 47); tr. *ANF* 3, 707–17

   De praescriptione haereticorum (*CC* 1)

Valerianus of Cimiez, *Homilia XV De bono martyrii* (*PL* 52)

Victricius, *De laude sanctorum* (*CC* 64)

Vita Caesarii Arelatensis (*MGH SRM* 3, 433–501)

Vita Genovefae virginis parisiensis (*MGH SRM* 3, 204–38). This gives the 'A' recension, *BHL* 3335, now accepted as the earliest version (see Heinzelmann and Poulin, *Vies anciennes de sainte Geneviève de Paris*). *AASS Ian.* 1, 138–43 gives the later 'B' recension, *BHL* 3334, tr. Joanne McNamara and John Halborg, *Sainted Women of the Dark Ages* (Durham and London, 1992)

Vita Gregorii, ed. and tr. B. Colgrave, *The Earliest Life of Gregory the Great by an Anonymous Monk of Whitby* (Cambridge, 1968)

Vita Monegundis, see Gregory of Tours, *Vita patrum*, as above

Zosimus, *Historia Nova*, ed. F. Paschoud, *Zosime, Histoire nouvelle* (Paris, 1979)

SECONDARY LITERATURE

Abbot, Frank Frost, and Allan Chester Johnson, *Municipal Administration in the Roman Empire* (Princeton, 1926)

Adams, J. N., *The Latin Sexual Vocabulary* (London, 1982)

Allard, Paul, 'Une grande fortune romaine au cinquième siècle', *Revue des questions historiques* 81 (1907), 5–30

Altaner, Bernd, 'Altlateinische Übersetzungen von Chrysostomusschriften', *Kleine patristische Schriften* (Berlin, 1967), 418–19

Altman, Charles F., 'Two Types of Opposition and the Structure of Latin Saints' Lives', *Medievalia et Humanistica* 6 (1975), 1–11

Amory, Patrick, *People and Identity in Ostrogothic Italy, 489–554* (Cambridge, 1997)

André, Jean-Marie, *L'Otium dans la vie morale et intellectuelle romaine: des origines à l'époque augustéenne* (Paris, 1966).

Anton, Hans Hubert, *Fürstenspiegel und Herrscherethos in der Karolingerzeit,* Bonner historische Forschungen 32 (Bonn, 1968)

Arjava, Antti, 'Paternal Power in Late Antiquity', *Journal of Roman Studies* 88 (1998), 147–65

    Women and Law in Late Antiquity (Oxford, 1996)

    'Family Finances in the Byzantine Near East: P. Petra inv. 68', in I. Andorlini et al., eds., *Atti del XXII Congresso Internazionale di Papirologia, Firenze 1998* (Florence, 2001), 65–70

Arnaoutoglu, P., 'Marital Disputes in Greco-Roman Egypt', *Journal of Juristic Papyrology* 25 (1995), 11–28

Bagnall, Roger, 'Church, State, and Divorce in Late Roman Egypt', in Robert E. Somerville and Karl-Ludwig Selig, eds., *Florilegium Columbianum: Essays in honor of Paul Oskar Kristeller* (New York, 1987), 41–61

    Egypt in Late Antiquity (Princeton, 1993)

Baldini Lippolis, Isabella, *La domus tardoantica: forme e rappresentazioni dello spazio domestico nelle città del mediterraneo* (Bologna, 2002)

Baluze, Étienne, *Miscellaneorum Liber Primus, hoc est, collectio veterum monumentorum quae hactenus latuerant in variis codicibus et bibliothecis* (Paris, 1678)

Banaji, Jairus, *Agrarian Change in Late Antiquity: Gold, Labour, and Aristocratic Dominance* (Oxford, 2001)

Barnish, S. J. B., 'Transformation and Survival in the Western Senatorial Aristocracy, c. AD 400–700', *PBSR* 56 (1988), 120–55

Bartlett, Richard, 'Aristocracy and Asceticism: The Letters of Ennodius and the Gallic and Italian Churches', in Mathisen and Shanzer, eds., *Society and Culture in Late Antique Gaul,* 201–16

Barton, Carlin A., *Roman Honor: The Fire in the Bones* (Berkeley, 2001)

Bergmann, Bettina, 'The Roman House as Memory Theater', *Art Bulletin* 73 (1994), 225–56

Baur, Chrysostomus, 'L'Entrée littéraire de saint Chrysostome dans le monde latin', *RHE* 8 (1907), 249–65

Beatrice, Pier Franco, *Tradux peccati: alle fonti della dottrina agostiniana del peccato originale,* Studia patristica mediolanensia 8 (Milan, 1978)

Berrouard, M.-F., 'Les Lettres 6* et 9* de saint Augustin', *REAug* 27 (1981), 264–77

Bisson, Thomas N., 'Reply [to Chris Wickham]', *Past and Present* 155 (1997), 208–25

Bitterman, H. R., 'The Council of Chalcedon and Episcopal Jurisdiction', *Speculum* 103 (1938), 198–203

Blecker, M. P., 'Roman law and consilium in the *Regula Magistri* and the *Regula Benedicti*', *Speculum* 47 (1972), 1–28

Bloomfield, Morton W., *The Seven Deadly Sins: An Introduction to the History of a Religious Concept, with Special Reference to Medieval English Literature* (Michigan State College Press [no place of publication], 1952)

Boatwright, Mary Taliaferro, 'Plancia Magna of Perge: Women's Roles and Status in Roman Asia Minor', in Sarah Booth Pomeroy, ed., *Women's History and Ancient History* (Chapel Hill, 1991), 249–72

Bolgar, R. R., *The Classical Heritage and its Beneficiaries* (Cambridge, 1958)

Bonner, Gerald, *Augustine and Modern Research on Pelagianism*, The Saint Augustine Lecture 1970 (Villanova, 1972)

Bourdieu, Pierre, 'Marriage Strategies as Strategies of Social Reproduction', in Roy Forster and Orest Ranum, eds., *Family and Society* (Baltimore, 1976) (first published in *Annales ESC* 27 (1972), 1105–25)

Boudreau Flory, Marleen, 'Family in *familia*: Kinship and Community in Slavery', *American Journal of Ancient History* 3 (1978), 78–95

Bowes, Kim, and Adam Gutteridge, 'Rethinking the Later Roman Landscape', *JRA* 18 (2005), 405–13

Boyarin, Daniel, *Carnal Israel: Reading Sex in Talmudic Culture* (Berkeley, 1993)

Bradley, Keith, *Slaves and Masters in the Roman Empire: A Study in Social Control* (Oxford, 1987)

Brakke, David, *Demons and the Making of the Monk: Spiritual Combat in Early Christianity* (Cambridge, Mass., 2006)

Brasington, Bruce C., 'Non imitanda sed veneranda: The Dilemma of Sacred Precedent in Twelfth-Century Canon Law', *Viator* 23 (1992), 135–52

Brooten, Bernadette, *Women Leaders in the Ancient Synagogue* (Chico, Ca., 1982)

Brown, Peter, 'Aspects of the Christianization of the Roman Aristocracy', *JRS* 51 (1961), 1–11

'The Later Roman Empire' (review of Jones, *The Later Roman Empire*), *The Economic History Review* n.s. 20 (1967), 327–43, repr. in Peter Brown, *Religion and Society in the Age of Saint Augustine* (London, 1972), 46–73

'The Rise and Function of the Holy Man in Late Antiquity', *JRS* 61 (1971), 80–101

'Sexuality and Society in the Fifth Century AD: Augustine and Julian of Eclanum', in Emilio Gabba, ed., *Tria corda: scritti in onore di Arnaldo Momigliano* (Como, 1983), 49–70

Power and Persuasion: Towards a Christian Empire (Madison, 1992)

'Enjoying the Saints in Late Antiquity', *Early Medieval Europe* 9 (2000), 1–24

The Rise of Western Christendom: Triumph and Diversity, AD 200–1000 (2nd edn, Oxford, 2003)

'Augustine and a Crisis of Wealth in Late Antiquity', *Augustinian Studies* 36 (2005), 5–30

Brown, T. S., *Gentlemen and Officers: Imperial Administration and Aristocratic Power in Byzantine Italy AD 554–800* (Rome, 1984)

Brubaker, Leslie, 'Memories of Helena: Patterns of Imperial Female Matronage in the Fourth and Fifth Centuries', in James, ed., *Women, Men and Eunuchs*, 52–75

Buckland, W. W., *A Text-Book of Roman Law from Augustus to Justinian*, 3rd edn, rev. by Peter Stein (Cambridge, 1963)

Bullough, Donald, 'Early Medieval Social Groupings: The Terminology of Kinship', *Past and Present* 45 (1969), 3–18

Burrus, Virginia, *The Sex Lives of Saints: An Erotics of Ancient Hagiography* (Philadelphia, 2004)

Cameron, Alan, 'The Date and Identity of Macrobius', *JRS* 56 (1966), 25–38
  'Paganism and Literature in Late Fourth Century Rome', in *Christianisme et formes littéraires de l'antiquité tardive en occident*, Fondation Hardt pour l'Étude de l'Antiquité Classique, Entretiens 22 (Geneva, 1977), 1–30

Cameron, Averil, 'Cassiodorus Deflated', *JRS* 71 (1981), 183–6
  Christianity and the Rhetoric of Empire: the Development of Christian Discourse, Sather Classical Lectures 55 (Berkeley, 1991)

Carandini, Andrea, ed., *Settefinestre: una villa schiavistica nell'Etruria Romana*, 3 vols. (Modena, 1985)

Cazelles, Brigitte, *Le Corps de sainteté d'après Jean Bouche d'Or, Jehan Paulus et quelques vies des XIIe et XIIIe siècles* (Geneva, 1982)

Cecchelli, Carlo, *Monumenti cristiano-eretici di Roma* (Rome, 1944)

Chadwick, Henry, *Boethius: The Consolations of Music, Logic, Theology, and Philosophy* (Oxford, 1981)

Charlet, Jean-Louis, 'Aesthetic Trends in Late Latin Poetry (325–410)', *Philologus*, 132 (1988), 74–85

Charlier, Celestin, 'Cassiodore, Pélage, et les origines de la Vulgate paulinienne', *Studiorum Paulinorum Congressus Internationalis* (Rome, 1963), 2, 461–70

Chastagnol, André, *La Préfecture urbaine à Rome sous le Bas-Empire* (Paris, 1960)

Chavasse, Antoine, 'Messes du pape Vigile dans le Sacrementaire léonien', *EL* 64 (1950); 66 (1952)

Christie, Neil, *From Constantine to Charlemagne: An Archaeology of Italy 300–800* (Aldershot, 2006)

Clark, Elizabeth A., ' "Adam's only companion": Augustine and the Early Christian Debate on Marriage', in R. R. Edwards and S. Spector, eds., *The Olde Daunce: Love, Friendship and Marriage in the Medieval World* (New York, 1991), 15–31 with notes at 240–54
  The Origenist Controversy: The Cultural Construction of an Early Christian Debate (Princeton, 1992)
  'Antifamilial Tendencies in Ancient Christianity', *Journal of the History of Sexuality* 5 (1995), 356–80
  '"The Lady Vanishes": Dilemmas of a Feminist Historian after "the Linguistic Turn"', *Church History* 67 (1998), 1–31

Clark, Gillian, *Women in Late Antiquity: Pagan and Christian Lifestyles* (Oxford, 1993)

Clark, Patricia, 'Women, Slaves, and the Hierarchies of Domestic Violence: The family of St Augustine', in Joshel and Murnaghan, eds., *Women and Slaves in Greco-Roman Culture*, 109–29

Clarke, J. R., *The Houses of Roman Italy, 100 BC–AD 250: Ritual, Space, Decoration* (Berkeley, 1991)

Cleary, Joseph F., *Canonical Limitations on the Alienation of Church Property: An Historical Synopsis and Commentary*, The Catholic University of America Canon Law Studies 100 (Washington, D.C., 1936)

Coates-Stevens, Robert, 'Housing in Early Medieval Rome, AD 500–1000', *PBSR* 64 (1996), 239–59

Colish, Marcia L., 'Why the Portiana? Reflections on the Milanese Basilica Crisis of 386', *JECS* 10.3 (2002), 361–72

Conant, Jonathan P., 'Staying Roman: Vandals, Moors, and Byzantines in Late Antique North Africa, 400–700' (Ph.D. dissertation, Harvard University, 2004)

Condello, E., *Una scrittura e un territorio: l'onciale dei secoli V–VIII nell'Italia meridionale* (Spoleto, 1994)

Cooper, Kate, 'Insinuations of Womanly Influence: An Aspect of the Christianization of the Roman Aristocracy', *JRS* 82 (1992), 150–64

'An(n)ianus of Celeda and the Latin Readers of John Chrysostom', *Studia Patristica* 27 (1993), 249–55

Concord and Martyrdom: Gender, Community, and the Uses of Christian Perfection in Late Antiquity (Ph.D. dissertation, Princeton University, 1993)

The Virgin and the Bride: Idealized Womanhood in Late Antiquity (Cambridge, Mass., 1996)

'The Voice of the Victim: Gender, Representation, and Early Christian Martyrdom', *Bulletin of the John Rylands University Library* 80 (1998), 147–57

'Contesting the Nativity: Wives, Virgins, and Pulcheria's *imitatio Mariae*', *Scottish Journal of Religious Studies* 19 (1998), 31–43

'The Martyr, the *Matrona* and the Bishop: Networks of Allegiance in Early Sixth-Century Rome', *Early Medieval Europe* 8.3 (1999), 297–317

'The Widow as Impresario: Gender, Legendary Afterlives, and Documentary Evidence in Eugippius' *Vita Severini*', in *Eugippius und Severin: Der Autor, der Text, und der Heilige*, ed. Walter Pohl and Maximilian Diesenberger (Vienna, 2001), 53–63

'Chastity', *Encyclopedia of Religion* (2nd edn, Framington Hills, Michigan, 2004) 3, 1557–60.

'Empress and *Theotokos*: Gender and Patronage in the Christolological Controversy', in R. N. Swanson, ed., *The Church and Mary* (Woodbridge, 2004), 39–51

'Ventriloquism and the Miraculous: Conversion, Preaching, and the Martyr Exemplum in Late Antiquity', in Kate Cooper and Jeremy Gregory, eds., *Signs, Wonders, and Miracles*, Studies in Church History 41 (Woodbridge, 2005), 22–45

'The Virgin as Social Icon: Perspectives from Late Antiquity', in Mathilde Van Dijk and Renée Nip, eds., *Saints, Scholars, and Politicians: Gender as a Tool in Medieval Studies*, Medieval Church Studies 15 (Leiden, 2005), 9–24

'The Household and the Desert: Monastic and Biological Communities in the *Lives* of Melania the Younger', in Anneke Mulder-Bakker and Jocelyn Wogan-Browne, eds., *Household, Women and Christianities in Late Antiquity and the Middle Ages* (Leiden, 2005), 11–35

'Approaching the Holy Household', *JECS* 15 (2007), 131–42

'Poverty, Obligation, and Inheritance: Roman Heiresses and the Varieties of Senatorial Christianity in Fifth-century Rome', in Kate Cooper and Julia Hillner, eds., *Religion, Dynasty, and Patronage Early Christian Rome, 300–900* (Cambridge, 2007)

'Gender and the Fall of Rome', in Philip Rousseau, ed., *The Blackwell Companion to Late Antiquity* (Oxford, forthcoming)

'Closely Watched Households: Visibility, Exposure, and Private Power in the Roman *Domus*' (*Past and Present* 197, forthcoming, 2007)

'Family, Dynasty, and Conversion in the Roman Gesta Martyrum', in *Hagiographische Überlieferung im Frühmittelalter – Zwischen Niederschrift und Wiederschrift*, ed. M. Diesenberger (Vienna, forthcoming)

'The date and authorship of *Ad Gregoriam in palatio*: An open question' (forthcoming)

Cooper, Kate, and Julia Hillner, eds., *Religion, Dynasty and Patronage in Early Christian Rome, 300–900* (Cambridge, 2007)

Cooper, Kate, and Conrad Leyser, 'The Gender of Grace: Impotence, Servitude and Manliness in the Fifth-Century West', *Gender and History* 12.3 (2000), 536–51

Consolino, Franca Ela, 'Sante o patrone? Le aristocratiche tardoantiche e il potere della carità', *Studi storici* 30 (1989), 971–91

Corbett, P. E., *The Roman Law of Marriage* (Oxford, 1930)

Cozic, Michel, *Le Liber ad Gregoriam d'Arnobe le Jeune: édition, traduction, étude historique, doctrinale et littéraire* (Villeneuve d'Ascq, 1997)

Cracco Ruggini, Lellia, *Il paganesimo romano tra religione e politica, 384–394 d. C.: per una reinterpretazione del Carmen contra paganos* (Rome, 1979)

Economia e società nell' 'Italia annonaria': rapporti fra agricoltura e commercio dal IV al VI secolo d. C. (2nd edn, Bari, 1995)

'Gregorio Magno e il mondo mediterraneo', in *Gregorio Magno nel XIV centenario della morte: convegno internazionale, Roma, 22–25 ottobre 2003*, Atti dei convegni Lincei 209 (Rome, 2004), 11–87

Crehan, Joseph H., 'Sinful Marriage and the Pseudo-Chrysostom', in *Kyriakon: Festschrift Johannes Quasten* (Münster, 1970) I, 490–8

Croke, Brian , 'AD 476: The Manufacture of a Turning Point', *Chiron* 13 (1983), 81–119

D'Arms, John, *Commerce and Social Standing in Ancient Rome* (Cambridge, Mass., 1981)

Dawson, David, *Allegorical Readers and Cultural Revision in Ancient Alexandria* (Berkeley, 1992)

Davidson, Ivor J., 'Ambrose's *De officiis* and the Intellectual Climate of the Late Fourth Century', *Vigiliae Christianae* 49 (1995), 313–33

de Gaiffier, Baldouin, Un prologue hostile au Décret de Gélase?' *Analecta Bollandiana* 82 (1964), 341–53

de Jong, Mayke, *In Samuel's Image: Child Oblation in the Early Medieval West* (Leiden, 1996)

Deleani, Simone, *Christum sequi: étude d'un thème dans l'oeuvre de saint Cyprien* (Paris, 1979) de Neeve, Peter Wim, 'A Roman Landowner and his Estates: Pliny', *Athenaeum* 78 (1990), 363–42

De Plinval, Georges, *Pélage: ses écrits, sa vie et sa réforme* (Lausanne, 1943), 44–5

De Salvo, L., '"*Navicularium nolui esse Ecclesiam Christi*": a proposito di Aug., *Serm*. 355.4', *Latomus* 46 (1987), 46–60

Davidoff, Leonora, and Carolyn Hall, 'The Architecture of Public and Private Life. English Middle Class Society in a Provincial Town 1780 to 1850', in Derek Fraser and Antony Sutcliffe, eds., *The Pursuit of Urban History* (London, 1983), 326–45

Diehl, Charles, *L'Afrique byzantine: histoire de la domination byzantine en Afrique (533–709)*, 2 vols. (New York, 1959)

Diepen; H. M, 'La Pensée christologique d'Arnobe le Jeune: théologie de l'assumptus Homo ou de l'Emmanuel?' *Revue Thomiste* 59 (1959), 535–64

Dixon, Suzanne, 'Family Finances: Tullia and Terentia', *Antichthon* 18 (1984), 78–101
'The Marriage Alliance in the Roman Élite', *Journal of Family History* 10 (1985), 353–78
The Roman Mother (London, 1988)
'Conflict in the Roman Family', in Rawson, ed., *The Roman Family*, 149–67
'The Sentimental Ideal of the Roman Family', in Rawson, ed., *Marriage, Divorce, and Children*, 99–113
The Roman Family (Baltimore, 1992)

Dumont, Louis, *Homo Hierarchicus: The Caste System and its Implications* (Chicago, 1986)
Affinity as a Value: Marriage Alliance in South India, with Comparative Essays on Australia (Chicago, 1983)

Ellis, Simon P., 'Late-Antique Dining: Architecture, Furnishings and Behaviour', in Laurence and Wallace-Hadrill, *Domestic Space in the Roman World: Pompeii and Beyond*, 41–51
'The End of the Roman House', *AJA* 92 (1988), 565–76
Roman Housing (London, 2000)

Elliot, Dyan, *Spiritual Marriage: Sexual Abstinence in Early Medieval Wedlock* (Princeton, 1993)

Elshtain, Jean B., *Public Man, Private Woman: Women in Social and Political Thought* (Princeton, 1981)

Engelbrecht, Jacobus H., *Het Utrechts Psalterium: een eeuw wetenschappelijke bestuderung (1860–1960)* (Utrecht, 1965)

Ermini, Filippo, *Il centone di Proba e la poesia centonaria latina* (Rome, 1909)

Étaix, Raymond, 'Sermon inédit de saint Augustin sur l'amour des parents', *RBen* 86 (1976), 38–48

Evans, Robert F., *Four Letters of Pelagius* (New York, 1968)

Evans Grubbs, Judith, 'Marriage More Shameful than Adultery: Slave–Mistress Relationships, "Mixed Marriages", and Late Roman Law', *Phoenix* 47 (1993), 125–54
Law and Family in Late Antiquity: The Emperor Constantine's Marriage Legislation (Oxford, 1995)

Women and the Law in the Roman Empire: A Sourcebook on Marriage, Divorce, and Widowhood (London, 2002)

'Parent–Child Conflict in the Roman Family: The Evidence of the Code of Justinian', in Michelle George, ed., *The Roman Family in the Empire: Rome, Italy, and Beyond* (Oxford, 2005), 93–128

'Marrying and its Documentation in Later Roman Law', in Philip L. Reynolds and John Witte, Jr., eds., *To Have and to Hold: Marrying and its Documentation in Western Christendom, 400–1600* (Cambridge, 2007), 43–94

Ferrari, Mirella, 'In margine ai Codices latini antiquiores: spigolature ambrosiane del sec. VIII', in Albert Lehner and Walter Berschin, eds., *Lateinische Kultur im VIII. Jahrhundert: Traube-Gedenkschrift* (St. Ottilien, 1989), 59–78

Filson, Floyd, 'The Significance of the Early House Churches', *Journal of Biblical Literature* 58 (1939), 105–12

Finley, M. I., *The Ancient Economy* (London, 1973)

Fontaine, Jacques, 'Unité et diversité du mélange des genres et des tons chez quelques écrivains latins de la fin du IVe siècle: Ausone, Ambroise, Ammien', in *Christianisme et formes littéraires de l'antiquité tardive en Occident*, Entretiens sur l'antiquité classique 33 (Geneva, 1976), 438–46

'Comment doit-on appliquer la notion de genre littéraire à la littérature latine chrétienne du IV e siècle?', *Philologus* 132 (1988), 53–73

Forbis, Elizabeth P., 'Women's Public Image in Italian Honorary Inscriptions', *American Journal of Philology* 111 (1990), 493–512

Fox-Genovese, Elizabeth, *Within the Plantation Household: Black and White Women of the Old South* (Chapel Hill, 1988)

Foxhall, Lin, 'The Dependant Tenant: Land Leasing and Labour in Italy and Greece', *JRStudies* 80 (1990), 97–114

Frier, Bruce W., 'Natural Fertility and Family Limitation in Roman Marriage', *Classical Philology* 89 (1994), 318–33

Frier, Bruce W., and Thomas A. McGinn, *A Casebook of Roman Family Law* (Oxford, 2004)

Gaca, Kathy L., *The Making of Fornication: Eros, Ethics, and Political Reform in Greek Philosophy and Early Christianity* (Berkeley, 2003)

Ganz, David, 'The Ideology of Sharing: Apostolic Community and Ecclesiastical Property in the Early Middle Ages', in Wendy Davies and Paul Fouracre, eds., *Property and Power in the Early Middle Ages* (Cambridge, 1995), 17–30

Gardner, Jane F., *Family and Familia in Roman Law and Life* (Oxford, 1998)

Garnsey, Peter, *Ideas of Slavery from Aristotle to Augustine* (Cambridge, 1996)

'The Land', in Alan K. Bowman, Peter Garnsey, and Dominic Rathbone, eds., *Cambridge Ancient History* 12, *The High Empire, AD 70–192* (Cambridge, 2000), 679–709

Gaudemet, Jean, *L'Église dans l'empire romain* (Paris, 1958)

George, Michelle, 'Repopulating the Roman House', in Rawson and Weaver, eds., *Roman Family*, 299–319

'*Servus* and *domus*: the Slave in the Roman House', in Laurence & Wallace-Hadrill eds., *Domestic Space in the Roman World: Pompeii and Beyond*, 15–24

Giardina, Andrea, 'Carità eversiva: le donazioni di Melania la Giovane e gli equilibri della società tardoromana', *Studi Storici* (1988), 127–42

Gibbon, Edward, *History of the Decline and Fall of the Roman Empire*, 7 vols., ed. J. B. Bury (London, 1902)

Gibson, Margaret, ed., *Boethius: His Life, Thought, and Influence* (Oxford, 1981)

Gillett, Andrew, *Envoys and Political Communication in the Late Antique West, 411–533* (Cambridge, 2003)

'The Purposes of Cassiodorus' *Variae*', in Alexander Callander Murray, ed., *After Rome's Fall: Narrators and Sources of Early Medieval History; Essays Presented to Walter Goffart* (Toronto, 1998), 37–50

Giuliani, E., and C. Pavolini, 'La "Biblioteca di Agapito" e la Basilica di S. Agnese', in William Harris, ed., *The Transformations of* Urbs Roma *in Late Antiquity*, *JRA* Supplementary Series 33 (Portsmouth, R.I., 1999), 85–107

Goffart, Walter, *Caput and Colonate: Towards a History of Late Roman Taxation* (Toronto, 1974)

Gordini, Gian Domenico, 'Il monachesimo romano in Palestina nel IV secolo', in *Saint Martin et son temps: memorial du XVIe centenaire des débuts du monachisme en Gaule, 361–1961*, Studia Anselmiana 46 (Rome, 1961), 85–107

Gorman, Michael M., 'Marginalia in the Oldest Manuscripts of St. Augustine's *De Genesi ad litteram*', *Scriptorium* 37 (1984), 71–7, now repr. in idem, *The Manuscript Traditions of the Works of St Augustine* (Florence, 2004), 249–55

Gould, Graham, 'Basil of Caesarea and the Problem of the Wealth of Monasteries', in *The Church and Wealth*, ed. William Sheils and Diana Woods, Studies in Church History 24 (Oxford, 1987), 15–24

Grahame, Mark, 'Public and Private in the Roman House: The Spatial Order of the *Casa del Fauno*', in Laurence and Wallace-Hadrill, eds., *Domestic Space in the Roman World: Pompeii and Beyond*, 137–64

Gregory, Christopher A., *Savage Money: The Anthropology and Politics of Commodity Exchange* (Amsterdam, 1997)

Guerra Medici, Maria Teresa, *I diritti delle donne nella società altomedievale* (Napoli, 1986)

Guidobaldi, Federico, 'L'edilizia abitativa unifamiliare nella Roma tardoantica', in Andrea Giardina, ed., *Società romana e impero tardantico*, 3 vols. (Rome, 1986) 2, 165–237, 446–60

'Le *domus* tardoantiche come "sensori" delle transformazioni culturali e sociali', in W.V. Harris, ed., *The Transformations of* Urbs Roma *in Late Antiquity*, *JRA* Supplementary Series 33 (Portsmouth, R. I., 1999), 53–68

Hadot, Ilsetraut, *Arts libéraux et philosophie dans la pensée antique* (Paris, 1984)

Haines-Eitzen, Kim, *Guardians of Letters: Literacy, Power, and the Transmitters of Early Christian Literature* (Oxford, 2000)

Hales, Shelley, *The Roman House and Social Identity* (Cambridge, 2003)

Halsall, Guy, *Barbarian Migrations and the Roman West* (Cambridge, 2007)

Hamerow, Helena, *Rural Communities in Early Medieval Europe: The Archaeology of Settlements* (Oxford, 2003)

Hammond, C. P., 'The Last Ten Years of Rufinus' Life and the Date of his Move South from Aquileia', *JThS* n.s. 28 (1977), 372–429

Harries, Jill, *Sidonius Apollinaris and the Fall of Rome* (Oxford, 1994)
  Law and Empire in Late Antiquity (Cambridge, 1998)

Heather, Peter, 'Literacy and Power in the Migration Period', in Alan Bowman and Greg Woolf, eds., *Literacy and Power in the Ancient World* (Cambridge, 1994), 177–97
  The Fall of the Roman Empire: A New History (London, 2005)

Hedrick, Charles W., *History and Silence: Purge and Rehabilitation of Memory in Late Antiquity* (Austin, 2000)

Heinzelmann, Martin, and Joseph-Claude Poulin, *Les Vies anciennes de sainte Geneviève de Paris, études critiques*, Bibliothèque de l'École des Hautes Études, IVe Section, Sciences Historiques et Philologiques 329 (Paris and Geneva, 1986)

Herlihy, David, *Medieval Households* (Cambridge, Mass., 1985)

Hillier, Bill, and Julienne Hanson, *The Social Logic of Space* (Cambridge, 1984)

Hillner, Julia, 'Monastic Imprisonment in Justinian's Novels', *JECS* 15 (2007), 205–37

Hopkins, Keith, 'Élite Mobility in the Roman Empire', *Past and Present* 32 (1965), 12–26
  Conquerors and Slaves (Cambridge, 1978)
  Death and Renewal: Sociological Studies in Roman History (Cambridge, 1983)
  'Taxes and Trade in the Roman Empire, 20 BC–AD 400', *JRS* 70 (1980), 101–25
  'Novel Evidence for Roman Slavery', *Past and Present* 138 (1993), 3–27.
  'Rents, Taxes and Trade in the City of Rome', in Elio Lo Cascio, ed., *Mercati permanenti e mercati periodici nel mondo romano: atti degli Incontri capresi di storia dell'economia antica, Capri, 12–15 ottobre 1997* (Bari, 2000), 253–67

Howell, Martha C., *Women, Production and Patriarchy in Late Medieval Cities* (Chicago and London, 1988)

Humbert, Michel, *Le Remariage à Rome: étude d'histoire juridique et sociale*, Università di Roma, Pubblicazioni dell'Istituto di diritto romano e dei diritti dell'oriente mediterraneo 44 (Milan, 1972)

Humphries, Mark, 'From Emperor to Pope? Ceremonial, space, and authority at Rome from Constantine to Gregory the Great', in Kate Cooper and Julia Hillner, eds., *Religion, Dynasty, and Patronage in Early Christian Rome, 300–900* (Cambridge, 2007), 21–58.

Hunter, David G., 'Resistance to the Virginal Ideal in Late-Fourth-Century Rome: the Case of Jovinian', *Theological Studies* 48 (1987), 45–64
  'Augustine and the Making of Marriage in Roman North Africa', *JECS* 11 (2003), 63–85, updated and expanded as 'Marriage and the *Tabulae Nuptiales* in Roman North Africa from Tertullian to Augustine', in Philip Reynolds and Witte, Jr., eds., *To Have and to Hold: Marrying and its Documentation in Western Christendom, 400–1600*, 95–113
  Marriage, Celibacy, and Heresy in Ancient Christianity: The Jovinianist Controversy (Oxford, 2007)

Jacobs, Andrew, 'Writing Demetrias: Ascetic Logic in Ancient Christianity', *Church History* 69 (2000), 719–48

Jahn, O., 'Über die Subscriptionen in den Handschriften römischer Classiker', *Berichte über die Verhandlungen der Königl.-Sächsischen Gesellschaft der Wissenschaften, Philologisch-Historisch Klasse* 3 (Leipzig, 1851), 327–73

James, Liz, ed., *Women, Men and Eunuchs: Gender in Byzantium* (London, 1997)

James, Montague Rhodes, *The Western Manuscripts in the Library of Trinity College Cambridge: A Descriptive Catalogue* (Cambridge, 1900)

Janson, Tore, *Latin Prose Prefaces: Studies in literary conventions*, Studia Latina Stockholmensia 13 (Stockholm, 1964)

Janssens, Jos, *Vita e morte del cristiano negli epitaffi di Roma anteriori al sec. VII* (Rome, 1981)

Johlen, Monika, *Die Vermögensrechtliche Stellung der weströmischen Frau in der Spätantike: zur Fortgeltung des römischen Rechts in den Gotenreichen und im Burgunderreich* (Berlin, 1998)

John, Eric, 'A Note on Bede's Use of "Facultas"', *RBen* 72 (1962), 350–5

Jordan, Mark, *The Ethics of Sex: New Dimensions to Religious Ethics* (Oxford, 2002)

Joshel, Sandra R., and Sheila Murnaghan, eds., *Women and Slaves in Greco-Roman Culture: Differential Equations* (London, 1998)

Jones, A. H. M., 'The Social Background of the Struggle between Paganism and Christianity in the Fourth Century', in Arnaldo Momigliano, ed., *Paganism and Christianity in the Fourth Century* (Oxford, 1963), 17–37

  The Later Roman Empire, 284–602: A Social, Economic, and Administrative Survey, 3 vols. (Oxford, 1964)

Karras, Ruth Mazo, 'The History of Marriage and the Myth of Friedelehe', *Early Medieval Europe* 14 (2006), 119–51

Kahlos, Maijastina, 'Fabia Aconia Paulina and the Death of Praetextatus – Rhetoric and Ideals in Late Antiquity (CIL VI 1779)', *Arctos* 28 (1994), 13–25

Kalas, Gregor, 'Sacred Image – Urban Space: Image, Installations, and Ritual in the Early Medieval Roman Forum' (Ph. D. dissertation, Bryn Mawr College, 1999)

Kaster, Robert A., *Guardians of Language: The Grammarian and Society in Late Antiquity* (Berkeley, 1988)

  'The Shame of the Romans', *Transactions of the American Philological Association* 127 (1997) 1–19

Katzenellenbogen, Adolf, *Allegories of the Virtues and Vices in Mediaeval Art from Early Christian Times to the Thirteenth Century*, tr. A. J. P. Crick (London, 1939)

Kelly, Christopher, *Ruling the Later Roman Empire* (Cambridge, Mass., 2004)

Kennell, S. A. H., *Magnus Felix Ennodius: A Gentleman of the Church* (Ann Arbor, 2000)

Kertzer, David I., 'Household History and Sociological Theory', *Annual Review of Sociology* 17 (1991), 155–79

  and Richard P. Saller, *The Family in Italy from Antiquity to the Present* (New Haven, 1991)

Kirkby, Helen, 'The Scholar and his Public', in Margaret Gibson, ed., *Boethius: His Life, Thought, and Influence* (Oxford, 1981), 44–69

Kirsch, J. P., 'I santuari domestici di martiri nei titoli romani ed altri simili santuari nelle chiese cristiane e nelle case private di fedeli', *Atti della pontificia accademia romana di archeologia* 2 (1924), 27–43

Klingshirn, William E., *Caesarius of Arles: The Making of a Christian Community in Late Anique Gaul* (Cambridge, 1994)

and Mark Vessey, eds., *The Limits of Ancient Christianity: Essays on Late Antique Thought and Culture in Honor of R. A. Markus* (Ann Arbor, 1999)

Knights, Clive, 'The Spatiality of the Roman Domestic Setting', in Michael Parker Pearson and Colin Richards, eds., *Architecture and Order: Approaches to Social Space* (London, 1994), 113–46

Koch, Claudia, 'Augustine's Letter to Ecdicia: A New Reading', *Augustinian Studies* 13 (2000), 173–80

Kolb, F., 'Der Bussakt von Mailand: Zum Verhaltnis von Staat und Kirche in der Spätantike', in H. Boockmann, K. Jürgensen and G. Stottenberg, eds., *Geschichte und Gegenwart: Festschrift für Karl Dietrich Erdmann* (Neumünster, 1980), 41–74

Krause, Jens-Uwe, *Spätantike Patronatsformen im Westen des Römischen Reiches* (Munich, 1987)

Krawiec, Rebecca, '"From the Womb of the Church": Monastic Families', *Journal of Early Christian Studies* 11 (2003), 283–307

Kreider, Alan, 'Changing Patterns of Conversion in the West', in idem, *The Origins of Christendom* (Edinburgh, 2001), 3–46

Kurdock, Anne N., *The Anician Women: Patronage and Dynastic Strategy in a Late Roman domus, 350 CE – 600 CE* (Phd dissertation, University of Manchester, 2003)

'*Demetrias ancilla dei*: The Problem of the Missing Patron', in Kate Cooper and Julia Hillner, eds., *Religion, Dynasty and Patronage in Early Christian Rome, 300–900* (Cambridge, 2007), 190–224

Lambert, David, 'History and Community in the Works of Salvian of Marseille' (D.Phil. thesis, Oxford University, 2003)

Lamberton, Robert, *Homer the Theologian: Neoplatonist Allegorical Reading and the Growth of the Epic Tradition* (Berkeley, 1986)

Lane Fox, Robin, 'Power and Possession in the First Monasteries', in *Aspects of the Fourth Century AD*, ed. H. W. Pleket and A. M. F. W. Verhoogt (Leiden, 1997), 68–95

Langlois, Pierre, 'Les Oeuvres de Fulgence le mythographe et le problème des deux Fulgence', *Jahrbuch für Antike und Christentum* 7 (1964), 94–105

Laurence, Ray, and Andrew Wallace-Hadrill, *Domestic Space in the Roman World: Pompeii and Beyond*, *JRA* Supplementary Series 22 (Portsmouth, R. I., 1997)

Leclercq, Jean, *The Love of Learning and the Desire for God*, tr. K. Misrahi (New York, 1961)

Lehmann, P., 'Mittelalterliche Beinahmen und Ehrentitel', *Historisches Jahrbuch* 49 (1929), 215–39

Lendon, J. E., *Empire of Honour: The Art of Government in the Roman World* (Oxford, 1997)

Lepelley, Claude, 'Mélanie la Jeune, entre Rome, la Sicilie, et l'Afrique: les effets socialement perniciuex d'une forme extrême de l'ascétisme', *Atti del IX congresso internazionale di studi sulla Sicilia antica, Kokalos* 43–4 (1997–8) I.1, 15–32

Les Cités de l'Afrique romaine au Bas-Empire 1, *La Permanence d'une civilisation municipale* (Paris, 1979)

Leppin, Hartmut, *Von Constantin dem Grossen zu Theodosius II: das christliche Kaisertum bei den Kirchenhistorikern Socrates, Sozomenus und Theodoret* (Göttingen, 1996)

Lesne, Émile, *Histoire de la propriété ecclésiastique en France*, 6 vols. (Lille, 1910–43)

Lévi-Strauss, Claude, *The Elementary Structures of Kinship*, tr. James Halre Bell, John Richard von Sturmer, and Rodney Needham (London, 1969)

Levy, Ernst, *West Roman Vulgar Law: The Law of Property* (Philadelphia, 1951)

Lewit, Tamara, '"Vanishing villas": what happened to élite rural habitation in the West in the 5th–6th Centuries?', *JRA* 16 (2003) 260–74

Leyser, Conrad, '"This Sainted Isle": Panegyric, Nostalgia, and the Invention of "Lerinian Monasticism"', in Klingshirn and Vessey, eds., *The Limits of Ancient Christianity*, 188–206

Authority and Asceticism from Augustine to Gregory the Great (Oxford, 2000)

'*Homo pauper, de pauperibus natus*: Augustine, Church Property, and the Cult of St Stephen', *Augustinian Studies* 36 (2005), 229–37

'Late Antiquity in the Medieval West', in Philip Rousseau, ed., *The Blackwell Companion to Late Antiquity* (Oxford, forthcoming), 190–224

'"A Church in the House of the Saints": Property and Power in the *Passion* of John and Paul', in Kate Cooper and Julia Hillner, eds., *Religion, Dynasty, and Patronage in Early Christian Rome, 300–900* (Cambridge, 2007), 140–62

Leyser, Karl, 'Maternal Kin in Early Medieval Germany: A Reply', *Past and Present* 49 (1970), 126–34

'The German Aristocracy from the Ninth to the Early Twelfth Century: A Historical and Cultural Sketch', *Past and Present* 41 (1968), 25–53

Liebeschuetz, Wolfgang, 'Administration and Politics in the Cities of the 5th and 6th Centuries with Special Reference to the Circus Factions', in Claude Lepelley, ed., *La Fin de la cité antique et le début de la cité médiévale de la fin du IIIe siècle à l'avènement de Charlemagne* (Bari, 1996), 160–82

Liebs, Detlef, *Die Jurisprudenz im spätantiken Italien (260–640 n.Chr.)*, Freiburger Rechtsgeschichtliche Abhandlungen n.f. 8 (Berlin, 1987)

Llewellyn, Peter, *Rome in the Dark Ages* (London, 1970)

Lo Cascio, E., and D. W. Rathbone, *Production and Public Powers in Classical Antiquity*, Cambridge Philological Society, suppl. vol. 26 (Cambridge, 2000)

L'Orange, H. P., *Art Forms and Civic Life in the Late Roman Empire* (Princeton, 1965)

and P. J. Nordhagen, *Mosaics*, tr. Ann E. Keep (London, 1966)

Lowe, E. A., *Codices latini antiquiores*, 13 vols. (Oxford, 1950–)

MacCormack, Sabine, *The Shadows of Poetry: Vergil in the Mind of Augustine* (Berkeley, 1998)

McCurry, Stephanie, *Masters of Small Worlds: Yeoman Households, Gender Relations, and the Political Culture of the Antebellum South Carolina Low Country* (New York, 1995)

MacDonald, Dennis, *The Legend and the Apostle: The Battle for Paul in Story and Canon* (Philadelphia, 1983)

MacDonald, Margaret Y., *Early Christian Women and Public Opinion: The Power of the Hysterical Woman* (Cambridge, 1996)

MacGeorge, Penny, *Late Roman Warlords* (Oxford, 2002)

Mackie, Nicola, *Local Administration in Roman Spain, AD 14–212*, British Archaeological Reports, International Series 172 (Oxford, 1983)

McLynn, Neil B., *Ambrose of Milan: Church and Court in a Christian Capital* (Berkeley, 1994)

MacMullen, Ramsay, 'Social Mobility and the Theodosian Code', *JRS* 54 (1964), 49–53
'Women in Public in the Roman Empire', *Historia* 29.2 (1980), 208–18

Maier, Harry O., '"Manichee!": Leo the Great and the Orthodox Panopticon', *JECS* 4 (1996), 441–60
'The Topography of Heresy and Dissent in Late Fourth-century Rome', *Historia* 44 (1995), 232–49
'Religious Dissent, Heresy and Households in Late Antiquity', *Vigiliae Christianae* 49 (1995), 49–63
'Private Space as the Social Context of Arianism in Ambrose's Milan', *JThS* n.s. 45 (1994), 72–93

Malingrey, Anne-Marie, 'La Traduction latine d'un texte de Jean Chrysostome: *Quod nemo laeditur*', *Studia Patristica* 7 (1966), 248–54

Manacorda, Daniele, 'The Ager Coasnus and the Production of the Amphorae of Sestius: New Evidence and a Reassessment', *JRS* 68 (1978), 122–31

Mantovanelli, Paolo, 'In difesa di Romilda: innamoramento classico e supplizio barbarico in Paolo Diacono, Boccaccio, Niccolò Canussio', in *Integrazione mescolanza rifiuto: incontri di popoli, lingue e culture in Europa dall'Antichità all'Umanesimo: Atti del convegno internazionale, Cividale del Friuli, 21–23 settembre 2000* (Rome, 2001), 337–54

Marazzi, Federico, 'The Destinies of the Late Antique Italies: Politico-Economic Developments of the Sixth Century', in Richard Hodges and William Bowden, eds., *The Sixth Century: Production, Distribution and Demand* (Leiden, 1998), 119–59

Marin, Marcello, 'Le *Tabulae matrimoniales* in s. Agostino', *Siculorum gymnasium* 29 (1976), 307–21

Markus, Robert, *The End of Ancient Christianity* (Cambridge, 1990)
'Manichaeism Revisited: Augustine's *Confessions* and the Controversy with Julian', *Collectanea Augustiniana: Mélanges T. J. Van Bavel* (Louvain, 1990), 913–25
Gregory the Great and his World (Cambridge, 1997)

Marrou, Henri-Irenée, *Saint Augustin et la fin de la culture antique*, Bulletin de l'École Française de Rome 145 (Paris, 1938)

Martin, Dale B., 'The Construction of the Ancient Family: Methodological Considerations', *JRS* 86 (1996) 40–60

Mathisen, Ralph W., *Roman Aristocrats in Barbarian Gaul: Strategies for Survival in an Age of Transition* (Austin, 1993)

and Danuta Shanzer, eds., *Society and Culture in Late Antique Gaul: Revisiting the Sources* (Aldershot, 2001)

Matter, E. Ann, 'Christ, God, and Woman in the Thought of St. Augustine', in Robert Dodardo and George Lawless, eds., *Augustine and his Critics: Essays in Honour of Gerald Bonner* (London, 2000), 164–75

Matthews, John, *Western Aristocracies and Imperial Court, AD 364–425* (Oxford, 1975)

'Anicius Manlius Severinus Boethius', in Margaret L. Gibson, ed., *Boethius: His Life, Thought, and Influence* (Oxford, 1981)

'The Poetess Proba and Fourth-Century Rome: Questions of Interpretation', in Michel Christol, Ségolène Demougin, Yvette Duval, Claude Lepelley, and Luce Pietri, eds., *Institutions, société et vie politique dans l'empire romain au IVe siècle ap. J.-C.: Actes de la table ronde autour de l'oeuvre d'André Chastagnol (Paris, 20–21 janvier 1989)* (Paris, 1992), 277–304

Middleton, John, *Lugbara Religion* (London, 1960)

Mohrmann, Christine, *Études sur le latin des chrétiens*, 4 vols. (Rome, 1958–77)

Molinier, A., *Catalogue des manuscrits de la Bibliothèque Mazarine* (Paris, 1885–92)

Momigliano, Arnoldo, 'Cassiodorus and the Italian Culture of his Time', in idem, *Studies in Historiography* (London, 1966), 181–210

'La caduta senza rumore di un impero', *Secondo contributo alla storia degli studi classici* (Rome, 1960), 159–79

'Gli Anicii e la storiografia latina del VI sec. d. C.', *Secondo contributo alla storia degli studi classici* (Rome, 1960), 191–229

Monachesi, Maria, 'Arnobio il Giovane ed una sua possible attività agiografica', *Bolletino di studi storico-religiosi* 1 (1921), 96–109

Moore, R. I. , 'Family, Community and Cult on the Eve of the Gregorian Reform', *Transactions of the Royal Historical Society* 5th series 30 (1980), 49–69

Moorhead, John, *Theoderic in Italy* (Oxford, 1992)

Morin, Germain, *Études, textes, découvertes* (Paris, 1913)

'Un commentaire romain sur saint Marc de la première moitié du Ve siècle', *RBen* 27 (1910), 352–62

'Un traité inédit d'Arnobe le Jeune', *RBen* 27 (1910), 153–71

'Fragments pélagiens inédits du manuscrit 954 de Vienne', *RBen* 3 (1922), 265–75

Morton Braund, Susanna, *Latin Literature* (London, 2002)

Nathan, Geoffrey S., *The Family in Late Antiquity: The Rise of Christianity and the Endurance of Tradition* (London, 2000)

Nelson, Janet, 'The Problematic in the Private', *Social History* 15 (1990), 355–64

Nevett, Lisa, 'Perceptions of Domestic Space in Roman Italy', in Rawson and Weaver, eds., *Roman Family*, 281–98

'Separation or Seclusion? Towards an Archaeological Approach to Investigating Women in the Greek Household in the 5th to 3rd Centuries BC', in Michael Parker Pearson and Colin Richards, eds., *Architecture and Order: Approaches to Social Space* (London, 1994), 98–112

Newhauser, Richard, ed., *In the Garden of Evil: The Vices and Culture in the Middle Ages.* Papers in Mediaeval Studies 18 (Toronto, 2005)

Newman, O., *Defensible Space: Crime Prevention through Urban Design* (New York, 1972)

Newton, Michael, *The Concept of Purity at Qumran and in the Letters of Paul* (Cambridge, 1985)

Nicols, J., 'Patrona Civitatis: Gender and Civic Patronage', *Latomus: Studies in Latin Literature and Roman History* 5 (1989), 117–42

Noonan, John, 'Marital Affection', *Studia Gratiana* 12 (1967), 479–509

North, Helen, *Sophrosune: Self-Knowledge and Restraint in Classical Antiquity* (Ithaca, 1966)

O'Donnell, James J., *Cassiodorus* (Berkeley, 1979)
  Avatars of the Word: From Papyrus to Cyberspace (Cambridge, Mass., 1998)
  'Liberius the Patrician', *Traditio* 37 (1981), 31–72
  Augustine, Sinner and Saint: A New Biography (London, 2005)

Oertel, F., 'The Economic Life of the Empire', in S. A. Cook, F. E. Adcock, M. P. Charlesworth, and N. H. Baynes, *Cambridge Ancient History* 12, *The Imperial Crisis and Recovery: AD 193–324* (Cambridge, 1939), 232–81

Orestano, Riccardo, *La struttura giuridica del matrimonio romano dal diritto classico al diritto giustinianeo* (Milan, 1951)

Osiek, Carolyn, 'The Family in Early Christianity: "Family Values" Revisited', *Catholic Biblical Quarterly* 58 (1996), 1–24

Parker, Holt, 'Loyal Slaves and Loyal Wives: The Crisis of the Outsider-within and Roman *Exemplum* Literature', in Joshel and Murnhagan eds., *Women and Slaves in Greco-Roman Culture*, 152–73

Papageorgiou, Panayiotis, 'Chrysostom and Augustine on the Sin of Adam and its Consequences', *St Vladimir's Theological Quarterly* 39 (1995), 361–78

Percival, John, 'Seigneurial Aspects of Late Roman Estate Management', *English Historical Review* 332 (1969), 449–73

Pietri, Luce, 'Évergétisme chrétien et fondations privées dans l'Italie de l'antiquité tardive', in Rita Lizzi Testa and Jean-Michel Carrié, eds., *'Humana sapit': études d'antiquité tardive offertes à Lellia Cracco Ruggini* (Turnhout, 2002), 253–63

Pölönen, Janne, 'The Division of Wealth between Men and Women in Roman Succession (ca. 50 BC–AD 250)', in Setälä *et al.*, eds., *Women, Wealth, and Power in the Roman Empire*, 147–79

Prete, S., 'Lo scritto pelagiano "De castitate" è di Pelagio?', *Aevum* 35 (1961), 315–22

Pricoco, Salvatore, *L'isola dei santi: il cenobio di Lerino e le origini del monachesimo gallico* (Rome, 1978)

Primmer, Adolf, 'Die Originalfassung von Anianus' Epistula ad Orontium', in Rudolf Hanslik, ed., *Antidosis: Festschrift für Walther Kraus* (Vienna, 1972), 278–89

Pringle, Denys, *The Defence of Byzantine Africa from Justinian to the Arab Conquest: An Account of the Military History and Archaeology of the African Provinces in the Sixth and Seventh Centuries*, British Archaeological Reports, International Series 99 (Oxford, 1981)

Radcliffe-Brown, A. R., and Daryll Forde, eds., *African Systems of Kinship and Marriage* (London, 1950)

Ramage, Edwin S., *Urbanitas: Ancient Sophistication and Refinement* (Norman, Oklahoma, 1973)

Rawson, Beryl, 'Roman Concubinage and Other *de facto* Marriages', *TAPA* (1974), 279–305

ed., *The Family in Ancient Rome: New Perspectives* (London, 1986)

ed., *Marriage, Divorce, and Children in Ancient Rome* (Canberra, 1991)

Rawson, Beryl, and Paul Weaver, eds., *The Roman Family in Italy: Status, Sentiment, Space* (Canberra, 1997)

Rémondon, Roger, 'L'Égypte au 5e siècle de notre ère: les sources papyrologiques et leurs problèmes', *Atti dell'XI Congresso Internazionale di Papirologia, Milano 2–8 Settembre 1965* (Milan, 1966), 135–48

'Situation présente de la papyrologie Byzantine', in Emil Kiessling and Hans-Albert Rupprecht, eds., *Akten des XIII internationalen Papyruskongresses, Marburg/Lahn, 2–6. August 1971* (Munich, 1974), 366–72

Reydellet, Marc, *La Royauté dans la littérature latine de Sidoine Apollinaire à Isidore de Seville* (Rome, 1981)

Reynolds, Philip L., *Marriage in the Western Church: The Christianization of Marriage During the Patristic and Early Medieval Periods* (Leiden, 1994)

and John Witte, Jr., eds., *To Have and to Hold: Marrying and its Documentation in Western Christendom, 400–1600* (Cambridge, 2007)

Riché, Pierre, *Éducation et culture dans l'Occident barbare, VIe–VIIIe siècles* (Paris, 4th edn, 1995)

Rives, James B., *Religion and Authority in Roman Carthage from Augustus to Constantine* (Oxford, 1995), 273–85

Roberti, M., '"Patria potestas" a "paterna pietas": contributo allo studio dell'influenza del cristianesimo sul diritto romano', in P. Ciapessoni, ed., *Studi in memoria di A. Albertoni I: diritto romano e bizantino* (Padua, 1935), 257–70

Roberts, Michael, *Biblical Epic and Rhetorical Paraphrase in Late Antiquity* (Liverpool, 1985)

'The Treatment of Narrative in Late Antique Literature: Ammianus Marcellinus (16.10), Rutilius Namatianus, and Paulinus of Pella', *Philologus* 132 (1988), 181–95

The Jeweled Style: Poetry and Poetics in Late Antiquity (Ithaca, 1989)

'Fortunatus' Elegy on the Death of Galswintha (*Carm.* 6.5)', in Mathisen and Shanzer, eds., *Society and Culture in Late Antique Gaul*, 298–312

Rouche, Michel, 'Des marriages païens au mariage chrétien: sacré et sacrament', *Segni* 2 (1987), 835–80

Rousseau, Philip, 'In Search of Sidonius the Bishop', *Historia* 25 (1976), 356–77

Ascetics, Authority, and the Church in the Age of Jerome and Cassian (Oxford, 1978)

Pachomius: The Making of a Community in Fourth Century Egypt (Berkeley, 1985; 2nd edn., 1999)

'The Pious Household and the Virgin Chorus: Reflections on Gregory of Nyssa's *Life of Macrina*', *Journal of Early Christian Studies* 13.2 (2005), 165–86

ed., *The Blackwell Companion to Late Antiquity* (Oxford, forthcoming)

Salamito, Jean-Marie, *Les Virtuoses et la multitude: Aspects sociaux de la controverse entre Augustin et les pélagiens* (Grenoble, 2005)

Saller, Richard P., '*Familia, Domus*, and the Roman Conception of the Family', *Phoenix* 38 (1984), 336–55

'*Patria Potestas* and the Stereotype of the Roman Family', *Continuity and Change* 1 (1986), 7–22

'*Pietas*, Obligation and Authority in the Roman Family', in Peter Kniessl and Volker Losemann, eds., *Alte Geschichte und Wissnschaftsgeschichte: Festschrift für Karl Christ* (Darmstadt, 1988), 393–410

'Corporal Punishment, Authority, and Obedience in the Roman Household,' in Rawson, ed., *Marriage, Divorce, and Children in Ancient Rome*, 124–56

Patriarchy, Property, and Death in the Roman Family (Cambridge, 1994)

'The Hierarchical Household in Roman Society: A Study of Domestic Slavery', in Michael Bush, ed., *Serfdom and Slavery: Studies in Legal Bondage* (London, 1996), 112–29

'Roman Kinship: Structure and Sentiment', in Rawson and Weaver, eds., *The Roman Family in Italy*, 7–34

'Symbols of Gender and Status Hierarchies in the Roman Household', in Joshel and Murnhagan, *Women and Slaves in Greco-Roman Culture*, 85–91

'*Pater familias, Mater familias*, and the Gendered Semantics of the Roman Household', *CPh* 94 (1999), 182–97

Saller, Richard P., and Brent Shaw, 'Tombstones and Roman Family Relations in the Principate: Civilians, Soliders, and Slaves', *JRS* 74 (1984), 124–56

Salzman, Michelle Renee, *The Making of a Christian Aristocracy: Social and Religious Change in the Western Empire* (Cambridge, 2002)

Salzman, Michelle Renee, and Claudia Rapp, eds., *Elites in Late Antiquity, Arethusa* 33.3 (Baltimore, 2000)

Samson, Ross, 'The Merovingian Nobleman's House: Castle or Villa?', *Journal of Medieval Archaeology* 13 (1987), 287–315

Santangeli-Valenziani, Riccardo, 'Residential Building in Early Medieval Rome', in Julia M. H. Smith, ed., *Early Medieval Rome and the Christian West: Essays in Honour of Donald A. Bullough* (Leiden, 2000), 101–12

Sarris, Peter, 'Rehabilitating the Great Estate: Aristocratic Property and Economic Growth in the Late Antique East', in Will Bowden, Luke Lavan, and Carlos Machado, eds., *Recent Research on the Late Roman Countryside*, Late Antique Archaeology 2 (Leiden, 2003), 55–71

von Savigny, Frederick K., *Jural Relations or the Roman Law of Persons as Subject of Jural Relations*, tr. W. H. Rattigan (London, 1884)

Savon, Hervé, 'Maniérisme et allégorie dans l'oeuvre d'Ambroise de Milan', *Revue des études latines* 55 (1977), 203–21

'Une Consolation imitée de Sénèque et de Saint Cyprien (Pseudo-Jérôme, *Epistula 5, ad amicum aegrotum*)', *Recherches Augustiniennes* 14 (1979), 153–90

Schnorr von Carolsfeld, Ludwig, 'Repraesentatio und Institutio: Zwei Untersuchungen über den Gebrauch dieser Ausdrücke in der römischen

Literatur', in Max Kaser, Hans Kreller, and Wolfgang Kunkel, eds., *Festschrift Paul Koschaker* (Weimar, 1939), 103–16

Schroeder, Joy A., 'John Chrysostom's Critique of Spousal Violence', *JECS* 12 (2004), 413–32

Scott, Sarah, 'Elites, Exhibitionism and the Society of the Late Roman Villa', in Neil Christie, ed., *Landscapes of Change: Rural Evolutions in Late Antiquity and the Early Middle Ages* (Aldershot, 2004), 39–65

Schlatter, Frederick, 'The Author of the *Opus imperfectum in Matthaeum*', *Vigiliae Christianae* 42 (1988) 364–75

Sears, Elizabeth, 'Louis the Pious as *Miles Christi*: The Dedicatory Image in Hrabanus Maurus's *De laudibus sanctae crucis*', in Peter Godman and Roger Collins, eds., *Charlemagne's Heir: New Perspectives on the Reign of Louis the Pious (814–840)* (Oxford, 1990), 605–28

Setälä, Päivi, *Private Domini in Roman Brick Stamps of the Empire* (Rome, 1977)
Female Networks and the Public Sphere in Roman Society (Rome, 1999)
'Women and Brick Production – Some New Aspects', in Setälä *et al.*, *Women, Wealth, and Power*, 181–201

Setälä, Päivi, *et al.*, *Women, Wealth, and Power in the Roman Empire* (Rome, 2002)

Sfameni, Carla, 'Residential Villas in Late Antiquity: Continuity and Change', in Will Bowden, Luke Lavan, and Carlos Machado, eds., *Recent Research on the Late Antique Countryside* (Leiden, 2003), 335–75

Shanzer, Danuta, *A Philosophical and Literary Commentary on Martianus Capella's De Nuptiis Philologiae et Mercurii Book 1*, Classical Studies 32 (Berkeley, 1986)
'The Anonymous *Carmen contra paganos* and the Date and Identity of the Centonist Proba', *RE Aug* 32 (1986), 232–48

Shaw, Brent, 'The Family in Late Antiquity: The Experience of Augustine', *Past and Present* 115 (1987), 3–51
'Latin Funerary Epigraphy and Family Relationships in the Later Empire', *Historia* 33 (1984), 457–97
'The Age of Roman Girls at Marriage: Some Reconsiderations', *JRS* 77 (1987), 30–46
'The Passion of Perpetua', *Past and Present* 139 (1993), 3–43
'The Cultural Meaning of Death: Age and Gender in the Roman Family', in Kertzer and Saller, eds., *The Family in Italy from Antiquity to the Present*, 66–90
review, *BMCR* (24 Feb. 2002), of Lo Cascio and Rathbone, eds., *Production and Public Powers*

Sieben, Hermann Josef, s.v. 'Jean Chrysostome (Pseudo-)', *Dictionnaire de Spiritualité* 8 (1974), cols. 362–9

Sivan, Hagith, 'Anician Women, the Cento of Proba, and Aristocratic Conversion in the Fourth Century', *Vigiliae Christianae* 47 (1993), 140–57

Smith, J. T., 'The Social Structure of Roman Villas', *Oxford Journal of Archaeology* 6 (1987), 243–55

Sotinel, Claire, 'Arator, un poète au service du la politique du pape Vigile', *MEFRA* 101 (1989), 805–20

Stark, Rodney, *The Rise of Christianity: A Sociologist Reconsiders History* (Princeton, 1996)

Stettiner, Richard, *Die illustrierten Prudentiushandschriften* (Berlin, 1895)

Stewart, Columba, *Cassian the Monk* (New York, 1998)

Sundwall, J., *Abhandlungen zur Geschichte des ausgehenden Römertums* (Helsinki, 1919)

Syme, Ronald, 'Les Alliances dynastiques dans l'aristocratie romaine', *Diogène* 135 (1986), 3–13

Thébert, Yvon, 'Private Life and Domestic Architecture in Roman Africa', in Paul Veyne, ed., *A History of Private Life* 1, *From Pagan Rome to Byzantium*, tr. Arthur Goldhammer (Cambridge, Mass., 1987)

Thomas, J. A. V. C., *Textbook of Roman Law* (Amsterdam, 1976)

Thonnard, François-Joseph, 'Saint Jean Chrysostome et Saint Augustin dans la controverse Pélagienne', Mélanges Venance Grumel II, *Revue des études byzantines* 25 (1967) 189–218

Tibiletti, Carlo, 'Teologia pelagiana su celibato/matrimonio', *Augustinianum* 27 (1987) 487–507

Tjäder, J.O., *Die nichtliterarischen lateinischen Papyri Italiens aus der Zeit 445–700*, 3 vols. (Lund, 1954–5)

Tomolescu, Constantin St., 'Léon Ier et le droit privé', *Accademia Romanistica Constantiniana* 5 (Perugia, 1983), 59–69

Toubert, Pierre, 'La Théorie du mariage chez les moralistes carolingiens', in *Il matrimonio nella società altomedievale*, Settimane di Studio del Centro Italiano di Studi sull'Alto Medievo 24, 2 vols. (Spoleto, 1977) 1, 233–85

Treggiari, Susan, 'Family Life among the Staff of the Volusii', *Transactions and Proceedings of the American Philological Association* 105 (1975), 393–401

    '*Iam proterva fronte*: Matrimonial Advances by Roman Women', in J. W. Eadie and J. Ober, eds., *The Craft of the Ancient Historian: Essays in Honor of Chester G. Starr* (Lanham, Md., 1985), 331–52

    Roman Marriage: Iusti Coniuges from the Time of Cicero to the Time of Ulpian (Oxford, 1991)

    review of Frier, 'Natural Fertility and Family Limitation in Roman Marriage', *Classical Philology* 89 (1994), 318–33

Troncarelli, Fabio, 'I codici di Cassiodoro: le testimonianze più antiche', *Scrittura e civiltà* 12 (1988), 47–99

    Vivarium, i libri, il destino, Instrumenta patristica 33 (Brepols, 1998)

Trout, Dennis E., *Paulinus of Nola: Life, Letters, and Poems* (Berkeley, 1999)

Urbainczyk, Theresa, *Socrates of Constantinople: Historian of Church and State* (Ann Arbor, 1997)

Van Bremen, Riet, *The Limits of Participation: Women and Civic Life in the Greek East in the Hellenistic and Roman Periods* (Amsterdam, 1996)

Van Ossel, Paul, *Établissements ruraux de l'antiquité tardive dans le nord de la Gaule*, 51e supplément à *Gallia* (Paris, 1992)

Vauchez, André, 'Saints admirables et saints imitables: les fonctions de l'hagiographie ont-elles changé aux derniers siècles du moyen-âge?', in *Les Fonctions des saints dans le monde occidental (IIIe–XIIIe siècle): Actes du Colloque organisé* par *l'École Française de Rome avec le concours de l'Université de Rome 'La Sapienza', Rome, 27–29 octobre 1988*, Collection de L'École Française de Rome 149 (Rome, 1991), 161–72

Vera, Domenico, 'Dalla "Villa perfecta" alla villa di Palladio: Sulle trasformazioni del sistema agrario in Italia fra Principato e Dominato', *Athenaeum* 83 (1995), 189–211

'Padroni, Contadini, Contratti: *realia* del colonato tardoantico', in Elio Lo Cascio, ed., *Terre, proprietà e contadini dell'impero romano: dall'affitto agrario al colonato tardoantico* (Rome, 1997), 185–224

'Le forme del lavoro rurale: aspetti della trasformazione dell'Europa romana fra tarda antichità e alto medioevo', in *Morfologie sociali e culturali in Europa fra tarda antichità e alto medioevo*, Settimane di studio sull' alto medioevo 45 (Spoleto, 1998), 293–338

Vessey, Mark, 'Introduction', in Cassiodorus, *Institutions of Divine and Secular Learning: On the Soul*, tr. James W. Halporn (Liverpool, 2004)

Vickery, Amanda, 'Golden Age to Separate Spheres? A Review of the Categories and Chronology of English Women's History', *Historical Journal* 36.2 (1993), 383–414

Villa, Claudia, 'Cultura e scrittura nell'Italia longobarda. Renovatio e translatio: centri amministrativi ed eredità culturale', in Walter Pohl and Peter Erhardt, eds., *Die Langobarden: Herrschaft und Identität* (Vienna, 2005), 502–23

von Harnack, Adolf, *Militia Christi: The Christian Religion and the Military in the First Three Centuries*, tr. David McInnes Gracie (Philadelphia, 1981)

von Moos, Peter, *Consolatio: Studien zur mittellateinischen Trostliteratur über den Tod und zum Problem der christlichen Trauer* (Munich, 1971)

von Schubert, Hans, *Der sogennante Praedestinatus: ein Beitrag zur Geschichte des Pelagianismus* (Leipzig, 1903)

Wallace-Hadrill, Andrew, 'The Social Structure of the Roman House', *Papers of the British School at Rome* 56 (1988), 43–97

'Houses and Households: Sampling Pompei and Herculaneum', in Rawson, ed., *Marriage, Divorce, and Children*, 191–227

Wallraff, Martin, *Der Kirchenhistoriker Socrates: Untersuchungen zu Geschichtsdarstellung, Methode und Person* (Göttingen, 1997)

Wang, Andreas, *Der 'Miles Christianus' im 16. und 17. Jahrhundert und seine mittelalterliche Tradition: ein Beitrag zum Verhältnis von sprachlicher und graphischer Bildlichkeit*, Mikrokosmos 1 (Frankfurt, 1975)

Ward-Perkins, Bryan, 'Continuitists, Catastrophists and the Towns of Post-Roman Northern Italy', *PBSR* 65 (1997) 157–76

The Fall of Rome and the End of Civilization (Oxford, 2005)

Wes, M. A., *Das Ende des Kaisertums im Westen des römischen Reiches* (The Hagve, 1967)

White, L. Michael, *Building God's House in the Roman World: Architectural Adaptation among Pagans, Jews, and Christians* (Baltimore, 1990)

Wickham, Chris, 'The Other Transition: From the Ancient World to Feudalism', *Past and Present* 103 (1984), 3–36 review of Banaji, *Agrarian Change in Late Antiquity*, in *Journal of Agrarian Change* 3 (2003), 434–6

Framing the Early Middle Ages: Europe and the Mediterranean, 400–800 (Oxford, 2005)

Wightman, Edith, 'Peasants and Potentates: An Investigation of Social Structure and Land Tenure in Roman Gaul', *American Journal of Ancient History* 3 (1978), 97–128

'North-Eastern Gaul in Late Antiquity: The Testimony of Settlement Patterns in an Age of Transition', *Berichten van de Rijksdienst voor het Oudheidkundig Bodemonderzoek* 28 (1978), 241–50

Will, E. L. 'Les Amphores de Sestius', *Revue Archéologique de l'Est et du Centre-Est* 7 (1956), 224–44

Wilmart, A., 'Les 38 sermons attribués à Saint Jean Chrysostome', *JThS* 19 (1917), 305–27

Wipszycka, E., 'Les Terres de la Congregation pachomienne dans une liste de payements pour les Apora', in Jean Bingen *et al.*, eds., *Le Monde Grec: Hommages à Claire Préaux*, (Brussels, 1975), 625–36

Wood, Ian, 'Administration, Law, and Culture in Merovingian Gaul', in R. McKitterick, ed., *The Uses of Literacy in Early Medieval Europe* (Cambridge, 1990), 63–81

The Merovingian Kingdoms: 450–751 (London, 1994)

The Missionary Life: Saints and the Evangelisation of Europe, 400–1050 (Harlow, 2001)

Wood, Kirsten E., *Masterful Women: Slaveholding Widows from the American Revolution through the Civil War* (Chapel Hill, 2004)

Woodruff, H., 'The Illustrated Manuscripts of Prudentius', *Art Studies* 7 (1929), 33–79

Wormald, Patrick, 'The Decline of the Western Empire and the Survival of its Aristocracy', *JRS* 66 (1976), 217–26

Yarborough, Larry O., *Not Like the Gentiles: Marriage Rules in the Letters of Paul* (Atlanta, 1985)

Zaccaria Ruggiu, Annapaola, *Spazio privato e spazio pubblico nella città romana* (Rome, 1995)

Zelzer, Klaus, 'Zur Beurteilung der Cicero-Imitatio bei Ambrosius', *Wiener Studien* n.f. 11 (1977), 168–91

Zetzel, James, *Latin Textual Criticism in Antiquity* (New York, 1981)

Index